Competitive Failures in Insurance Markets

CESifo Seminar Series
Edited by Hans-Werner Sinn

Competitive Failures in Insurance Markets

Theory and Policy Implications

Edited by
Pierre-André Chiappori and
Christian Gollier

CESifo Seminar Series

The MIT Press
Cambridge, Massachusetts
London, England

MIT Press books may be purchased at special quantity discounts for business or sales promotional use. For information, please e-mail ⟨special_sales@mitpress.mit.edu⟩ or write to Special Sales Department, The MIT Press, 55 Hayward Street, Cambridge, MA 02142.

This book was set in Palatino on 3B2 by Asco Typesetters, Hong Kong and was printed and bound in the United States of America.

Library of Congress Cataloging-in-Publication Data

Competitive failures in insurance markets : theory and policy implications / Pierre-André Chiappori and Christian Gollier, editors.
    p.   cm. — (CESifo seminar series)
Includes bibliographical references and index.
ISBN 0-262-03352-6 (alk. paper)
1. Insurance—Mathematical models. 2. Insurance, Health—Mathematical models.
I. Chiappori, Pierre-André. II. Gollier, Christian. III. Series.

HG8051.C574   2006
368'.01—dc22   2005058020

10 9 8 7 6 5 4 3 2 1

Contents

Series Foreword

Edited by Hans-Werner Sinn

This book is part of the CESifo Seminar Series in Economic Policy, which aims to cover topical policy issues in economics from a largely European perspective. The books in this series are the products of the papers presented and discussed at seminars hosted by CESifo, an international research network of renowned economists supported jointly by the Center for Economic Studies at Ludwig-Maximilians-Universität, Munich, and the Ifo Institute for Economic Research. All publications in this series have been carefully selected and refereed by members of the CESifo research network.

Acknowledgments

We wish to acknowledge the support of CESifo—an international platform of the University of Munich's Center for Economic Studies (CES) and the Ifo Institute for Economic Research—for its technical and financial support in the organization of the conference held in San Servolo (near Venice, Italy) in July 2003 on which this conference volume is based. The assistance of Roisin Hearn and Marko Koethenbuerger has been particularly helpful and efficient. We also wish to acknowledge all the contributing authors and the referees for their significant contributions.

Pierre-André Chiappori
Columbia University

Christian Gollier
University of Toulouse

Competitive Failures in Insurance Markets

Introduction

The Insurability Problem

Risk sharing is a cornerstone of modern economies. It is valuable to risk-averse consumers and essential for entrepreneurship. Without mechanisms for allowing risk transfer, what single individual could have borne the risks involved in building skycrapers and airplanes and investing in major research and development programs? Historians have documented the role played by private risk-sharing devices in the development of trade in the Middle Ages, particularly in the case of sea transport. The successes of the Netherlands in the seventeenth century and of England in the eighteenth century are strongly correlated with the emergence of financial markets and insurance companies in those countries. The prohibition against insurance companies in France during the same period is one explanation for the late start of the industrial revolution there.

The adverse consequences of the limits to insurability are overwhelmingly underestimated. The management of risks and the management of production cannot be disentangled. Having limits on insurability forces small entrepreneurs to bear the risks linked to their investment, leading to a reduction in investment, employment, and growth. In addition, the inefficiency of our economies in transferring risks that affect human capital forces households to bear larger risks over their lifetime. Given risk aversion, it has a sizeable adverse effect on welfare.

There are several ways to share risk in society. Historically, before the emergence of a market economy, risks were shared within families or small rural communities. This is still largely the case in developing countries. Private contracts usually include several risk-sharing clauses, such as limited liability and others. Long-term labor contracts, cost-plus industrial contracts, and fixed-rate credit contracts are a few examples of such risk-sharing devices. Stocks and bonds can be seen as tradable versions of the same. Still, although risk-sharing clauses are present in most trades, insurance contracts are the only ones for which transfer of risk is the essence of the exchange.

The standard economic model of risk exchanges predicts that competition in insurance markets leads to a Pareto-efficient allocation of risks in the economy. In particular, it states that all diversifiable risks in the economy will be washed away through mutual risk-sharing arrangements. All risks will be pooled in financial and insurance markets. Moreover, the residual systematic risk in the economy will be born by the agents who have a comparative advantage in risk management as insurers and investors. In short, all individual risks will be insured. This prediction, however, is contradicted by casual observations. Many diversifiable risks are still borne by individuals. Indeed, individual consumption levels are not perfectly correlated in the population—that is, for every shock in the economy, they are winners and losers. This is the expression of an inefficient risk sharing ex ante. To illustrate, most of the risks related to human capital, such as long-term unemployment and fluctuations of labor incomes, cannot be insured. Many environmental, catastrophic, and technological risks are not covered by an insurance contract. Risks linked to terrorism may be difficult to insure.

The possibility of transferring a risk to the marketplace is contingent on whether the buyer is ready to pay a larger price than the minimum price at which the seller is ready to sell. Consequently, the concept of a limit to insurability cannot be defined only on the basis of the distributional characteristics of the risk, but it should also take into account the economic environment. Berliner (1982) enumerates the criteria required to define insurability. The actuarial view of this problem is usually summarized by stating that a risk is insurable if the law of large numbers may be applied. This means that the maximum potential loss may not be infinite or very large. Similarly, risks should not be too positively correlated. In addition, the risk must exist: a realized risk cannot be insured. The legal environment must be stable or predictable. Finally, an objective distribution function should be subject to quantification.

This definition, however, remains insufficient, and the actuarial view on the limits to insurability appears to be too narrow. After all, Lloyd's agreed to underwrite the risk of the capture of the monster of Loch

Ness, and more standard insurance companies cover the risk of failure of *Ariane V*, the new European satellite launcher on which no data are available. Conversely, many risks to which the law of large numbers could be applied are beyond the limits of insurability. No insurers would accept the risk of the absence of promotion or divorce.

A transaction on a market is possible if two parties are willing to transfer the underlying good at a specific price. This joint willingness can exist only if the seller and the buyer find it advantageous to exchange. We define a risk as being uninsurable if, given the economic environment, no mutually advantageous risk transfer can be exploited by the consumer and the suppliers of insurance. Partial uninsurability occurs when the parties can exploit only part of the mutually advantageous transfer of risk.

The objective of this book is to provide new insights into recent developments in the economic analysis of the limits of insurability. The main message is that asymmetric information is a central reason that competition in insurance markets may fail to guarantee that all mutually advantageous risk exchanges are realized in our economies. In particular, adverse selection and moral hazard can explain why competitive insurance markets fail to provide an efficient level of insurance and why public interventions are required to cure the problem.

Asymmetric Information and Commitment

In the classical model, it is assumed that all agents share the same information about the likelihood of the various states. This allows for heterogeneous populations as long as the characteristics of the risk borne by each agent is common knowledge. For example, the fact that young women are safer drivers than young men is compatible with full insurance of every driver at the competitive equilibrium with a risk-neutral insurance industry. The premium rate for every category of risk will be fair (hence gender-specific), thereby inducing each individual to purchase full insurance at the optimum.

Adverse Selection

A problem arises when the population is heterogeneous but the observable characteristics of the agents do not perfectly reveal their risk. The adverse-selection problem initially pointed out by Akerlof (1970) in the case of secondhand vehicles originates from the observation that if insurance companies calculate the premium rate on the basis of the average probability distribution in the population, the less risky agents will purchase less insurance than riskier agents. In the extreme case, the low-risk agents will find the premium rate too large with respect to their actual probability of loss. They will prefer not to insure their risk. Insurers will anticipate this reaction, and they will increase the premium rate to break even only on the population of high-risk policy-holders. In summary, the presence of high-risk agents generates a negative externality to lower-risk agents who are unable to find an insurance premium at an acceptable premium rate.

The literature on adverse selection is devoted to defining and characterizing an equilibrium. A basic insight (Rothschild and Stiglitz, 1976) is that when contracts are exclusive, insurers may use the fact that low-risk agents and high-risk agents behave differently in the face of a large set of insurance contracts. In particular, low-risk agents could credibly signal their type by selecting a contract with a large deductible, something that high-risk agents dislike.

Adverse selection can reflect the limits on the information that is available to insurance companies, but it may also stem from specific regulations restricting or prohibiting some forms of discrimination. Such regulations, in turn, may aim at increasing ex ante efficiency. For instance, increasing the availability of predictive tests (based in particular on advances in genetic biology) may be globally beneficial but may limit the scope of insurance coverage for individual, since the *classification risk* (the risk of being predisposed to a particular disease) may be both considerable and hard to insure. A prohibition on the use of genetic tests for insurance underwriting has thus often been proposed as a means of increasing insurability. Clearly, the potential benefits of such regulations have to be compared to their adverse consequences, in particular in terms of market inefficiencies induced by adverse selection. This is the topic of the chapters by Pierre-André Chiappori and Roland Eisen in this volume (chapters 2 and 3).

Moral Hazard
The population of risks can be heterogeneous not only because agents bear intrinsically different risks but also because they do not invest the same amount of their energy, wealth, or time to risk prevention. In particular, it has long been recognized that individuals that are better covered by insurance invest less in risk prevention ex ante and risk mitigation ex post if the link between the premium rate and the size of these investments is weak. It will be the case if insurers are not in a po-

sition to observe the investment in risk prevention by the policyholder. In that case, the premium rate is not sensitive to the efforts made by the policyholder to prevent losses. Contrary to the result of the classical model, the inverse relationship between risk prevention and insurance coverage thus generated will lead to an inefficiently low level of risk prevention. This is ex ante moral hazard. Anticipating this low degree of prevention and the higher frequency of losses that it entails, insurers will raise their premium rates. Full insurance will not be optimal for agents. At the limit, no insurance can be an equilibrium. Moral hazard is often invoked to explain why it is not possible to insure against (lack of) promotion at work, failure at school or university, divorce, or the lack of demand for a new product. In some instances, this is also why it is hard to insure against unemployment or against environmental and technological risks.

In health insurance, there have been various attempts to control moral hazard by better management of care, a problem that is examined by Hansjörg Lehmann and Peter Zweifel in chapter 6. Using a latent health status from panel data in Switzerland, they identify the risk-selection effects of the different insurance plans that are available, but this can explain only a fraction of the differences in expenditures of these plans. This seems to confirm the suspicion that the considerable cost savings achieved by Swiss managed-care plans emanate from risk selection rather than from changed contractual incentives limiting moral hazard.

An area in which this conflict between insurance and incentives is paramount is agriculture. Historically, various types of contracts between tenants and landlords have been implemented, with different impacts on risk sharing and contrasted incentives properties. Chapter 11 by Luis H. B. Braido surveys the literature devoted to these issues. He shows that while theory is by now well understood, empirical evidence is somewhat mixed. He emphasizes how the exogenous (and sometimes unobserved) elements underlying the choice of different contractual forms should play a key role in any assessment of the magnitude of the incentive effects.

Limited Commitment
Another potential limitation of efficiency in insurance markets arises from commitment problems. In many cases (health being a prominent example), welfare maximization requires long-term contracts to be signed and implemented. An individual may want to be covered not

only against the risk of being found to be a bad risk (the classification risk) but also against the risk of becoming a bad risk. The ability of markets to provide these types of contracts has often been questioned. Mark V. Pauly addresses this issue in chapter 1. Pauly argues that insurance markets have actually set up institutional structures that appear to deal in a good (though not perfect) way with this problem. The key innovation was the introduction of contracts involving guaranteed renewability, whereby the insurance company formally commits not to readjust the terms of the agreement in response to changes in the individual actual (or perceived) risk.

Empirical Applications

Several essays published in this volume reexamine the asymmetric information problems in insurance markets from an empirical viewpoint. Lucien Gardiol, Pierre-Yves Geoffard, and Chantal Grandchamp (chapter 4) provide a careful investigation of asymmetric information in health insurance, using a remarkable Swiss database. They show that adverse selection is indeed pervasive in this market. For instance, there exists a significant correlation between contractual choice and future mortality. They also find that the positive correlation between coverage and outpatient expenditure is not fully explained by selection effects and conclude that moral-hazard effects are of the same order of magnitude.

A second empirical application of the ideas developed above is provided by Mark J. Browne's analysis of the market for long-term care insurance (chapter 5). Currently, this market is surprisingly small: private long-term care insurance pays approximately 5 percent of all nursing home costs in the United States. The chapter focuses on one possible explanation for this apparent failure—namely, contracting problems arising from asymmetric information and one-sided commitment. Empirical results turn out to be consistent with both interpretations. The chapter provides empirical evidence that contracting problems in the private insurance market have led government insurance programs, rather than private insurance, to be the primary financing source for long-term care losses.

The econometrics of asymmetric information are tricky. In chapter 8, Georges Dionne, Christian Gouriéroux, and Charles Vanasse analyze the methodological issues that arise in that context. They propose the notion of conditional independence as a key concept for this purpose and show how a parametrically misspecified framework may induce spurious conclusions. The insight is that it may be difficult to distinguish between the decision variables' information content and an omitted nonlinear effect of the initial exogenous variables. Applying their approach to the analysis of automobile accidents in Quebec and to the demand for life insurance in France, they conclude that the additional information provided by the decision variables is rather weak and often insignificant as soon as the nonlinear effect of the initial exogenous variables has been introduced in a suitable way.

Irena Dushi and Anthony Webb (chapter 9) tested for the presence of adverse selection on the annuity market in the United States. They show that although there is evidence that information asymmetries contribute to the low mortality of annuitants and the small size of the voluntary annuity market, there is another equally important factor. The high proportions of preannuitized wealth held by poorer and on average higher-mortality households will lead them to place such a low value on the longevity insurance provided by annuities that they will find annuitization unattractive over a wide range of subjective mortality beliefs. In other words, the lower mortality of annuitants may be the result not only of traditional adverse selection arising out of asymmetric mortality information but also of passive selection in which wealth affects both preferences and outcomes.

Paul Kofman and Gregory P. Nini (chapter 12) derive three testable predictions from a theoretical model of asymmetric learning that is characterized by an incumbent insurance company gaining private information about the risk of their customers. Using Australian time-series data of automobile insurance contracts, they conclude that this market has developed an efficient mechanism for sharing relevant information through the use of a publicly available set of rating characteristics.

In chapter 10, Luigi Guiso and Monica Paiella show that there is much heterogeneity in the degree of risk aversion among consumers. Moreover, they show that, as predicted by economic theory, the individual degree of risk aversion has much predictive power to explain individual decisions under uncertainty as the choice of insurance deductibles. This implies that asymmetric information and self-selection on insurance markets has two dimensions—one on the risk and the other on risk aversion.

Erik Grönquist (chapter 7) investigates the decision to opt out of an insurance pool based on updated assessments of risk based on experience. A simple model is presented to show that opting out never occurs if both the insurer and insured learn symmetrically from the insured's experience but may occur if the policyholder comes to believe that the correct risk class is lower than the one assigned by the insurer's reassessment and the adjusted premium for the policy is more than the insured is willing to pay. This happens when the insurer reclassifies the insured into a lower (higher) risk class and the insured believes the risk class should be lower still (not as high). The dropout decision is examined empirically using Swedish dental insurance data.

Two conclusions emerge from this rapid overview. First is that the analysis of insurance markets raises complex issues that require precise and detailed theoretical investigations. Small differences of context may lead to significantly divergent policy recommendations; and a simple, one-size-fits-all approach is unable to capture these subtleties. Second, theory by itself is not sufficient. Most of the time, optimal policy responses depend on the respective magnitude of the effects at stake. These can be measured only through careful empirical investigations. We believe that a deeper integration of theoretical and empirical methods and concepts is what is presently needed. And we hope that the present book will be perceived as a step in this fruitful direction.

References

Akerlof, G. A. (1970). "The Market for 'Lemons': Quality Uncertainty and the Market Mechanism." *Quarterly Journal of Economics* 84(3): 488–500.

Berliner, B. (1982). *Limits of Insurability of Risks.* Englewood Cliffs, NJ: Prentice Hall.

Rothschild, M., and J. Stiglitz. (1976). "Equilibrium in Competitive Insurance Markets: An Essay on the Economics of Imperfect Information." *Quarterly Journal of Economics* 80: 629–649.

I Theoretical Models

1

Time, Risk, Precommitment, and Adverse Selection in Competitive Insurance Markets

Mark V. Pauly

Many of the risks an individual faces evolve and change over a lifetime. Not only do risks change, but they change in different ways for different people so that the distribution of risks becomes more diverse over time. While individual risks of death, illness, and wealth reduction differ to some extent at young ages (because of inheritance of wealth and because of observed aspects of inheritance of genetic makeup), for the most part the passage of time is associated with the evolution of different risks for individuals as they change in different ways or as their characteristics become gradually more apparent throughout life. Moreover, the knowledge of a risk is dependent to some extent on its longevity: old risks that remain with an individual or the individual's assets can become better known than risks reflecting changes that are recent or yet to occur.

The passage of time thus presents the conflicting trends of greater ability to measure existing risk differences and greater opportunity for risks to change. So how might or does insurance work for a set of agents who begin their (economic) lifetime with roughly similar perceived risks but gradually experience (as they age) greater divergence in the risk of future adverse events? Basic insurance theory tells us that competitive insurance markets can work efficiently in dealing with adverse events whose probabilities are known to all and stable over time. How do markets work when it is certain that risks will change according to a predictable pattern but when it is uncertain which persons will experience those changes at which time?

In this chapter, I informally review some recent research that develops the theory for how insurance markets develop methods to deal with risks that evolve over time. I discuss policy provisions involving guaranteed renewability as one such device that not only deals with what Kenneth Arrow (1963) calls "insurance with a long time perspective" but also may go much of the way toward solving the problem of adverse selection.

Information Structures

I distinguish three different possible structures for risk information for insurance consumers and firms. One case, which I save for later, is the situation in which at least some of the information is known only to the consumer and to none of the insurers; this is classic *adverse selection*. The second case is one in which all insurers know what consumers know about risks at every point in time; this is the case that leads to *risk rating*, in which premiums vary with risk and change when (perceived) risk changes. The third case is one in which the consumer and the consumer's current insurer (the one sold insurance to the consumer in the last period) have the same information about the consumer's risk but other insurers have less complete information. I begin with a special version of this third case.

Models of Insurance with Constant But Initially Unknown Risk

In the first set of models, risk truly differs even in the first period, but information that establishes these differences takes time to accumulate. We assume that, initially, the (representative) consumer and insurer do not know the consumer's particular risk level but that time permits the accumulation of evidence, equally available to both but hidden from other insurers, that leads to more precise estimates of individual risk. The classic example here is automobile insurance. Even if there are (intrinsically) good drivers and bad drivers, newly licensed drivers will not be able to be categorized and so would initially be assigned, by consumer and insurer alike, the average risk (which, of course, could be higher for new drivers than for experienced drivers). As time passes, however, events occur (or do not occur) that help to sharpen estimates. Accidents happen, and traffic citations are accumulated, which help to distinguish (though not perfectly) between drivers of different risk levels. A key assumption in these models is that at least some of this driving record (the frequency of claims) is known to the consumer and to the consumer's current insurer but not to other potential insurers.

Given these assumptions, models generally indicate that insurers may well underprice products initially to collect this private knowledge but will eventually earn profits on those they identify as low risks

(Kunreuther and Pauly, 1985). Whether they choose to backload in this fashion or frontload depends on the degree of information asymmetry that can be created by keeping knowledge private and on the extent of risk aversion by consumers facing a risk of future reclassification. Other models indicate that the effect of insurance on premiums may be different for those consumers who initially represented themselves as low risk than for those who represented themselves as high risks. In this discussion, I ignore the possibility that the consumer has some influence over the initial classification (Cooper and Hayes, 1987). Those who turn out to be high risks will engage in adverse selection but will do so against other insurers whose information on the person's driving record is imperfect.

These models differ from the classic model of incomplete but evolving information (applied to labor markets) of Harris and Holmstrom (1982). In their model, information is symmetric; all agents (firms and workers) share common beliefs, and all new information is common knowledge.

Models of Insurance with Changing Risk

A second case has recently become a topic of discussion—a situation in which a consumer's risk level is perfectly known to all at any point in time but that may change in the future in unpredictable ways. Health insurance is the most common example, in which the onset of a previously unsuspected high-cost chronic condition changes the person's risk level in the future. This phenomenon also potentially applies to other insurance in which the risk depends on individual health, such as life insurance and nursing-home (long-term care) insurance.

In this case, I argue that the optimal insurance is frontloaded, with initial premiums above actuarially determined values. This argument is based on papers by Pauly, Kunreuther, and Hirth (1995) (hereafter PKH), Cochrane (1995), and, more recently, for the specific case of term life insurance without formal guaranteed renewability, Hendel and Lizzeri (2003). I provide a simple example to illustrate the main idea of these papers. I further show that, in some circumstances, the equilibrium premiums are efficient, solving the problem of both premium risk and adverse selection. I also summarize more recent empirical evidence suggesting that actual markets may approximate this ideal rather well, despite some threats to equilibrium and efficiency. Finally, in addition to explaining in more detail what some recent research tells us (theoretically and empirically) about the changing risk model, I offer some thoughts on what happens if the two models are combined.

This frontloading property is also present in the Harris-Holmstrom model, even though in their case the unknown potentially stochastic variable (a worker's "true" productivity) does not change over time. But in a similar fashion, agents observe new information that causes them to change their beliefs about the expected value. Whether these distinctions make a difference to all aspects of the model has, to my knowledge, not been investigated.

A population is assumed to begin its life cycle with equal apparent risk, but events occur over time that in part measure the initial (but unknown) differences in risk and in part signal changes in risk. Will the final market equilibrium be one with frontloaded, backloaded, or actuarially based premiums? And can we say anything about its efficiency?

Guaranteed Renewability as a Solution to Insurance Market Problems

I first explain and summarize with a simple example some recent research that demonstrates a solution to the problem of risk variation. Suppose each of a set of similar persons is at risk of an adverse event per time period with probability p. Suppose there are two periods. If a loss occurs in period 1, those persons who incur the loss (high risks) are assumed to have higher loss probability p' in period 2; if a loss does not occur, the probability in period 2 remains at p for those who continue to be low risks. (The onset of chronic illness would produce roughly this pattern.) Full-coverage insurance (with benefits equal to the loss) is offered by competitive insurers, and every insurer knows each person's loss probability.

Ignoring administrative costs, the break-even premium for any insurer in period 1 is p. In period 2, in the absence of anything else, insurers would charge p' to those high risks who had suffered a loss in period 1 because of a continuing chronic condition and p to those who had not. A uniform premium of $pp' + (1 - p)p = \bar{p}$ would also cover losses in period 2. However, any insurer who tried to charge $\bar{p}$ would only be selected by the high risks; the low risks would defect to an insurer charging them just p.

Risk-averse consumers would presumably prefer to avoid the risk of having to pay a high-risk premium in period 2. An insurer could guarantee not to do so, still attract the lower risks, and (ignoring interest) just cover its cost by charging a premium of $p + p(p' - p)$ in period 1 and a uniform premium of p in period 2. That is, the insurer would provide *guaranteed renewability (GR) at nondiscriminatory premiums* for period 2. It is easy to see that such a schedule would be incentive compatible in the sense that (1) all consumers would be willing to pay the period 1 premium and (2) all consumers would be willing to pay the period 2 premium. Clause 1 is true because all insureds initially assume themselves to be the same risk and would prefer to pay the two-period premium to bearing the risk of losses in period 1 and uncertain premiums in period 2. Clause 2 is true because both high and low risks would be willing to pay the low-risk premium in period 2. The insurer would break even since its per person premium collections over both periods, $p + p(p' - p) + p$, would equal its expected losses over both periods in either case $(p + pp' + (1 - p)p)$. That is, both revenue and cost equal $2p + pp^i - p^2$.

This is a specific example of a set of incentive compatible premium schedules proposed by PKH (1995) and by Cochrane (1995). There are relatively minor differences between the two models in the extent of "lock in" to a given insurer, depending on what one assumes about whether a high-risk consumer is permitted to and is able to recover the excess prepaid premium; there are administrative advantages and disadvantages of either approach.

Making GR Theoretically Bullet-Proof

The policy provision called *guaranteed renewability* (GR) means that the insurer agrees to renew a policy at the next policy anniversary period at a premium that is nondiscriminatory. Such a provision is actually common and well known in insurance practice (if not to insurance theorists). Under this provision, future premiums can change, but they must do so to the same extent for all in the (initial) rating class.

Administering this provision is in practice almost surely less costly than continual individual risk rating. It means that the insurer need determine only the new (average) premium for the coverage purchased by people in a risk class for the next time period and does not need to assemble or analyze data on the claim or risk levels of individual members of the class. In a practical sense, individual reunderwriting is costly, but failure to reunderwrite is free of cost. The life insurer need not administer another medical examination, the health insurer need not assemble data on individual health claims, and the long-term care insurer need not inquire about chronic conditions or frailty.

If some insurers engage in guaranteed renewability as a policy feature, is this behavior consistent with market equilibrium? The only conceptual treatment of this subject as applied to insurance that I have found before the Cochrane (1995) and PKH (1995) papers was in Peter Diamond's (1992) 1991 Econometric Society presidential address. After noting that guaranteed renewability was common in individual term life insurance (but failing to note that it was also common in individual health insurance), he says (correctly) that "the restriction on price changes coming from this contract clause will depend on the marketing strategy being followed by the company for the set of current insurees." Even under GR, a company could stop selling insurance altogether, for example. But he also argues that "this guarantee could be of little value." His example is that of a life insurance company that initially charges the same rate to smokers and nonsmokers. "Then some companies introduce new policies only available to nonsmokers. By evaluating new applicants, unhealthy non-smokers are excluded from buying these policies. All healthy non-smokers switch to this new class of policies," while the unhealthy nonsmokers are now lumped together with the smokers in a higher premium policy (Diamond, 1992, p. 1238). The problem with this example is that if the nonsmokers were all equally healthy initially, the premium that would be charged to all nonsmokers in each future period by their original insurer would be no higher than the premium a new insurer would propose to charge to those nonsmokers who remained healthy. There would be no new applicants. That is, under incentive-compatible GR, the premium charged to the healthy in any period makes renewed insurance purchase by them as or more attractive than switching to a new company or a new policy.

To be sure, in all periods (but the last) the premium charged to the healthy for insurance for next year would be higher than a premium charged by an insurer who just wanted to offer one year of coverage without GR. But risk-averse people would prefer the higher one-period premium with GR protection to the lower non-GR premium that buys one year of coverage but leaves the person exposed to the chance of a substantial jump in premium for the years following. This is the meaning of *incentive compatibility*.

The more serious threat to GR is whether a contract that delivers what is promised can be written and enforced. In one sense, any solution here is bedeviled by the usual problem of long-term contracting in economics. Once payment has been made for some types of costly long-term contract provision, it is always to the advantage of the agent who would have to pay to try to renege on the contract—and it is usually impossible to write a contract so detailed that there is no possibility for the agent bearing the cost to refuse to pay on some part of the deal. The standard solution to this problem (despair being disproved by the existence in the real world of long-term arrangements and contracts that seem to work) is to invoke some assumption of either repeat dealing or reputation that serves to force both agents to live up to the contract. Our empirical research in fact suggests that insurance brokers know which insurers play games at renewal time and either advise their customers to avoid them or at least to pay a lower price (Pauly, Rosenbloom, Herring, Szrek, and Rosenquist, 2003).

The other solution is a kind of second-best one: as long as the major or most important features can be specified in a contract, the outcome can be pretty good, even if not perfect. To be specific: it is important for buyers to be able to anticipate what the path of future premiums will be and to be assured that future premiums will change only if marketwide expected expenses truly do change.

For life insurance, this is not a serious problem. Benefits are stated in nominal monetary terms, and there is usually good agreement on what death probabilities are represented in the mortality tables. In contrast, health insurance premiums in the future depend in part on how frequently people get sick but even more on the cost of treating them, and that cost is affected by new technology, health worker wages, and the extent of insurance coverage itself. In the face of medical spending growth, Diamond argues that "premiums can rise enormously" and (he might have added) unpredictably. The question then is: to what is the future GR insurance premium indexed?

This is a serious problem. Suppose a company that sold GR health coverage raised its premiums (equally) for all of those in rating class, those who had contracted chronic conditions and those that had not. If it raised its premium by less than the increase in marketwide insurance cost, it would suffer losses. If it raises its premium by more than

marketwide insurance costs rose, it (or another insurer) could propose
to charge a premium based more accurately on those costs for a new
rating class that included only good risks and that the good risks
would find attractive. That would leave only the bad risks in the original pool, and the company could and would raise the premium it
charges (nondiscriminatorily) to those remaining in the poll. In effect,
it could pocket the excess premiums it collected in previous years by
driving off the good risks (Rothschild and Stiglitz, 1976). In doing so,
it would not have violated any terms of the GR feature. Here again,
repeated play of this strategy by an insurer would eventually bring
recognition and retaliation, but it does appear that GR contracts are
fragile. Such pricing mistakes, whether intentional or unintentional,
make GR less valuable as a solution than the theoretical models would
suggest. Moreover, consumers would have difficulty determining
whether a given increase was or was not justified on the basis of cost
and thus difficulty detecting the kind of strategy just described. I deal
further with strategies that could and actually have been used to deal
with this problem when I discuss the behavior of insurers in practice.

The other aspect of an insurance contract that can be difficult to specify exactly is what we might loosely call *quality*. For example, the speed
at which questions are answered, disputes resolved, and claims pro-
cessed could be reduced in a discriminatory fashion for those the insurer identifies to have become higher risks. This problem is most
acute in managed-care health insurance, where the insurer delivers
health care as well as wealth transfers conditional on poor health. It
will be hard to specify in the contract all the dimensions of access to
care and quality of services specifically used by higher-risk people.

Because of this transaction or contracting cost, insurance provision in
markets where risk variation over time is important may be limited (to
a greater extent than is ideal) to those features that can be specified and
monitored. This might explain, for example, why managed-care long-
term care insurance has so far failed to emerge and why such policies
typically are limited to specifying indemnity benefits.

"Sure, It Works in Practice, but Can It Work in Theory?"

Despite the prominence in insurance economics of theoretical arguments about problems raised by adverse selection and single-period
risk rating, guaranteed renewability (in some form or other) exists in
many insurance markets. It emerges and continues to survive even

when not required by law or regulation and therefore (by the usual Darwinian model of positive economics) must be performing some useful function in some way. Our recent empirical research has developed some evidence on how guaranteed renewability works in actual individual health insurance markets in the United States, which are relatively lightly regulated in most states, and so it is perhaps worthwhile to summarize that research.

While insurance with GR is theoretically frontloaded, the risk of death or illness rises with age even for apparently healthy people. This means that, even with guaranteed renewability, premiums would be expected to rise with age—just not as steeply as in the absence of GR.

Our recent research has examined the way in which premiums for individual health insurance vary with age. One empirical discovery, which turned out to be highly consistent with the hypothesis of effective GR coverage, was the finding that premiums rose with age at a much lower rate than did expected (average) expenses. That is, relative to a premium that would cover current period costs, younger buyers of insurance were being overcharged much more than older buyers (Pauly and Herring, 1999). But this is exactly the pattern we would expect to prevail under GR.

Following this hint, we examined the actual path of premiums with age more directly. Using data on the probability of contracting a costly chronic condition at any age and on the persistence of high spending, we developed a model to predict or estimate the time path of premiums that would prevail under optimal GR—in which the premium at each age had to cover costs but to continue to appeal to the low risks (Herring and Pauly, 2003). Both interest rates and a forecast of the rate of growth of medical spending were included in the model. We then compared this theoretically optimal and equilibrium path with the actual path of premiums insurers charge. The results for males, shown in figures 1.1 and 1.2, are striking. Figure 1.1 shows three alternative actuarially fair premium or average benefits paths for a standard policy. It shows the premium of low risks (those with no chronic conditions), high risks (those with one or more such conditions), and the average break-even premium, all for a standardized policy. As expected, all premiums rise with age.

Next we solved for the incentive-compatible premium—the premium that (in any time period) covered both the costs incurred in that period by low risks and the expected discounted future premiums for those who become high risks in that period. (Both death and recovery

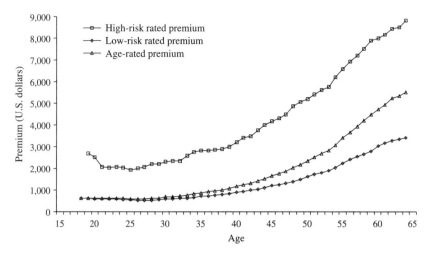

Figure 1.1
Male risk-rated premium schedules
Note: These estimates are given in 2003 dollars.

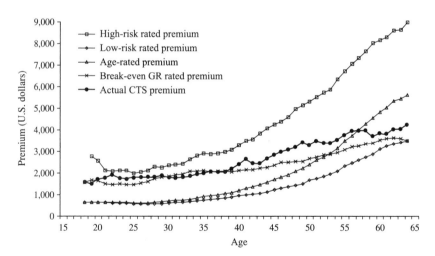

Figure 1.2
Male actual Community Tracking Survey nongroup premiums
Note: These values are given in 2003 dollars.

are taken into account.) Finally, from the Community Tracking Survey (CTS), a large household survey of insurance purchasers, we calculated the actual premiums paid for the standardized policy as a function of age. These two premium paths are overlaid on the other paths in figure 1.2. The comparisons are striking. First, actual premiums definitely deviate from the single-period break-even age-rated premium for both good risks and average risks. The margin of the actual premium over the age-rated average premium is high at younger ages but eventually becomes negative. Second and even more surprising, the optimal time path and the actual time path are fairly similar, as indicated in figure 1.2. (The similarity still exists but is less precise for females, perhaps because the expenditures due to childbearing do not reflect an unexpected chronic condition for which GR funding is most appropriate.) In any case, the overall pattern is one in which reality, once observed, is highly consistent with the recently developed theory.

In quantitative terms, the average additional lifetime premium for guaranteed renewability in this data is about 35 percent of the average premium for a standardized policy ($658 versus $1,854). These calculations do not take turnover into account. This additional amount is similar for men and women and roughly constant in absolute dollar amount over most of the lifetime (until the last few years). Because the average expense of young men (age eighteen to thirty-four) is lower than the overall average, this incremental premium constitutes about 77 percent of their average premium. While the judgment is subjective, it does not appear that the amount of frontloading is substantial relative to average premiums or that it is high relative to a person's total income.

Modifications to the Market-Equilibrium Guaranteed-Renewability Model

The theoretically optimal equilibrium guaranteed-renewability (GR) schedule charges the good risks at any age a premium that they are willing to pay and at the same time collects enough to cover all future above-good-risk costs of those who become chronically ill. Here I consider some possible modifications of this basic model.

Level Premiums

First, it is clearly possible to think of setting future premiums below the premiums good risks would be willing to pay, while at the same time having yet higher frontloading. The most extreme version of this would be to charge a single lump sum for lifetime coverage at some age and zero thereafter. While that strategy would not seem reasonable, another similar approach apparently has attracted the attention of private insurers and insurance regulators in Germany: a requirement that plans charge level premiums that vary with the age at which the person first begins insurance with a particular firm but not thereafter. Compared to the optimal schedule at any age, this factor will yield higher initial premiums and lower ones later in life. It will be stable, but as with a lump-sum premium the important question is whether this pattern is efficient. If we assume that capital markets are imperfect, so that young consumers would prefer to minimize the premiums they pay when wealth is low, this pattern is less than ideal. It also complicates the problem of calculating reserves by requiring larger future reserves.

Presumably this pattern exists in Germany because of the need to compete with the statutory health insurance that charges premiums based only on earnings (up to a limit); the "lock in" thus keeps people from defecting to that insurance as they age. What would emerge without the presence of such funding for quasi-public plans is an open question. My conjecture is that flat premium plans would not survive in competition with plans with GR whose premiums grow moderately with age.

Lock-In

One of the problems with frontloading is the mirror image of the protection the firm agrees to provide against increases in premiums: those who become high risks are locked in to the insurance policy and insurance firm they initially chose. It is important to note that the more numerous low risks are definitely *not* locked in; they can switch insurers or switch policies as they wish. Only those who are high risks at the moment are locked in. The possibility of lock-in presumably motivates people to search more intensively among insurers in making their initial purchase and to choose those with a reputation for treating high risks well. However, people may not want to make a binding commitment to a particular insurer if they become high risks. The data suggest that those with chronic conditions who survive often do not remain high expected expenses for the rest of their lives; cancer survivors, for example, eventually become close to average risks. But people may well still be concerned with lock-in to individual insurance, just as they are supposedly concerned with lock-in to a job in the case of job-based insurance (Madrian, 1994).

There are ways to mitigate the lock-in effect, but they raise problems of their own. For example, the insurer could be required, as Cochrane has suggested, to pay a lump-sum bonus, reflecting the expected value of future above-average premiums, to those high risks who wish to leave; they could then use this amount to cover their premiums at other insurers. However, following this procedure then requires determining precisely what the person's risk level is, which reinstitutes costly underwriting and is sure to be controversial. The PKH approach does not explicitly permit opting out and therefore would require prospective buyers to put more effort into searching for good insurance from good firms in the first instance.

One issue here raises one of the paradoxes of economics. If competition based on reputation, say, is vigorous, consumers who select a firm in the market will probably get a price close to cost and future performance that does not permit the insurer to take advantage of them. (More on this later on.) But for competition to be most vigorous, consumers should not only have an opportunity to choose initially but also an opportunity to leave firms that try to take advantage of them. More generally, the portability of initial excess premiums and the method of determining the amount of any exit payment to high risks is something that competitive markets could determine.

Apparently, in individual health insurance in the United States, the problem of lock-in is not severe enough to make it worthwhile for any insurer (life or health) to follow the Cochrane model. However, it is instructive that individual health insurance is much less likely to be a "preferred-provider" model with limited but changing panels of providers (rather than indemnity, all-provider insurance). The additional premium that would need to be charged at young ages is not negligible but is not high relative to income. At younger ages, the onset of long-term chronic conditions is rare, and many persons who contract them recover, die, or drop their individual health insurance. A key issue is whether there are good reasons why a person's demand for insurance (and therefore the specifics of a policy) should change. Lock-in is a problem only if there are likely to be reasons why one would want to change insurers or coverage. One reason for desired change should probably be ruled out: an increase in demand for coverage of a particular type of care after a person discovers a chronic condition that uses that type of care. This would ordinarily represent adverse selection.

At a more general level, the question is whether the demand for insurance would be expected to change when risk changes, given that premiums also change in response to risk. As Ehrlich and Becker (1972) point out, the demand for insurance should respond primarily to loading, not to loss probability; the only effect that the latter would have is as an income effect, which should be minor. Thus an optimal indemnity policy may depend on the person's extent of risk aversion and on the loading but could and should be written in such a way that the form of the contract can remain the same even as risk changes. Proportional coinsurance, for example, displays this property: when risk increases, expected out-of-pocket payment also increases (proportionately), even with no changes in explicit policy provisions.

Changes in a person's circumstances (income, location, family structure) are more plausible reasons for seeking a change in the form of insurance. Many insurers will permit changes in coverage and still continue GR for such explicit and documented alterations of characteristics. Clearly, lock-in need not be absolute but must still be present to some extent; the real problem arises when it is hard to distinguish objectively between changes in the person's demand for insurance, the given risk, and any changes in the risk.

The other reason that lock-in would be a problem is if the insurer changes behavior even while the consumer's demand remains constant. As already noted, the danger of reneging on explicit or implicit long-term contracts is always present, and the changing cost and quality of medical care made it harder to monitor what the insurer is providing. One would think that if this were a serious problem in practice, safeguards would be built into actual policies. The apparent absence of safeguards is consistent with the hypothesis that reputation provides a sufficient constraint on opportunistic behavior by insurers. It would also be consistent with the hypothesis that consumers are totally unaware of their vulnerability to lock-in—but then one would have to explain why they value GR protection that is empty. Empirical work seems to be the best way to make progress on these issues.

Time Period between Changes
While the theory envisions that GR provides a guarantee for a lifetime, there may be reasons to shorten the time period—without going all the way to the one-year interval typical of ordinary insurance plans. Term life insurance provides a model here, with term insurance available for periods of one, five, or ten years—over which interval not only re-

newal but premiums themselves are guaranteed. Buyers can choose the time period, and there is generally a tradeoff between length of commitment and premium.

Requiring a waiting period before a change in coverage can be made is equivalent to choosing the term of insurance. Single-year term insurance permits changes every year, but ten-year term insurance permits changes only every decade. The primary advantage of ten-year term insurance over single-year term insurance is that the latter specifies not what the premium will be for the next time period but only that evidence of insurability will not be required so that there will be no discrimination.

The longer the time period between a decision to increase, reduce, drop, or change insurance and the time at which that change becomes effective, the lower the chance of adverse selection by the buyer or reunderwriting by the seller. The veil of ignorance becomes more opaque, and decisions will be made in a less opportunistic fashion. But the longer the lag, the less closely coverage can be tailored to the person's current circumstances. (This raises again the issues associated with lock-in.) Again there is a tradeoff, with greater ability to change insurance associated on average with a longer time period between changes.

It seems that markets could solve the problem of optimal waiting period for changes in coverage. It can offer insurances for which premium change can be rapid or slow, at different premiums, and let buyers choose what they want. While a shorter waiting period will be associated with more adverse selection, there should not be adverse selection associated with making the choice of a shorter waiting period itself. Instead, the frequency of changes in external circumstances, the person's taste for bearing the cost of change, and the elasticity of the person's demand function (as a proxy for lost consumers' surplus from the wrong quantity) should influence this choice.

Guaranteed Renewability in Term Life and Long-Term Care Insurance

It appears that the first and most common use of guaranteed renewability was in life insurance (Harrington and Niehaus). Under this provision, the person who has paid premiums for a given amount of coverage for the current term is permitted to renew the same policy without the need to take a physical exam or provide other evidence on health. It is also even common (more so in whole life insurance) to buy a supplementary policy that allows the person to increase coverage at the anniversary date without providing evidence of insurability.

The premium for life insurance policies typically increases with age; the new premium is at the discretion of the insurer. The premiums for policies with longer terms either remain constant or increase with age according to a prespecified schedule. This is the case in which it is clearest that the GR is really passive rather than active; it simply represents the absence of effort to determine the buyer's current-period risk level. Because the payout of life insurance is in monetary terms and because mortality tables are general knowledge, insurers set aside a portion of the premiums collected as a reserve against the GR promise.

As far as I am aware, the guaranteed renewability feature in life insurance works very well. Those who survive and have good health do not drop coverage in a future year even if, by that time, it will be apparent which of the original purchasers have a chronic condition and therefore which are more likely to claim death benefits. The premium must be low enough to keep the good risks renewing from the initial firm and not volunteering for new medical examinations to get lower premiums from new firms.

Whole life insurance and long-term care insurance share the property that the premium depends on the age at which the contract begins and generally does not increase over time even though the probability of making a claim of either type surely does increase over time. As in German private health insurance, this feature implies even more frontloading of the premium and even less likelihood of adverse selection by those who turn out to be good risks. In essence, the person prepays part of the future premium. In whole life, a person who decides to drop out can claim some of this prepayment back—the so-called surrender value of the policy—although the frontloading of expenses (especially commissions) means that the surrender amount is initially low relative to the present value of the amounts used for prepayment.

Long-term care insurance in the United States also has a similar prepayment feature but usually does not offer a cash value if the policy terminates or lapses. Not only is the premium lower the younger the age at which the person starts to pay for long-term care insurance, but the difference between the "spot" premium and the present value of prefunded premiums at an earlier age is positive. The insurer is assuming adverse selection.

Long-term care insurers initially determined the amount of front-loading based on assumptions about the proportion of policies that would lapse. What they found was that the lapse rate was both lower than expected and skewed toward heavier users of long-term care, so that the prefunding was inadequate.

Adverse Selection and Guaranteed Renewability

One of the aspects of insurance that has most intrigued and bothered economic theorists is the problem of adverse selection. I suggest that GR provides a solution to much of the problem of adverse selection. The solution is not quite complete in theory but perhaps close enough in practice.

Suppose that, in contrast to the earlier model, no insurer can tell which insureds develop the chronic condition in period 1, so that there is informed asymmetry. However, the insurance has a GR provision. Would this situation be vulnerable to adverse selection?

Given the assumption of the Cochrane and PKH models, the answer is negative. Both of those models assume that the amount of insurance in the policy is given or fixed over time, and it is the premium for just this fixed amount of coverage that is guaranteed. That is, neither model assumes that the individual obtains the privilege of buying more insurance at the average premium or of recovering some of the excess premium if he subsequently decides to buy less. In effect, in these models the consumer's only choice is either to buy the predetermined level of coverage or none at all, at least from this insurer.

To see why the GR equilibrium is stable and is not subject to adverse selection, consider whether, in the spirit of the Rothschild-Stiglitz (1976) (RS) model, it is possible for a new insurer to profitably offer a different policy to those with the GR-or-nothing option. Would low risks be able to be attracted away? The negative insurer has already been given: in the next period or periods, the low risks expect to pay only their own expected expenses to the current insurer, so the new insurer has nothing to offer them.

In the RS model, the key reward to low risks from being separated from a pooling equilibrium is the chance to avoid transfers to high risks. But with GR, there are no transfers ex post from those who know themselves to be low risks to those who know themselves to be high risks. Thus, in this model, there is equilibrium and no adverse selection, without even invoking the alternative concepts of equilibrium.

What about the people who know they have become high risks? If a new insurer proposed to charge the high-risk premium, either for the current level of coverage or some different amount, the high risks would also not be attracted, since, having prepaid the difference between high- and low-risk premia, they would expect to pay the latter in the future.

We do not need to require that the quantity be the original or standard quantity and zero. Insurers could be free to sell less generous policies; low risks would not be induced to reduce the quantity below their original level, since the premium was and is based on the low-risk probability.

One possible vehicle for adverse selection to occur would be if insurers were willing to sell more coverage than the initial or standard amount. The possibility here is that those consumers who (secretly) know they have become high risk might be more likely to buy more coverage because the premium has fallen well below one based on their risk level. This sort of behavior is effectively ruled out in simple Rothschild-Stiglitz models by the assumption that insurers know the insured's demands (conditional on type) and would refuse to sell coverage higher than the higher risks would efficiently demand. In a more realistic model in which demand varies because risk aversion varies, an insurer might be willing to sell high levels of coverage. But what premium would insurers charge for such additional coverage after the first period, given that they know that some of the potential buyers of additional coverage have now become high risk? The answer depends on the reason they imagine that someone might want additional coverage. If the reason is always because the person has become high risk, insurers would then propose to charge the high-risk premium for such coverage, and high risks would have no special incentive to buy more coverage.

If the only change that was occurring for consumers was the change in loss probability, we know (as Ehrlich and Becker, 1972, have shown) that change in probability, loading held constant, should not change the desired level of coverage (except for minor income effects). However, there might be good reasons why some consumers would want to buy more coverage. They might have new dependents or a higher level of income. They might experience a change in the value of health that would affect the level of health insurance coverage they desire. Then some consumers seeking more coverage might be low risks. The insurer might be able to identify risk levels by discovering the reason for changing coverage. If that proved difficult, however, there could be adverse selection applied to *increments* in coverage, above the standard or average quantity chosen when insurance is first purchased.

Insurer Inside Information and Guaranteed Renewability

In this last section, I combine the model of guaranteed renewability, which both smooths risks over the lifetime and strongly inhibits adverse selection, with a model, especially valid for automobile insurance, in which the insurer from which coverage is bought learns through a consumer's claims history what that person's risk level is. However, other insurers, without access to as accurate a claims history, will be less adept at identifying specific risks. Will the current insurer try to exploit its informational advantages, and where will there be an equilibrium?

The insurer might plan to raise the premium it charges to especially good risks up to the higher premium they would be charged by outside insurers. One factor that would inhibit this behavior would be fear of a bad reputation, but the imprecision of what expected expenses are for coverages with necessary "repair costs," like auto and health, gives an insurer some leeway. If reputation fails to discipline adequately, however, insurers could expect to earn profits on those they know to be better risks than the market judges; in turn, this would provide a motivation for offering low prices initially to "buy" this information, as Kunreuther and Pauly (1985) have suggested. Such backloading of profits and administrative costs would offset the frontloading inherent in GR.

It seems that the question is ultimately an empirical one of which influence is stronger. We know that, on balance, individual health insurance is frontloaded. The elasticity of premiums with respect to changes in expected expense due to age is substantially less than unity, in the range of 0.2 to 0.45 (Pauly and Herring, 1999). I am less familiar with such information on automobile insurance. But generally it does not seem that backloading or initial-period discounts are common.

Conclusion

In ways largely unrecognized by insurance theorists, some insurance markets have set up institutional structures that appear to deal in a good (though not perfect) way with both risk rating/time consistency and adverse selection. There is a problem in insurance markets if people wait to buy insurance until risk differentiation occurs or becomes apparent. Guaranteed renewability tends to inhibit such behavior, offering a strong incentive to buy insurance *before* events that increase risk occur, but customer ignorance may mean that some consumers still wait to seek coverage until they become high risk. The political sensitivity to having such high risks then pay high premiums or be refused coverage at reasonable premiums frequently motivates what in my view are ill-considered, unnecessary, inefficient, and inequitable efforts at ex post risk pooling. Regulations forbidding insurers from risk rating those who do delay destroys the incentive to take GR coverage. In this sense, community rating is a humanitarian temptation that needs to be resisted in favor of more efficient ways to deal with high risks. To be sure, differences in risk level at the start of (adult) life that come from genetics or misfortune in childhood *do* deserve to be averaged or pooled across everyone in the community. But the fraction of the eighteen-year-old population with a chronic condition is less than 3 percent, so this cannot be a problem that requires heavy-handed interaction in the insurance transactions for the great majority of consumers.

Insurance theorists may have devoted excessive attention to the theory of adverse selection, relative to the real-life relevance of the problem in markets that actually exist. Most of the examples of severe adverse selection come from situations in which community rating or some other deviation from risk rating are required by law. We need to recognize that markets that are more complex than those usually used in the theoretical models have developed ways to capture, at least in part, the efficiency that would be lost in market failure.

Note

1. If it were forbidden to discriminate its premium or a new contract, it could still get the risks to self-select by offering a Rothschild-Stiglitz policy (Rothschild and Stiglitz, 1976).

References

Arrow, K. J. (1963). "Uncertainty and Welfare Economics of Medical Care." *American Economic Review* 53(5): 941–973.

Cochrane, J. (1995). "Time-Consistent Health Insurance." *Journal of Political Economy* 103(3): 445–473.

Cooper, R. W., and B. Hayes. (1987). "Multiperiod Insurance Contracts." *International Journal of Industrial Organization* 5: 221–232.

Diamond, P. (1992). "Organizing the Health Insurance Market." *Econometrica* 60(6): 1233–1254.

Ehrlich, I., and G. S. Becker. (1972). "Market Insurance, Self-Insurance, and Self-Protection." *Journal of Political Economy* 80(4): 623–648.

Harrington, S. E., and G. R. Niehaus. (1999). *Risk Management and Insurance.* Boston: Irwin/McGraw-Hill, 1999.

Harris, M., and B. Holmstrom. (1982). "A Theory of Wage Dynamics." *Review of Economic Studies* 49(3): 315–333.

Hendel, I., and A. Lizzeri. (2003). "The Role of Commitment in Dynamic Contracts: Evidence From Life Insurance." *Quarterly Journal of Economics* 118(1): 299–327.

Herring, B., and M. V. Pauly. (2003). "Incentive-Compatible Guaranteed Renewable Health Insurance." NBER Working Paper 9888, July. ⟨http://www.nber.org/papers/w9888⟩, September 10, 2003.

Kunreuther, H., and M. V. Pauly. (1985). "Market Equilibrium with Private Knowledge: An Insurance Example." *Journal of Public Economics* 26(3): 269–288.

Madrian, B. (1994). "Employment-Based Health Insurance and Job Mobility: Is There Evidence of Job-Lock?" *Quarterly Journal of Economics* 109(1): 27–54.

Pauly, M. V., and B. Herring. (1999). *Pooling Health Insurance Risks.* Washington, DC: AEI Press.

Pauly, M. V., H. Kunreuther, and R. Hirth. (1995). "Guaranteed Renewability in Insurance." *Journal of Risk and Uncertainty* 10(2): 143–156.

Pauly, M. V., J. Rosenbloom, B. J. Herring, H. Szrek, and J. N. Rosenquist. (2003). "Guaranteed Renewability in Individual and Group Health Insurance: Functioning and Future Prospects." Final Report on Robert Wood Johnson Foundation Grant 44065. Wharton School, University of Pennsylvania.

Rothschild, M., and J. E. Stiglitz. (1976). "Equilibrium in Competitive Insurance Markets: An Essay on the Economics of Imperfect Information." *Quarterly Journal of Economics* 90(4): 630–649.

2

Adverse Selection in the Health Insurance Market after Genetic Tests

Roland Eisen

Introduction

On June 26, 2000, scientists from two major research institutions declared that a draft of the human genetic code was completed, and it was expected that the human genome will be fully sequenced by 2003. The sequencing was completed on February 15, 2001. But sequencing is just the first major step toward understanding the human genetic code. What is really needed is the identification of the location, length, and function of each gene. Furthermore, mutations of genes must also be studied because they may indicate future health problems. To date, mutations that affect the likelihood of developing breast, ovarian, or colon cancer, Alzheimer's disease, and Huntington's disease have been discovered. Much research is also directed at estimating the likelihood that people who have a genetic mutation will develop other particular diseases.

All this currently and soon to be available information will have different effects. First, it puts the individual in an informational lottery: would you want to know whether your genetic code indicates an increased likelihood to develop (or even to have) a particular disease? Second, knowledge of a mutation's existence (wherever this information comes from, either a genetic test or the use of a family's history of diseases) could encourage an individual to undergo periodically preventive measures to maintain his health. Or this knowledge may lead to the eventual discovery of cures for the tainted genes and for these diseases. Third, should society and insurers use the available information efficiently to write different insurance policies with different fair premia or to reach a separating equilibrium (with only private information) in the sense of Rothschild and Stiglitz (1976)?[1] Fourth, given the information and the possibilities of insurers using this information for risk classification and pricing, which arrangement is Pareto superior: the separating equilibrium of Rothschild/Stiglitz, the subsidizing of the bad risks to get a pooling equilibrium in the sense of Wilson (1977) and others, or the combination of a basic compulsory insurance together with a voluntary insurance contract?[2] These questions are discussed in this chapter, which takes into account the costs of prevention, the value of a treatment option, and the problem that even the information content of genetic tests is uncertain.

The chapter is organized as follows. The information lottery is presented and put in an arrangement where there is insurance, a treatment option exists, and information is symmetric or public (everybody, the insurer as well as the potential policyholder, has the same information relevant for risk assessment). Also considered is asymmetric information, where there is a difference between private and public information (in other words, access to information is restricted to the person concerned). The case for subsidization or the mix of compulsory and voluntary insurance is discussed, and the different information states of compulsory and private insurance are compared. The problem of uncertainty of genetic tests and therefore uncertainty in risk classification are also taken into account. A summary and some policy conclusions with respect to further problems are given at the end of the chapter.

Genetic Tests and Health Insurance with Symmetric (or Public) Information

Would you want to know whether your genetic code indicates an increased probability to develop (or to have) a particular disease? An individual's answer will depend on what else the individual knows, if there is a cure for or method to prevent the disease, and whether this information (or the genetic test itself) can be used for therapeutical purposes. Therefore, the decision must be put into a more sophisticated environment.

The environment of the individual is as follows (see, e.g., Doherty and Posey, 1998). Everybody knows the proportion of high $(1 - \rho)$ and low risks (ρ) in the population $(0 < \rho < 1)$, and the respective disease probabilities of the risk classes (π_H, π_L) are also common knowledge. It is the purpose of genetic tests to reveal these morbidity probabilities before the ailment appears.[3] These probabilities, however, can be reduced by treatment for those revealed to be in the high-risk class.

The production function for treatment, $\pi_H(V)$, is known to all, and only high risks need treatment. The costs of prevention V are of two kinds: (1) the costs of providing professional medical treatment and (2) personal costs, mainly unobservable by others (like a special diet, pain, and discomfort), that are related to the preventive measures. Besides high and low risks who know their risk type, some individuals are *uninformed* about their conditions. However, they can get a genetic test at zero cost. This checkup will reveal information on the morbidity probability. Consumers are risk averse, and insurance companies are risk neutral. Utility is assumed to be separable in the chosen level of treatment V. Therefore, treatment costs can be measured in money terms and in psychic terms (such as discomfort). The utility function is state independent. All consumers have an initial wealth of W_0; the inherent loss L is fixed and the same for all who suffer it.[4]

The following assumptions are made with respect to the loss probabilities π_i and the treatment technology:

$$\pi_H(V), \pi_U, \pi_L > 0; \tag{2.3a}$$

$$\pi_H'(V) < 0; \quad \pi_H''(V) > 0; \tag{2.3b}$$

$$\pi_H(\infty) > \pi_U > \pi_L; \tag{2.3c}$$

$$\pi_U = \rho\pi_L + (1 - \rho)\pi_H(0); \tag{2.3d}$$

where π_i is loss probability of risk class i ($i = H, L$, and $U =$ uninformed), V is treatment cost, and ρ is proportion of low risks in the population.

As mentioned before, only high risks need treatment, and there are decreasing returns (assumption 2.3b) such that the high risks stay in this category even when they spend unlimited amounts of resources (assumption 2.3c). This ensures the single crossing property (see Hoy, 1989) of the indifference curves.[5]

This situation is depicted in figure 2.1: the two risk types and the uninformed individuals are characterized by three different indifference curves. Since everybody is fully informed (information is public) and all three types can be distinguished, these three risk classes would be offered full insurance at actuarially fair rates. This gives the policies H^*, U^*, and L^* offered respectively to high risks, uninformed individuals, and low risks. Treatment affects both the probability of loss and the endowment point by the direct and indirect costs. The first effect is embodied in the slope of the high-risk indifference curve and the

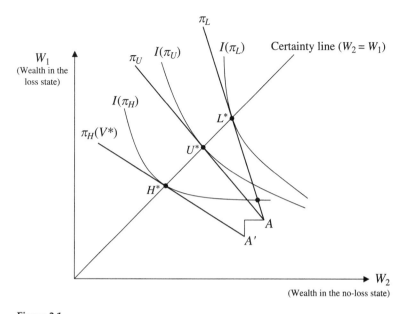

Figure 2.1
Full-information equilibrium
Notes: The original endowment point is A; the low-risk price line is labeled π_L, the high-risk price line after treatment is labeled $\pi_H(V^*)$; the indifference curves of the different risk types are denoted by $I(\pi_i)$; the first-best policies are $\{H^*, U^*, L^*\}$.

budget line, the second effect in the shift of the endowment point from A to A'.

The insurance policies are fairly priced, the premiums therefore are given by

$$\alpha_i = \frac{\pi_i}{1 - \pi_i} \cdot \beta_i,$$

with β_i as the payout net of the premium. For high risks, the optimal policy solves

$$\max_{\beta, V} EU = \pi_H(V)\upsilon(W_0 - L + \beta_H)$$
$$+ (1 - \pi_H(V))\upsilon\left(W_0 - \frac{\pi_H(V)}{1 - \pi_H(V)} \cdot \beta_H\right) - V. \tag{2.4}$$

The first-order conditions for an inner optimum are

$$\frac{\partial EU}{\partial \beta_H} = \pi_H(V) \cdot \upsilon_H^{S'} - (1 - \pi_H(V))\frac{\pi_H(V)}{1 - \pi_H(V)} \cdot \upsilon_H^{N'} = 0; \tag{2.5}$$

$$\frac{\partial EU}{\partial V} = \pi'_H(V)\left[v_H^S - v_H^N - \beta_H \frac{1}{1-\pi_H}v_H^{N'}\right] - 1 = 0; \tag{2.6}$$

where $v_H^S = v(W_0 - L + \beta_H)$,

$$v_H^N = v\left(W_0 - \beta_H \frac{\pi_H(V)}{1-\pi_H(V)}\right),$$

and $v_H^{N'}$ and $v_H^{S'}$ are the respective derivatives.

In equation (2.5), it is clearly visible that the marginal utility in the loss-state $v_H^{S'}$ equals marginal utility in the no-loss state $v_H^{N'}$. This implies equal wealth in both states and hence *full insurance*.

In equation (2.6), the marginal costs of treatment are 1 and equal to the marginal benefits, which consist of two components—the reduction in the loss probability and the value of this reduction in utility terms.

If there is a genetic mutation without a treatment, then $\pi'_H(V) = 0$, and the necessary condition for the optimal treatment level cannot be fulfilled (however, there can exist a corner solution).

One can now put the above-mentioned question in a new form: is the uninformed individual interested in making a genetic test taking into account that the information is public and shared with the insurance company? Since the contracts of the (informed) high and low risks remain the same after the acquisition of information by the uninformed individual, he or she is faced with a choice between the contract U^* and a lottery over the two contracts H^* and L^*. The private *and* social value of the information for the uninformed (VI_U) is given by

$$VI_U = \rho v[L^*, \pi_L] + (1-\rho)\{v[H^*, \pi_H(V^*)] - V^*\} - v[U^*, \pi_U]. \tag{2.7}$$

The first two elements of equation (2.7) show the expected value of the lottery (one can call this the *premium risk*), and the third term shows the sure value of the state of ignorance. If we take into account that the way from U^* to H^* is over H^0, where the individual is known as a high risk but has not taken any decision with respect to treatment, the value of information can be written—by adding and subtracting $(1 - \rho)v[H^0, \pi_H(0)]$—in the following form:

$$VI_U = (1-\rho)\{v[H^*, \pi_H(V^*)] - V^* - v[H^0, \pi_H(0)]\}$$
$$+ \{(1-\rho)v[H^0, \pi_H(0)] + \rho v[L^*, \pi_L] - v[U^*, \pi_U]\}. \tag{2.8}$$

Now, the value of the genetic information consists of two terms:

• *The value of the treatment option*   With probability $(1 - \rho)$, the individual is recognized as a high risk, which brings him the risky utility $v[H^0, \pi_H(\mathbf{0})]$. However, this information opens the possibility of treatment to reduce the loss probability from $\pi_H(\mathbf{0})$ to $\pi_H(V^*)$ by spending V^*. Hence, the treatment is socially efficient (a positive marginal productivity) when this term is positive—that is,

$$V^* < \{v[H^*, \pi_H(V^*)] - v[H^0, \pi_H(\mathbf{0})]\}. \tag{2.9}$$

• *The value of the insurance classification lottery*   The decision to take the test exposes the individual to a lottery, either to turn out as a high risk with probability $(1 - \rho)$ or as a low risk with probability ρ. On the other hand, if uninformed, the individual has a policy offering full insurance at a fair price π_U, which satisfies the above given assumption (see eq. (2.3d)). Thus, this decision is—at the most—a fair lottery, and for a risk-averse individual the fair lottery reduces expected utility, implying that the second term is negative.

These two arguments can be summarized in the following proposition.

Proposition 2.1   The (public) value of genetic information—which is also known by the insurance company—is ambiguous even when there is a treatment option, which is, by itself, sufficiently productive. When there is no treatment option, the value of genetic information is unambiguously negative since the first term (treatment option) is equal to zero, and the second term is negative.

From equation (2.9), one can see that testing is less likely to be the chosen alternative, compared to no test and prevention, the higher the cost (V^*) and the less effective (the difference between the two probabilities of getting the ailment) are preventive measures. Furthermore, the second part of equation (2.8) shows that testing is less likely chosen the more risk averse is the uninformed individual. In other words, the more risk averse the person is, the larger is the (absolute) value of the insurance classification risk. Together one notes that even when the treatment is socially efficient not everybody will undertake the test.

Difference between Private and Public Information of Genetic Tests

Genetic testing is an important health policy issue because genetic tests will have important effects on the health insurance system. Some people even express the apprehension that insurers, making use of the information, may deny coverage for individuals with a genetic mutation or may require prohibitively high premia for insurance coverage of these diseases. Therefore, society has to decide how to handle this problem.

In the case of genetic tests, in praxi *four* different regimes of information regulation could be distinguished:

• *Strict regulation,* where insurers do not inquire and are not allowed to use or to ask for information connected with genetic tests. Here, information is (strictly) private.

• *Consent law,* where insurers are allowed to use genetic information but are not allowed to ask for genetic tests prior of contract agreement. In other words, the individuals *can* reveal test results.

• *Revelation duty,* where insurers can use available genetic information. Insurers are permitted to ask whether consumers have taken tests or not and then to use this information.

• *Laissez faire,* where insurers may ask for genetic tests or otherwise; the contract will be signed by the insurer only if a test is made.

Different countries use different regulations. Austria, Belgium, Denmark, France, and Norway (cf. Berberich, 2001, p. 318) have enacted laws prohibiting insurance companies or employers from asking for a genetic test. In other countries (such as Finland, France, Germany, Sweden, and Switzerland), insurers have chosen a moratorium. Furthermore, in the United Kingdom, a Genetics and Insurance Committee (GAIC) has been established to decide whether certain genetic test results can be used in the underwriting decision.

The problem now is the following: when the individual takes a (genetic) test that gives information on his or her state of health and—if high-risk type is revealed—permits treatment *V*, should the individual make this information public? In this case, the information about health status and prevention costs is private. Therefore, insurance contracts cannot be made contingent on whether preventive measures have been taken. However, insurers can react by offering a menu of contracts so that individuals will self-select.

Doherty and Posey (1998) also take up this question and generalize their argument for the case where the insurance company cannot observe the results of the tests. In this case, the insurance companies must have some beliefs about whether the uninformed have taken the test and become informed or not. In overall equilibrium, these beliefs must be consistent with the actual behavior of the uninformed. Hence, the insurance company offers a menu of contracts to induce consumers to self-select the appropriate policy for them. Doherty and Posey (1998) calculate the value of information for the uninformed consumers under each of the contract menus. They show "that *becoming informed is a dominant strategy for the uninformed* consumers" when there is a treatment option, *and* "high risks invest in the level of treatment which is optimal for them *ex post*" (p. 203). We can summarize this result in the following proposition.

Proposition 2.2   "The private value of information is strictly positive under asymmetric information" (Doherty and Posey, 1998, p. 203).

This means, however, since the insurance company cannot observe the test results, that "it is the ability to hide information status, rather than the ability to hide test results that is pivotal in determining the value of information" (Doherty and Posey, 1998, p. 203). Furthermore, even when the private value of information to the uninformed is zero (because there is no treatment option), taking the test and allowing the risk-selection process increases the utility of the low risks who have then lower signaling costs. As shown by Doherty and Posey (1998, p. 205), we can summarize this in the following proposition.

Proposition 2.3   The social value of information revealed by genetic tests is positive whether or not there is a treatment option. Thus, "the presence of the treatment option is the key to the private market's ability to provide socially optimal incentives for acquiring hidden information" (Doherty and Posey, 1998, p. 205).

However, in this context, the uninformed must signal that they really are uninformed and cannot only pretend to be uninformed. To separate the wolves in sheep's clothing from the (uninformed) sheep, the insurer will offer a new set of contracts. Therefore (see figure 2.2), the uninformed must accept a contract that fulfills the self-selection constraint of high risks. This contract is U^{**}. If the uninformed chooses this contract, which one should be offered to the good risks so that the uninformed does not choose the contract offered to the good risks (e.g., L^{**})? Hence, this contract must satisfy the self-selection constraint of the uninformed, which is L_2. Now, is the triple $\{H^*, U^{**}, L_2\}$ an equilibrium? The answer to this question depends on the costs of information. The uninformed chooses either to keep U^{**} *or* to get informed *and*

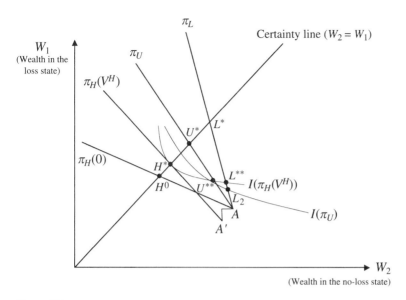

Figure 2.2
Two or three contracts separating equilibria
Notes: A is the initial endowment; the low-risk price line is labeled π_L; the high risks spend V on safety, resulting in the high-risk price line labeled $\pi_H(V^H)$; when high-risk individuals do not undertake prevention, the budget line is $\pi_H(0)$; in equilibrium, high risks are indifferent between having policy H^* (which means spending V^H on safety) and policy L^{**} (which means less insurance but at a lower price).

to choose the lottery between H^* and L_2. The value of the test (and hence of information) is positive: although the test implies more risk, this is compensated by a factor that shifts the weight in favor of the lottery. To stay uninformed is accompanied by a real cost because the contract U^{**} must bear the risk of fulfilling the self-selection constraint of high risks. Hence, an uninformed will stay uninformed only if the costs of the test are high enough. If the costs of tests are low, then $\{H^*, U^{**}, L_2\}$ is no equilibrium.

If insurers expect that all uninformed will make the test but they cannot observe the risk status after the test, then they will offer the Rothschild-Stiglitz pair of contracts $\{H^*, L^{**}\}$, which fulfills the self-selection constraint of the high risks. Now it is evident that for the uninformed to stay uninformed, she or he will prefer L^{**} over H^*. Hence, the choice for the uninformed is to keep L^{**} (which is optimal also without knowing the risk status) *or* to take a lottery between H^* (which is preferred if one has full information of the high-risk status) and L^{**} (which is preferred if one comes out as a good risk). The value of this lottery is clearly zero. Therefore, if the costs of the test are zero and one uses a tie-breaker rule, then the uninformed will take the test, and the contract pair $\{H^*, L^{**}\}$ is a Nash-Cournot equilibrium.[6] If the test is costly, however, this is no equilibrium. These arguments lead to the following proposition.

Proposition 2.4   With private information and sufficiently high test costs, $\{H^*, U^{**}, L_2\}$ is an equilibrium. If test costs are below some threshold, then there is no Nash-Cournot equilibrium. Furthermore, there is an equilibrium "on the knife edge" if test costs are zero: $\{H^*, L^{**}\}$.

However, things may be different if the *consent-law* case is in force. This case was analyzed by Tabarrok (1994). He concluded that the individual will choose the test. This case was further analyzed by Doherty and Thistle (1996b). Informed good risks will present their test results. Informed high risks will not do this. Hence, the triple $\{H^*, U^{**}, L^*\}$ or the pair $\{H^*, L^*\}$ are potential equilibria. $\{H^*, L^*\}$ has a positive value of information; hence, this is an equilibrium only if the information value is higher than the test costs. $\{H^*, U^*, L^*\}$ is an equilibrium only if the uninformed stay uninformed. Since the value of information is positive, he or she will stay uninformed only if the test costs are high enough. One can summarize this in the following proposition.

Proposition 2.5   Under consent law, the uninformed stay uninformed only when test costs are sufficiently high. If test costs are zero, nobody will stay uninformed, and taking the test is the optimal strategy. Hence, $\{H^*, L^*\}$, is the resulting equilibrium. This is also true for the two other information regimes.[7]

Given these results, the challenge for the insurance companies and the general public is to select those tests that are combined with a sufficiently productive treatment option and to offer this option without payment.

A Case for Subsidization or Compulsory Insurance

The results thus far show that with private information the equilibrium is characterized by two or three contracts, depending on the cost of the test and the legal regime with respect to the information about genetic tests. Therefore, a first policy result will be to offer the test without payment. Then it is optimal for the uninformed individuals to take the test.

Hence, given these (negative) informational external effects, market equilibria are only second best. Therefore, the question can be posed, whether (to collect the benefits of the positive social value of information; see propositions 2.3 and 2.5) there is some form of state intervention, regulation, or compulsory or social insurance leading to Pareto superior results.

In the literature about insurance equilibria, Spence (1978) and Miyazaki (1977) have generalized the result of Wilson (1977)[8] and introduced the concept of *transfer equilibrium*. Such a transfer equilibrium is characterized by the low risks subsidizing the high risks, but both risk classes together fulfill the zero-profit constraint of the insurer.

Figure 2.3 provides an illustration of such a tax-transfer system, where the low risks are taxed by an amount t, while the high risks will get the transfer or subsidy s per policy. Given the proportion ρ of low risks in the population and under the zero-profit condition of the insurance company, this implies

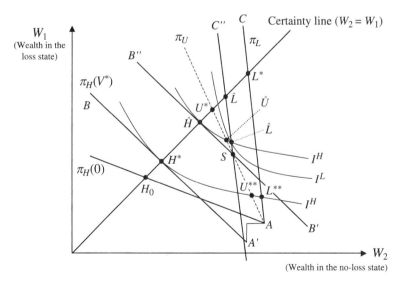

Figure 2.3
Transfer equilibrium with asymmetric information and a tax-subsidy system
Notes: The original endowment point is A; the low-risk price line AC is shifted to $C'C''$; the high-risk price line $A'B$ is shifted to $B'B''$ by the tax-transfer mechanism; the old equilibrium $\{H^*, L^{**}\}$ is changed to the transfer equilibrium $\{\hat{H}, \hat{L}\}$; optimal policies lay on the line $U^*\hat{L}L^{**}$ (not shown).

$(1 - \rho)s = \rho \cdot t.$ $\qquad\qquad\qquad\qquad\qquad\qquad\qquad\qquad$ (2.10)

The tax shifts (see figure 2.3) the budget line of low risks from AC to $C'C''$; the subsidy shifts the budget line of high risks from $A'B$ to $B'B''$. The indifference curve of high risks is tangential to $B'B''$ in $\hat{H}$ and cuts the new budget line $C'C''$ at $\hat{L}$. This shows that with the use of this tax-subsidy mechanism the high risks can get an insurance contract $(\hat{H})$ that is strictly preferred to H^*, and the low risks will get the policy $\hat{L}$ that is (in this example) also strictly preferred to L^{**}. By varying the tax and the subsidy, a curve $U^*\hat{L}L^{**}$ can be constructed (not shown in the figure), and the best contract for the low risks is that where the indifference curve of the low risks is tangential to $U^*\hat{L}L^{**}$.

The pair of contracts $\{\hat{H},\hat{L}\}$ is a reaction equilibrium with transfers (under private information and zero tests costs) and Pareto efficient; however, it is no Nash-Cournot equilibrium (see also Eisen, 1986, p. 350). Furthermore, these equilibria[9] are by themselves Pareto ordered—that is,

$$\{H^*, L^{**}\} < \{\hat{H}, \hat{L}\}.$$

This market outcome is equivalent to a compulsory (or social) insurance where everybody must buy the same policy S—in this case, however, with partial coverage only (see also Dahlby, 1981). Varying the tax and subsidy, every policy S between A and U^* can be chosen. The insurance premium is independent of the individual risk. There is, however, the possibility to buy (additional) voluntary insurance according to the individual risk class along the changed budget lines.

Private and Compulsory Insurance under Private or Public Information

Recall now the assumptions about (1) the institutional constraint of the insurers (the insurance contract cannot depend on whether an individual is tested or not or on the test result) and (2) private information. Now assume that the insurers expect individuals to be informed about their health or risk status. If there is full insurance coverage, then there will be no prevention because prevention is costly. Hence, when there is voluntary (additional) insurance, this insurance must be offered with the premium $\pi_H(0)$, leading to full coverage of the high risks (somewhere between $\hat{H}$ and H^*). In other words, given S, it might be cheaper for the high risk to pay the higher premium $\pi_H(0)$ for additional or supplementary insurance of a small amount to reach full insurance than to undertake prevention at a cost that is independent of the loss. Since the indifference curve of the high risks through the (new) full insurance policy is higher than that through H^*, the low risks also can get more insurance than L^{**} or even L_2 (in figure 2.2). Using the same argument as in Doherty and Thistle (1996a), it can be shown that taking a test is the optimal choice. Therefore, these results can be summarized (without giving a rigorous proof) in the following proposition.

Proposition 2.6   When we define compulsory insurance as a contract with equal (but not necessary full) coverage and equal premium for both risk classes, then

1. There is a transfer equilibrium combining compulsory (to the level of S) and supplementary voluntary insurance.

2. This equilibrium is characterized by two contracts because it is optimal for uninformed individuals to take a (zero cost) test: $\{\hat{H}, \hat{L}\}$.

3. To maintain the incentive for high risks to undertake preventive measures, the contract $\hat{H}$ may not be a full-coverage insurance contract.

4. But full insurance for the high-risk individuals can be offered only at the fair premium $\pi_H(0)$ for additional insurance, implying that they will not undertake prevention.

5. Whatever the contract offer (either case 2 or 4 above, depending on whether we take moral hazard into account), there is a social loss compared to the public information case $\{\hat{H}, \bar{L}\}$, since at least the low risks get less coverage.

Even this transfer equilibrium does not fully eliminate the negative informational externality. However, this result is (Pareto) superior to the equilibrium without compulsory insurance, described in proposition 2.5. To raise efficiency, there is some redistribution.

Given this fact, it is possible to take into account explicitly (societal) *goals of redistribution*. As can be seen from figure 2.3, the higher the degree of compulsory insurance (policy S), the less variation there is in the different insurance premiums of high and low risks. With private insurance, the high-risk individuals have to pay the high-risk premium, independent of the information regime. In the private-information regime, the outcome (the insurance contract) may even be worse[10] than in the public-information regime. So there are good reasons to offer a social insurance scheme and to make information public. Besides this *distributional dimension*, there are two other tradeoffs that should be mentioned (also discussed in Hoel and Iversen, 2002). Under the *public-information regime*, full coverage can be offered regardless of the degree of compulsory (or social) insurance. Under the *private-information regime*, full coverage can be offered to both risk classes only with compulsory insurance. Due to adverse selection, full private insurance can be offered only for high-risk individuals who choose not to prevent. Those high-risk individuals who undertake prevention and the low-risk individuals get only partial insurance.

Under the *public-information regime*, reducing the part of compulsory (social) insurance may discourage (socially efficient) testing because of the increasing classification risk. Under the *private-information regime*, reducing the part of compulsory insurance may lead to more (socially efficient) testing and prevention. The reason is that the premium of private insurance of the uninformed individuals increases due to adverse selection. Because the insurer cannot distinguish between the truly uninformed and those high-risk individuals pretending to be uninformed, taking both the test *and* preventive measures is the dominant strategy. However, if prevention is *not* socially efficient (or effective) (see equation (9)) or if there are no preventive measures at all, then testing is still (see proposition 2.2) the dominant strategy under the private information regime and private insurance.

Uncertain Risk Classification

In the foregoing, it was assumed that information *after* the test was perfect. However, the predictive power of genetics in particular in multifactorial diseases is exaggerated. Consider the case of Huntington's disease. This disease is genetically transmitted, and the risk at birth of developing this disease for someone with an ill parent is 50 percent. A person at risk will have a confirmatory test that will refine the prior probability to either 5 or 95 percent (see Meissen, Myers, Mastromauro, et al., 1988). However, in most cases, the onset of the disease is usually late in life, and there is still a high degree of uncertainty. Metaphorically or figuratively, it means that to take this second-degree uncertainty into account, the budget lines for the three different risk classes look more like bands. This argument can be applied in particular for the high-risk class where insurers can identify high risks but are not able to calculate exactly the loss probability. The fixed loss L in the above model represents normally a skewed loss distribution, where the high risks get the high losses that are sometimes so unusual as to preclude an exact calculation of the loss probability. This uncertainty leads to an increased risk that will be taken into account by a high loading factor. In other words, with adverse selection or moral hazard, this second-degree risk has to be borne by the high-risk individuals. One can now ask whether it is possible to improve the situation not only by compulsory or social insurance but also by using additional (although incomplete) information?

Doherty and Thistle (1996a) discuss this problem for the individual who knows that his or her family history (or anamnesis) indicates a higher or lower probability of disease. This divides the group of *uninformed* individuals into two subgroups. Then they show (p. 97, proposition) that "If information were costless, then becoming informed would again be a dominant strategy." Hence, "uninformed consumers remain uninformed simply because information costs are too high" (p. 98).[11]

These results depend critically on the assumptions that insurers cannot observe the risk type directly and that informed and uninformed consumers cannot be distinguished.

However, insurers also can use such information relating to anamnesis as signals or monitors. The main question then is how reliable this additional information is. Doherty and Thistle (1996a) use a signal s_i ($i = 1, 2$) that when observed determines that the individual is with probability μ_i a high risk. In the literature, different signals also are discussed, mostly in the case of moral hazard (see, e.g., Harris and Raviv, 1978, 1979; Shavell, 1979; Holmström, 1979; Eisen, 1981). When insurers can use this additional information (without knowing whether the individual has taken a test and afterward will be revealed as low or high risk), then the cases discussed by Doherty and Thistle (1996a) with only private information are not (empirically) relevant. This is the result even when the law does not permit insurers to inquire whether applicants (customers) have taken the test (consent-law case). In a certain sense, this brings insurance markets nearer to efficiency. Insofar as the private value of information is positive (because there is a sufficiently effective treatment), tests will be taken and the public-health externality will be mitigated or even resolved. The equilibrium in the insurance market will be a full-information equilibrium with no uninformed policyholders. However, this favorable result depends crucially on the argument that information is public. With private information about tests and their results, because of adverse selection both risk classes get less than full insurance.

However, when there is no treatment option (or no socially efficient treatment option), then testing is still the dominant strategy under the private-information regime and private insurance. This inefficiency (as Hoel and Iversen, 2002, p. 266, called it) "is likely to be more prevalent the less compulsory insurance a system contains."

With private (voluntary) insurance and under the public-information system, it is possible that insurance is too costly or pro-hibitive for those testing positive (or having inherited the wrong parents)—even without taking into account that tests are costly. This implies, as discussed already by Tabarrok (1994), that genetic insur-ance is necessary to deal with the risk of an increased insurance pre-mium when someone is identified as a high-risk individual.

In the recent literature, two solutions are discussed for the pre-mium risk attached to worsening risk conditions—the guaranteed-renewability insurance proposed by Pauly, Kunreuther, and Hirth (1995) (see also Pauly, 2006) and the time-consistent health insurance discussed by Cochrane (1995). Although in both models the time pro-file of premiums is decreasing in time ("high-balling"), the main differ-ence consists in a severance payment. While in the Pauly, Kunreuther, and Hirth proposal all insurance buyers pay the expected increase in risk in advance (and are therefore dependent on the long-term commit-ment of the insurer), with Cochrane's proposal the severance payment functions like a bond whose value allows the individual to pay the higher premiums (and this bond is transferable between insurance companies). However, in both proposals the (stochastic or probabilis-tic) changes in risks must balance over the insureds (they are only white noise). Therefore, nondiversifiable shocks and medical and tech-nological progress are outside these contracts. Furthermore, because of the extreme experience rating within the insurance contracts, there are great problems for individuals who are sick at the beginning or show genetic defects or poor family history. So we are back to our starting point. Until now there have been no possibilities for insuring this pre-mium risk except by some sort of social (compulsory) insurance.

To make (private) insurance policies affordable also for the high risks, the consumer can buy insurance contracts precluding some pre-specified illnesses or certain treatment alternatives (with especially high costs) (see the model of Strohmenger and Wambach, 2000, and the comments by Eisen and Zweifel, 2003). In other words, instead of buying an overall coverage with an equal distribution, the money can be put—according to the different risks of illnesses—into different treatments or the exclusion of certain treatments. The individual may still retain coverage of some dread disease (like heart attacks), particularly by excluding a few other conditions (identified by the genetic test) from his or her health insurance policy.

This solution is not without its problems, either. For one, Fuchs (1979, p. 170) has argued that individuals may desire comprehensive health insurance coverage not only to reduce uncertainty (as is normally assumed) but also to obviate the need for troublesome moral choices between money and medical treatment during episodes of illness.

Second, the decision to exclude some conditions is likely to cause regret. Experience shows that the insured frequently go to court. The question then becomes whether this type of contract will hold up in court (see Kolata, 1994, p. A1).

When insurers are allowed to require genetic tests and to use this kind of information or information from other sources, there might then exist a tendency to privately insure only low risks, while high risks are referred to compulsory or social insurance. Until now, social health insurance is usually rated according to income and not to risk. However, this tendency may raise the costs of social insurance, making it less attractive for the low risks with the consequence that these individuals will leave social insurance. This in turn raises the premium even further. This problem can be solved only by compulsory insurance because then adverse selection cannot occur. In this case, (compulsory) social insurance can Pareto-improve the situation as shown above.[12]

Conclusions and Policy Implications

Genetic tests and their possible use in insurance have released hopes and fears (even of the impossibility of private insurance). Pivotal for this discussion is the possibility of adverse selection—the use of hidden information by applicants to buy an insurance contract that is too inexpensive. This may be a real problem in life and annuity insurance, where with asymmetric information the price of insurance for low risks is too high and for high risks is too low. This leads to underinsurance of low risks and to overinsurance of high risks, resulting in an increase in the break-even premium. If insurance contracts are tradable, then there will be a secondary market for life insurance policies, and the high risks may realize risk-free arbitrage gains. This can lead to a breakdown of the (life) insurance market.

In health insurance markets, the situation is different. On the one hand, whether or not the insurance company knows the risk types, the break-even policy for the overall population (cf. condition (2.3d)) does not change. The genetic test reveals only the risk types.[13] On the other hand, as shown here, when there is a treatment option or when the private value of information is nonnegative, then insurance markets are (second-best) efficient. Hence, even under the private-information regime where the individual can hide his or her (unfavorable) test result, insurance companies can design a menu of contracts so that taking tests is the dominant strategy (and the public can support this equilibrium by offering genetic tests at zero costs).

Furthermore, it is shown here that the social value of (genetic) information is always positive, independent of whether there is a treatment option. The reason is that the low and the high risks must bear lower signaling costs; everybody can get a better insurance contract (this is in particular true for the low risks). However, there might exist a conflict between efficiency and the social value of insurance or ethics: when the information about the possibility (or probability) of getting certain illnesses is available, insurers want to use it for risk classification. This results, however, in decreased insurance coverage because those individuals who are almost sure to get the illness will not be offered coverage, while those who are almost sure to be immune will not need coverage. Hence, society will be tempted (because of ethical considerations) to ban the use of this information for risk-classification purposes (see Rothschild and Stiglitz, 1997).

Moreover, it was shown that there exists the possibility of changing the equilibrium concept and using a tax-subsidy system to improve on the result of the (Nash-Cournot) market equilibrium. Together with the problem of uncertainty *after* the test—which may result in a too-high loading factor for high risks—this shows the advantage of alternative institutional arrangements. To mitigate the problems of adverse selection and to secure insurability of high risks, either compulsory or social insurance should be considered as solutions.[14]

Given the different tradeoffs discussed above, an important implication relates to the *information-regime* society should choose. To stay in the state of ignorance is better preserved under the public-information regime than under the private-information regime. Therefore, if society gives the *right not to know* a high value, then the chosen regime should be category (2.3) with revelation duty. The costs of this policy could be dealt with either by social insurance or by some sort of (publicly provided) genetic insurance.

At the end, one problem left over should be touched. Even when we allow for costs of the genetic test, the utility loss of the individual is hardly taken into account. In other words, individuals with a genetic peculiarity should know what this means for them (with or without a treatment option). This in turn shifts the responsibility of physicians from diagnosis and therapy of illness to consultation about genetic tests and their consequences ('genetic counsellor').

Acknowledgments

This is a thoroughly revised version of the paper presented at the Venice Summer Institute Workshop on Insurance: Theoretical Analysis and Policy Implications, July 23–24, 2003. Preliminary versions were presented at the Economic Seminar of Goethe University in Frankfurt and at the Twenty-eighth Seminar of the European Group of Risk and Insurance Economists in Strasbourg, September 2001.

I am indebted to Friedrich Breyer, Arnold Chassagnon, Frank Sloan, Achim Wambach, the participants at the Venice Summer Institute Workshop, and especially Mark Browne, P. A. Chiappori, and two anonymous referees for their comments. Errors are mine.

Notes

1. An informationally efficient equilibrium is one where different risks get different insurance policies with full coverage and pay according to their risk class different premiums.

2. Typically, the compulsory insurance will be publicly organized (like social insurance), while voluntary insurance (or supplementary insurance) will be privately supplied.

3. Here the (potentially) positive value of information about one's health gained by testing is not taken into account. This chapter deals only with asymmetric information and its consequences, not the human-capital accumulation aspects.

4. It is an interesting question to vary the loss of income when sick with income (or productivity) when healthy. With this assumption, one can model also the consequences of illness on income distribution (cf. Hoel and Iversen, 2002). Furthermore, Strohmenger and Wambach (2000) analyze the case with state-dependent utility and the peculiarity that treatment costs are higher than the willingness to pay.

5. The editor and an anonymous referee pointed out that this assumption of *immutable characteristics* or traits is important and limiting. And there are examples showing that in

reality treatment (or operations) can result in bringing the individual from the high-risk class into the low-risk class. However, taking into account most treatment possibilities (such as breast cancer), only some harmful consequences can be avoided, so in effect most people with genetic mutations—unless these can be "pulled up by the roots"—stay in the high-risk class.

6. As shown by Rothschild and Stiglitz (1976), this statement also depends on a critical ratio of low to high risks in the market.

7. It is obvious for a laissez-faire regime because then the insurer can ask for genetic tests and use the results, and it is also clear for a revelation-duty regime because taking the test is the dominant strategy.

8. Contrary to the NC-concept of Rothschild and Stiglitz (1976) with "myopic insurers," Wilson (1977) takes into account that insurers *react* to the introduction of new insurance policies.

9. If there exists only one Nash-Cournot equilibrium, then it is also a reaction equilibrium (or Wilson equilibrium), and both coincide with the transfer equilibrium where the best policy for the low risks is L^{**} on $U^*\hat{L}L^{**}$.

10. Compare the contract H^* (where some high-risk individuals take genetic tests and preventive measures and some do not, depending, for example, on the effectiveness of prevention and the coefficient of risk aversion) with the contract $\hat{H}$ (where all high-risk individuals take the test and preventive measures, and due to moral hazard, the high-risk individuals cannot be offered full coverage).

11. It is an interesting question whether genetic tests contain more information than (family) anamnesis (see Taupitz, 2000).

12. The discussion about when social insurance can Pareto-improve the situation is too large to be presented here. Zweifel and Eisen (2003, chap. 9.2) give an overview.

13. Moral hazard, which plays a greater role in life insurance, is not treated here or is treated only in passing (cf. the full-insurance contract $\hat{H}$).

14. A tax on the low risks introduces an underwriting restriction that may result in a second-degree adverse-selection problem, as M. Browne pointed out. To circumvent this problem, a general tax-transfer system may be preferable. However, this solution is beyond the limits of the (partial) model considered here.

References

Berberich, Kerstin. (2001). "Genetische Tests und Privatversicherung (Genetic tests and private insurance)." *Versicherungswirtschaft* 56(5): 313–320.

Cochrane, John H. (1995). "Time-Consistent Health Insurance." *Journal of Political Economy* 103: 445–473.

Dahlby, B. G. (1981). "Adverse Selection and Pareto Improvements through Compulsory Insurance." *Public Choice* 37: 547–558.

Doherty, Neil A., and Lisa L. Posey. (1998). "On the Value of a Check Up: Adverse Selection, Moral Hazard and the Value of Information." *Journal of Risk and Insurance* 65(2): 189–211.

Doherty, Neil A., and Paul D. Thistle. (1996a). "Adverse Selection with Endogenous Information in Insurance Markets." *Journal of Public Economics* 63: 83–102.

Doherty, Neil A., and Paul D. Thistle. (1996b). "Advise and Consent: HIV Tests, Genetic Tests and the Efficiency of Consent Laws." Working Paper, Wharton School, University of Pennsylvania.

Eisen, Roland. (1981). "Information and Observability: Some Notes on the Economics of Moral Hazard and Insurance." *Geneva Papers* 21: 22–33.

Eisen, Roland. (1986). "Wettbewerb und Regulierung in der Versicherung. Die Rolle asymmetrischer Information (Competition and Regulation in Insurance: The Role of Asymmetrical Information)." *Schweiz. Zeitschrift für Volkswirtschaft und Statistik*: 339–358.

Eisen, Roland, and Peter Zweifel. (2003). Comments to Adverse Selection and Categorical Discrimination in the Health Insurance Market: The Effects of Genetic Tests by Strohmenger and Wambach (*JHE* 19, 2000). Unpub. ms, University of Frankfurt, Department of Economics.

Fuchs, Victor R. (1979). "Economics, Health and Post-industrial Society." *Health and Society* 57: 153–182.

Harris, Milton, and Artur Raviv. (1978). "Some Results on Incentive Contracts with Application to Education and Employment, Health Insurance and Law Enforcement." *American Economic Review* 68: 20–30.

Harris, Milton, and Artur Raviv. (1979). "Optimal Incentive Contracts with Imperfect Information." *Journal of Economic Theory* 20: 231–259.

Hoel, Michael, and Tor Iversen. (2002). "Genetic Testing When There Is a Mix of Compulsory and Voluntary Health Insurance." *Journal of Health Economics* 21: 253–270.

Holmström, Bengt. (1979). "Moral Hazard and Observability." *Bell Journal of Economics* 10: 74–91.

Hoy, Michael. (1989). "The Value of Screening Mechanisms under Alternative Insurance Possibilities." *Journal of Public Economics* 39(2): 177–206.

Kolata, Gina. (1994). "Patients' Lawyers Lead Insurers to Pay for Unproven Treatments, Coverage Even When Policy Excludes a Therapy." *NYT*, March 28, pp. A1, A7.

Meissen, G. J., R. H. Myers, C. A. Mastromauro, et al. (1988). "Predictive Testing of Huntington's Disease with Use of a Linked DNA Marker." *New England Journal of Medicine* 318: 535–542.

Miyazaki, Hajme. (1977). "The Rat Race and Internal Labor Markets." *Bell Journal of Economics* 8(2): 394–418.

Pauly, Mark V. (2006). "Time, Risk, Precommitment, and Adverse Selection in Competitive Insurance Markets." This volume, chapter 1.

Pauly, Mark, Howard Kunreuther, and Richard Hirth. (1995). "Guaranteed Renewability in Insurance." *Journal of Risk and Uncertainty* 10: 143–156.

Rothschild, Michael, and Joseph E. Stiglitz. (1976). "Equilibrium in Competitive Insurance Markets: The Economics of Markets with Imperfect Information." *Quarterly Journal of Economics* 90: 629–649.

Rothschild, Michael, and Joseph E. Stiglitz. (1997). "Competition and Insurance Twenty Years Later." *Geneva Papers on Risk and Insurance Theory* 22: 73–79.

Shavell, Steven. (1979). "On Moral Hazard and Insurance." *Quarterly Journal of Economics* 93: 541–562.

Spence, Michael. (1978). "Product Differentiation and Performance in Insurance Markets." *Journal of Public Economics* 10: 427–447.

Strohmenger, Rainer, and Achim Wambach. (2000). "Adverse Selection and Categorial Discrimination in the Health Insurance Markets: The Effects of Genetic Tests." *Journal of Health Economics* 19: 197–218.

Tabarrok, Alexander. (1994). "Genetic Testing: An Economic and Contractarian Analysis." *Journal of Health Economics* 13: 75–91.

Taupitz, Jochen. (2000). "Genetische Diagnostik und Versicherungsrecht (Genetic Diagnostic and Insurance Law)." *Frankfurter Vorträge zum Versicherungswesen*, No. 32. Karlsruhe.

Wilson, C. A. (1977). "A Model of Insurance Markets with Incomplete Information." *Journal of Economic Theory* 16(2): 167–207.

Zweifel, Peter, and Roland Eisen. (2003). *Versicherungsökonomie* (Insurance economics). 2nd ed. Berlin: Springer.

3 The Welfare Effects of Predictive Medicine

Pierre-André Chiappori

Introduction

One of the striking achievements of modern science is the progress of medical diagnosis and predictive medicine. Most infections can be detected long before the appearance of the first symptoms of actual illness (HIV testing being only one spectacular example). Even more remarkable are the recent improvements in our understanding of genetic mechanisms that allow us to unveil predispositions to a number of diseases. In some cases (monogenic diseases, typically), a genetic test enables a physician to predict with near certainty the future occurrence (or not) of the pathology. Even in more difficult cases, in which the disease results from complex interactions between genetic and environmental factors, evidence of a genetic predisposition can significantly modify the ex ante probability of occurrence, with potentially major consequences on markets for health and life insurance. Because these progresses are expected to continue at a rapid pace, insurance markets ten or twenty years from now may differ markedly from the current situation. The ex ante heterogeneity of individual status regarding insurance may increase dramatically, leading to a much wider dispersion in premium and coverage; some individuals may even be unable to acquire any coverage at all.

For an economist, the resulting dispersion can be analyzed from two different viewpoints. Ex post (once tests are available), interindividual differences can be viewed as inequalities that governments may (or may not) be willing to alleviate. A more interesting perspective relies on an ex ante analysis. The prospect of future improvements in insurers' ability to predict raises for all agents a *classification risk*—the risk of being found to be a bad risk. Risk-averse agents may be willing to buy an insurance against this risk. In the absence of predictive tests, a standard health insurance policy that charges a similar premium to all agents provides coverage against both the risk of illness and the classification risk. However, the availability of a test may, under circumstances that are discussed below, restrict (or destroy) the feasibility of a coverage against the classification risk. In a world of risk-averse agents, such restrictions of the scope of insurance unambiguously decrease welfare. This is the well-known *Hirshleifer effect*, whereby the availability of more accurate information may be harmful from a Pareto point of view.[1]

The analysis just sketched is familiar to economists. It describes only one side of the consequences of predictive medicine, although probably an important one. While better information may be detrimental to risk-averse agents by restricting the scope of efficient risk-sharing contracts, it may also improve decision making in a number of ways. Often enough, early knowledge of a risk allows individuals to alleviate or eliminate its consequences through adequate prevention. The discovery of a predisposition to breast cancer may lead to systematic investigations and preventive treatments, ultimately reducing mortality. Another example is provided by hemochromatosis, the most frequent genetic disease affecting Caucasian populations.[2] When undetected, hemochromatosis causes serious lesions to several organs, including liver, brain, and lungs, and may generate lethal cancers. However, simple treatments are available that allow doctors to fully control the evolution of the disease and eliminate all harmful consequences. In the latter case, early information is unambiguously good.

In some cases, however, no preventive measures or treatments are available. A typical example is provided by Huntington disease, a lethal degeneracy of the nervous system. Huntington is a monogenic disease; a genetic test has been available for several years that detects the presence of the gene and hence predicts either that the illness will certainly not occur or that it will occur with probability almost one.[3] Even in this extreme situation, though, the availability of the test enables individuals to make more accurate choices regarding intertemporal allocation of resources. Major decisions regarding marriage, fertility, investment, and other events may be dramatically improved. The choice of a spouse and the decision to have children should take into account the genetic risks involved.[4] Similarly, the optimal investment in human capital crucially depends on the time period during which returns will be received. Again, a more precise knowledge of the risk can significantly ameliorate the efficiency of the decision to attend college or invest in specialized training, leading to potentially important gains in welfare.

Theory thus suggests that the development of predictive medicine will have a range of opposite consequences, with an ambiguous final impact on welfare. Hence, any welfare analysis must ultimately rely on an evaluation of the magnitude of the various effects at stake. The goal of this chapter is to propose a first and partial attempt at such a quantification. As is made clearer below, some key parameters (such as the joint distribution of income and risk aversions) are largely unknown, and some aspects of the decision processes (such as the subjective costs of learning about personal exposure to a lethal risk) have not (yet) been fully explored. As such, the computations proposed here provide at best a partial and preliminary analysis of this difficult issue. We believe, however, that this attempt, imperfect as it may be, still constitutes a step in the right direction. The development of predictive medicine may have a deep impact on our lives and raise difficult problems regarding regulation and health policy. It is unlikely that much progress can be made from a normative point of view without a more precise understanding of the main issues at stake, including the size of the welfare effects involved.

The Costs of Information Availability: How Large Is the Hirshleifer Effect?

The focus throughout this chapter is on the impact of predictive medicine on the market for insurance. Early knowledge of unfavorable predispositions may affect other aspects of economic life, most notably employment and housing; these issues are not studied here. We consider the typical situation of an individual who, in the absence of the test, would be considered by insurance companies as average in her risk class; however, an unfavorable test outcome increases the predicted risk of this individual relatively to her class. Note that, in practice, individual risk can often be assessed even in the absence of sophisticated tests, although less precisely. Insurance companies routinely ask questions about the health status of the subscriber's parents. Should the latter suffer from health problems that are known to involve some genetic component, this information will be used for the underwriting process. In that sense, genetic testing is an old practice.[5] Even when the disease has no known genetic component (AIDS being a typical case), proxy can be used to detect higher-risk individuals.[6]

For these reasons, what predictive medicine provides is simply a more precise assessment of probabilities, resulting (potentially) in an exacerbation of existing inequalities. The analysis below should thus be understood as *conditional* on the individual's risk class (on all relevant observable characteristics). It applies within a cell as defined by insurers from observable characteristics for underwriting purposes.

Finally, we assume in this section that any information resulting from a medical test is publicly revealed and that insurance companies can freely require and use this information for underwriting. This needs not be the case. The information could be revealed exclusively to the individual, and regulations could prohibit insurance companies from imposing the test, asking about privately undertaken tests, or simply using the outcome of any such test for underwriting purposes. The scope and the problems of such a regulation are discussed in the final section of the chapter.

The Hirshleifer Effect: Theoretical Background

Consider a disease that affects a proportion π of a given population.[7] In the absence of predictive testing, all individuals in the population are facing the same probability π of getting the disease. As argued above, this assumption does not contradict the fact that some factors (such as age or gender) may influence the probability of getting the disease, since the population may be defined in a narrow sense (say, all Caucasian females between age twenty and thirty), and the analysis below can be repeated for various all such cells of the total population. In the initial situation, we assume that agents can purchase full insurance coverage for a premium $\gamma\pi$ proportional to the probability of occurrence (γ denoting the corresponding loading coefficient).[8]

We are interested in a situation in which a test allows us to make a precise assessment of the risk of each individual. Assume, for simplicity, that there are only two classes: high-risk agents, in proportion λ, face a probability of occurrence P, while low-risk agents, in proportion $1 - \lambda$, face a smaller probability p (with $\lambda P + (1 - \lambda)p = \pi$). Since the information is publicly revealed, high-risk individuals will be charged a fair rate, corresponding to P, instead of the average rate based on the ex ante probability π. Note that even when π is small, the conditional probability P may be large (it is close to one in the case of Huntington disease), resulting in a major increase of the premium. This is exactly the definition of the classification risk. Assuming that the premium is always proportional to the probability of occurrence (γ denoting the corresponding loading coefficient), the initial, sure premium $\gamma\pi$ is replaced with a random premium that equals either γp (with probability $1 - \lambda$) or γP (with probability λ). While, in expected terms, the change is revenue neutral, the introduction of a risk implies for risk-averse agents a welfare loss, the magnitude of which depends on the (relative) size of the potential loss and the degree of risk aversion. A standard measure of the loss is its *risk premium* (defined as the certain amount the agent would be willing to give up in the initial situation (before the test is introduced) to avoid the risk).[9] Technically, the risk premium r is defined by

$$u(W - \gamma\pi - r) = \lambda u(W - \gamma P) + (1 - \lambda)u(W - \gamma p), \tag{3.1}$$

where u is the agent's Von Neumann-Morgenstern utility and W her wealth.

This formula relies on two implicit assumptions. The first assumption is that the agent would still be willing to pay the insurance premium, even if she was found to be of the high-risk type. When found at risk, however, she may prefer to give up the insurance coverage altogether. The decision, again, depends on the agent's risk aversion and also on the efficiency of the treatment that the insurance would cover. The agent may decide to pay for the required treatment out of her own pocket and not to buy the insurance. This attitude is unlikely from a risk-averse agent, at least for reasonable values of the loading factor. She also may decide, should the disease occur, to opt for an alternative and cheaper (although less efficient) treatment or even to give up the treatment altogether. The analysis here varies with the details of the context at stake and should depend on the type of disease, its consequences on life expectancy and quality of life, the range of treatments available, and so on. An investigation devoted to a particular disease should consider these possibilities. Given the general scope of the present chapter, we stick to the assumption that the agent will always prefer to purchase a coverage. The analysis here thus fits cases in which either an expensive but (reasonably) efficient treatment exists (as for AIDS) or the disabilities provoked by the disease require expensive care (as for Huntington).

More generally, the second assumption (shown in equation (3.1)) assumes that the classification risk affects only the premium. This implies that the level of coverage is not affected—say, because the coverage is complete in all cases. As before, this assumption, made for simplicity, does not sound particularly unrealistic.[10] The possible distortions due to partial coverage are of second order with respect to the main issue—namely, the welfare loss due to the classification risk.

The Distribution of Risk Aversion: Empirical Evidence

In equation (3.1) above, a key parameter is the form of the utility function, particularly the resulting degree of risk aversion. Any tentative assessment of the cost of early information, as measured by the risk premium r, will heavily rely on the choice made at this level. A standard conclusion of most empirical studies, in insurance as well as finance, is that constant relative risk aversion (CRRA) utilities tend to provide a good fit to existing data. However, the value of the coefficient of relative risk aversion is not clear. Different sources have been used to estimate this crucial parameter:

• Many experiments have been designed to study risk aversion, but these attempts have recently been questioned. Rabin (2000) argues that small-scale lotteries cannot provide adequate estimates of people reactions when faced with significant risks.[11] Perhaps more convincing are the various attempts based on natural experiments, an interesting example being provided by Beetsma and Schotman's (2001) study of the television game show *Lingo*. Despite the flaws inherent in these approaches (including specificity of the context and selection of participants), these real-life situations do provide useful information. Beetsma and Schotman (2001) find that CRRA preferences provide a good fit and that their estimate of the coefficient of relative risk aversion is around 7.

• Another source comes from the analysis of portfolio composition, particularly the division of total wealth between risky and nonrisky assets. Under CRRA preferences, the share of wealth invested in risky assets does not depend on wealth. This assumption fits existing data reasonably well, at least for portfolios with nonzero risky assets.[12] Several existing works (for instance, Campbell, 1996, and Blake, 1996) find a high value for the coefficient of relative risk aversion (between 8 and 30).

• The returns on risky assets can also be used to measure risk aversion. According to standard theory, the expected returns of stocks should exceed that on government bonds by a risk premium that directly reflects risk aversion. However, standard estimates using historical data find an implausibly high value for the coefficient of relative risk aversion (50 or more). This equity premium puzzle has generated a huge literature (surveyed, for instance, in Cochrane, 2005).

• The analysis of saving behavior, based on the estimation of individual Euler equations, provides a joint estimation of risk aversion and intertemporal substitutability. First-generation models were using intertemporally separable preferences of the CRRA (or constant elasticity) family. A standard criticism addressed to this literature was that the two determinants of intertemporal choices—risk aversion and income smoothing—were represented by the same coefficient, characterizing the concavity of the utility function. A second generation of models, using a more flexible specification, tries to disentangle the two effects. The estimation of such models leads to complex identification problems. Still, Attanasio and Weber (1989) find a coefficient of relative risk aversion varying from 5 to 25 depending on the functional form.

• In principle, insurance behavior should provide an ideal context for studying risk aversion. In practice, however, such an investigation faces important technical difficulties. A few studies, starting with Drèze (1960), try to recover risk aversion from the observation of individual choices among various contracts offering different premium and coverages. Usually, the CRRA assumption is not rejected, and the estimated coefficient is high (around 8). One problem with these results is that they require the strong assumption that people are aware of their *true* accident probability; the realism of this assumption may vary with the context.

• Finally, some surveys ask questions about choices in hypothetical lotteries ("Would you accept a new job that would ultimately, with equal probabilities, either increase your wage by 50 percent or decrease it by 30 percent?"). Despite the well-known problems affecting this type of data, such studies present a significant advantage, since they allow a tentative estimation of the *distribution* of the coefficient of relative risk aversion in the population. One of the most widely used estimations was provided by Barsky, Juster, Kimball, and Shapiro (1997). Table 3.1 summarizes its main findings. In this table, the four classes are defined from the answers to two hypothetical questions, and expected relative risk aversions are computed assuming a lognormal distribution of risk tolerance with additional noise. According to these estimates, about two-thirds of the population exhibit a level of risk aversion above a lower bound of 3.8, for an average over this class estimated to more than 16, while only 13 percent of the responses are compatible with a

Table 3.1
Risk premium for various relative risk aversion coefficients ($L/W = 5\%$, $p = 1\%$)

	Class			
	I	II	III	IV
Percentage of total population	65%	11%	11%	13%
Expected relative risk aversion[a]	15.7	7.2	5.7	3.8

a. Conditional on survey response.

Table 3.2
Risk premium (in percentage of the ex ante fair price)

	Coefficient of relative risk aversion				
Characteristics of the risk	1	2	3	5	10
$L/W = 5\%$, $p = 1\%$	3	5	8	15	31
$L/W = 5\%$, $p = 10\%$	2	5	7	12	26
$L/W = 10\%$, $p = 1\%$	5	11	17	31	74

low level. Moreover, average risk aversion does not seem to vary much between different levels of wealth, suggesting that the distributions of wealth and risk aversion are roughly independent.[13]

The Distribution of Risk Aversion: A Simple Calibration

A remarkable feature of the previous studies is that despite the diversity of the approaches adopted, the estimations of the coefficient of relative risk aversion are consistently quite high (above 5). A simple calibration exercise confirms that such values should not be considered unrealistic. Consider the benchmark case of a 1 percent probability of losing an amount L equal to 5 percent of the person's total wealth, W; one may think, for instance, of the risk of car theft for a middle-class household. The first row in table 3.2 summarizes the risk premium as a percentage of the ex ante fair rate π for CRRA preferences and various values of the coefficient of relative risk aversion.

A remarkable feature of this table is that the risk premium exceeds the standard loading factor on theft insurance (usually between 20 and 30 percent) only for high levels of relative risk aversion (close to 10). Moreover, this result is largely robust to changes in the occurrence probability, provided that it remains reasonably small. For instance, the second row in table 3.2 shows the result if the probability is increased to 10 percent.

The results are sensitive to the magnitude of the loss. Keeping the probability at 1 percent but increasing the relative loss to 10 percent gives the results shown in the third row of table 3.2.

This is in line with standard intuition about risk aversion: the benefits of insurance increase rapidly with the size of the loss—a property that plays a key role in what follows. Still, even in the latter case, insurance coverage with a 30 percent loading factor will not be purchased by individuals whose coefficient of risk aversion is smaller than 5. Altogether, the purchase of insurance against a risk of this size—a commonly observed behavior—indicates a large coefficient of risk aversion. This conclusion is pretty much in line with the previous results in suggesting that a significant fraction of the population may exhibit a large (above 5) degree of relative risk aversion.

The Hirshleifer Cost: A First Approximation
Using the results described above, it is possible to propose a preliminary calibration of the size of the loss resulting from the absence of insurance against the classification risk. A key parameter is the size of the potential loss—that is, the ex post premium P charged to a high-risk individual as a proportion of the individual's wealth. At this point, a calibration requires more precise hypothesis. If the amount at stake is relatively small (say, less than 10 percent of total wealth or, equivalently, if the annual cost of insurance for high-risk individuals is small with respect to their annual income), the tables above indicate that the welfare loss resulting from inability to cover the classification risk, as measured by the risk premium, remains low (certainly less than the fair ex ante premium for reasonable levels of risk aversion). The picture is totally different in the case of large risks (when the ex post cost of insurance for high-risk agents represents a significant proportion of disposable income). Table 3.3 is based on the same parameter values as table 3.2, except that the size of the annual loss is now assumed to be 50 percent of disposable income.

Table 3.3
Risk premium (in percentage of the ex ante fair price) for $p = 1\%, L/W = 50\%$

Coefficient of relative risk aversion				
1	2	3	5	10
39	98	194	590	3560

The risk premium is now considerably higher than the fair premium —three times as much for a relative risk aversion coefficient of 3, seven time as much for a coefficient of 5, more than thirty-six times as much for a coefficient of 10. Not surprisingly, these numbers increase even further for larger relative losses. Even when the RRA coefficient is fixed at the modest level of 3, the risk premium is represents about thirty times the fair premium when the potential loss represents 80 percent of income.

How relevant are these calibrations? Unfortunately, for many diseases and most income levels, treatment costs representing of 50 percent or even 80 percent of disposable income is by no means unrealistic. The annual cost of treatment of an HIV positive patient receiving a preventive tritherapy is of the same order of magnitude as the median per capita net disposable income in the United States. Anecdotal evidence abounds of cases in which noncovered individuals lose a large fraction or even the totality of their wealth after a severe illness. Accepting the conclusion put forth by Barsky et al. (1997) that the correlation between wealth and risk aversion is weak, it is probably fair to say that the financial risk linked to the inability to cover the classification risk, for serious diseases such as AIDS, represents for a large fraction of the population a significant proportion of disposable income.[14]

A more difficult issue is the relevance of CRRA with a relatively large coefficient for such large risks. Although we tend to believe that the estimates provided represent a reasonable best guess, it is fair to say that the question is largely open. Not much exists on the empirical estimation of risk aversion in the case of large financial risks.

Assuming that the calibration above provides a good first approximation of the phenomenon at stake, then the amount paid on insurance premium, a number often used to quantify the importance of the insurance business, may provide a dramatically biased estimation of the magnitudes at stake. In the case of major financial risks, our estimates suggest that premiums may underestimate the true welfare cost by a factor of twenty (or more). Just to provide an order of magnitude, assume, following Barsky et al., that two-thirds of the population have a large level of relative risk aversion, and let us adopt for them the (very) conservative average value of 8 (remember that Barsky et al. estimate their mean relative risk aversion at 15). Assume that treatment costs, relative to the income distribution, are such that for 15 percent of this sample, the cost of the treatment would average (or exceed) 50 percent of the household's disposable income—again, a conservative assumption in the case of AIDS. We thus isolate a subpopulation, representing 10 percent of the total, which is particularly vulnerable to the classification risk. For these agents alone, the welfare loss resulting from the loss of coverage against the classification risk—as estimated by the risk premium—would represent about $2,000 per household, hence an aggregate welfare loss exceeding probably $20 billion. If one further assumes that the AIDS risk is actually larger than average for this poorer fraction of the population, the number could be even higher; and, again, we are considering only a small fraction of the total population. The striking conclusion is that the potential losses due to the Hirshleifer effect may in some cases be huge.

The Benefits of Early Knowledge
As stressed in the introduction to this chapter, early information about a predisposition to some disease may (and will, in many cases) lead to efficient prevention or treatment, thus considerably increasing welfare. In such contexts, the Hirshleifer effect vanishes (with the notations above, p and P are equally small), and early information has a strictly positive value. In this section, we consider the opposite extreme situation of a pathology for which early detection has no direct medical benefit. Huntington's disease is a typical example of such a context. The presence of the genetic anomaly causing Huntington's simply predicts a largely ineluctable and almost always fatal evolution. Even in this case, early knowledge can affect long-term behavior and result in significant economic gains.

Stoler (2004) has recently proposed a preliminary investigation of the impact of such early knowledge on investment in human capital, with an emphasis on the decision to attend college. Clearly, the benefits of human-capital accumulation increase with the length of the horizon during which the returns will be received. Huntington's disease reduces the expected length by one-half on average, with an additional uncertainty on the age of occurrence. A key characteristic of many genetic diseases, including Huntington's, is that almost all patients know early (when one of their parents starts developing the disease) that they are at risk. If one parent carries the gene, the probability that each child will also carry it (and hence develop the disease) is exactly 50 percent. The impact of the test is to replace this 50 percent probability with a certainty in one direction or the other. Stoler computes the benefit of this shift as a function of the individual-specific college premium—the expected gain in income resulting from college attendance for the

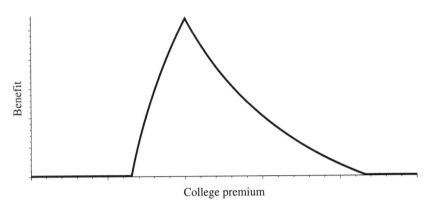

Figure 3.1
Ex ante benefits of early detection of Huntington's disease, as a function of the college premium (CES utility, perfect financial markets)
Source: Stoler (2004).

individual under consideration. The general shape of the gain is given in figure 3.1.

For a low level of the premium, college attendance is not profitable even for an healthy agent; hence the benefit of early knowledge is null. At a higher premium, a healthy individual would choose to attend college, but the 50 percent uncertainty is sufficient to discourage college attendance. The healthy children of a Huntington's patient thus benefit from the test by deciding to attend college, and their gain increases with the premium. Then a threshold is reached, beyond which college attendance is the optimal decision even under the 50 percent uncertainty, although not for an individual knowing for sure she will develop the disease. The benefit of the test goes only to agents who are found to carry the gene and therefore avoid attending college; note that this benefit decreases with the premium. Finally, for very high levels of the college premium, agents will attend college irrespective of the test outcome, and the benefit is again null.

Simplistic as this figure may be, it emphasizes that the benefits of early detection are linked with a key, individual-specific parameter—namely, the potential benefits of human-capital accumulation. In general, these are modeled as determined by agents' ability, a characteristic that is (partially) unobservable by the econometrician and heterogeneously distributed in the population. Again, a cost-benefit analysis of early detection must involve the joint distribution of ability and risk aversion, on which little is known. Empirical work currently in progress on Huntington patients may help clarify this complex issue.

Regulating Discrimination: The Curse of Adverse Selection?

Regulation: A Strategic Analysis

Given the potential magnitude of the Hirshleifer effect, a natural question is whether government intervention could alleviate the resulting loss in welfare. It has often been argued that the access of insurance companies to the results of genetic or other tests should be strictly regulated. Various levels of regulation have been proposed, which can be broadly summarized as follows:

• *Level 0* Insurance companies are allowed to require any test to be undertaken by the subscriber during the underwriting process.

• *Level 1* Insurance companies are not allowed to require a test but may ask questions about any test that may have been privately undertaken by the subscriber in the past; the subscriber cannot decline to answer.

• *Level 2* Explicit questions about past tests are prohibited; however, subscribers are allowed to voluntarily communicate to their insurer any test result they may have, and insurers are then allowed to use this information for underwriting.

• *Level 3* Insurance companies are not allowed to use test information for underwriting, even when this information has voluntarily been supplied by the subscriber.

Various versions of these four levels have been proposed and sometimes implemented. A basic principle governing medical ethics is that no information about health status, including the outcome of a test, should be disclosed (including to an insurance company) without the patient's informed consent.

From an economic viewpoint, however, many of the distinctions sketched above appear spurious. A simple, game-theoretic analysis of this issue relies on two preliminary remarks.[15]

Remark 3.1 If free, anonymous tests are feasible, then an agent always benefits from privately acquiring information about her health status.

The key word, here, is *anonymous*. Indeed, a crucial issue is whether the fact that the agent has undertaken the test is public information or can be kept secret by the agent. In the former case, an agent can readily avoid the Hirshleifer effect by deciding not to get the information. In the hypothetical case in which the test has no benefit (no treatment is available, prevention is not possible, and the agent's investment decisions are inelastic to her life expectancy), no agent will ever choose to take the test, and the competitive equilibrium is ex ante efficient. Note that such an outcome obtains under one condition only: the agent must be able to prove that she did not undertake the test.

Let us now consider the alternative case in which such a proof does not exist—that is, the claim that the test has not been taken cannot be verified by the insurance company. Then the Hirshleifer effect becomes an Hirshleifer curse. Indeed, an agent cannot lose by *secretly* acquiring the relevant information, since she can either use it, discard it, or even claim she never acquired it. The curse comes from the fact that this private benefit for each participant may ultimately result in a public loss for all agents because of the externality induced by adverse selection.

Remark 3.2   In a competitive market, a patient who finds she belongs to the low-risk type always gains in freely revealing this information to the insurance company. If free, anonymous tests are feasible and if the patient can, if she wants, freely communicate hard evidence of their result to insurers, then regulation levels 0, 1, and 2 above are equivalent and result in full revelation of information (associated to the corresponding contract discrimination) at equilibrium.

The economic intuition is clear. In a competitive market, an agent who is known to belong to the low-risk type will be charged a smaller premium than both high-risk agents and agents of unknown type. It follows that, at equilibrium, all agents will privately acquire the information, and those for whom the news is good will forward the result to their insurer. Insurance companies, in turn, anticipate this pattern and will tend to treat similarly the agents who were found to be high risk and those who (claim they) did not undertake the test.[16] Ultimately, this treatment will justify both the decision to privately undertake the test and the decision to forward the favorable result to the insurer.

How empirically relevant is this game-theoretic analysis? In practice, anonymous tests are hard to eliminate. In the case of AIDS, for instance, such tests are essential.[17] Assuming that costs are negligible may be more questionable, especially when the psychological costs of learning about one's true condition are taken into account. In practice, patients are often reluctant to undertake a test and cite as their main motivation the fact that "living with such a knowledge can be an excessively heavy burden."[18] However, in the equilibrium structure just described, the potential gain from learning may be significant (if the result is a low-risk classification) with a zero downside (since no difference is made between high-risk and unknown agents). In the end, the answer will depend, among other things, on the magnitude of the potential gain from being found to be a low risk with respect to the financial and psychological costs of undertaking the test. Empirical evidence sugegsts that, in some cases, the impact is indeed minimal.[19] In other situations (AIDS being an obvious but by no means unique example), the opposite logic prevails. Then it is safe to consider, at least for diseases that are not too rare, that the patient's free access to the result of the test constitute a natural benchmark case for evaluating the impact of regulation.

The most problematic assumption is probably the free revelation of information to the insurer. A situation where no agent chooses to disclose the information relative to her health status is in principle not stable (in the usual, Nash equilibrium sense) because any low-risk agent would have an incentive to privately inform her insurer. Assume, however, that the proportion of high-risk agents λ is very small. The difference in risk between a low-risk insuree and the average individual in the population may then be negligible or at least insufficient to justify a new contract. Then the incentives to privately undertake the test and communicate its results (if favorable) disappears altogether. In technical terms, for rare diseases, even small transaction costs may stabilize a pooling equilibrium.

It should however be stressed that this point holds true only insofar as the proportion of high-risk individuals *within the population under consideration* is small—which is often not the case in practice because insurers use existing information to isolate particular subpopulations of potentially at risk individuals. Testing each American citizen for Huntington would not make much sense because the proportion of individuals carrying the gene is so small that costs would be proportionally excessive. However, the problem typically arises for the specific subpopulation of persons who have a parent suffering from the disease. Then the probability is large (50 percent), and the argument just sketched fully applies—as it may apply to the subpopulation of single males working in artistic professions for AIDS, and other examples can readily be found.

At any rate, the previous arguments indicate that regulation of information diffusion is a complex issue because of the externality inherent to any adverse-selection context. It suggests in particular that the emphasis generally put on voluntary disclosure of information is partly misplaced. Forwarding an information against the will of the patient is clearly unacceptable in most cases,[20] and everyone agrees on the necessary enforcement of this prohibition. The previous analysis shows, however, that such a prohibition is generally not sufficient: a world in which information can be only voluntarily supplied (our level 2) is likely to result in exactly the same discrimination as complete disclosure of information because insurance companies are likely to consider any agent as a high risk unless proved otherwise. To be effective, a regulation must probably prohibit the use of test outcomes altogether, even when they are voluntarily supplied by the subscriber. This corresponds to our level 3 regulation, which can be called *comprehensive*.

Comprehensive Regulation and Adverse Selection
We now consider the case of level 3 regulation, whereby insurers are not allowed to take into account any information. Such a ban creates a typical situation of adverse selection on the insurance markets: a relevant piece of information (the test outcome) is known by the agent but cannot be used by the insurance company. It is useful, at this point, to briefly review the standard analysis of competition under adverse selection. A basic distinction should be established between exclusive and nonexclusive contracts. In a world of exclusive contracts (health insurance being a typical illustration), insurees can freely choose the company from which they buy coverage, but their contractual relationship with this company is exclusive, in the sense that they cannot simultaneously buy insurance from another provider. Annuity contracts provide the opposite example of nonexclusive relationship, since any agent can simultaneously buy annuities from different firms.

Exclusive contracts involve a stronger commitment from one of the parties; not surprisingly, it tends to generate more efficient relationships, since some contracts are simply not available in the absence of exclusivity (see Bennardo and Chiappori, 2003, for a precise discussion). Technically, a crucial difference is that exclusivity is necessary to implement *convex pricing*, a natural tool in a context of asymmetric information.[21] The consequences of adverse selection on competitive markets markedly differ in the two contexts.

Nonexclusive Contracts   In the absence of exclusivity, contracts typically involve linear pricing, the unit price being identical for all agents.[22] The consequences of adverse selection in this context are well known. High-risk agents will, everything else being equal, purchase larger amounts of coverage, driving up the unit price. If the proportion of high-risk agents is small and low-risk agents are sufficiently risk averse, an equilibrium exists in which low-risk individuals subsidize high-risk agents—a property that can actually improve welfare from an ex ante point of view. However, with many high-risk individuals or insufficient risk aversion, low-risk agents may stop purchasing insurance altogether, which results in a collapse of the market: only high-risk individuals are left, and they pay their fair rate. The comparison with the full-information-disclosure context is thus delicate and depends on the parameters of the model at stake. The welfare analysis will typically rely on the following conditions:

• When the proportion of high-risk agents is low and risk aversion is important (say, because the risk at stake is large), then the prohibition may be ex ante welfare increasing by alleviating the ex post discrimination between high- and low-risk agents.

• In the opposite situation (a significant number of high-risk individuals and a lower degree of risk aversion in general), the regulation is unambiguously harmful, since it cannot avoid discrimination (high-risk types are charged an ex post fair price) and implies the additional cost that low-risk agents are not covered at all.

• In both cases, an additional regulation imposing a ceiling on the amount purchased can be useful. In complex cases of multidimensional adverse selection, optimal contracts are typically more complex and may involve full disclosure for higher levels of purchase.

A final remark is that the previous discussion implicitly assumes that agents are committed to their contract and cannot renegotiate or resell it once purchased. In the life insurance framework, for instance, this implies that the purchased contract will be carried over until it expires (or the patient dies). However, recent innovations contradict this assumption. The development of the market for viaticals, whereby agents sell the rights stemming from their life insurance contract to a third party at a fair price minus a fee, has dramatically altered the picture. The theoretical analysis of viaticals is particularly interesting because it provides a typical example of a contractual innovation that is both remarkably efficient ex post and remarkably inefficient ex ante. Ex post efficiency comes from the fact that an agent who simultaneously learns (say, from an HIV or a genetic test) that her life expectancy is much shorter than expected *and* that large sums will have to be spent on health in the next future may greatly benefit from immediate availability of (a fraction of) her life insurance coverage. However, the availability of viaticals essentially forbids ex ante any significant cross-subsidization between risk classes. Given the existence of a resale market on which the insurance contract can be sold *at a fair price*, an initial premium significantly smaller than the fair amount would result in huge arbitrage opportunities and the predictable collapse of the market altogether. From an ex ante perspective, thus, viaticals destroy the possibility of a coverage against the classification risk.

Exclusive Contracts The case of exclusive contracts is more difficult to analyze, if only because no general agreement has been reached so far about the optimal equilibrium concept. The general intuition stemming from the classical (Rothschild and Stiglitz, 1976; Hellwig, 1987) as well as the more recent (Bisin and Gottardi, 1999; Dubey and Geanakoplos, 2002) literature is that competition typically result in the apparition of a range of contracts that may de facto implement a full separation of types. The basic idea is that companies will try to attract particular subsegments of the subscriber population through an adequate design of the proposed contracts. For instance, a basic contract may offer full coverage at a high unit price, but clients may choose much cheaper options involving specific limitations of coverage. For a relevant definition of the limitations, the options may attract the low-risk fraction of the population, while high-risk individuals will remain covered by the basic contract, probably at a fair ex post rate.[23] In other words, such menus, which are standard in insurance and seem difficult to prohibit, are likely to result in full discrimination, at least insofar as adequately designed menus can be used to fully separate the various types.

Should such an outcome be predicted, then the judgment that can be formulated about the regulation would be negative: not only would discrimination be just as strong as in the case of complete disclosure of information, but in addition low-risk agents would face strong limitations of coverage. Whether this separation can be achieved as an *equi-*

librium outcome is unclear and depends on the particular equilibrium concept used. In the initial Rothschild-Stiglitz contribution, no equilibrium exists when the proportion of high-risk agents is small—although the empirical meaning of such a conclusion is somewhat ambiguous. Various alternative concepts have been developed, leading to different predictions (the equilibrium is always separating for some concepts but may be pooling for others)—although it can be noted that several recent approaches, based either on game-theoretical refinements or on a more Walrasian perspective, seem to support separation.

Conclusion

The first conclusion emerging from this brief presentation is that many questions remain open, especially from an empirical viewpoint. The consequences of competition under adverse selection are crucially relevant for any normative analysis of these issues. It is fair to say that the *theoretical* understanding of these problems has not yet reached a state of general agreement. More damaging is the fact that the empirical knowledge of these issues is scarce.[24]

A second conclusion is that any cost-benefit analysis of early information disclosure must adopt a case-by-case approach and consider each disease as specific. Diseases for which an early diagnosis leads to an improved treatment differ deeply from those, such as Huntington's, for which no cure exists. From a regulatory perspective, scarce pathologies should also be distinguished from frequent ones.

A third implication is that in any case, regulation is a complex issue for which an explicit and precise economic analysis is necessary. One pattern emerging from the above discussion is that for regulation to be effective, it must be quite comprehensive. Prohibiting the use of genetic testing against the will of the patient is certainly necessary, if only to protect individual rights, but is probably not sufficient to avoid discrimination. Even a general ban on the use of test outcomes for underwriting may in some cases be counterproductive, resulting in full-scale discrimination plus severe restrictions on access to coverage by low-risk agents. Again, more work is needed, especially from an empirical perspective.

Various policies have been proposed—from lax regulation that acknowledges discrimination as unavoidable but tries to limit its most shocking excesses to compulsory public coverage of all large risks.

Intermediate solutions have been proposed. Some advocate a lump-sum payment to people carrying adverse genes. Diamond (1992) has proposed a system of group insurance whereby a government agency would divide the population into large groups and private firms would bid for the coverage of an entire group. The recently introduced Swiss regulation provides an interesting example. It explicitly restricts the firms' ability to offer options and menus of contracts—a feature clearly aimed at avoiding the implementation of revelation mechanisms.

Finally, it should be stressed that the classification risk issue goes well beyond the impact of predictive medicine. Classification into a high-risk group may also result from exterior events, such as the occurrence of a serious health problem.[25] One of the basic challenges facing any health-coverage system is precisely its ability to provide long-term contracts covering these types of risks. In chapter 1 in this volume, Mark V. Pauly (2006) shows how the market developed adequate responses to this problem. For instance, most *individual* health insurance contracts in the United States contain guaranteed renewability provisions (required now by law) that protect insureds against selective increases in premiums based on their health state or health insurance. The case of group health (or life) insurance is more complex. On the one hand, contracts are usually such that premiums do not increase for an individual based on a test result or drugs in health state. On the other hand, a worker who loses his job after a significant increase in his health risk is likely to pay a significant higher premium for his health coverage in the future. In another worst-case scenario, the worker belongs to a firm that is small, so that his increased risk raises significantly the total cost of health coverage to the employer, who reacts either by dropping the coverage altogether or by switching to a new contract entailing low caps on some treatments.[26] And millions of individuals are currently not covered. This suggests that classification risk and the Hirshleifer effect may remain major issues for policymakers in the future.

Acknowledgments

I received useful comments from Georges Dionne, an anonymous referee, and the workshop participants. Errors are mine. Financial support from the National Science Foundation (NSF Grant No. 0096516) is gratefully aknowledged.

Notes

1. The intuition that information availability may decrease welfare was initially mentioned by Drèze (1960). See Hirshleifer (1971) for a formal definition and a detailed discussion.

2. About one person in ten carries at least one gene, resulting in one in four hundred developing the disease.

3. The age of occurence cannot be fully predicted, which explains the residual uncertainty. In the vast majority of cases, the disease occurs between the ages of thirty and forty-five. Although the disease itself cannot be cured, the disabilities it provokes require expensive care.

4. The number of cases of Tay-Sachs disease, a lethal illness that affects mostly members of the Ashkenazic Jewish community, has been considerably reduced through a careful monitoring of marriages by the community. The explicit aim of the monitoring was to avoid situations in which spouses would both carry the (recessive) gene.

5. During the recent debate on the access of insurance companies to the outcome of genetic tests of Huntington's disease, an argument often used in support of free access was precisely that discrimination already existed based on family history. The test, it was argued, would allow children of Huntington's patients who did not carry the gene to access insurance in normal conditions.

6. Anecdotal evidence suggests that in situations where HIV tests were either unavailable or prohibited for underwriting purposes, single males between age twenty-five and forty-five and working in specific professions were charged an extremely high price for life insurance.

7. For a detailed presentation, see Hirshleifer (1971) and Crocker and Snow (2000).

8. Note that, in theory, whenever the insurance is priced above the fair rate, agents should be willing to purchase only partial coverage. We thus disregard the various limitations (such as deductible and copayments) that would lead to some risk being born by the insured agent. This assumption, made for simplicity, allows us to concentrate on the main issue while avoiding tedious background-risk computations.

9. Other measures could be used. For instance, one could compute the certain amount that should be paid to the agent, once the test is available, to compensate her for the uncertainty.

10. A well-known puzzle of insurance is precisely that people tend to buy full insurance even when the price is above the fair rate. This effect is magnified when agents can self-insure through accumulated savings (see Gollier, 2003).

11. Rabin's claim is actually stronger: he argues that expected utility theory is not adequate for modeling small bets.

12. A significant number of low-wealth portfolios do not include risky assets at all, a feature that is usually explained by the existence of fixed information and transaction costs.

13. However, Guiso and Paiella (2006, this volume, chapter 10), in a similar context, question the adequacy of the CCRA form.

14. The Medicaid system has sometimes been described as "an implicit insurance contract with a deductible equal to your wealth."

15. The analysis sketched below summarizes classical results of the literature, starting with Rothschild and Stiglitz (1976) and including contributions by Hoy (1989), Tabarrok (1994), Doherty and Thistle (1996) and recently Doherty and Posey (1998), Hoy, Orsi, Eisinger, and Moatti (2003), and Eisen (this volume 2006, chapter 2). For a recent survey, see, for instance, Dionne, Doherty, and Fombaron (2000).

16. The latter claim should be qualified in the case in which insurers can implement full separation through the offer of an adequate menu of contracts. In that case, three contracts will be offered, corresponding to the three categories of agents (tested positive, tested negative, untested). See Doherty and Posey (1998) for a careful analysis of this model. In practice, full separation may be difficult to obtain when adverse selection is in fact multidimensional (that is, agents might differ in risk but also risk aversion, in wealth, and so on).

17. The case of AIDS is specific because of the contamination risk: uninformed agents are a danger for their potential partners. This externality may well justify the availability of anonymous tests despite the induced Hirshleifer curse. Such arguments do not apply to genetic tests.

18. This conclusion, for instance, comes out clearly in Stoler's (2004) survey.

19. For an example dealing with breast cancer genetic testing and life insurance markets, see Subramanian et al. (1999).

20. A possible exception could be health-policy considerations in the case of severe epidemics.

21. Convex pricing implies that the unit price increases with the quantity purchased. Such a feature cannot be implemented if agents can independently buy small quantities from different providers.

22. Life insurance is a good example. According to Cawley and Philipson (1999), price schedules are actually slightly concave, probably reflecting a technology in which fixed costs play an important role, while under adverse selection optimal pricing tend typically to be convex (although this property may depend on the form of preferences).

23. Typical examples include contracts imposing a ceiling on lifetime expenditures for some specific diseases, such as AIDS.

24. One can mention, among others, Cutler and Zeckhauser (1998), Browne (1992), and Buchmueller and DiNardo (2002).

25. For instance, it is well known that an agent who suffered from a heart attack faces a significantly higher risk of future health problems.

26. In December 1987, John McGann was diagnosed with AIDS. His (small) employer opted out its previous HMO coverage and adopted a self-financed plan. The new plan entailed a $5,000 ceiling for lifetime expenditures related to AIDS (as oposed to a ceiling of $1,000,000 in the initial plan). All court rulings were favorable to the employer.

References

Attanasio, O., and G. Weber. (1989). "Intertemporal Substitution, Risk Aversion and the Euler Equation for Consumption." *Economic Journal* 99(395): 59–73.

Barsky, Robert B., Thomas F. Juster, Miles S. Kimball, and Matthew D. Shapiro. (1997). "Preference Parameters and Behavioral Heterogeneity: An Experimental Approach in the Health and Retirement Study." *Quarterly Journal of Economics* 112(2): 537–580.

Beetsma, R., and P. Schotman. (2001). "Measuring Risk Attitudes in a Natural Experiment: Data from the Television Game Show Lingo." *Economic Journal* 111(474): 821–848.

Bennardo, A., and P. A. Chiappori. (2003). "Bertrand and Walras Equilibria under Moral Hazard." *Journal of Political Economy* 111(4): 785–817.

Bisin, A., and P. Gottardi. (2002). "Competitive Equilibria with Asymmetric Information." *Journal of Economic Theory* 87(1): 1–48.

Blake, D. (1996). "Efficiency, Risk Aversion, and Portfolio Insurance: An Analysis of Financial Asset Portfolios Held by Investors in the United Kingdom." *Economic Journal* 106(438): 1175–1192.

Browne, M. (1992). "Evidence of Adverse Selection in the Individual Health Insurance Market." *Jouranl of Risk and Insurance* 59(1): 13–33.

Buchmueller, T., and J. DiNardo. (2002). "Did Community Rating Induce an Adverse Selection Death Spiral? Evidence from New York, Pennsylvania, and Connecticut." *American Economic Review* 92(1): 280–294.

Campbell, J. (1996). "Understanding Risk and Return." *Journal of Political Economy* 104(2): 298–345.

Campbell, J., and J. Cochrane. (2000). "Explaining the Poor Performance of Consumption-Based Asset Pricing Models." *Journal of Finance* 55(6): 2863–2878.

Cawley, J., and T. Philipson. (1999). "An Empirical Examination of Information Barriers to Trade in Insurance." *American Economic Review* 89(4): 827–846.

Cochrane, J. H. 2005. *Asset Pricing*. Princeton: Princeton University Press.

Crocker, K., and A. Snow. (1986). "The Efficiency Effect of Categorical Discrimination in the Insurance Industry." *Journal of Political Economy* 94: 321–344.

Crocker, K., and A. Snow. (2000). "The Theory of Risk Classification." In G. Dionne (Ed.), *Handbook of Insurance*. London: Kluwer.

Cutler, D., and R. Zeckhauser. (1998). "Adverse Selection in Health Insurance." *Frontiers in Health Policy Research* 1: 1–31.

Diamond, P. (1992). "Organizing the Health Insurance Market." *Econometrica* 60(6): 1233–1254.

Dionne, G., N. Doherty, and N. Fombaron. (2000). "Adverse Selection in Insurance Markets." In G. Dionne (Ed.), *Handbook of Insurance*. London: Kluwer.

Doherty, N., and P. Thistle. (1996). "Adverse Selection with Endogenous Information in Insurance Markets." *Journal of Public Economics* 63(1): 83–102.

Doherty, N., and L. Posey. (1998). "On the Value of a Checkup: Adverse Selection, Moral Hazard and the Value of Information." *Journal of Risk and Insurance* 65(2): 189–211.

Drèze, J. (1960). "Le paradoxe de l'information." *Economie Appliquée* 13: 71–80.

Dubey, P., and J. Geanakoplos. (2002). "Competitive Pooling: Rothschild-Stiglitz Reconsidered." *Quarterly Journal of Economics* 117(4): 1529–1570.

Eekhoudt Louis, and Miles Kimball. (1992). "Background Risk, Prudence and the Demand for Insurance." In G. Dionne (Ed.), *Contributions to Insurance Economics*. London: Kluwer.

Eekhoudt, L., C. Gollier, and H. Schlesinger. (1996). "Changes in Background Risk and Risk Taking Behavior." *Econometrica* 3(64): 683–689.

Eisen, R. (2006). "Adverse Selection in the Health Insurance Market after Genetic Tests." This volume, chapter 2.

Gollier, C. (2003). "To Insure or Not to Insure? An Insurance Puzzle." *Geneva Papers on Risk and Insurance Theory* 28(1): 5–24.

Guiso, L., and M. Paiella. (2001). "Risk Aversion, Wealth and Background Risk." Mimeo, Bank of Italy.

Guiso, L., and M. Paiella. (2006). "The Role of Risk Aversion in Predicting Individual Behavior." This volume, chapter 10.

Hellwig, M. (1987). "Some Recent Developments in the Theory of Competition in Markets with Adverse Selection." *European Economic Review* 31(1/2): 319–325.

Hirshleifer, J. (1971). "The Private and Social Value of Information and the Reward of Inventive Activity." *American Economic Review* 61: 561–574.

Hoy, M. (1989). "The Value of Screening Mechanisms under Alternative Insurance Possibilities." *Journal of Public Economics* 39(2): 177–206.

Hoy, M., F. Orsi, F. Eisinger, and J. P. Moatti. (2003). "The Impact of Genetic Testing on Healthcare Insurance." *Geneva Papers on Risk and Insurance: Issues and Practice* 28(2): 203–221.

Pauly, M. (2006). "Time, Risk, Precommitment, and Adverse Selection in Competitive Insurance Markets." This volume, chapter 1.

Rabin, Matthew. (2000). "Risk Aversion and Expected Utility Theory: A Calibration Theorem." *Econometrica* 68: 1281–1292.

Rothschild, M., and J. Stiglitz. (1976). "Equilibrium in Competitive Insurance Markets: An Essay on the Economics of Imperfect Information." *The Quarterly Journal of Economics* 90(4): 629–649.

Stoler, A. (2004). "Economic Implication of Genetic Testing and Mortality Risk." Mimeo, University of Chicago.

Subramanian, K., et al. (1999). "Estimating Adverse Selection Costs from Genetic Testing for Breast and Ovarian Cancer: The Case of Life Insurance." *Journal of Risk and Insurance* 66(4): 531–550.

Tabarrok, A. (1994). "Genetic Testing: An Economic and Contractarian Analysis." *Journal of Health Economics* 13(1): 75–91.

II

Empirical Analysis in Health Insurance

4

Selection and Incentive Effects: An Econometric Study of Swiss Health-Insurance Claims Data

Lucien Gardiol, Pierre-Yves Geoffard, and Chantal Grandchamp

Introduction

This chapter presents an empirical analysis of the links between health-insurance coverage and the level of health-care expenditures. Standard insurance theory predicts that expenditures and coverage should be positively correlated for two main reasons. First, individuals who expect high health-care costs may choose a more extensive coverage (*selection effect*).[1] Second, a more extensive coverage may increase health costs (*incentive effect*), either through an increase in the probability to experience sickness (ex ante moral hazard) or through an increase in expenditures in a given health state (ex post moral hazard).

Even if these two explanations revert the causality relationship between costs and coverage, they are quite difficult to separate empirically, especially on cross-sectional data (see, e.g., Chiappori and Salanié, 2000). However, the implications in terms of regulation policies are quite different. If moral hazard is an important phenomenon, a mandatory reduction of insurance coverage reduces the level of aggregate risk and may therefore increase efficiency. In contrast, if the correlation is due to selection, reducing coverage (such as mandatory minimum deductibles) would simply limit the scope of mutually beneficial contracts without affecting the level of risk, which is clearly inefficient (Chiappori, Durand, and Geoffard, 1998). On the other side, if selection effects are important, then a competitive market may be subject to adverse selection, which requires an adequate regulation. Moreover, from an empirical point of view, if selection is an important phenomenon, then estimates of moral hazard obtained on cross-sectional data are upward biased, since the correlation between expenditures and coverage is captured by the moral-hazard effect. However, the empirical evidence of (adverse) selection in insurance markets is weak (Chiappori and Salanié, 2000).

This chapter uses administrative data from a major Swiss health-insurance fund to perform a joint estimation of moral hazard and selection effects. An important point is that the menu of contracts offered to each individual is perfectly known, which gives a way to measure the opportunity cost of the contract chosen by each individual.

The main finding of the chapter is that even though incentive effects are important, selection effects are also present and far from being negligible. After the Swiss health-insurance system and our data are introduced, an analysis of mortality rates provides a strong evidence of self-selection behavior, and our empirical strategy and results for estimating incentive and selection effects are presented.

The Swiss Health-Insurance System

Overall Description

The Swiss health-insurance system offers interesting features that can be used to test for the presence of asymmetric information. Even if it seems reasonable that, in any system, each individual selects the best contract given his or her preferences and information, selection occurs only when this information is hidden to the insurer or when it is observed but cannot be used for risk selection or contract pricing. This latter case corresponds to the Swiss health-insurance system.

In Switzerland, health insurance is a two-tier system. Since 1996, according to the federal Law on Health Insurance (LAMal), all individuals must subscribe to one of several sickness funds. Each fund covers outpatient expenditures (a defined bundle of health goods and services) and half of inpatient expenditures (the other half being covered by the state).

All insurance contracts include a deductible on yearly expenditures, a copayment rate of 10 percent once the deductible level has been reached (and a fixed daily contribution of SFr 10 in case of hospitalization), and a cap on yearly payments equal to SFr 600 (approximately 400 euros) in addition to the deductible. Private not-for-profit insurance firms offer a menu of such contracts, which differ in terms of deductibles and premiums. Since 1998, deductibles can be equal to SFr 230, 400, 600, 1,200, or 1,500.[2] Premiums vary across insurance funds but are identical for all risk groups for a given deductible. In particular, no price discrimination based on age, gender, or health condition is allowed. Moreover, the range of premium reductions for individuals who choose a higher deductible rather than the basic one of SFr 230 is also limited by law. The explicit motivation of such a regulation was to implement some redistribution between risk groups, since it was assumed that high-risk individuals would opt for small deductibles.

In short, the law introduced mandatory deductibles and copayments to address moral-hazard issues, imposed uniform premiums to address selection issues, and regulated premium reductions to implement some form of redistribution explicitly based on self-selection. Finally, redistribution to some specific groups (low income) took the form of premium subsidies directly paid by each state (canton).

In addition to this mandatory health insurance, individuals may also subscribe to a supplementary insurance that covers additional goods and services considered to be "comfort" services, such as a private hospital room and coverage of alternative medicine. The supplementary insurance contract may be purchased from a different insurance firm than the mandatory one, even though it seems that not many individuals use this option.

A particularly interesting feature of the Swiss system is that, as far as basic insurance is concerned, the menu of contracts offered to each individual is the same for every individual. This is an important element. Put simply, theory predicts a selection effect:[3] each individual chooses the best contract, and empirical estimation needs to compare the preferred contract with other alternatives, which determine the opportunity cost (Cardon and Hendel, 2001).

A first question we may ask is why different individuals choose different levels of deductibles. The main reason seems to be related to health states: different expectations about future expenditures may lead high-risk individuals to self-select among plans with more extensive coverage. Other reasons may play a role (such as differences in risk aversion, time preference, or cash constraints if the premium must be paid in advance), but the data do not contain the information needed to analyze these points.

Data

We use administrative data, provided by CSS, one of the largest private (not-for-profit) insurance firms in Switzerland. For each adult individual covered, we observe the amount of yearly health-care expenditures (as known by CSS) for individuals living in the Canton de Vaud, the Swiss state that includes the city of Lausanne. The data set contains information on 62,415 individuals, covers four years (1997 to 2000), and represents 199,019 observations.

Individuals need to address all health-care bills to the insurer if they want to be reimbursed. In some cases (mostly for inpatient care and for some drugs), the insurer first pays the bill and then charges the amount due (deductible, copayment, daily contribution to hospital housing costs) to the insured. Therefore, the bill may be received by the insurer even before the deductible level has been reached, and the individual has an incentive to report an expenditure. This administrative data can reasonably be assumed to be highly reliable (at least above the deductible level) in the sense that they include most actual health-care expenditures (and all inpatient-care expenditures) for the given population. Another benefit of such data is the number of observations: exhaustive health-care expenditures for more than 60,000 individuals followed up for four years is certainly highly valuable information.

Unfortunately, administrative data usually provide few variables (with respect to survey data), which strongly conditions the econometric analysis. The following variables are available in our data set:

• Gender (0 = woman and 1 = man),

• Birth year,

• Annual outpatient costs per insured (including drugs) for 1997 to 2000,

• Annual inpatient costs per insured for 1997 to 2000,

• Deductible for 1997 to 2000,

• Rural or urban area (0 = urban and 1 = rural),

• Supplementary insurance (alternative medicine, semiprivate, private), and

• Death.

Our sample may not be representative of the Swiss population or even of the population of the Canton de Vaud. However, concentrating on a specific geographic area may reduce unobserved heterogeneity and increase robustness of results. The descriptive statistics of our work data set are presented later in this chapter.

As a first outline of the distribution of total health costs, table 4.1 summarizes the distribution of total annual health costs per deductible.

Table 4.1
Distribution of annual health expenditures across deductible

	Deductible (Swiss francs)				
	230 $n = 91,831$	400 $n = 42,581$	600 $n = 34,090$	$\geq 1,200$ $n = 30,517$	All $n = 199,019$
Mean	4,205.95	2,443.83	2,128.21	1,278.03	3,024.08
Standard deviation	7,795.21	5,467.80	4,846.92	3,742.65	6,475.16
	%	%	%	%	%
[0]	12.32	17.21	25.08	43.80	20.38
[0; 1,500]	33.46	42.41	39.08	35.53	36.65
[1,500; 7,500]	40.00	33.85	30.22	17.27	33.52
[7,500]	14.23	6.54	5.61	3.40	9.45

The table gives the mean (in current SFr) and the standard deviation of the annual health expenditure and, over four ranges of expenditures, the proportion of observations that lie in this interval.

The proportion of agents with no health expenditures dramatically increases with the deductible level. On the other side, the proportion of high health expenditures decreases strongly with the deductible. As expected, there is a positive correlation between insurance coverage and health expenditure. This chapter shows that this correlation is due to both incentive and selection effects.

Nonparametric Evidence of Selection Effects

In Switzerland, no discrimination based on age, gender, or health condition is allowed for mandatory health insurance. It is then not surprising to find a selection effect since we observe variables (age and gender) that are also observed by the insurer but that cannot be used to differentiate the premiums. If we still find a selection effect, evidence, even after controlling for age and gender, tells us that another unobserved information matters to the choice of an insurance contract (as health condition).

Lets denote D the deductible, h the health state, and x some observable component of the risk. For instance, x may denote an index of health-care consumption (such as number of doctor visits or hospital stays or annual inpatient or outpatient expenditures) or may denote mortality.

Many observable variables x signal bad health. Some may be subject to incentive effects (such as ambulatory care, demand for which is known to be price elastic). But for some other variables, it is reasonable to assume that there is no incentive effect. A striking example is mortality: given a health condition h, the deductible level should have no impact on the probability to die, at least in the short run. A second example is inpatient expenditures: standard results in the empirical literature are that price elasticity of demand for hospital care is close to zero (Manning et al., 1987; Newhouse and the Insurance Experiment Group, 1996).

Death and the Deductible
An interesting feature of our administrative data set is its size. Indeed, the followup of more than 60,000 individuals over four years provides a rare opportunity to study the determinants of the mortality rate. This analysis is usually impossible on survey data, given that the average mortality rate is below 1 percent per year, and sample sizes are rarely larger than 10,000 individuals.

For this analysis, we select the subpopulation of individuals between age twenty and sixty-four in 1997 who did not exit the sample except in case of death. This subsample contains 25,314 individuals, among whom 360 died during the four years of observation.

Mortality data are highly interesting for our purposes. In the presence of selection, individuals with a higher probability to die will tend to select lower deductibles, since health-care expenditures are usually very high at the end of life. This is actually what the data show in a quite striking way. First, we look for a selection effect without taking into account observable variables that cannot be used by the insurer to differentiate premiums.

As expected, table 4.2 shows that the death rate strongly decreases with the deductible. Then we control for observable variable (age and gender) in a simple logit model where the dependent variable is 1 if the insured died between 1997 and 2000 and 0 if not. Independent variables X are gender (reference category is female), age, age squared, and deductible in 1997 (reference category: deductible 400 SFr).

These results (table 4.3) show that a small deductible is an indicator of higher mortality, even after controlling for gender and age. Table 4.4 gives the probability of death in the following year by gender and deductible at age thirty, forty, fifty, and sixty. Such a pattern cannot be caused by an incentive effect, since (as table 4.1 shows) health-care

Table 4.2
Death rates per deductible

Deductible (Swiss francs)	n	Number of Deaths					Death Rate (Mil)
		1997	1998	1999	2000	Mean	
230	12,362	75	56	58	68	64.25	5.20
400	4,195	12	8	11	11	10.50	2.50
≥600	8,757	12	21	16	12	15.25	1.74
Total	25,314	99	85	85	91	90	3.56

Table 4.3
Probability of death between 1997 and 2000 ($n = 25,314$)

Variables (x)	Coefficients	Odds Ratio	z
Constant	−7.1000		−6.92
Gender	0.8376	2.3108	7.66
Age	0.0075	1.0076	0.17
Age squared	0.0007	1.0007	1.53
Deductible SFr 230	0.6657	1.9459	3.95
Deductible ≥ SFr 600	−0.3671	0.6927	−1.81

Table 4.4
Estimated probability of death during the following year (in Millions)

Sex	Deductible (Swiss francs)	Age			
		30	40	50	60
Women	230	0.95	1.66	3.35	7.70
	400	0.49	0.86	1.73	4.02
	≥600	0.34	0.60	1.20	2.80
Men	230	2.17	3.81	7.61	17.10
	400	1.12	1.97	3.97	9.09
	≥600	0.78	1.37	2.77	6.37

expenditures also decrease with the deductible, and health-care consumption does not (in general) increase the mortality risk. These results strongly support the selection-effect assumption: people in bad health select low deductible levels.

A Parametric Analysis of Selection and Incentive Effects

Data Preparation and Descriptive Statistics

The original data set contains 62,415 individuals. To focus only on our specific problem and to consider yearly observations of each individuals as independent, we exclude all observed sources of exogenous heterogeneity. We restrict the empirical analysis to a subsample composed of the following individuals:

• Men (in our data, we cannot identify pregnancy costs, which the insurance fully covers by law),

• Those who stayed at the CSS from January 1, 1997, until December 31, 2000 (this excludes people who died or shifted to another insurance fund),

• Those who kept the same deductible during the whole period (only 13 percent of our sample changed their deductible at least once during the four years),

• Those who were older than twenty-five in 1997 (children and younger adults face a different menu of contracts),

• Those who did not receive a premium subsidy (eligibility is based on income, and subsidized individuals have a stronger incentive to opt for a low deductible),

• Those who were not eligible for disability pension benefits in any of the four years (eligibility is based on severe health conditions, and a specific public insurance fund covers health-care expenses).

The final data set contains 7,885 individuals observed between 1997 and 2000 (which means 31,540 observations). Table 4.5 presents the population descriptive statistics of our work data set.

Estimation and Testing Strategy

In the previous section, we show, in a simple way, evidence of selection effects. We propose in this section a simplified linear structural model for separating selection and incentive effects.

Table 4.5
Population descriptive statistics

Variables ($n = 31{,}540$)		Mean	Standard Deviation
Age in 1997		52.68	14.92
Outpatient expenditures (SFr)		1,854.17	3,288.77
Frequency of inpatient costs > 0 (SFr)		9%	—
Inpatient expenditures (if > 0) (SFr)	$n = 2{,}848$	6,706.22	8,537.38
Total health-care costs (SFr)		2,478.86	5,240.32
Rural area		30%	—
Deductible (SFr)	230	40%	—
	400	16%	—
	600	26%	—
	1,200	10%	—
	1,500	8%	—
Supplementary insurance	Alternative	58%	—
	Semiprivate	15%	—
	Private	14%	—

We denote by X the observed health expenditure, by Z a vector of individual characteristics, by D the deductible level, and by h the unobserved health status of the individual:

$$E(X|D, Z, h) = \alpha + \beta D + \gamma Z + \phi h.$$

The parameter β represents the deductible effect on X; presumably, this price effect is negative. The parameter ϕ represents the direct effect of health on X—that is, $\frac{\partial}{\partial h} E(X|D, Z, h)$—which is presumably negative (better health leads to lower spending). However, since h is not observed, the law of iterated conditional expectations gives the following:

$$E(X|D, Z) = \alpha + \beta D + \gamma Z + \phi E(h|D, Z).$$

Taking the difference between the expected health expenditures given for Z for two different deductible levels gives the following:

$$E(X|D, Z) - E(X|D', Z) = \underbrace{\beta(D - D')}_{\text{Incentive effect}} + \underbrace{\phi[E(h|D, Z) - E(h|D', Z)]}_{\text{Selection effect}}.$$

The first part of this difference represents the incentive effect: the impact of a change in deductible level on health expenditures, controlling for health status and other individual characteristics. The second part represents the selection effect: the impact on expenditures of a different distribution of h as revealed by the choice of deductible D. We do not observe h, but we assume a linear relation $E(h|D,Z) = kD + mZ$, with $k > 0$ if there is a selection effect. Under this specification, we have

$$E(X|D,Z) - E(X|D',Z) = \beta(D - D') + \phi k(D - D').$$

Estimating β by a direct regression of X on D (and other observable variables Z) will lead to a biased estimate $\hat{\beta} = \beta + \phi k$, and k is not identifiable when h is not observed.

However, we observe two kinds of health expenditures: outpatient (x) and inpatient (y). We may therefore write

$$E(x|D,Z) - E(x|D',Z) = \beta(D - D') + \phi k(D - D')$$

$$E(y|D,Z) - E(y|D',Z) = b(D - D') + \psi k(D - D').$$

We assume that $b = 0$ for two reasons: first, the price elasticity of hospital care has usually been found to be close to zero (Newhouse and the Insurance Experiment Group, 1996); second, in the Swiss institutional framework, the total health expenditures of an individual who spends at least one night at the hospital is systematically larger than the higher deductible level and in many cases exceeds the cap on annual payments. Therefore, even if the price elasticity was not zero, the price effect would be negligible on hospital care. Under this assumption, we have that $b = 0$, so that $\hat{b} = \psi k$. Moreover, we assume that the effect of a change in health is larger on hospital expenditures than on outpatient expenditures and that both are negative—that is, that $\psi \leq \phi < 0$.

Under these two assumptions, we may perform two tests on the estimated parameters $\hat{b}$ and $\hat{\beta}$. First, if $\hat{b} < 0$, this reveals that $k > 0$—that is, that there is a selection effect. Second, since $\hat{\beta} = \beta + \phi k$, $\hat{\beta} < \hat{b}$ is equivalent to $\beta < (\psi - \phi)k$. Therefore, a *sufficient* condition for the presence of incentive effects on outpatient care $(\beta < 0)$ is that $\hat{\beta} < \hat{b}$. However, notice that if the difference between ψ and ϕ is large, this may provide a very conservative test: β may well be larger than $(\psi - \phi)k$ but still negative.

In summary,

- If $\hat{b} < 0$, there is a selection effect;
- If $\hat{\beta} < \hat{b}$, there is also an incentive effect.

Econometric Estimation

We estimate two separate equations, one for each kind of health-care expenditure (outpatient and inpatient). For each equation, we run a two-step regression: the first step represents the probability to have nonzero expenditures (interpreted as the probability of illness), and the second step represents the amount of expenditures that are conditional on the occurrence of illness.

In the first step, a logistic model is estimated such that the odds ratio can be compared in any point of the distribution; hence we can also compare the odds ratio of outpatient and inpatient estimations. In the second step, a log-linear model is estimated for outpatient and inpatient expenditures, given that expenditures are positive.

In both steps, we have a multiplicative model. In this context, in the first step the assumption $\psi \leq \phi < 0$ means that a marginal decrease of h (worse health) increases the probability of an inpatient stay more than the probability of outpatient expenditures. In the second step, it means that the elasticity of expenditures with respect to health is larger for inpatient than for outpatient expenditures.

Results   We first perform unconstrained estimations for outpatient and inpatient expenditures in both steps. In each regression, we also test if the three deductible coefficients are jointly equal to zero. Table 4.6 presents the results of the two estimations for outpatient and inpatient expenditures and for the likelihood ratio test $(LR - test)$.

Age has a global positive effect on both outpatient and inpatient expenditures. This effect is larger for outpatient than for inpatient expenditures.[4]

The effect of living area (reference is urban) shows a different pattern for inpatient care than for outpatient expenditures. Living in a rural area decreases significantly the probability of nonzero outpatient-care consumption and the conditional outpatient expenditure. This may indicate that access to outpatient services is less costly (especially in terms of transportation costs) for urban individuals. For inpatient care, the increase in expenditures is not significant.

For outpatient care, supplementary health-insurance dummies all have a positive effect on expenditures, which is important for semiprivate and private insurance. This effect is not significant for alternative-medicine insurance, but such contracts cover some goods and services not covered by the mandatory insurance. It is interesting

Table 4.6
Unconstrained logistic and log-linear estimations

	Outpatient		Inpatient	
Logistic Estimation	Odds Ratio	t-stat	Odds Ratio	t-stat
Age	1.0475	46.43	1.0462	30.90
Deductible level (SFr)				
400	0.9286	−1.84	0.7745	−4.37
600	0.5130	−20.04	0.7881	−4.48
1,200 or 1,500	0.1672	−46.54	0.5492	−8.40
Rural area	0.8226	−6.81	1.0729	1.58
Supplementary health insurance				
Alternative medicine	1.0087	3.83	1.0055	1.57
Semiprivate	1.0344	10.25	1.0156	3.22
Private	1.0380	11.05	1.0205	4.34
Maximum likelihood	−17,246.64		−8,859.75	
LR test $\chi_2(3)$		2,580.16		84.23
Log-linear estimation	Coefficient	t-stat	Coefficient	t-stat
Constant	1.0237	32.68	2.2860	25.51
Age	0.0190	42.26	0.0118	9.83
Deductible level (SFr)				
400	−0.0617	−3.53	−0.1314	−2.71
600	−0.1689	−10.25	−0.1776	−3.98
1,200 or 1,500	−0.3352	−14.11	−0.1699	−2.80
Rural area	−0.0669	−4.68	0.0187	0.50
Supplementary health insurance				
Alternative medicine	0.0009	0.82	−0.0038	−1.33
Semiprivate	0.0095	6.25	−0.0076	−1.89
Private	0.0141	9.28	0.0017	0.44
Maximum likelihood	−26,377.40		−3,697.18	
LR test $\chi_2(3)$		244.60		21.12

to note that people who buy an alternative medicine insurance contract do not spend less on traditional normal care.

The deductible coefficients show in a general way the negative association between deductible and health expenditures: the larger the deductible, the smaller the probability is of having positive health expenditures, and the smaller any positive expenditures are (for those who have them).

All these results are of the expected sign and stress once again the positive correlation between insurance coverage and health-care expenditures.

Selection and Incentive Effects

• *Selection effects* The first test we propose is that the coefficients of deductibles are significantly different from zero for inpatient expenditures ($\hat{b} < 0$). In table 4.6, we can see that the LR tests are all highly significant ($p < 0.01$), meaning that in each estimation the deductible effects are jointly different from zero. For the inpatient equation and under our assumptions, this reveals the presence of a selection effect. Therefore, the correlation between coverage and health expenditures present in the outpatient equation cannot be attributed a priori to only an incentive effect.

• *Incentive effects taking into account for selection effects* The second test is that the coefficients of deductibles in the outpatient equation are smaller than the coefficients in the inpatient equation ($\hat{\beta} < \hat{b}$). We perform this test for both steps separately. We use an LR test in the outpatient constrained model where the coefficients of insurance variables are constrained to be the same as in the inpatient equation. We obtain significant $LR - tests$ for both steps: the likelihood ratio for the first step is 1,298.4 and for the second step 81.9 (critical value at 5 percent is 7.8). We can therefore argue that $\hat{\beta}$ is significantly smaller than $\hat{b}$, which reveals the presence of an incentive effect on outpatient expenditures, controlling for selection effects.

Conclusion

This chapter provides three main empirical conclusions. The observed correlation between mortality rates and chosen deductible levels proves the presence of self-selection. This self-selection effect remains significant when we control for age and gender, proving that self-selection is also done according to private information that is unknown by the insurer. Second, inpatient spending is negatively correlated with deductible levels, which is another indication of self-selection. Third, the correlation between expenditures and deductible levels is significantly larger for outpatient care than for inpatient care. We interpret this difference as being due to incentive effects that add to selection effects. The test for the presence of incentive effects is indeed very conservative, and it seems reasonable to believe, in view of the results, that both effects are positive and significant. However, the relative share of each effect in the observed correlation between coverage and expenditures may not be accurately estimated. A more detailed investigation of the differences between the whole distribution of expenditures for different deductible levels is the object of an ongoing research project by the same authors.

This chapter contributes to the existing empirical evidence of adverse selection on health-insurance markets (as reviewed by Cutler and Zeckhauser, 2000) and also confirms other growing evidence on Swiss data (Schellhorn, 2001; Werblow and Felder, 2003). We emphasis that in the Swiss context, adverse selection (strategic response to self-selection behavior by competing insurers) is not possible. Therefore, our empirical strategy offers some direct evidence of self-selection effects.

The consequences of these findings are twofold. First, empirical analysis of incentives effects needs to control carefully for selection effects. Second, self-selection behavior may lead to a failure of insurance markets. Therefore, competition in health-insurance markets should be carefully regulated to prevent such failures. In particular, mandatory insurance and some form of contract standardization may limit indirect risk selection and reduce welfare losses due to asymmetries of information.

Acknowledgments

We thank Konstantin Beck for the provision of data, Ramses Abul Naga, Pierre-André Chiappori, Alberto Holly, Stefan Felder, and Martin Schellhorn for discussions and suggestions, seminar and conference participants at Toronto (CHERA: the Ninth Canadian Conference on Health Economics), Taipei (National Taiwan University), Paris (the Fifth European Congress in Health Economics), Saõ Paulo (LAMES), Lund (the Eleventh European Workshop on Econometrics and Health

Economics), and Venice (the CES-ifo Summer Institute, 2003). Financial support from the Swiss National Fund for Scientific Research (PNR 45) is gratefully acknowledged. Remaining errors are ours.

Notes

1. We limit the term of adverse selection to the situation in which insurance firms compete in contracts and attempt to selectively attract good risks. This is possible only if there is a selection effect in the sense defined above, but market regulation in Switzerland prevents adverse selection as far as basic health insurance is concerned.

2. Since January 1, 2004, the cap on yearly payments is equal to SFr 700, and the lower deductible is equal to SFr 300 rather than SFr 230.

3. Since insurance funds cannot compete in contracts, there is no adverse selection, in a strict sense, in Switzerland. However, individuals may self-select themselves into the most adapted contracts, given their private information.

4. We tested a polynomial occurrence of age and found that the linear specification fits best.

References

Cardon, J. H., and I. Hendel. (2001). "Asymmetric Information in Health Insurance: Evidence from the National Medical Expenditure Survey." *RAND Journal of Economics* 32(3): 408–427.

Chiappori, P.-A., F. Durand, and P.-Y. Geoffard. (1998). "Moral Hazard and the Demand for Physician Services: First Lessons from a French Natural Experiment." *European Economic Review* 42: 499–511.

Chiappori, P.-A., and B. Salanié. (2000). "Testing for Asymmetric Information in Insurance Markets." *Journal of Political Economy* 108(1): 56–79.

Cutler, D., and R. Zeckhauser. (2000). "The Anatomy of Health Insurance." In A. Culyer and J. Newhouse (Eds.), *Handbook of Health Economics*. Amsterdam: Elsevier/North-Holland.

Manning, W. G., J. P. Newhouse, N. Duan, E. B. Keeler, B. Benjamin, A. A. Leibowitz, M. S. Marquis, and J. Zwanziger. (1987). "Health Insurance and the Demand for Medical Care: Evidence from a Randomized Experiment." *American Economic Review* 77(3): 251–277.

Newhouse, J., and the Insurance Experiment Group. (1996). *Free for All? Lessons from the RAND Health Insurance Experiment*. Cambridge, MA: Harvard University Press.

Schellhorn, M. (2001). "The Effect of Variable Health Insurance Deductibles on the Demand for Physicians Visits." *Health Economics* 10: 441–456.

Werblow, A., and S. Felder. (2003). *Der Einfluss von freiwilligen Selbstbehalten in der gesetzlichen Krankenversicherung: Edivenz aus der schweiz*. *Schmollers Jahrbuch* 123: 235–264.

5   Adverse Selection in the Long-Term Care Insurance Market

Mark J. Browne

Introduction

The aging of societies in many countries around the world is creating an increasing need for long-term care. For instance, the size of the United States population over age eighty-five, a group at great risk of needing long-term care, grew 274 percent between 1960 and 1994. As the baby-boom generation of many industrialized countries ages, the population in need of long-term care is expected to grow. In many European and Asian countries, particularly Japan, the aging of society is expected to have profound social implications as the need for long-term care by a growing proportion of the population becomes acute.

The need for long-term care strikes many in their elderly years who do not have the financial resources to pay for care. Some receive care from family members. Others qualify for government-supported coverage of their long-term care needs. In spite of the apparent need for long-term care insurance, this market is relatively small. One reason long-term care insurance may not be commonly purchased is because this market may be plagued by information asymmetries that limit the transfer of risk. A second possibility is that one-sided commitment, an important characteristic of multiyear long-term care insurance contracts, fails to lock in lower-risk insureds. Failure of the contracts to lock in low risks may result in unstable risk pools. The data analysis reported in this study suggests contracting problems exist in the private long-term care insurance market. The analysis leaves open the question whether this is due to information asymmetries in the market or difficulties arising from one-sided commitment.

Aging and the Need for Long-Term Care

The average age of people living in the United States, and in many other developed countries, is increasing. Important factors contributing to an aging population are an increase in life expectancy and an aging post–World War II baby-boom generation. According to the U.S. Census Bureau, 12.4 percent of the population was over age sixty-five in 2001. This was a dramatic change from 1900, when 4.1 percent of the population was over age sixty-five. Even greater has been the percentage increase since 1900 in the number of people in the two highest age groups: the size of the age cohort seventy-five to eighty-four has increased by a factor of 16, and the size of the age cohort eighty-five and over has increased by a factor of 33. The number of people over age sixty-five is expected to double in the next thirty years.

The increase in the elderly population has created significant social and financial concerns in the United States, which are reflected in debates over the future direction of social security, the public retirement pension system in the United States. The Social Security Administration reports that without reforms the system will be unable to fulfill its financial obligations past the year 2034. In large part, this situation is attributable to a significant decline in the ratio of workers to retirees in the United States, which is the product of the growing size of the elderly population and a decline in the birthrate. The stress placed on the working population by the increasingly large retiree population has been noted in numerous newspaper and magazine articles, which report on a "sandwich generation" of middle-age workers who are attempting to care for both children and the elderly.

The need for professional managed care for many elderly becomes clear when one considers the demographics of the population over the age of sixty-five. Because males have a shorter life expectancy, this group is largely female, and the ratio of females to males increases as age increases. In large part due to death, many in the elderly cohort are not married: 25 percent of elderly men and 57 percent of elderly women are unmarried. Although the majority of the noninstitutionalized elderly live in a family setting, the proportion doing so decreases with age. This decrease is due largely to the death of spouses. Less than half of those over age eighty-five live in a family setting: about 31 percent of the noninstitutionalized elderly lived alone in 1998, and almost 60 percent of women over age eighty-five live alone. The loss of a spouse, who may have provided care during a time of illness at an earlier point in life, leaves many elderly individuals in a situation where they must rely on professional care provided by either a nursing home or visits from health professionals (AARP, 1999).

In part because women have longer life expectancies than men, long-term care nursing facilities serve largely the elderly female population. The average age a woman is admitted into a nursing home is eighty-three. Women account for roughly 80 percent of the population over age eighty-five in nursing homes. If one averages over all ages, 75 percent of nursing home residents are women.

The task of paying for nursing home care for many women is daunting for two reasons. First, many women have limited incomes during their retirement years. In 1996, the median income of unmarried women over age sixty-five was only $10,483, which was less than half of the median income of married couples over age sixty-five that year. Many elderly women live in poverty. The Social Security Administration reports that over 30 percent of both African American and Hispanic women over age sixty-five live in poverty and that approximately 17 percent of white women over age sixty-five live in poverty.

The second reason many women have a difficult time affording long-term care is because it is expensive. The average annual cost of care in a nursing home in 1997 was roughly $48,000. Care provided on an out-of-facility basis, commonly called *home care*, is also expensive. The average cost of a single visit by a health professional is $77. Regular care over the course of a year can easily exceed $15,000.

Lacking a spouse to provide needed care and the financial resources to access professional care, many elderly individuals rely on care provided on a voluntary basis. Often children provide this assistance. This volunteer care can be extremely taxing on children. A typical volunteer caregiver spends eighteen hours per week providing assistance to an elderly individual. Almost 40 percent of those who provide volunteer assistance provide more than forty hours per week. To accommodate this demanding schedule, many caregivers adjust their employment conditions by either seeking jobs with fewer hours or modifying the hours they work at their jobs. Many caregivers quit their jobs or take leaves of absence (Adams, Nawrocki, and Coleman, 1999).

Government and Private Insurance for Long-Term Care
Government funding of long-term care in the United States is provided primarily to those who qualify under the Medicaid program. While eligibility criteria differ from state to state, the program is available only to those meeting both income and asset tests of need. Elderly

individuals may make themselves eligible for Medicaid coverage by depleting their resources. Resource depletion may occur as a result of out-of-pocket financing for long-term care over an extended period. In addition to its eligibility restrictions, there are several additional drawbacks to Medicaid as a funding vehicle for long-term care. One drawback is that the reimbursement levels paid by Medicaid to nursing homes are insufficient to cover the costs of some nursing homes. A second drawback is that impoverishing oneself to qualify for Medicaid may have significant negative consequences for a spouse, when the individual in need of long-term care is married.

The increasing need for long-term care suggests a potentially significant marketing opportunity exists for insurers who can successfully write this coverage. The need for this form of coverage results not only from the aging of society but also from the adverse consequences and inherent difficulties associated with financing this risk through private savings, charity, or governmental assistance. This potential opportunity has been known to the insurance community since at least the mid-1980s. Nonetheless, private insurance financing of this risk continues to be relatively minor. Table 5.1 reports sources of long-term care financing in 1997.

One reason that private insurance may not be an important financing mechanism for this risk is that insurers may not be able to classify

Table 5.1
Sources of long-term care financing, 1997

	Home Health Care		Nursing-Home Care	
	U.S. Dollars (Billions)	Percentage	U.S. Dollars (Billions)	Percentage
Private				
Out-of-pocket payments	7.0	21.7	25.7	31.0
Private health insurance	3.7	11.5	4.0	4.8
Other payments	3.9	12.1	1.6	1.9
Total private	$14.7	45.3%	$31.3	37.8%
Government				
Federal	15.4	47.7	34.5	41.7
State and local	2.3	7.1	16.9	20.4
Total government	$17.7	54.8%	$51.4	62.1%
Total	$32.3	100%	$82.8	100%

Source: "National Health Expenditures," (1998).

risks with precision. In this chapter, longitudinal data from the long-term care insurance market are used to test whether risk-pooling problems are present in the market. The chapter presents different explanations that have been provided in prior research for the relatively small size of the long-term care insurance market. The model used to test the hypothesis of the study and the data that are used to estimate the model are discussed, and empirical findings are presented, along with a discussion of the empirical findings and their implications for the funding of long-term care.

Explaining the Small Size of the Market for Long-Term Care Insurance

As noted above, the Medicaid program in the United States provides coverage for long-term care expenses for individuals with little to no income and minimal assets. Pauly (1990) argues that the presence of this public insurance coverage decreases the demand for private insurance by some individuals. For an individual without a spouse and no bequest motive, the use of wealth to purchase private insurance that would provide a level of care equal to that funded by Medicaid would not be utility maximizing. This is because payment of the insurance premiums would result in a decrease in the consumption of other goods when premiums are paid but would provide no benefit greater than that provided by Medicaid when the loss occurs. If the need for long-term care arises, the individual lacking private insurance coverage could simply spend down his or her wealth to become eligible for Medicaid. Maximizing utility over a lifetime, individuals would choose not to purchase the insurance coverage unless the cost of coverage was cheaper than the actuarially fair price. An assumption in Pauly's argument is that entrance into a nursing home is invariably followed by death. Dick, Garber, and MaCurdy (1994) show that some individuals do return to the community after a nursing-home stay.

If private insurance would allow one to access higher-quality nursing-home care, Pauly argues that utility-maximizing individuals would demand insurance coverage that would pay for the difference in the cost between the higher-quality nursing-home care and that financed by Medicaid. He points out, however, that Medicaid rules preclude coverage of this type by taking into consideration private insurance before paying.

The preceding argument by Pauly assumes that individuals do not have a bequest motive. He finds that relaxing this assumption does not affect the demand for long-term care insurance in most situations. The preceding argument also assumes that the individual does not have a spouse. The presence of a spouse may result in the demand for long-term care insurance, but the policy would have a significant deductible. In general, Pauly finds that the presence of public coverage serves as a substitute for private coverage for many individuals.

In addition to the crowding-out effect that Pauly asserts Medicaid exerts on the private market for long-term care insurance, several other explanations have been offered for the relatively small size of this market. A federal government study undertaken by the Task Force on Long-Term Care Health Policies (1987) argues that people are not fully aware of the risk of needing long-term care services. As a consequence, they do not demand as much insurance to cover the risk as they would if better informed. A survey taken in 1993 supports this. The survey found that 76 percent of Americans surveyed felt they would never have a need for any long-term care services (Marer, 1999). A related argument is that individuals do not purchase long-term care insurance because they feel they have coverage through the federal government's Medicare program. In fact, Medicare covers only the first one hundred days of a stay at a nursing home and then only in certain cases. Individuals may be ill informed about both the risks of needing long-term care and the social insurance coverage that exists for this potential loss. Calling for federal legislation to address the issue of long-term care, Senator Bob Graham of Florida stated, "Most Americans spend more time planning for their two-week summer vacation" than for retirement (Jacoby, 2000).

Davis and Rowland (1986) offer another possible explanation for the small size of the long-term care insurance market. They suggest adverse selection may be present in this market. While Doerpinghaus and Gustavson (1999) do not test whether adverse selection is present in the long-term care insurance market, they report evidence that policy characteristics linked to the control of adverse-selection and moral-hazard problems are important determinants of insurance policy prices.

In the seminal work on adverse selection, Akerlof (1970) describes an insurance market in which buyers of insurance are better informed about the risk that is being insured than the insurers. In his model, the individuals seeking insurance differ in their expected loss. Insurers are unable to perceive the difference in expected losses between individuals of different risk types. As a result, they price the insurance policy at a price that represents the expected loss for the group as a whole. When faced with a price of insurance representing an average for the group as a whole, the better risks in the group choose not to purchase coverage. They choose not to purchase insurance as they feel the price is too expensive relative to their risk. In contrast, the higher risks perceive that they are being offered insurance at a favorable price. They purchase coverage. With only the higher risks purchasing coverage at a rate that is based on the expected loss experience of the group as a whole, the insurers lose money. The insurer raises its premium in an attempt to restore profitability. This induces the better risks of those that are still in the pool to drop their coverage, resulting in further losses for the insurance company. The cycle of premium increases and individuals dropping their coverage continues until only the very worst risks purchase insurance coverage at a very high price. This cycle is frequently referred to as a *death spiral*.

According to Akerlof's model, the inability of insurers to discern between different risk types leads to a market outcome in which the very worst risks are able to obtain insurance coverage at a price that is fair for them. Other potential purchasers of insurance are unable to acquire insurance at a price that is fair given their risk level. They wind up uninsured. Rothshchild and Stiglitz (1976) reach similar but somewhat different conclusions in their study of market equilibrium in an insurance market characterized by asymmetric information. In their study, they assume that there are only two risk types—high risks and low risks. Just as Akerlof did, they assume that insurers are unable to perceive a difference in risk between the risk types. Like Akerlof, they find that adverse selection may result in the low risks getting no coverage and the high risks getting full coverage at a high price. However, they also describe situations in which the high risks may purchase full coverage at a high price and the low risks purchase less than full coverage at a low price. Finally, they describe the possibility that the market for insurance may not reach equilibrium when information is asymmetric in favor of the buyer of insurance. Wilson (1977) develops a model similar to that of Rothschild and Stiglitz but adds the assumption that insurers will not offer an insurance product if they know that it will become unprofitable as a result of other insurers introducing products to the marketplace. In Wilson's model, the possibility that high risks and low risks purchase the same insurance policy at a pooled price exists.

Several empirical studies suggest that adverse selection does occur in health insurance markets. Browne (1992) provided statistical evidence that adverse selection is present in the market for individual health insurance. His study suggests that cross-subsidization of high risks by the low risks does occur in this market. Browne and Doerpinghaus (1993) also focused on the market for individual health insurance. They report that the characteristics of the insurance policies purchased by high and low risks and the premiums paid by high and low risks are similar but that high risks derive more indemnity benefits from their insurance coverage than do low risks. They noted that this finding suggests that adverse selection in the market for individual health insurance results in a pooling of risk types. Browne and Doerpinghaus (1994) report obtaining similar results in a study of the Medicare supplemental-insurance market.

Finkelstein and McGarry (2003) find that purchasers of long-term care insurance are better informed about their risk of needing long-term care than insurers. They further find that individuals' risk assessments are correlated with their insurance purchases. Nonetheless, they find that long-term care insurance purchases are not correlated with the occurrence of a loss. They explain this apparent contradiction by arguing that more cautious individuals are more likely to purchase insurance and less likely to require nursing-home care.

If information is asymmetric in favor of the buyer of insurance in the long-term care insurance market, purchases of insurance coverage by lower risks may be significantly lower than they would be in a market free of adverse selection. As a result of the implicit cross-subsidization of high risks by low risks that may occur in a market with adverse selection, higher risks may be charged premiums less than their actuarially fair price. This may result in greater insurance purchases by higher risks than would occur in a market with complete information.

Pauly, Kunreuther, and Hirth (1995) describe how insurance written with a guaranteed renewability provision may be written at a break-even rate that would be attractive to both low and high risks. Their policy entails frontloading, a feature that discourages low risks from leaving the policy as information becomes known over time. Hendel and Lizzeri (2003) report evidence from the life insurance market that frontloading does create a partial lock-in of lower-risk insureds. They also find that more frontloading is associated with lower lapse rates. Insufficient frontloading may result in lower-risk insureds lapsing coverage over time. If long-term care insurance contracts do not include an adequate frontload to lock in low risks, it is reasonable to assume the contracts would be less desirable to consumers seeking extended-period coverage against the risk of long-term care. This is an additional explanation for the relatively small size of the private long-term care insurance market.

The current study attempts to provide information on whether contracting problems, whether arising from adverse selection or the failure of contracts to lock in lower risks, plague the market for long-term care insurance. The study analyzes data from one long-term care insurance pool that experienced annual rate increases over a series of years. The rate increases applied equally to all policies in the insurance pool. For instance, if a rate increase was 10 percent, all of the policies in the pool experienced a 10 percent increase in premium, regardless of the prior loss experience of individual policies in the pool. The policies sold to the individuals in this pool had a guaranteed renewable provision. The study tests whether the higher risks in the pool were more likely than the lower risks to retain coverage following a rate increase. Although the policies were written with a guaranteed renewable provision, the rate increases indicate initial pricing did not adequately account for loss trends.

Methodology

To test whether the lower-risk individuals in the data sample are more likely to drop their insurance coverage than higher-risk individuals, it is first necessary to classify the individuals in the data set by their risk type. The predicted losses of insureds are used as a proxy for their risk type. Predicted losses are estimated with an equation of the form

$$Loss_{i,t} = a_1 + a_2(Density_{i,t}) + a_3(Female_{i,t}) + a_4(Age_{i,t}) + a_5(Year_t)$$
$$+ a_6(Underwriting_{i,t}) + e_{i,t},$$

where $Loss_{i,t}$ is the insured loss incurred by individual i during time period t. $Density_{i,t}$ is a series of dummy variables representing the population density of the area in which individual i resides during time period t. This is included to proxy the likelihood that a policyholder lives near a family member, such as an adult child, who can provide assistance with activities of daily living. $Female_{i,t}$ takes the value 1 if

Table 5.2
Prediction equation variables, descriptive statistics

Variable	Mean	Standard Deviation	Minimum	Maximum
Claim size	3,285.920	8,426.500	0	63,118.090
Large urban	0.278	0.448	0	1.000
Rural	0.007	0.081	0	1.000
Female	0.230	0.421	0	1.000
Age	83.007	5.695	58.000	99.000
Year	8.248	2.689	5.000	16.000
UW1	0.084	0.278	0	1.000
UW2	0.015	0.120	0	1.000
UW3	0.405	0.491	0	1.000
UW4	0.020	0.141	0	1.000
UW5	0.052	0.223	0	1.000
UW6	0.056	0.231	0	1.000
UW7	0.123	0.328	0	1.000
UW8	0.126	0.332	0	1.000
UW9	0.102	0.303	0	1.000
UW10	0.010	0.097	0	1.000

individual i was a female during time period t and 0 otherwise. $Age_{i,t}$ is the age in years of individual i during time period t. $Year_t$ is a count variable that takes the value of the last two digits of the calendar year of the observation. The term $Underwriting_{i,t}$ represents a series of dummy variables for ten underwriting questions related to the health of individual i. Each variable takes the value 1 if individual i answered affirmatively to the question during the underwriting process. Otherwise, the variable takes the value 0. The model's intercept is a_1. The coefficients are a_2 through a_6. The standard error is $e_{i,t}$.

Table 5.2 reports descriptive statistics for the variables used to estimate the model. Table 5.3 reports the estimated parameters of the model. The model was estimated by the method of ordinary least squares. The model has an R^2 value of .156. While the model does not explain a considerable amount of the variation in the dependent variable, this is not surprising as insured losses are largely random events. Considerable unexplained variation is expected.

The central hypothesis of this study—that adverse selection occurs in the market for long-term care insurance—is tested with the following logit model:

Table 5.3
Prediction equation estimation (Adj $R^2 = 15.5$, $n = 12{,}492$)

Variable	Parameter Estimate	$Pr > |t|$
Intercept	−19,987	<0.0001
Large urban	−679.693	<0.0001
Rural	637.189	0.4572
Female	−114.357	0.5521
Age	189.816	<0.0001
Year	945.388	<0.0001
UW1	−256.603	0.3212
UW2	2,541.794	<0.0001
UW3	−591.434	0.0001
UW4	−569.099	0.2509
UW5	−279.052	0.3788
UW6	−50.805	0.8693
UW7	384.650	0.0746
UW8	269.537	0.2081
UW9	842.034	0.0003
UW10	1,628.646	0.0233

$$Insured_i = b_1 + b_2(Female_i) + b_3(Age_i) + b_4(Deductible_i)$$
$$+ b_5(Medium\ Limit_i) + b_6(High\ Limit_i)$$
$$+ b_7(Predicted\ Loss_i) + e_i,$$

where $Insured_i$ takes the value 1 if individual i had insurance coverage and 0 otherwise. The variables $Female_i$ and Age_i represent the gender and age in years of individual i. These variables are included in the model to proxy for income. They also serve to control for differences in the utility functions of the individuals in the sample.

The variables $Deductible_i$, $Medium\ Limit_i$, and $High\ Limit_i$ represent characteristics of the insurance policy held by individual i. The variable $Deductible$ takes the value 1 if the individual's insurance policy has a time deductible and 0 if it provides first-day coverage. Insureds in the pool held policies that had either a low, medium, or high policy limit. The variables $Medium\ Limit_i$ and $High\ Limit_i$ take the value 1 if individual i's policy had a medium or high limit, respectively, and takes the value of 0 otherwise. The policy-provision variables serve as proxies for the price of insurance coverage. They also are proxies for risk type. Rothschild and Stiglitz (1976) contend that in a market with incomplete information high-risk individuals may purchase policies that provide greater insurance coverage than those purchased by lower-risk individuals. A shortcoming of using policy provisions as an indicator of risk type in the model is that individuals, if they do self-sort by risk type into policies with different provisions, may sort by policy provisions that are not included in the model.

The variable *Predicted Loss$_i$* is used to test whether high risks are more likely to drop insurance coverage than low risks following a rate increase. The predicted loss for each individual is derived from the prediction equation described earlier. A positive relationship between predicted loss and insured status would suggest that lower risks are more likely to drop coverage than higher risks in response to a rate increase. This would be indicative of contracting problems in the long-term care insurance market, whether due to adverse selection or failure of the insurance contracts to achieve a lock-in of the lower risks.

Empirical Results

The test equation is estimated seven times, once for each of the years of the data period. Rate increases occurred on a yearly basis during this time period. Table 5.4 reports the estimated parameters of each of the models.

In the first two years of the analysis, years t and $t + 1$, the test variable *Predicted Loss* is insignificant. This suggests that individuals with higher predicted losses were neither more nor less likely to renew their insurance coverage following a rate increase than individuals with lower predicted losses. In the middle years of the analysis—years $t + 2$, $t + 3$, and $t + 4$—the variable is significant and is positive as hypothesized. In years $t + 2$ and $t + 4$, the variable is significant at the .05 level. In year $t + 3$, it is significant at the .10 level. The sign on the variable *Predicted Loss* is positive, and the variable is highly significant at the .01 level in the last three years of the analysis. These results provide support for the hypothesis that those with higher predicted losses are more likely to retain coverage in response to rate increases.

In the first two years of the analysis, the variables *Gender*, *Age*, and *Deductible* were all significant. Females were less likely to renew their policies than males. This may be an income effect. At advanced ages, women are more likely to be single than men. As was noted earlier, the average income of elderly single women over age sixty-five is less than half that of married couples. In each year of the analysis, the gen-

Table 5.4
Logit model, test equation estimations

Variable	Year						
	t	$t+1$	$t+2$	$t+3$	$t+4$	$t+5$	$t+6$
Intercept	−7.507***	−6.374***	−4.905***	−5.184***	−3.728***	−3.166***	−3.689***
Gender	−0.465***	−0.716***	−0.821***	−0.637***	−0.714***	−1.620***	−1.762***
Age	0.079***	0.063***	0.034**	0.033*	0.003	−0.018	−0.022
Deductible	0.624***	0.598***	0.573***	0.520***	0.449**	0.469**	0.302
Medium max	0.405	0.043	−0.180	−0.079	−0.262	−0.322	−0.129
Long max	0.544	0.105	−0.185	−0.123	−0.312	−0.261	−0.146
Predicted loss	9.4E-5	1.12E-4	1.93E-4**	1.41E-4*	2.38E-4***	3.01E-4***	3.21E-4***

Notes: *Significant at .10 level.
**Significant at .05 level.
***Significant at .01 level.

der variable is highly significant. The age variable is highly significant in the early years of the analysis but is not in the later years. The positive sign of the variable in the earlier years is suggestive of contracting problems.

In all but the last year of the analysis, individuals who had purchased policies with deductibles were more likely to continue coverage than those who purchased policies without deductibles. This is counter the expected result that those with deductibles would be more likely to relinquish coverage in response to rate increases. Prior work on adverse selection suggests that low-risk individuals are more likely than high-risk individuals to purchase policies with deductibles. The positive sign of the deductible variable may be due to a price effect. Since policies with deductibles are initially less expensive than policies without deductibles, uniform percentage-rate increases on all policies would result in greater dollar-rate increases on policies without deductibles than on policies with deductibles.

Conclusion

The potential size of the market for long-term care insurance is large and growing. Nonetheless, the portion of long-term care costs paid by insurance is small. Out-of-pocket payments and government insurance programs provide the bulk of funding for long-term care. This study tests whether the relatively minor role played by insurance in the long-term care market is due to contracting problems that limit risk transfer. The empirical analysis provides support for this explanation, although the analysis does not address whether the breakdown in risk transfer results from adverse selection or the failure of one-sided long-term contracts to achieve a lock-in of lower risks. The results must be interpreted with caution as the data are from a single insurer. In addition, age and gender variables were included in the empirical model to proxy income and risk aversion. To the degree these are inadequate proxies, the results may be biased.

This study tested whether individuals with different predicted losses differed in their likelihood of retaining coverage following rate increases of a uniform percentage. Consistent with theory, the data indicate that individuals with higher predicted losses are more likely to retain coverage than individuals with lower predicted losses. Implicit in this empirical test is the assumption that the pool of risks subjected to rate increases is not made up of homogeneous risks. The finding that coverage continuation is correlated positively with predicted losses provides support for this assumption. This result is consistent with evidence reported by Finkelstein and McGarry (2003) that purchasers of long-term care insurance are better informed about their potential need for long-term care than insurers. While Finkelstein and McGarry find that private information in favor of the insurance consumer does not result in a greater likelihood that higher risks will purchase insurance, this study finds that higher risks are more likely to retain coverage than lower risks in response to a rate increase imposed on a contract with one-sided commitment.

Many during their lifetimes will have a need for long-term care. As this need hits when an individual is in a vulnerable position, the need to preplan for this risk is important. While insurance against this risk would seem to be a prudent purchase, many in fact do not purchase long-term care insurance. The research reported here suggests that one reason for this apparent paradox is that adverse selection adversely affects the market for insurance. As a result, it is not surprising that government has played an important role in financing this risk. The most recent data from the United States show that government programs pay over 50 percent of long-term care costs. In many other countries, government also plays an important role in financing long-term care. If the contracting problem in the long-term care market that is studied here is not solved, perhaps through innovations in policy design or underwriting, the role of government in financing this risk may well increase. Recently, Japan instituted a tax of approximately $25 per month that every individual over age forty is required to pay to a government pool ("The April Almanac," 2000). The pool will subsidize nursing-home and home-care costs arising from aging-related diseases. The adoption of this program reflects the Japanese government's specific recognition of its role in financing long-term care. The government's intent to meet this increasing need through this program rather than through the promotion of private insurance may indicate the government's belief that this is a very difficult, if not at times impossible, peril to insure through a private market.

References

Adams, Stephanie, Heather Nawrocki, and Barbara Coleman. (1999). *Women and Long-Term Care*. Washington, DC: Public Policy Institute. ⟨http://research.aarp.org/health/fs77_women.html⟩.

Akerlof, George A. (1970). "The Market for 'Lemons': Quality Uncertainty and the Market Mechanism." *Quarterly Journal of Economics* 84: 488–500.

American Association of Retired Persons (AARP). (1999). *A Profile of Older Americans*. Washington, DC: AARP.

"The April Almanac." (2000). *Atlantic Monthly* (April): 24.

Browne, Mark J. (1992). "Evidence of Adverse Selection in the Individual Health Insurance Market." *Journal of Risk and Insurance* 59(1): 13–33.

Browne, Mark J., and Helen Doerpinghaus. (1993). "Information Asymmetries and Adverse Selection in the Market for Individual Medical Expense Insurance." *Journal of Risk and Insurance* 60(2): 300–312.

Browne, Mark J., and Helen Doerpinghaus. (1994). "Asymmetric Information and the Demand for Medigap Insurance." *Inquiry* 31(4): 445–450.

Davis, Karen, and Diane Rowland. (1986). *Medicare Policy: New Directions for Health and Long-Term Care*. Baltimore: Johns Hopkins University Press.

Dick, Andrew, Alan Garber, and Thomas McCurdy. (1994). "Forecasting Nursing Home Utilization of Elderly Americans." In David Wise (Ed.), *Studies in the Economics of Aging*. Chicago: University of Chicago Press.

Doerpinghaus, Helen, and Sandra Gustavson. (1999). "The Effect of Firm Traits on Long-Term Care Insurance Pricing." *Journal of Risk and Insurance* 66(3): 381–400.

Finkelstein, Amy, and Kathleen McGarry. (2003). "Private Information and Its Effect on Market Equilibrium: New Evidence from Long-Term Care Insurance." NBER Working Paper 9957, September.

Hendel, Igal, and Alessandro Lizzeri. (2003). "The Role of Commitment in Dynamic Contracts: Evidence from Life Insurance." *Quarterly Journal of Economics* 118: 229–327.

Jacoby, Mary. (2000). "Long-Term Care Plan Has a Chance This Year." *St. Petersburg Times*, March 9.

Marer, Eva. (1999). "Short-Term View on Long-Term Care: New Laws and Benefits Programs Are Being Designed to Jar a Procrastinating Public." *Financial Planning* 29, no. 9.

"National Health Expenditure, 1997." (1998). *Health Care Financing Review* 20(1): 83–126.

Pauly, Mark V. (1990). "The Rational Nonpurchase of Long-Term Care Insurance." *Journal of Political Economy* 98(1): 153–168.

Pauly, Mark V., Howard Kunreuther, and Richard Hirth. (1995). "Guaranteed Renewability in Insurance." *Journal of Risk and Uncertainty* 10: 143–156.

Rothschild, Michael, and Joseph Stiglitz. (1976). "Equilibrium in Competitive Insurance Markets: An Essay on the Economics of Imperfect Information." *Quarterly Journal of Economics* 90: 629–649.

Task Force on Long-Term Health Care Policies. (1987). *Report to the Congress and the Secretary*. Washington, DC: U.S. Government Printing Office.

Wilson, Charles. (1977). "A Model of Insurance Markets with Incomplete Information." *Journal of Economic Theory* 97: 167–207.

6

Choice of Managed Care and Cost Savings: The Role of Latent Health Status

Hansjörg Lehmann and Peter Zweifel

Introduction and Motivation

Premium regulation in social health insurance creates powerful incentives for the selection of favorable risks. Offering managed-care (MC) plans can be seen as an attempt at risk selection, by allowing favorable risks to be attracted within the cells distinguished by risk-adjustment schemes (Van de Ven and Ellis, 2000). In Switzerland, the choice of plan within the social health insurance is an entirely individual decision, with no involvement of employer or government. Premiums are regulated and are uniform for all adult enrollees of a given insurer, apart from an adjustment for regional cost differences. At the same time, the Swiss risk-adjustment scheme is based only on age and sex, leaving much scope for use of private information by insurers (Spycher, 2002). In this situation, there is a particularly strong suspicion that the considerable cost savings achieved by Swiss MC plans emanate from risk selection rather than changed contractual incentives.

For evaluating the relevance of this suspicion, the experience of a major Swiss health insurer is of particular interest. Unlike most competitors, this insurer not only writes policies with different annual deductibles but also offers a choice of managed-care plans. Among these alternatives, the health-maintenance organization (HMO) plan stands out with average treatment costs that are 62 percent lower than in the conventional fee-for-service setting. At the same time, HMO enrollees are some seven years younger than enrollees of conventional plans, pointing to risk selection. The objective of this contribution thus is twofold. First, it seeks to determine the extent to which the choice of an MC plan may be associated with risk selection. Second, it purports to estimate the importance of risk selection as a cause of the cost savings achieved by MC plans. Should risk selection dominate in both cases, then an argument can be made in favor of a uniform health insurance scheme that is not fraught with the considerable loading for acquisition costs incurred with the marketing of differentiated insurance products.

Therefore, the task at hand is to control for risk selection in a nonexperimental situation. The traditional approach has been to view choice of plan as well as spending on health-care expenditures (HCE) as being determined by the same set of unobserved variables, creating an identification problem. The most important of these variables presumably is latent health status. If a reliable indicator of latent health were available, this identification problem could be solved or at least mitigated. This possibility exists here because the database contains repeated measurements of the same individuals. Specifically, latent health status can be inferred from previous health-care expenditures, both in conventional and managed-care contracts.

After a review of the literature on risk selection associated with the choice of managed-care plans and on risk selection as the likely cause of their cost advantage, latent health is introduced as an enabling factor for risk selection and its statistical determination from previous observations of health-care expenditures described. The database and the variables used are defined, and the estimation results are presented. The main findings are that both contract choice and spending on health-care expenditures reflect risk-selection effects; however, risk selection explains only a minor part of the cost differential in favor of managed care. Thus, MC plans may well achieve true cost savings thanks to changed contractual incentives, and a discussion of the reasons for and possible criticisms of this result concludes the chapter.

Literature Review

The Role of Risk Selection in the Choice of Managed-Care Plans
Since managed care was introduced in the United Sates and the experiences of Switzerland and the first trials in Germany have not yet documented in the published literature, table 6.1 features only U.S. contributions. Here managed care is understood to be a health insurance policy that limits patients' choice of physician and gives participating physicians increased incentives or possibilities to contain the cost of treatment (a more detailed typology follows in the next section). Also, the term *risk selection* comprises both the active form, with an insurer making efforts to attract favorable and eschew unfavorable risks

Table 6.1
Evidence concerning the role of risk selection in the choice of managed-care plans

Authors	Findings	Effect of Risk Selection
A. Observable indicators of health status		
Bice (1975)	Bad health status and high expected health-care expenditures	Reverse
Scitovsky et al. (1978)	More young and married individuals, more parents	Favorable
Hudes et al. (1980)	More pregnant women	Reverse
Juba et al. (1980)	Good health status (self-declared)	Favorable
Merrill et al. (1985)	More young people, men, chronic sicks	Ambiguous
Gordon and Kaplan (1991)	Equal health status	None
Robinson (1993)	More pregnant women	Reverse
B. Utilization and HCE as indicators of health status		
Jackson-Beeck and Kleinman (1983)	53% fewer inpatient days the year before HMO enrollment	Favorable
Buchanan and Cretin (1986)	Lower prior spending	Favorable
Lairson and Herd (1987)	Equal prior spending	None
Brown (1988)	21% lower prior spending for HMO enrollees, 54% higher prior spending for HMO disenrollees	Favorable
Kasper et al. (1988)	24% to 42% lower prior spending	Favorable
Langwell and Hadley (1989)	44% lower prior spending	Favorable
Feldman et al. (1989)	Equal prior spending	None
Hill (1992)	23% lower prior spending among HMO enrollees	Favorable
Billi et al. (1993)	19% lower prior spending among PPO enrollees	Favorable
Brown (1993)	10% lower prior spending	Favorable
Cutler and Reber (1998)	20% lower prior spending among HMO enrollees	Favorable
Nicholson et al. (2003)	10% lower prior spending among HMO enrollees, 18% higher prior spending among HMO disenrollees	Favorable

(often called *cream skimming*) and the passive form, with the insureds choosing a contract also in view of their risk status. Under either form, if the insured's risk status (which can be equated to health status in the present context) helps to predict enrolment in a MC plan rather than a conventional fee-for-service alternative, then risk selection is said to be associated with this choice.

A first group of studies cited in table 6.1 relies on easily observable indicators of health status, such as age, marital status, and pregnancy, and self-declared health (panel A). In the majority of cases, the evidence suggests that those opting for a managed-care plan are more likely to be young, married individuals and the declared healthy. However, both Hudes, Young, Sohrab, et al. (1980) and Robinson (1993) find that pregnant women are overrepresented in MC compared to the conventional alternative. A second group of contributions uses utilization and health-care expenditures incurred before the change to MC as an indicator (panel B). This is an observable quantity for the insured but not necessarily for the receiving MC insurer (unless conventional and MC plans are written by the same organization, which typically does not happen in the United States). Again, movers to MC are characterized by low prior health-care expenditures, although Lairson and Herd (1987) and Feldman, Finch, and Dowd (1989) fail to find a significant difference between movers and stayers (with conventional care). This ambiguity is of particular interest because previous health-care expenditures are used later in this chapter to derive an indicator of latent health in a novel way to serve as a predictor of the choice of several MC plans.

The evidence of table 6.1 does not directly bear on the issue of whether indicators of latent health contribute to predicting the choice of a managed-care plan. Taking this choice as given, it is about postdiction rather than prediction. On balance, however, it still supports the notion that risk selection may be associated with the choice of a MC plan.

The Contribution of Risk Selection to Cost Savings by Managed-Care Plans

Once more, table 6.2 is limited to U.S. contributions. Panel A contains a selection of works analyzing preferred provider organizations (PPOs). In PPOs, employers negotiate with physician and or hospital groups for lower fees. In return, their employees must call on participating health-care providers in the event of illness. As evidenced already by

Table 6.2
Cost comparisons between managed-care and conventional health plans

Authors	Way of Controlling for Differences in Patient Characteristics	Cost Difference between Managed-Care and Conventional Plans
A. PPO		
Hosek et al. (1990)	Socioeconomic characteristics, health status	−11% to +9%
Wells et al. (1992)	Mental health status, level of prior care, age, sex, education	−3%
Smith (1997)	Socioeconomic characteristics	−12%
B. IPA		
McCombs et al. (1990)	Socioeconomic characteristics, prior care	+11%
Stapleton (1994)	Socioeconomic characteristics	−23%
Christensen (1995)	Socioeconomic characteristics	−4%
C. HMO		
Manning et al. (1984)	Randomized assignment, age, sex	−28%
McCombs et al. (1990)	Socioeconomic characteristics, prior care	−39%
Hill (1992)	Socioeconomic characteristics	−11%
Christensen (1995)	Socioeconomic characteristics	−20%
Buchanan et al. (1996)	Age, family size, education, prior care, subjective health status	−29%

the early study by Hosek, Marquis, and Wells (1990), PPOs need not result in a reduction of health-care expenditures once workers' socio-economic characteristics (among them health status) are taken into account. A possible explanation is that providers, who continue to be paid fee-for-service, simply compensate by stepping up the intensity of their treatment.

In panel B of table 6.2, the experience with independent-practice associations (IPAs) is reviewed. Participating physicians agree to act as gatekeepers and to accept peer review; however, payment can still be fee-for-service. The evidence presented suggests that as long as the mode of payment is not uniformly capitation, health-care expenditures may not be significantly reduced (Christensen, 1995). Again, the characteristics of the insureds are statistically controlled for in the majority of studies.

Panel C turns to health-maintenance organizations (HMOs of the group and staff type) as the most prominent managed-care alternative.

Here, physicians also participate in the financial proceeds of the plan, giving them a strong incentive to avoid costly referrals to specialists outside the HMO and to hospitals. After taking differences in patient characteristics into account, cost savings reach as much as 39 percent, compared to the conventional setting.

To sum up, even with risk selection effects taken into account, the HMO variant of managed care features a sizable cost reduction from conventional fee-for-service care, with IPAs and PPOs characterized by much smaller amounts.

Inferring Latent Health Status from Previous Health-Care Expenditures

The literature reviewed agrees on the hypothesis that both the choice of contract and spending on health-care expenditures may depend on unobserved health status. The novelty of the present work lies in the construction of an indicator $\hat{h}$ of latent health status. Specifically, $\hat{h}$ is to be inferred from previous $LHCE = ln(HCE + 1)$. This indicator should have two properties. First, since risk-selection effects result from insurer as well as enrollee behavior, it should be relevant to both. For the insurer, $\hat{h}$ should reflect a systematic deviation from expected health-care expenditures characterizing a population cell as defined by the risk-adjustment scheme. Therefore, a positive value of $\hat{h}$ would be reason to eschew that risk. For the insured, such a systematic deviation is expected to trigger a reassessment of his or her own risk and hence a modified choice of plan. Therefore, inferring $\hat{h}$ from previous health-care expenditures is appropriate for modeling both active selection by the insurer and passive selection by the insured.

The second desired property is that a systematic deviation from expected value of health-care expenditures should exclusively reflect $\hat{h}$; if it does reflect a second factor, this factor needs to be uncorrelated with $\hat{h}$. However, a likely second factor is the generosity of the plan, and it will be correlated with $\hat{h}$ to the extent that individuals with unfavorable latent health choose more generous plans. One way to break this correlation consists in limiting the sample to individuals who have switched between plans in the recent past. These enrollees presumably have retained their value of $\hat{h}$ when switching plans, causing their chosen generosity to be uncorrelated with $\hat{h}$.[1]

The previous health-care expenditures of enrollees who have switched between plans from 1997 to 1999 therefore may be used for deriving an unbiased indicator of latent health. More specifically, the idea is to estimate a panel model of health-care expenditures and to use the individual, time-invariant component of the residual as an indicator of health status. Now the decision to use health-care services can be split into the decision to initiate a treatment episode and a decision concerning the amount of health-care expenditures given initiation. The main alternatives here are the two-part model and the Tobit model. In the present context, the latter alternative has the advantage of generating a complete residual vector. Its covariates are identical to the ones used for the equation pertaining to health-care expenditures in the year 2000 (see table 6.7, left-hand side).

Estimating a Tobit model requires a random-effects specification rather than a fixed-effects specification (StataCorp., 2001, 4: 475). Therefore, the Tobit error term for latent health-care expenditures is given by

$$\varepsilon_{it} = \xi_{it} + u_i, \tag{6.1}$$

with u_i denoting the time-invariant individual effect that will be interpreted as latent health. Both components are assumed to be normally distributed with expectation zero and constant variances σ_ξ^2 and σ_u^2. Moreover, they are assumed independent such that

$$\mathrm{Var}[\varepsilon_{it}] = \sigma_\xi^2 + \sigma_u^2. \tag{6.2}$$

However, there is correlation between different years caused by the time-invariant individual component. The correlation coefficient ρ is given by

$$\rho := \mathrm{Corr}[\varepsilon_{it}, \varepsilon_{is}] = \sigma_u^2 / (\sigma_\xi^2 + \sigma_u^2). \tag{6.3}$$

A preliminary estimate yielded $\rho = 0.53$, which suggests that the time-invariant component may indeed have some importance (details are shown in the appendix to this chapter). Unfortunately, however, the Tobit model does not allow the individual error components to be directly calculated. In the specific case, the decision was made to use the observations from 1997 through 1999 for averaging the residuals, thus calculating

$$\hat{h}_i = \bar{\varepsilon}_i = \frac{\hat{\varepsilon}_{i99} + \hat{\varepsilon}_{i98} + \hat{\varepsilon}_{i97}}{3} = \hat{u}_i + \frac{\hat{\xi}_{i99} + \hat{\xi}_{i98} + \hat{\xi}_{i97}}{3} = \hat{u}_i + \bar{\xi}_i. \tag{6.4}$$

In this way, $\hat{h}_i$ resembles a fixed effect, albeit with a large variance because the number of repeated observations falls far short of infinity. In addition, Tobit residuals for observations with $LHCE = 0$ have the property of reflecting the distance between the horizontal axis and the extrapolated regression line, resulting in a tendency towards positive residuals. This censoring can be corrected by calculating the expected value of the residual (Chesher and Irish, 1987),

$$E[\varepsilon|LHCE = 0] = \frac{-\sigma\phi((x\beta)/\sigma)}{1 - \Phi((x\beta)/\sigma)}, \quad \text{with } \sigma := \text{var}(\varepsilon). \quad (6.5)$$

To conclude, an indicator of latent health can be constructed from a Tobit random-effects estimate of previous latent health-care expenditures, associating latent health status with the individual, time-invariant component of the residual.

Insurance Plans, Database, and Estimation Results

Description of Contracts Written
As stated above, the health insurer considered writes both conventional fee-for-service and several managed-care plans. Both sets feature a choice of annual deductibles and a uniform rate of coinsurance of 10 percent prescribed by the law. However, different deductibles aggravate the problem of censoring of the HCE distribution. In addition, the choice of the deductible would constitute another dimension for risk selection as well as the determination of health-care expenditures. For this reason, only the plans with the minimum deductible (amounting to approximately U.S. $170 at 2003 exchange rates) are retained.

Among the managed-care alternatives, there is one that comes close to a PPO, the main difference being that the insurer does not negotiate a fee reduction but seeks to form a provider group that excludes the most expensive practitioners in terms of ambulatory care cost. It is labeled *PPO* in the following. The second managed-care plan limits primary physician choice more severely to a set of gatekeepers that agree to avoid hospitalization if possible. The majority of these gatekeepers continue to be paid fee-for-service. This alternative thus resembles an independent-practice association and is called *IPA* in the following. Finally, insureds can agree to be treated at a health maintenance organization (typically a local group practice with salaried physicians); this plan is labeled *HMO*. The market shares of the four alternatives (*CONVENTIONAL* serving as the reference category) are shown in table 6.3 below. Among switchers, the managed-care alternatives dominate with a total share of 61 percent compared to the conventional contract

Table 6.3
Description of explanatory variables and of sample

Variable	Description	Minimum	Maximum	Mean	Standard Error
PREMIUM	Annual premium of health plan	1,411	3,986	1,948	366
PREMIUM_AVG	Premium of conventional and averaged premium of managed care plans	1,930	3,986	2,388	518
AGE	Age of the insured	26	98	51.5	15.9
SEX_M	1 = male 0 = female	0	1	0.44	0.50
URBAN	1 = Residence in urban area 0 = Residence in rural area	0	1	0.71	0.45
SUBSIDY	1 = Recipient of premium subsidy 0 = otherwise	0	1	0.21	0.41
HMO_RES	1 = HMO in the community of residence 0 = otherwise	0	1	0.26	0.44
HMO	1 = HMO plan 0 = otherwise	0	1	0.13	0.34
IPA	1 = IPA plan 0 = otherwise	0	1	0.39	0.48
PPO	1 = PPO plan 0 = otherwise	0	1	0.09	0.28

Number of individuals who had switched from managed care to conventional between 1997 and 99: 7,219
Number of individuals who had switched from conventional to managed care between 1997 and 99: 1,159

with 39 percent, which is on the same footing as the IPA variant of managed care.

Description of Explanatory Variables

The explanatory variables and their statistics reflecting the characteristics of some 8,500 individuals who had switched between plans during the years 1997 to 1999 are gathered in table 6.3. In principle, the price of insurance is given by the premium paid relative to the expected future value of benefits. This latter quantity has to be extrapolated from previous health-care expenditures, causing it to be highly collinear with latent health $\hat{h}$ (in a preliminary estimate, their correlation coefficient exceeded 0.91). Since $\hat{h}$ is the variable of crucial interest, actual premiums paid ($PREMIUM$) has been retained as one of two price variables. The other price variable, $PREMIUM\_AVG$, reflects the first stage of plan choice in the year 2000, between $CONVENTIONAL$ and a managed-care plan. For individuals having a conventional plan, $PREMIUM\_AVG$ is the average of the three managed-care variants. For individuals having one of the three managed-care variants, $PREMIUM\_AVG$ takes on the one value per region of the conventional plan. Apart from age and sex, the communities of residence were consolidated into an urban ($URBAN = 1$) category and a rural category according to criteria defined by the Federal Statistical Office that are similar to those used for delineating Standard Metropolitan Statistical Areas (SMSAs) in the United States. The dummy variable HMO_RES takes on the value of one if there is an HMO in the community of residence.

The dummy variable $SUBSIDY$ indicates whether the individual receives a means-tested premium subsidy. In Switzerland, inhabitants are required by law to have health insurance. In return, those whose premium exceeds 8 to 10 percent of their taxable income (depending on canton of residence) are entitled to a personal subsidy. The subsidy does not entail any restriction in the choice of insurer or plan, making $SUBSIDY$ mainly an inverse indicator of income. However, it might also reflect latent health to the extent that unfavorable health triggers the subsidy through its association with lower taxable income.

The table does not show a total of ten dummy variables, designed to take heterogeneities between eleven cantons (with Zurich serving as the benchmark) into account. Cantons differ markedly in terms of fee levels, presence of specialized physicians and hospitals, and density of medical supply in general. While the insurer does business in all twenty-six cantons, individual insurance records contain information with regard to *SUBSIDY* in only eleven of them. Finally, inferred health status $\hat{h}$, being an averaged residual, has a mean value of practically zero (not shown in table 6.3). The expected sign of the coefficients belonging to these explanatory variables appears in the tables containing the regression results.

Estimation Results

Choice of Health Plan Health insurance contracts constitute discrete multidimensional alternatives that cannot easily be ordered. The theoretical basis for modeling the choice between such alternatives is the random-utility model (McFadden, 1974). For the stochastic specification, the standard alternatives are probit and logit. For computational reasons, the logit specification is retained; however, this has the disadvantage of requiring independence of irrelevant alternatives. The specification test of Hausman and McFadden (1984) can be used to check this independence requirement. The test statistic suggests rejection of the null hypothesis of independence. A reasonable structuring of the alternatives is to pit the conventional contract against the three managed-care plans. Applying the specification test of Hausman and McFadden once more, one finds that the null hypotheses of independence of irrelevant alternatives between the three managed-care plans can be maintained. This result requires that the choice of plans be modeled in a sequential way (see figure 6.1). In a first stage, the individual chooses between conventional and managed-care plans; in a second stage, he or she selects one of the three managed-care alternatives.

The estimation results for the first stage are shown in table 6.4. The dependent variable takes on the value of one if the individual is enrolled in a managed-care rather than a conventional plan as of the

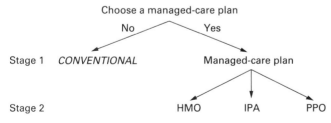

Figure 6.1
Choice of health plan in 2000

Table 6.4
Conditional logit estimation of choice of managed-care versus conventional health plans

	Coefficient	Standard Error	Odds Ratio
PREMIUM_AVG	−0.0012***	0.0002	0.891[a]
MC-SEX_M	0.3044	0.0699	1.354
MC-AGE	−0.0277	0.0158	0.970
MC-AGE^2	0.0003*	0.0001	1.001
MC-URBAN	−0.5047***	0.0938	0.600
MC-HMO_RES	0.2531***	0.1143	1.286
MC-$\hat{h}$	−0.1364***	0.0130	0.793
MC-SUBSIDY	−0.0965	0.0828	0.908

Number of observations: 25,112
$LR\ \chi^2(17) = 12{,}699$ Prob $> \chi^2 = 0.0000$
Pseudo $R^2 = 0.55$

*$p \le 0.05$.
**$p \le 0.01$.
***$p \le 0.001$.
a. Odds ratio calculated for a change of 100 CHF.

year 2000. The higher the premiums for the managed-care contracts (*PREMIUM_AVG*), the lower the odds ratio of choosing one of them. Increased age has an unclear effect since the coefficient of *AGE* is negative but insignificant while that of AGE^2 is very small. The presence of an HMO at the community of residence ($HMO\_RES = 1$) serves to boost this propensity (odds ratio = 1.286).

Since the enrollees sampled all had switched plans during the previous three years, the latent health status of a given enrollee should not depend on the plan. However, a given predetermined value of $\hat{h}$ should in its turn influence plan choice. Indeed, the odds ratio of a managed-care alternative being selected decreases with a higher value of $\hat{h}$ (worse latent health). This finding adds to that part of the literature that associates the choice of a managed-care plan with the selection of favorable risks.

In view of the strong significance of the coefficient for $\hat{h}$, latent health status presumably is controlled for. This means that the premium subsidy (*SUBSIDY* = 1) may justifiably be interpreted as an inverse income rather than a risk indicator. Its lack of statistical significance then provides preliminary evidence in favor of the view that the targeted premium subsidy preserves free choice of health insurance for low-income individuals.

Table 6.5
Conditional logit estimation of choice of HMO or PPO versus IPA

	Coefficient	Standard Error	Odds Ratio
PREMIUM	−0.0021***	0.0002	0.814[a]
HMO-SEX_M	0.2001**	0.0760	1.222
HMO-AGE	−0.0958***	0.0106	0.909
HMO-AGE^2	0.0005***	0.0001	1.001
HMO-URBAN	0.4339***	0.1039	1.543
HMO-HMO_RES	1.1382***	0.0886	3.713
HMO-SUBSIDY	−0.0181	0.0899	0.982
HMO-$\hat{h}$	−0.1059***	0.01258	0.899
PPO-SEX_M	−0.0858	0.0958	0.918
PPO-AGE	0.0531***	0.0083	1.072
PPO-AGE^2	−0.0005***	0.0001	0.999
PPO-URBAN	1.0001***	0.1429	2.718
PPO-HMO_RES	−0.8337***	0.1067	1.026
PPO-$\hat{h}$	0.0258	0.0167	1.031
PPO-SUBSIDY	−0.0474	0.1142	0.954

Number of observations = 21,768
$LR\ \chi^2(25) = 8{,}445$ Prob $> \chi^2 = 0.0000$
Pseudo $R^2 = 0.53$

*$p \leq 0.05$.
**$p \leq 0.01$.
***$p \leq 0.001$.
a. Odds ratio calculated for a change of 100 CHF.

The second stage constitutes the choice of one out of three managed-care alternatives (see table 6.5). The benchmark category is IPA, a physician network with fee-for-service payment. *PREMIUM* is statistically significant, the odds ratio indicating that all variants are less likely to be chosen if they cost more. With regard to the HMO, increased age (*AGE, AGE^2*) goes along with a decreased propensity of enrollment, up to age ninety again. As expected, the presence of an HMO in the community of residence (*HMO_RES* = 1) proves even more decisive than at the first stage of choice. The lower odds ratio associated with a higher value of $\hat{h}$ again points to risk-selection effects working in favor of the HMO. On the other hand, the premium subsidy (*SUBSIDY* = 1) does not favor HMOs, confirming the impression that low-income individuals enjoy full freedom of choice.

For the PPO, higher age makes their choice more likely over the relevant age range. This time however, there is no statistical evidence of risk-selection effects, judging from the lack of statistical significance of $\hat{h}$. Finally, once again *SUBSIDY* has no recognizable effect on plan choice.

In sum, there is evidence of risk selection at both stages of contract choice. First, favorable risks seem to prefer managed-care over conventional plans. Second, within managed-care plans, they tend to prefer the HMO over the IPA and the PPO.

Utilization and Health-Care Expenditures   The specification in this section follows the two-part model mainly for two reasons. First, Tobit estimation links the decision to initiate treatment and intensity of treatment (reflected by health-care expenditures spent during an illness episode) through a joint error distribution. However, the issue of whether the first decision is made already with regard to the second is still not settled (Leung and Yu, 1996; Manning et al., 1987). Second, comparison with existing research is facilitated on the basis of the two-part model (a Tobit estimate was also performed with roughly comparable results).

Thus, turning to the likelihood of initialization of an episode, table 6.6 shows two probit equations, one without $\hat{h}$, the other, including $\hat{h}$. Without $\hat{h}$, differences in health status are already controlled for to the extent that they correlate with known socioeconomic characteristics such as age. In the case of the HMO, this causes the observed gross likelihood differential of fifteen percentage points to even increase, to an estimated 18.2 points. The PPO and IPA variants have estimated effects roughly one-third as strong.

Inclusion of $\hat{h}$ does change the estimated effects of the managed-care alternatives. First, the HMO variant loses roughly two-thirds of its previously estimated effect, amounting to about seven percentage points. Second, the IPA variant does not differ significantly anymore from the conventional setting. Third, the PPO variant is associated with a reduction effect that now comes close to that of the HMO (almost five percentage points). By way of contrast, the estimated effects of socioeconomic characteristics remain quite stable in the main, which supports the notion that latent health $\hat{h}$ contains information that is independent of these known characteristics. This is also confirmed by the very high level of significance of $\hat{h}$ and the jump from 0.09 to 0.30 in the pseudo R^2.

Table 6.6
Probit estimation of the likelihood of initialization of an episode

	Expected Sign	Estimation without $\hat{h}$			Estimation with $\hat{h}$		
		Coefficient	Standard Error	Influence in Percentage Points	Coefficient	Standard Error	Influence in Percentage Points
HMO	−	−0.577***	0.061	−18.2	−0.278***	0.068	−6.9
IPA	−	−0.212***	0.054	−5.7	−0.078	0.062	−1.7
PPO	−	−0.260***	0.071	−7.6	−0.193*	0.079	−4.7
AGE	+	−0.013	0.008	−3.5ª	−0.002	0.009	−0.5ª
AGE²	+	0.001***	0.000	0.08ª	0.001**	0.000	0.06ª
SEX_M	−	−0.412***	0.032	−11.4	−0.491***	0.037	−11.6
URBAN	+	0.012	0.038	3.3	0.070***	0.043	−0.2
SUBSIDY		−0.069	0.039	−1.9	−0.036	0.044	−0.8
$\hat{h}$	+				0.246***	0.006	5.6
Constant		1.087***	0.220		0.672**	0.248	

Number of observations = 8,363
$LR \chi^2(16) = 727.77$; Prob $> \chi^2 = 0.0000$
Pseudo $R^2 = 0.09$

Number of observations = 8,363
$LR \chi^2(17) = 2{,}580.69$; Prob $> \chi^2 = 0.0000$
Pseudo $R^2 = 0.30$

* $p \leq 0.05$.
** $p \leq 0.01$.
*** $p \leq 0.001$.
a. Calculated for a change of 10 years.

As to health-care expenditures given initialization, the log transformation was deemed appropriate because the objective is to simply estimate percentage differences that may be caused by differing contractual incentives. In table 6.7, the left-hand side again contains regression results without $\hat{h}$. Cost reductions can be associated with all three managed-care variants, with the HMO plan amounting to 44 percent. The estimated effects of the PPO and IPA plans are clearly less marked, which does not come as a surprise in view of the fact that these plans pay fee-for-service in the main. Estimated influences of the socioeconomic variables conform to expectations; specifically, the total effect of aging is positive within the sampled domain. A detail of interest is the observation that *SUBSIDY* lacks statistical significance (as already with regard to initialization), suggesting that neither access to medical care nor intensity of treatment received correlates with income.

With $\hat{h}$ accounted for, estimated cost effects of managed-care alternatives drop throughout by fifteen (HMO) and by five (IPA, PPO) percentage points. This still leaves cost reductions between 31 percent (HMO) and 19 percent (IPA) that cannot be attributed to risk selection effects. Also, the rank ordering of cost savings (HMO > PPO > IPA) corresponds to that found in research from the United States (see table 6.2). It is not affected by the inclusion of $\hat{h}$, which nevertheless is a highly significant explanatory variable, occasioning an increase in adjusted R^2 from 0.09 to 0.24.

In conclusion, the managed-care alternatives studied in this contribution are estimated to reduce the likelihood of initializing a treatment episode (except IPA) as well as health-care expenditures given initialization. When differences in latent health are accounted for, these reductions are cut by up to two-thirds in the case of initialization but only one-third in the case of HCE given initialization. This means that while risk selection certainly plays a role (as found in the preceding section), it falls far short of explaining the observed differences in health-care expenditures. Managed-care plans therefore are found to have a true cost-saving effect.

Summary and Concluding Remarks

Ever since the inception of managed-care plans, there has been a debate about whether the cost savings they achieve are due to improved contractual incentives rather than risk selection. When differences in health-care expenditures are controlled for risk selection, a review of

Table 6.7
OLS estimation of logarithmic treatment costs (given initialization)

	Expected Sign	Estimation without $\hat{h}$			Estimation with $\hat{h}$		
		Coefficient	Standard Error	Influence in Percentage	Coefficient	Standard Error	Influence in Percentage
HMO	−	−0.586***	0.069	−44.3%	−0.367***	0.063	−30.7%
IPA	−	−0.271***	0.055	−23.7%	−0.206***	0.050	−18.6%
PPO	−	−0.350***	0.072	−29.5%	−0.276***	0.067	−24.1%
AGE	+	−0.007	0.008	−6.6%[a]	−0.011**	0.007	−10.5%[a]
AGE²	+	0.001***	0.000	0.3%[a]	0.001***	0.000	0.4%[a]
SEX_M	−	−0.173***	0.036	−15.9%	−0.364***	0.034	−30.5%
URBAN	+	0.077	0.041	8.0%	0.084***	0.038	8.8%
SUBSIDY		0.044	0.045	4.5%	−0.030	0.041	−3.0%
$\hat{h}$	+				0.235***	0.007	0.24%[b]
Constant		6.747***	0.229		6.456***	0.211	

Number of observations = 6,593

$F(17; 6,593) = 40$; Prob $> F = 0.0000$

Adj. $R^2 = 0.09$

Number of observations = 6,593

$F(18; 6,593) = 112$; Prob $> F = 0.0000$

Adj. $R^2 = 0.24$

$* p \leq 0.05.$
$** p \leq 0.01.$
$*** p \leq 0.001.$
a. Calculated for a change of 10 years.
b. The coefficient of latent health is an elasticity, since the values of $\hat{h}$ are in logarithms.

the U.S.-based literature suggests that the health maintenance organization (HMO) variant of managed care features the maximum
cost reductions from conventional fee-for-service practice, with the
independent-practice association (IPA) and the preferred-provider organization (PPO) achieving much smaller reductions.

Evidence from Switzerland on this issue should be of interest because social health insurance, while mandatory, is individually contracted without any involvement of employers or the government.
Therefore, there is much scope for passive risk selection by the individual insured. This contribution introduces a novel approach to the
problem that both the choice of plan and health-care expenditure are
influenced by the same unobserved characteristics, including latent
health status. This variable is defined in a way as to make it useful for
modeling risk selection effects both in the choice of managed-care
plans and the determination of health-care expenditures. A major
Swiss health insurer provided access to repeated observations covering
the years 1997 to 2000, permitting an estimation of a Tobit random-
effects model for health-care expenditures, yielding residuals whose
time-invariant components reflect latent health status.

When analyzing contract choice in the year 2000, the evidence
pointed to two stages in the decision making. First, individuals seem
to decide between conventional and managed-care in general. Lower
latent health status is associated with a preference for managed-
care, as predicted by the risk-selection hypothesis. Within the three
managed-care alternatives written by the insurer, risk-selection effects
tend to favor the HMO more than either the IPA or the PPO. Since the
HMO imposes the most stringent restrictions on physician choice and
referrals to specialists, followed by the IPA and by the PPO, this finding again supports the risk-selection hypothesis.

With regard to utilization in the year 2000, the HMO plan and
more weakly the PPO plan are found to lower the likelihood of
initialization of a treatment episode when risk-selection effects are
accounted for. For health-care expenditures given initialization, all
three managed-care variants compare favorably with the conventional
alternative. They therefore generate true cost savings, with an ordering
HMO > PPO > IPA that is compatible with the existing evidence (see
table 6.2).

In all, there is considerable evidence of risk selection in the Swiss
market for health insurance. Expected future health-care expenditures

(which include latent health in this estimation) clearly is associated with plan choice. Differences in latent health do explain part of the cost advantage of the managed-care plan over conventional plans. However, they fall far short of explaining this advantage.

These results need to be qualified in several ways. First, only risk-selection effects within the population of one particular insurer are controlled for. Risk-selection processes may well occur between insurers, although the annual rate of migration is only 2 to 3 percent in Switzerland. Next, the high gross cost reductions observed may be due to the fact that the market share of managed care has been too small (7 percent) to force adjustments in conventional medical care. It is an open question for future research whether the amount of true savings achieved by manage-care plans will change in the event that conventional care and managed care should converge in the future. Moreover, since the analysis is limited to individuals switching between health plans, generalizing the results to the whole population of insurance purchasers may appear problematic. However, estimation results based on both switchers and nonswitchers (not presented here) are very similar. A related issue is that individuals typically moved from more conventional to more restrictive plans, which again may detract from generalizability. However, additional analysis (again not presented here) suggests that there is no systematic difference between those switching to more and those switching to less generous alternatives.[2] On both counts, it therefore appears that the results of this study have a reasonable degree of generality.

Finally, a more comprehensive set of observable socioeconomic characteristics of the insured might have resulted in different estimates of latent health status. To the extent that the present estimates of these regressors contain measurement error, the importance of risk-selection effects in the determination of health-care expenditures may still be underestimated. However, the counter hypothesis that the true cost savings are all zero has little credibility because the ranking of the HMO, PPO, and IPA variants corresponds to theoretical expectations and existing empirical evidence.

Acknowledgments

The authors wish to acknowledge helpful suggestions from H. E. Frech (UCSB), M. König, and H. Telser (University of Zurich).

Appendix

Table 6A
Tobit random effect estimation of logarithmic treatment costs

	Expected Sign	Coefficient	Standard Error
HMO	−	−0.4748***	0.0682
IPA	−	−0.0256	0.0436
PPO	−	−0.0939	0.0843
AGE	+	−0.0055	0.0136
AGE^2	+	+0.0006***	0.0001
SEX_M	−	−1.6204***	0.0642
URBAN	+	0.1601*	0.0725
SUBSIDY		0.1513*	0.0597
Constant		3.9441***	0.3551

Number of observations = 25,089
Wald $chi^2(17) = 1,669$; Prob > $chi^2 = 0.0000$
$\rho = 0.53$

*$p \leq 0.05$.
**$p \leq 0.01$.
***$p \leq 0.001$.
a. Calculated for a change of 10 years.

Notes

1. We are grateful to an anonymous referee for pointing out the problem and suggesting this solution.

2. As agents switching to the least (most) generous plan, HMO (*CONVENTIONAL*) can switch only from more (less) generous plans, any asymmetry could be tested only for individuals originally enrolled in the two plans of medium generosity, IPA and PPO.

References

Bice, T. W. (1975). "Risk Vulnerability and Enrollment in a Prepaid Group Practice." *Medical Care* 13: 698–703.

Billi, J. E., C. G. Wise, S. I. Sher, et al. (1993). "Selection in a Preferred Provider Organization Enrollment." *Health Services Research* 28: 563–575.

Brown, R. S. (1988). *Biased Selection in the Medicare Competition Demonstrations*. Princeton, NJ: Mathematica Policy Research.

Brown, R. S. (1993). *The Medicare Risk Program for HMOs: Final Summary Report on Findings from the Evaluation*. Princeton, NJ: Mathematica Policy Research.

Buchanan, J. L., and S. Cretin. (1986). "Risk Selection of Families Electing HMO Membership." *Medical Care* 24: 39–51.

Buchanan, J. L., A. Leibowitz, and J. Keesey. (1996). "Medicaid Health Maintenance Organizations: Can They Reduce Program Spending?" *Medical Care* 34: 249–263.

Chesher, Andrew, and Margaret Irish. (1987). "Residual Analysis in the Grouped and Censored Normal Linear Model." *Journal of Econometrics* 36: 33–61.

Christensen, S. (1995). *The Effects of Managed Care and Managed Competition.* Washington, DC: Congressional Budget Office.

Cutler, D.-M., and S.-J. Reber. (1998). "Paying for Health Insurance: The Trade-Off between Competition and Adverse Selection." *Quarterly Journal of Economics* 113: 433–466.

Feldman, R., M. Finch, and B. Dowd. (1989). "The Role of Health Practices in HMO Selection Bias: A Confirmatory Study." *Inquiry* 26: 381–387.

Gordon, N.-P., and G.-A. Kaplan. (1991). "Some Evidence Refuting the HMO 'Favorable Selection' Hypothesis: The Case of Kaiser Permanente." *Advances in Health Economics and Health Services Research* 12: 19–39.

Hausman, J., and D. McFadden. (1984). "Specification Tests for the Multinomial Logit Model." *Econometrica* 52: 1219–1240.

Hill, J. (1992). *The Impact of the Medicare Risk Program on Use of Services and Cost to Medicare.* Princeton, NJ: Mathematica Policy Research.

Hosek, S. D., M. S. Marquis, and K. B. Wells. (1990). *Health Care Utilization in Employer Plans with Preferred Provider Organization Options.* Santa Monica, CA: Rand Corporation, RAND R-3800-HHS/NIMH.

Hudes, J., C. A. Young, L. Sohrab, et al. (1980). "Are HMO Enrollees Being Attracted by a Liberal Maternity Benefit?" *Medical Care* 18: 635–648.

Jackson-Beeck, M., and J. H. Kleinmann. (1983). "Evidence for Self-Selection among Health Maintenance Organization Enrollees." *Journal of the American Medical Association* 250: 2826–2829.

Juba, D. A., J. R. Lave, and J. Shaddy. (1980). "An Analysis of the Choice of Health Benefits Plans." *Inquiry* 17: 62–71.

Kasper, J. D., G. F. Riley, J. S. McCombs, et al. (1988). "Beneficiary Selection, Use, and Charges in Two Medicare Capitation Demonstrations." *Health Care Financing Review* 10: 7–49.

Lairson, D.-R., and J. A. Herd. (1987). "The Role of Health Practices, Health Status, and Prior Health Care Claims in HMO Selection Bias." *Inquiry* 24: 276–284.

Langwell, K. M., and J. P. Hadley. (1989). "Evaluation of the Medicare Competition Demonstrations." *Health Care Financing Review* 11: 65–80.

Leung, S. F., and S. Yu. (1996). "On the Choice between Selection and Two-Part Models." *Journal of Econometrics* 72: 197–229.

Manning, W. G., et al. (1987). "Health Insurance and the Demand for Medical Care: Evidence from a Randomized Experiment." *American Economic Review* 77: 251–277.

Manning, W. G., A. Leibowitz, G. A. Goldberg, et al. (1984). "A Controlled Trial of the Effects of a Prepaid Group Practice on the Use of Services." *New England Journal of Medicine* 310: 1505–1510.

McCombs, J. S., J. D. Kasper, and G. F. Riley. (1990). "Do HMOs Reduce Health Care Costs? A Multivariate Analysis of Two Medicare HMO Demonstration Projects." *Health Services Research* 25: 593–613.

McFadden, D. (1974). "Conditional Logit Analysis of Qualitative Choice Behavior." In P. Zarembka (Ed.), *Frontiers in Econometrics* (pp. 105–142). New York: Academic Press.

Nicholson, S., et al. (2003). "The Magnitude and Nature of Risk Selection in Employer-Sponsored Health Plans." NBER Working Paper w9937.

Robinson, J. C. (1993). "Payment Mechanisms, Nonprice Incentives, and Organizational Innovation in Health Care." *Inquiry* 30: 328–333.

Smith, D. G. (1997). "The Effects of Preferred Provider Organizations on Health Care Use and Costs." *Inquiry* 34: 278–287.

Spycher, S. (2002). *Risikoausgleich in der Krankenversicherung* (Risk Adjustment in Health Insurance). Bern: Haupt.

Stapleton, D. (1994). *New Evidence on Savings from Network Models of Managed Care.* Washington, DC: Lewin-VHI.

StataCorp. (2001). *Stata Statistical Software: Release 7.0.* College Station, TX: Stata Corporation.

van de Ven, W. P. M. M., and R. P. Ellis. (2000). "Risk Adjustment in Competitive Health Plan Markets." In J. P. Newhouse and A. J. Culyer (Eds.), *Handbook of Health Economics* (pp. 757–845). Amsterdam: Elsevier.

Wells, K. B., S. D. Hosek, and M. S. Marquis. (1992). "The Effects of Preferred Provider Options in Fee-for-Service Plans on Use of Outpatient Mental Health Services by Three Employee Groups." *Medical Care* 30: 412–427.

7   Information Updating and Insurance Dropout: Evidence from Dental Insurance

Erik Grönqvist

Introduction

Asymmetric information in insurance markets may reduce the extent of insurance coverage and thereby induce welfare costs. In a survey of the empirical literature, Chiappori and Salanié (2003) find the extent of asymmetric information to vary across different types of insurance markets. Testing the extent of asymmetric information in health insurances and whether agents act on informational advantages is therefore important to determine the viability of health insurance markets. Already Akerlof (1970) noted that adverse selection can motivate public intervention in health insurance markets.

The evidence of adverse selection in health insurance is mixed. Most empirical studies on health insurance markets use cross-sectional data to observe whether the market equilibrium has properties consistent with adverse selection (see, for example, Savage and Wright, 2003; Sapelli and Vial, 2003; Thomasson, 2002; and Cardon and Hendel, 2001). Little is however learned about the dynamics of adverse selection.

Testing how agents react to exogenous shocks can be one strategy for capturing the evolution of an adverse-selection externality. Changes in the incentive structure can be one such shock. Buchmueller and DiNardo (2002) study the dynamics of the health insurance market in New York (state) when mandatory community rating was implemented in some segments of the market. They find that healthier agents are more prone to switch into less generous policies (such as HMO plans). In a similar way, Cutler and Reber (1998) study the evolution of selection in health plans offered to Harvard University employees following a price reform, where the marginal price of coverage was increased. They observe that younger and healthier agents tend to switch from more generous to less generous insurance policies, rather than older

and less healthy agents switching in the opposite direction. One remarkable result is the potential speed of an adverse-selection death
spiral as the most generous health plan collapsed only three years after
the price reform. In a similar vein, Nicholson, Bundorf, Stein, and
Polsky (2003) study health-care spending among individuals switching between HMO and non-HMO plans. They find that individuals
switching from a non-HMO to a HMO plan used 11 percent fewer
resources prior to switching than those remaining in the non-HMO
plan. Individuals switching from an HMO to a non-HMO plan, on the
other hand, used 18 percent more resources prior to switching than
those staying within the HMO.

The way that the contracting parties are updating their information
on risk has consequences for the persistence of information asymmetries. If updating is asymmetric, either one party may gain an informational advantage over time, or the existing asymmetries will be
reduced. There is some indirect evidence about the learning process on
health risks. Hendel and Lizzeri (2003) find the premium profiles on the
U.S. life insurance market to be consistent with a model of symmetric
learning and commitment from the insurer on reclassification risk.
Crocker and Moran (2003), in turn, find evidence that the coverage in
employer-based health plans is consistent with a model of symmetric
learning and friction in the mobility between jobs. The empirical research on how insurers and policy holders update their information on
health risks is limited, however.

In this study, micro data is used to analyze why agents opt out of insurance in a setting where the premium can be changed due to risk
reclassification. The purpose is to analyze how the decision to leave insurance coverage is related to new information on risk acquired by the
policy holder and the insurer.

The data comes from a dental insurance natural experiment provided by the National Dental Service[1] in the county of Värmland, Sweden. The insurance was introduced in 1999 and offers full coverage
during a two-year contract period. After the initial contract period, 9.6
percent of the policyholders decided not to renew their insurance. This
decision is here related to new information on dental health. The
results indicate that the updating of information is asymmetric. Policyholders tend to view a higher premium, due to reclassification of risk,
as a price increase rather than a signal of worse dental health. They
also tend to be more responsive to higher premiums than to private
signals of changed dental risk.

The next section gives a description of the institutional setting and the data and is followed by first a simple theoretical framework for insurance lapsation when information is asymmetrically updated and then the empirical results.

Empirical Setting

Dental care in Sweden is provided by both private, mainly self-employed dentists and the National Dental Service. From the year an individual turns age twenty, he is covered by a public dental insurance scheme to which both private and public dentists are affiliated.[2] The public dental insurance was initially designed as a progressive subsidy, with a coverage up to 80 percent of dental costs. Over time, the generosity of the scheme has gradually been reduced in an effort to cut public spending on dental care, making individuals more exposed to the risk of high dental costs. Since 1999, the subsidy is linear, covering around 30 percent of all dental costs (Olsson, 1999).

Dental Insurance with Risk Reassessment

To counteract the increased risk exposure, the National Dental Service in Värmland, Sweden, introduced a voluntary insurance in January 1999 that offered dental patients an opportunity to subscribe to dental care.[3] The term *insurance* is not explicitly used by the National Dental Service, but the subscription is in effect a full-coverage voluntary dental insurance provided by a public monopolist. At a fixed annual fee, the subscription provides free dental services during a two-year contract period. Dentists within the National Dental Service are employed with a fixed salary and have no direct private interest in the insurance.

The subscription fee is set after an oral examination of the patient. The oral examination evaluates dental risk in four dimensions (general risk, technical risk, caries risk, and parodental risk), and for each dimension there are six to eight risk indicators, where each indicator is rated on a four-graded scale. The risk indicators for each dimension are summed up, and patients are clustered into one of sixteen risk classes based on this sum. Contracts are then priced according to risk class. The risk classification is assessing patients' dental health. Dental health never improves, so a patient being upgraded to a higher risk class has experienced a deterioration in his dental health and is viewed as a higher risk. Any downgrading of a patient to a lower risk class follows from new information indicating that the initial classification was erroneous. The National Dental Service only uses these risk indicators when assessing risk and does not take realized dental costs explicitly into account.

In 1999, around 60 percent of all patients registered with the National Dental Service in Värmland had a valid risk classification and were thus given the opportunity to purchase insurance. About 23 percent of these patients—roughly seven thousand individuals— purchased a dental subscription in 1999. The introduction of the dental insurance in 1999 constitutes an ideal situation for studying adverse selection, as no voluntary insurance was available to these individuals before 1999. It was also unanticipated from the patients' perspective, making dental-care utilization exogenous to the insurance decision. The launch of the dental plan thus constitutes a natural experiment. The initial decision of whether to purchase insurance is analyzed by Grönqvist (2004) and results differ across risk classes. The estimated evidence of adverse selection is concentrated to high-risk classes. Within low-risk classes, however, there is evidence consistent with advantageous selection; here, the probability of purchasing dental insurance is increasing with lower expected dental consumption. This latter finding is consistent with findings of Cawley and Philipson (1999) and Finkelstein and McGarry (2003). The results can be explained by heterogeneity in both risk aversion and the effectiveness of prevention in a model similar to that of de Meza and Webb (2001), where the level of self-protection increases with risk aversion. The overall evidence from the initial decision to purchase insurance suggests that adverse selection may not be a problem at the aggregate level.

The introduction of the dental insurance in 1999 also creates a setting for studying selection in terms of insurance lapsation. After the two-year contract period, agents must decide whether to continue their subscription for another contract period. Before the insurance can be renewed, patients have their dental risk and thus their premium reassessed by the dental service. It turns out that about 10 percent of those agents who found the insurance worth purchasing in 1999 choose not to renew it in 2001.[4] Thus, there must be some new circumstance that makes these agents reconsider their initial decision. Within this dental insurance setting, it is possible to link the decision to lapse from the insurance to proxies of new information. The new information on risk, received by the insurer, cannot be directly observed but can be inferred through the upgrading or downgrading of agents into new risk classes.

For agents, dental care consumed within the insurance is used as a proxy for new private information. Consumption of dental care and dental cost has a high correlation over time (see, for example, Powell 1998). A person with a history of prior caries has a higher probability of getting new problems. Bacteria will easily grow if the enamel has been coarsened by prior caries or will grow in the seam between a prior filling and the tooth. A filled tooth will also need future maintenance or replacement and will be more fragile. Past dental consumption is thus a good predictor of dental risk and future dental consumption. Consequently, if agents have private information, this could be proxied with past costs, since the National Dental Service in Värmland does not explicitly use realized dental costs in their risk assessment. So if an agent has an unexpectedly high (low) dental consumption within the insurance, he can be viewed as receiving a signal of the dental risk being higher (lower) than his prior expectations.

The risk classification is assessing the long-run risk level, not explicitly the expected expenditures during the upcoming two-year contract period. Asymmetric information in this setting may also result from dental consumption potentially following cyclical patterns longer than the two-year contract period. The idea being that high dental consumption (such as from investing in a denture) would be followed by a period of low expenditures before the denture needs to be repaired or replaced.

An important question at this stage is whether past dental consumption contains any private information on dental risk, as oral examinations are used by the National Dental Service in Värmland to assess dental risk. To this end, a validity test of the proxy for private information and whether it is due to a cyclical pattern in dental consumption is performed. Dental cost for the two years 2000 to 2001 is regressed on dental costs during the two preceding years (1998 and 1999) and on dummy variables for each of the sixteen risk classes. Dental costs for the additional preceding two-year period (1996 and 1997) are also added to the analysis to capture the long-run patterns of dental consumption. If the proxy contains private information, dental consumption during the preceding two years should explain costs in the upcoming two-year period, in excess of the risk-classification system. The test is performed on the agents not buying the insurance within the period 1999 to 2001 ($n = 36,241$). The reason for using this group is that dental care within the insurance may be guided by clinical guidelines related to risk classes, thus generating a spurious relation.

Table 7.1 reports that past dental costs (1998 and 1999) alone explain 9 percent of future costs, whereas the risk-classification system alone explains 11 percent of the variation.[5] The risk classes are better predictors of future dental costs and contain more information on dental risk than do past costs. When both past dental costs (1998 to 1999) and the risk classes are used as regressors, 14 percent of the variation in costs in 2000 and 2001 is explained. Hence, a large part, but not all, of the information contained in past dental consumption is also captured by the risk-classification system. There is still scope for private information to act on. Past dental consumption captures an additional 27 percent (three percentage points) of the variation in future dental costs not captured by the risk-classification system. The coefficient on *Cost 98–99* is positive, demonstrating that high dental consumption during the previous two-year period indicates higher dental-care expenditures in the next two years. This rejects the notion that any private information would be due to cyclical patterns in dental consumption not captured by the risk-classification system. Instead, the predictive power would be due to the anatomy of dental problems giving a positive correlation over time. Next, when dental consumption for the period 1996 to 1997 is added to the analysis the explanatory power increases; 16 percent of the variation in dental costs in 2000 and 2001 is explained. The predictive power of *Cost 96–97*, in excess of *Cost 98–99* and the risk classification, indicates that there is a cyclical component in dental care, even if this component does not explain predictive power of the chosen proxy for private information.

Data
Data come from an administrative database on dental care. The sample consists of those patients who started to subscribe to dental care in 1999 and who were registered with the dental service in Värmland during the period 1997 to 2001.[6] Patients needed to be registered until 2001 so that they could be observed throughout the contract period. They also needed to be registered from 1997 so that their dental consumption could be tracked during the two-year period before the insurance purchase.

The sample consists of 5,998 patients, of whom 9.6 percent, or 575 individuals, choose to drop out after the initial two-year contract period. Policy holders are mainly clustered in the low- and middle-risk classes, with over 90 percent of the individuals in the sample belonging

Table 7.1
Regression of dental costs, 2000 to 2001

	Model 1		Model 2		Model 3		Model 4	
	Coefficient	t-value	Coefficient	t-value	Coefficient	t-value	Coefficient	t-value
Cost 00–01								
Const.	1,478	93.2	740	8.11	615	6.86	521	5.87
Cost 98–99	0.308	58.3			0.200	36.1	0.175	31.4
Cost 96–97							0.163	27.1
D gr2			97.5	0.87	78.6	0.71	75.4	0.69
D gr3			208	1.92	170	1.59	162	1.53
D gr4			394	3.98	325	3.34	290	3.01
D gr5			636	6.48	515	5.34	453	4.74
D gr6			907	9.32	737	7.7	648	6.84
D gr7			1,247	12.9	995	10.5	850	9.0
D gr8			1,626	17.0	1,306	13.9	1,124	12.0
D gr9			2,040	20.9	1,626	16.9	1,391	14.5
D gr10			2,262	22.6	1,787	18.0	1,505	15.2
D gr11			2,495	24.1	1,935	18.8	1,648	16.1
D gr12			2,920	25.2	2,272	19.7	1,933	16.8
D gr13			3,421	24.6	2,705	19.6	2,291	16.7
D gr14			2,869	14.8	2,093	10.9	1,669	8.8
D gr15			2,900	8.8	2,318	7.2	1,893	5.9
D gr16			−306	−0.5	−886	−1.3	−1,247	−1.9
n	36,241		36,241		36,241		36,241	
Adj. R^2	0.086		0.114		0.144		0.161	

to the eight lowest-risk classes. None of the policy holders in the sample belong to any of the three top risk classes (14 to 16). The decision to opt out is slightly increasing with higher-risk classes.

Private information on risk is proxied with past dental costs. The variable *Pre-cost* contains the cost of dental care during the two-year period prior to the insurance purchase[7] and gives a measure of agents' private information at the time when the initial decision to sign up was made. *Diff-cost*, in turn, captures the signal received by the agent during the insurance period, and it is defined as the cost of dental care within the insurance minus *Pre-cost*.[8] A high value of *Diff-cost* indicates an unexpectedly high dental consumption, as compared to the prior period. *Pre-cost* and *Diff-cost* are measured in SEK (1 SEK = U.S. $0.128 in January 1999).

The signal received by the dental service can be inferred from the risk reclassification and is measured as premium changes in SEK, so *Diff-prem* is measured in the same units as *Diff-cost* and is directly comparable in numbers. The variable *Diff-prem* includes only premium changes due to patients being reclassified into higher- or lower-risk classes and does not capture the general price increase over all risk classes. Between January 1999 and May 2001, all premiums increased by 11 percent. Consumer prices increased by 5 percent during the same period, while the general price level for medical and dental services increased by 16 percent (Statistics Sweden, n.d.).

The data also include information on patient age and gender. The decision to opt out may be influenced by the attitudes of the treating dentist. To capture this influence, a dummy variable for each of the forty-three clinics is used. Descriptive statistics of the variables are displayed in table 7.2.

Table 7.2
Descriptive statistics

Variable	n	Mean	Standard Deviation	Minimum	Maximum
Opt-out	5,998	0.096	0.294	0	1
Pre-cost	5,998	652	920	0	22,999
Gender	5,998	0.506	0.500	0	1
Age	5,998	37.6	13.4	20	85
Diff-prem	5,998	77.1	382	−3,801	3,570
Diff-cost	5,998	454	1031	−22,419	10,642

Dropout under Asymmetric Updating

If agents lapse in their insurance coverage, there must be some new circumstance that makes the insurance no longer worth buying. There are a number of reasons for opting out, such as premiums that increased due to higher loading or dental consumption that increased due to moral hazard. Also, policyholders' wealth circumstances or their degree of risk aversion may have changed. The focus here, however, is how the decision to opt out is related to new information on risk and whether updating of information is asymmetric. The decision to opt out is viewed as a response to new information on risk obtained by the insurer and the policyholder in a setting that captures the dental insurance in Värmland.

Dropout Decision

Agents are assumed to live in a world where they face the risk of a financial loss and where an insurer offers a full-coverage insurance. Neither the agent nor the insurer has perfect knowledge of the risk level, but each makes an assessment of the risk. The policy is priced based on the insurer's inference of the agent's risk level.

For an agent to find a full-coverage insurance worth buying, it must give him an assured wealth level Z_i at least as high as the certainty equivalence CE_i. Hence, if the agent initially bought the insurance in the beginning of period 0, then $CE_{i0} < Z_{i0}$.

During period 0, both the agent and the insurer receive new information, making them reassess the agent's risk level. If the agent decides to opt out at the beginning of period 1, at least one part—the agent or the insurer—must have obtained new information on the agent's risk level. If the learning process is symmetric, the agent adjusts his willingness to pay for the insurance by the same amount as the insurer changes the premium, and there is no lapsation due to updating. If signals are asymmetric, on the other hand, agents may in fact discontinue their insurances either (1) when the agent lowers the assessed risk level more than the insurer does or (2) when the insurer receives a signal to raise the assessed risk level and it is not matched by the signal received by the agent. In both cases, the insurance becomes relatively more expensive from the agent's perspective.

In the first situation, the agent gets a signal indicating that his risk is lower than expected, reducing his assessed risk level at the beginning of period 1. With a lower perceived risk, his cost of being uninsured is reduced, implying that $CE_{i1} > CE_{i0}$. If the insurer also gets a signal indicating that the agent has a lower risk, the updated risk assessment will make him reduce the insurance premium, thereby increasing the wealth level assured by the insurance $Z_{i1} > Z_{i0}$. Whether the agent will continue to purchase insurance in period 1 depends on the size of these signals. If the signal received by the agent is sufficiently large relative to that of the insurer, the certainty equivalent will become larger than the wealth assured by insurance, $CE_{i1} > Z_{i1}$. Thus, even if the premium has been reduced, the agent will no longer find the insurance worth its price and will opt out.

In the second situation, the insurer receives a signal to raise the assessed risk level not matched by the agent. The updated risk assessment will make the insurer raise the insurance premium for period 1, which implies that the wealth assured by having insurance is reduced, $Z_{i1} < Z_{i0}$. If the agent also gets a signal during period 0 indicating that the risk level is higher than anticipated, he will be willing to purchase a more expensive insurance in period 1, $CE_{i1} < CE_{i0}$. When the signal received by the insurer is sufficiently large relative to that received by the agent, the income with insurance will become lower than the certainty equivalent, $CE_{i1} > Z_{i1}$. The price of the insurance has increased more than what the agent is willing to accept, so he drops out.

If the responsiveness to signals is not sufficiently large, however, or if asymmetric updating makes the policy relatively cheaper from the agent's perspective, he will not opt out.

Dropout Consequences

Insurance lapsation due to updating follows from signals of new information being asymmetric in a certain way. The consequences of insurance dropout depend on the quality of new information.

At signals indicating better than expected health, agents lapse their contract only if they reduce the assessed risk level more than the insurer. The agents opting out are those believing that they have lower risk than previously expected. If this belief is correct, lapsation will lead to problems of adverse selection, since the risks opting out are the good ones. If the signal is false and the insurer's assessment is more correct, there will be no problems of adverse selection.

When new information indicates higher risk, on the other hand, there is lapsation only if the insurer increases the assessed risk level more than the agent does. If the insurer's reassessment is correct, the self-selection out of insurance occurs because the insurer has improved on its risk classification, which can be viewed as reducing the problems of adverse selection. If, however, the insurer's signal is erroneous— and the agent's assessment is more correct—the risks of opting out are the good ones, thereby aggravating the problem of adverse selection.

Hence, lapsation will lead to adverse selection if agents' risk reassessment is more accurate than that of the insurer, irrespective of whether lapsation follows from good or bad news. Adverse selection has negative welfare consequences as the scope of coverage provided by the market is reduced, potentially eliminating the insurance in a death spiral.

Even if the insurer's reassessment is more correct, agents lapsing their contract imply an inefficiency as risk-averse agents always take a fair insurance. Agents here opt out even though the policy becomes more fair and also fairer than their preferred policy.

Empirical Strategy

If a patient gains from not renewing the contract, $U^I < U^{NI}$, there is some new information that makes him reconsider his initial decision. The decision to opt out is related to signals on risk and analyzed with a binary-choice model.

With symmetric learning, the decision to opt out of insurance is not related to signals of new information; that is, if the insurer gets a signal indicating the risk level of an agent to be higher than expected, he will raise the agent's premium accordingly. The agent, in turn, will regard the increase in the premium as fair and will not opt out as he receives an equivalent signal. Likewise, if the agent receives a signal indicating lower risk, his willingness to pay for insurance is reduced. The agent will still not opt out as the insurance premium is accordingly reduced while the insurer receives an equivalent signal. The hypothesis of symmetric updating can be tested by estimating the following model—

$$Prob(y_{i1} = 1) = Prob(U_{i1}^{NI} > U_{i1}^I) = g(S_{i0}^j, P_{i0}^A, P_{i0}^I, X_i, \varepsilon_{i1}) \tag{7.1}$$

—and by testing for $g_1 = 0$, where S_{i0}^j for $j = I, A$ is the signal of new information received during period 0 by the insurer and the agent, respectively. Positive (negative) values on the signal implies that new information indicate the risk to be larger (smaller) than expected. P_{i0}^j for $j = I, A$ is the prior on risk in the beginning of period 0 for the insurer and the agent, respectively, and ε_{i1} is the error term in the econometric model. Individual specific reasons for opting out—other than asymmetric updating—are captured by the error term, assuming them to be independent of the signals of new information. The general tendency to opt out is captured by the constant term in the regression model. The covariate vector X_i contains age and gender to capture socioeconomic and behavioral differences and a dummy variable for each clinic to capture potential differences in praxis style. If $g_1 = 0$ cannot be rejected, agents lapse their coverage for reasons other than asymmetric updating.

If the hypothesis of symmetric learning is rejected, asymmetric updating is studied by estimating the following model:

$$Prob(y_{i1} = 1) = Prob(U_{i1}^{NI} > U_{i1}^{I}) = f(S_{i0}^{A}, S_{i0}^{I}, P_{i0}^{A}, P_{i0}^{I}, X_i, \varepsilon_{i1}). \qquad (7.2)$$

In the dental-insurance setting, the signal received by the insurer is not really private. It can be inferred by observing the premium changes due to risk reclassification. These signals are thus public and available to the agents. If an agent believes the insurer to be guided by new and valid information, he should incorporate this information and act only on his private information. That is, the decision on whether to opt out should not be influenced by premium change as this change reflects new information on risk obtained by the insurer. If agents incorporate the insurer's signal in addition to their private signals, the marginal effects will be $f_1 < 0$ and $f_2 = 0$.

If the agent does not incorporate (or only partially incorporates) information obtained by the insurer, the contracting parts will have disjoint information sets if updating is asymmetric, and the marginal effects will be $f_1 < 0$ and $f_2 > 0$. The two situations where asymmetric updating lead to lapsation generate the same reduced-form predictions. In both cases, the insurance policy becomes relatively more expensive from the agent's perspective: (1) when new information indicates that the agent has a higher risk than expected, he will opt out if the premium increase is higher than the increase in his willingness to pay (that is, the higher the insurer's signal, conditional on the agent's signal, the greater is the likelihood of the agent opting out); (2) when new information reveals that the agent has lower risk than expected, the agent opts out if his willingness to pay is reduced more than the premium (that is, the lower the agent's signal, conditional on the insurers signal, the greater the likelihood that the agent will opt out).

To analyze whether the response to asymmetric updating is the same when premiums are not reduced sufficiently as when premiums are raised too much, dropout behavior is analyzed separately for premium decreases and increases.

From the reduced-form model, it is not possible to determine who has the informational advantage, only whether updating is asymmetric or not.

Results

A first conclusion from the empirical results is that the hypothesis of symmetric updating is not supported by the data. In model 1, table 7.3, the decision to opt out of insurance is regressed only on the proxy for the insurer's signal (*Diff-prem*) and not on the signal received by agents (*Diff-cost*). Dummy variables for each risk group and previous dental costs are included to control for the information available at the

Table 7.3
Probit estimates of failure to renew insurance, I

	Model 1		Model 2		Model 3	
	Coefficient	t-value	Coefficient	t-value	Coefficient	t-value
D gr2	0.237	1.38	0.244	1.43	0.254	1.48
D gr3	0.508	3.04	0.506	3.05	0.543	3.24
D gr4	0.549	3.37	0.573	3.54	0.598	3.66
D gr5	0.578	3.52	0.612	3.74	0.656	3.96
D gr6	0.598	3.57	0.622	3.71	0.705	4.15
D gr7	0.554	3.17	0.621	3.52	0.713	3.98
D gr8	0.858	4.74	0.868	4.72	1.052	5.60
D gr9	0.908	4.52	0.932	4.54	1.174	5.54
D gr10	1.241	5.47	1.185	5.10	1.554	6.47
D gr11	0.982	2.75	0.937	2.69	1.367	3.68
D gr12	1.279	3.17	1.199	2.91	1.794	4.21
D gr13	2.506	3.50	1.748	2.29	3.251	4.41
Age	−0.092	−9.29	−0.092	−9.42	−0.091	−9.11
Age sqrt	9.50E-04	8.54	9.91E-04	9.15	9.30E-04	8.30
Gender	−0.133	−2.68	−0.126	−2.58	−0.139	−2.81
Pre-cost	−1.49E-04	−3.69	−2.04E-04	−3.83	−3.09E-04	−5.42
Diff-prem	5.88E-04	9.87			6.27E-04	10.36
Diff-cost			−1.03E-04	−2.53	−1.71E-04	−3.97
Const.	−0.421	−1.34	−0.341	−1.12	−0.391	−1.24
Fe clinics	Yes		Yes		Yes	
n	5998		5998		5998	
LRI	0.161		0.136		0.165	
Log-likelihood	−1,590.63		−1,636.54		−1,582.21	

time of the initial decision to enter the insurance. In addition, the effects of age, gender, and variation across clinics are controlled for. The results show *Diff-prem* to be positive and highly significant. Agents are more likely to drop out when the insurer increases its assessment of the risk level. Replacing *Diff-prem* by *Diff-cost* in model 2 gives similar results; *Diff-cost* is negative and significant. Agents receiving a signal of risk being lower than expected are more likely to drop out, indicating that the premium is not accordingly reduced. Had learning on risk been symmetric, these signals would not have been significant.

To identify the determinants of selection out from insurance, both *Diff-prem* and *Diff-cost* are included as explanatory variables in model 3. Both variables are significant, and the responsiveness to *Diff-prem* is more than three times as large as to *Diff-cost*. This rejects the hypothesis that agents deduce the insurer's signal through the observed risk reclassification and then append this additional information to their information sets. Instead, agents and insurer have, at least in part, different information sets. The higher responsiveness to *Diff-prem* may be due to higher premium representing a loss with certainty, while a lower *Diff-cost* represents uncertain gains in risk. Increases and decreases in premiums are included as separate variables in model 4, table 7.4. The parameter estimate for premium increases is considerably larger than the estimate for reductions, but the difference does not reach significance (p-value $= 0.210$). A premium increase, net of private signals, is at least partly regarded by agents as a price increase, rather than a fair-risk reassessment. The risk reclassification by dentists is based on specific risk indicators within the scope of an oral examination, and the outcome is available to patients via their dentist. Therefore, it would have been natural if patients had seen this risk reassessment as legitimate and based on objective criteria.

The responsiveness of new information may differ across risk classes, as the relative impact of a Krona's worth of change in premium and dental consumption differs. Different slopes are therefore allowed for low-, medium-, and high-risk classes, where risk classes 1 to 4 are defined as low, risk classes 5 to 8 as medium, and risk classes 9 to 13 as high. In model 5, table 7.4, where different slopes are allowed for *Diff-prem*, the effect does not differ between high- and low-risk classes. *Diff-prem* is positive and significant throughout. The hypothesis of equal slopes cannot be rejected (p-value $= 0.458$); higher premiums are viewed as the same type of price increases, regardless of risk class. For *Diff-cost*, on the other hand, the effect differs across risk classes

Table 7.4
Probit estimates of failure to renew insurance, II

	Model 4		Model 5		Model 6	
	Coefficient	t-value	Coefficient	t-value	Coefficient	t-value
D gr2	0.254	1.47	0.253	1.47	0.262	1.52
D gr3	0.542	3.24	0.542	3.24	0.555	3.31
D gr4	0.595	3.64	0.599	3.67	0.623	3.79
D gr5	0.650	3.92	0.647	3.87	0.607	3.62
D gr6	0.694	4.07	0.697	4.07	0.654	3.80
D gr7	0.696	3.87	0.703	3.88	0.661	3.63
D gr8	1.026	5.44	1.047	5.54	0.997	5.25
D gr9	1.142	5.35	1.197	5.61	1.053	4.84
D gr10	1.511	6.23	1.565	6.51	1.436	5.88
D gr11	1.291	3.44	1.398	3.80	1.234	3.28
D gr12	1.724	4.02	1.807	4.25	1.642	3.83
D gr13	2.970	3.82	3.138	4.20	2.995	3.95
Age	−0.091	−9.12	−0.091	−9.13	−0.091	−9.05
Age sqrt	9.32E-04	8.32	9.29E-04	8.29	9.25E-04	8.26
Gender	−0.139	−2.81	−0.141	−2.84	−0.142	−2.87
Pre-cost	−3.09E-04	−5.41	−3.11E-04	−5.45	−3.05E-04	−5.40
Diff-prem					6.27E-04	10.33
l diff-prem			6.05E-04	3.38		
m diff-prem			6.83E-04	8.88		
h diff-prem			5.27E-04	5.11		
neg diff-prem	4.16E-04	2.37				
pos diff-prem	6.63E-04	9.89				
Diff-cost	−1.73E-04	−4.00	−1.74E-04	−4.03		
l diff-cost					−3.77E-04	−3.99
m diff-cost					−1.72E-04	−3.47
h diff-cost					−1.01E-04	−1.67
Const.	−0.398	−1.26	−0.368	−1.17	−0.365	−1.15
Fe clinics	Yes		Yes		Yes	
n	5,998		5,998		5,998	
LRI	0.165		0.165		0.167	
Log-likelihood	−1,581.44		−1,581.43		−1,578.73	

(*p*-value = 0.031). In low-risk classes, high values of *Diff-cost* will reduce the probability of lapsation more than in high-risk classes.

A noteworthy result is that *Pre-cost*—agents' information at the time of the initial insurance decision—is negative and significant. Lower dental cost prior to purchasing insurance increases the probability of opting out. This information was available already in the decision to sign up and should therefore have no bearing on the decision to lapse the insurance.

Another remarkable result is that the constant term is increasing with higher-risk classes. That is, controlling for the effect of both old and new information, agents in higher-risk classes have higher probabilities of opting out. During the period, all risk classes were subject to a proportional price increase (11 percent between January 1999 and June 2001), which translates into larger out-of-pocket costs for higher-risk groups. One interpretation would be that patients are more sensitive to larger nominal premium increases, being liquidity constrained.

The probability of opting out of insurance is reduced with higher age, the interpretation of which is ambiguous. It might be that age contains information on changes in risk that is not captured in the risk classification or in past dental consumption. It also might be the case that the propensity to insure risk increases with age. Moreover, men are less likely to opt out than women.

The results can also be captured by depicting the typical patient lapsing the insurance. Table 7.5 reports that the National Dental Service in Värmland makes larger profits on patients that opt out,[9] which implies that, on average, patients opting out have lower dental costs than their peers in the same risk class. Patients who opt out also receive higher average premium increases, as seen in table 7.6. However, considering all patients receiving higher premiums, in table 7.7, it is seen that the profit on these agents is negative. For patients remaining

Table 7.5
Mean profit by renewal status

| Opt Out | Profit | | P-Values for Differences | |
	Mean	Standard Deviation	*t*-test	Mann-Whitney
No	68	663	0.013	<0.001
Yes	145	708		

in the same risk class, the profit is positive, and it is positive and still higher for patients reclassified into a lower-risk class. Hence, patients upgraded to a higher-risk class are, on average, those having generated losses to the dental service, but there is a large variability.

The National Dental Service is reassessing patients' risk level on basis of certain risk indicators. These indicators do not only pick up information contained in dental cost. Thus, some patients receiving higher premiums actually have a lower dental cost relative to peers in the same risk class. The typical patient leaving the insurance is someone generating profits but still receiving a higher premium. Whether lapsation is due to an adverse-selection process depends on who is making the best assessment on future risk. If the risk indicators go wrong for this group of patients, there is adverse selection, but if the indicators actually pick up new risk not contained within realized dental consumption, there is instead inefficiency due to a communication problem between dentist and patient.

A next issue is whether insurance dropout due to asymmetric updating has an economic importance. To get an impression of the economic significance of the estimated effects in model 3, table 7.3, the

Table 7.6
Mean premium change by renewal status

	Diff-prem		P-values for Differences	
Opt Out	Mean	Standard Deviation	t-test	Mann-Whitney
No	60	348	<0.001	<0.001
Yes	241	592		

Table 7.7
Mean profit by risk reclassification

	Profit		P-values for Differences	
Diff-prem	Mean	Standard Deviation	t-test	Mann-Whitney
Neg	229	746	<0.001	<0.001
0	132	603	<0.001	<0.001
Pos	−109	725		

Note: The p-values tests for differences in profit against the group for which *Diff-prem* is positive.

Table 7.8
Impact of asymmetric updating

| | Probability at | | | |
	Mean	1 Standard Deviation	Change	Percentage Change
Diff-prem	0.069	0.107	0.038	54.7
Diff-cost	0.069	0.096	0.027	38.6

Note: The probability of buying insurance is evaluated (1) at the sample mean of all variables and (2) when *Diff-prem* is increased, and *Diff-cost* is decreased, with one standard deviation, respectively.

probability of opting out is first evaluated at the sample mean of all included variables and then compared to the probability when *Diff-prem* is increased and *Diff-cost* is reduced with one standard deviation, respectively, see table 7.8. At the sample mean, the probability of dropping coverage is 6.9 percent. When *Diff-prem* is increased with one standard deviation the probability of opting out increases with 55 percent—to 10.7 percent. A decrease in *Diff-cost* with one standard deviation, in turn, raises the probability of dropping coverage with 39 percent—to 9.6 percent. Hence, the behavioral response to asymmetric learning on risk is substantial in the present setting.

Discussion

There are many reasons why agents may fail to renew an insurance. The aim here is to analyze how the decision is affected by new information on risk. Asymmetric updating of information may lead agents' to terminate their insurance. In the context of a voluntary dental insurance, proxies for new information are related to the decision to opt out. Past dental costs can be used as a proxy for private information due to the set up of the insurance. A potential problem of using dental costs within the insurance to capture new information is that agents with a skill to extract services would be more likely to stay insured. These agents would have an unexpectedly high dental consumption without necessarily having a higher risk. Still, it is a signal of higher future dental-care consumption.

The results show that patients respond to economic circumstances in making their decision to leave or keep the insurance. Patients are more prone to opt out when reclassified into higher premium classes or when they have an unexpectedly low dental consumption. They are more responsive to higher premiums than to reduced expected costs.

If updating were symmetric, patients would not respond to a higher premium since it would be regarded as a fair assessment of increased risk. The results indicate updating on dental risk to be asymmetric, leading to partly different information sets. New information obtained by the insurer can be inferred by observing premium changes, but patients do not fully incorporate this public information. A higher premium is viewed as a higher price on insurance contracts rather than as a fair risk reassessment. The results may follow from the insurer making an erroneous updating of the patients' risk. However, if the insurer's updating does contain valid new information on risk, the results are consistent with the literature on loss aversion and fairness of pricing, where the outcomes of transactions are evaluated against a reference point. Kahneman, Knetsch, and Thaler (1986) find that price increases that deviate from the reference price (and are not justified by increasing costs) are perceived as unfair by agents. Increased risk is an abstract notion, and dentists may have problems in communicating why a contract has a higher expected cost. Higher premiums may therefore be viewed as breaking the reference price of an insurance contract.

The cyclical pattern of dental care is not responsible for the asymmetric updating. If this was the case, a high consumption within the insurance would increase the probability of lapsing dental coverage—a pattern that is not observed in the data.

The fact that *Pre-cost* is significant indicates that the impact of new information to the agent accumulates over time. This result may, however, be due to the cyclical pattern, giving *Pre-cost* predictive power of the dental-care needs in the upcoming contract period. Indeed, in table 7.1 it is seen that dental consumption four years back has predictive power on current consumption. Agents not taking full account of new signals might also be due to a slow cognitive process of updating information.

The consequences of asymmetric updating depend on which of the contracting parts has the advantage in updating. Within the present data, the question of whether lapsation is due to a process of adverse selection cannot be determined. It can be noted that the risk-assessment system used by the National Dental Service in Värmland does about 30 percent better in predicting future dental costs than do past dental costs. Nonetheless, past dental consumption captures some of the variations in future dental cost that are not captured by risk classification.

Acknowledgments

I am grateful to the National Dental Service in Värmland, Sweden, and especially to Jörgen Paulander for providing data and odontologic expertise and to Ann-Britt Emilsson for generously answering questions about registration practices. Financial support has been provided by Apoteksbolagets Fond för Forskning och Studier i Hälsoekonomi och Samhällsfarmaci. Comments and suggestions from two anonymous referees, Magnus Johannesson, Mark V. Pauly, and seminar participants at the Stockholm School of Economics, Swedish Institute for Social Research, and the Trade Union Institute for Economic Research are gratefully acknowledged.

Notes

1. Folktandvården.

2. Dental care is provided free of charge for individuals below the age of twenty.

3. For patients age twenty, the insurance was introduced in September 1998.

4. This number is net of agents who die or leave the county during the period.

5. For risk classes 14 to 16, the coefficients do not follow the increasing pattern expected for higher-risk classes. This is due to the low number of patients, 229 out of the 36,241 (0.64 percent) belonging to any of the top three risk classes in the chosen sample. Chance thus has a larger scope.

6. Patients age twenty in 1998 were given the offer in September 1998 as part of a pilot project. These patients are included in the sample, even if they bought the insurance at the end of 1998. In this case, they need to have been registered with the National Dental Service since 1996 but need not be registered in 2001.

7. *Pre-cost* is the amount charged by the National Service in Värmland and calculated by applying the gross price list to procedures chargeable to patients.

8. Dental care within the insurance is not registered as specific procedures. Instead, it is registered within broader groups of procedures and as the time used by the relevant staff category (dentist, hygienist, nurse). To calculate dental cost, the time usage is summed up using the time tariff. From 1999, there are, however, no explicit time tariffs for hygienist and nurse services. These are calculated as fractions of the time tariff for dentists, using the price list in 1995 to 1998 as a key.

9. The profit for each patient is calculated by subtracting the cost of his dental care (within the contract) from the revenue he generates. The revenue consists of the premium

paid by the patient, plus a lump sum of 200 SEK from the Public Insurance Office (Försäkringskassan). This lump sum corresponds to the average reimbursement from the public dental insurance scheme, covering all adults in Sweden. It is paid out to induce neutrality toward patients outside the voluntary dental insurance.

References

Akerlof, G. (1970). "The Market for Lemons: Quality Uncertainty and the Market Mechanism." *Quarterly Journal of Economics* 84: 488–500.

Buchmueller, T., and J. DiNardo. (2002). "Did Community Rating Induce an Adverse-Selection Death Spiral? Evidence from New York, Pennsylvania, and Connecticut." *American Economic Review* 92: 280–294.

Cardon, J., and I. Hendel. (2001). "Asymmetric Information in Health Insurance: Evidence from the National Health Insurance Survey." *RAND Journal of Economics* 32: 408–427.

Cawley, J., and T. Philipson. (1999). "An Empirical Examination of Information Barriers to Trade in Insurance." *American Economic Review* 89: 827–846.

Chiappori, P. A., and B. Salanié. (2003). "Testing Contract Theory: A Survey of Some Recent Work." In M. Dewatripont, L. P. Hansen, and S. J. Turnovsky (Eds.), *Advances in Economics and Econometrics*. Cambridge: Cambridge University Press.

Crocker, K. J., and J. R. Moran. (2003). "Contracting with Limited Commitment: Evidence from Employment-Based Health Insurance Contracts." *RAND Journal of Economics* 34: 694–718.

Cutler, D. M., and S. J. Reber. (1998). "Paying for Health Insurance: The Trade-off between Competition and Adverse Selection." *Quarterly Journal of Economics* 113: 433–466.

de Meza, D., and D. Webb. (2001). "Advantageous Selection in Insurance Markets." *RAND Journal of Economics* 32: 249–262.

Finkelstein, A., and K. McGarry. (2003). "Private Information and Its Effects on Market Equilibrium: New Evidence from Long-Term Care Insurance." NBER Working Paper 9957.

Grönqvist, E. (2004). "Does Adverse Selection Matter? Evidence from a Natural Experiment." SSE/EFI Working Paper Series in Economics and Finance No. 575. Stockholm School of Economics.

Hendel, I., and A. Lizzeri. (2003). "The Role of Commitment in Dynamic Contracts: Evidence from Life Insurance." *Quarterly Journal of Economics* 118: 299–326.

Kahneman, D., J. L. Knetsch, and R. Thaler. (1986). "Fairness as a Constraint on Profit Seeking: Entitlements in the Market." *American Economic Review* 76: 728–741.

Nicholson, S., K. M. Bundorf, R. M. Stein, and D. Polsky. (2003). "The Magnitude and Nature of Risk Selection in Employer-Sponsored Health Plans." NBER Working Paper 9937.

Olsson, C. (1999). *Essays in the Economics of Dental Insurance and Dental Health*. Umeå Economic Studies No. 494, Umeå University.

Powell, L. V. (1998). "Caries Prediction: A Review of the Literature." *Community Dental Oral Epidemiology* 26: 361–371.

Sapelli, C., and B. Vial. (2003). "Self-Selection and Moral Hazard in Chilean Health Insurance." *Journal of Health Economics* 22: 459–476.

Savage, E., and D. J. Wright. (2003). "Moral Hazard and Adverse Selection in Australian Private Hospitals: 1989–1990." *Journal of Health Economics* 22: 331–359.

Statistics Sweden. (n.d.). "Sweden's Statistical Databases." ⟨http://www.scb.se/indexeng .asp⟩.

Thomasson, M. A. (2002). "Did Blue Cross and Blue Shield Suffer from Adverse Selection? Evidence from the 1950s." NBER Working Paper 9167.

III

Empirical Analysis in Nonhealth Insurance

8

The Informational Content of Household Decisions with Applications to Insurance under Asymmetric Information

Georges Dionne, Christian Gouriéroux, and Charles Vanasse

Introduction

Under asymmetric information, empirical studies of household behavior involving financial products or insurance contracts are generally designed to predict some individual endogenous variable related to individual risk or insurance demand. The prediction formula is then used to classify (score) individuals and construct homogenous subpopulations.

If the choice is qualitative, the variable of interest is often predicted by means of a nonlinear regression model including, as explanatory variables, some exogenous characteristics such as age, occupation, housing district, and income level. But other variables summarizing the endogenous choices of the agents may also be introduced, and this raises questions about the additional information they provide.

For instance, the type of automobile insurance contract selected (that is, its level of deductible) can be introduced to predict the number and cost of the policyholder's car accidents. The choice of a graduated monthly payment instead of a regular monthly payment or the choice of a collateral can provide information on potential payment default. Since they can approximate risk aversion, types of financial assets held in an individual's portfolio may help to predict life insurance coverage.

The theoretical arguments proposed for introducing such decision variables among the regressors are twofold. First, the individual may know more than the econometrician or the insurer about his type of risk (and his risk aversion), and some of this additional information may be revealed through such decision variables. This is the standard argument in adverse-selection literature, where the choice of an automobile insurance contract with a large deductible reveals a better risk (Rothschild and Stiglitz, 1976; Wilson, 1977; see Dionne, Doherty, and Fombaron, 2000, for a survey).

Second, the individual may take combined decisions. In such cases, the analysis of one decision component irrespective of the other ones may prove inefficient. Combined decisions regarding life insurance and financial securities offer a good example, since the choice of a particular portfolio may reveal information about risk aversion.[1]

These two arguments may also be combined. In the case of moral hazard, additional individual-specific information (the individual's effort) can be chosen along with other assets or insurance contracts. This dimension of the problem will not be explicitly discussed in this chapter, although it is an underlying factor (see, however, Dionne, Gourieroux, and Vanasse, 1998; Chassagnon and Chiappori, 1996).

This chapter extends the article of Dionne, Gouriéroux, and Vanasse (2001) with a detailed discussion of the different econometric issues related to the methodology. We propose the notion of conditional independence and explain how it can be used in our framework. We also define a measure of the informational content of these decision variables, introduce test statistics for the null hypothesis on no informational content, and study how these notions and statistics depend on the initial exogenous information.

In practice, this conditional dependence analysis is usually performed in a parametric framework where the model is a priori constrained. This practice may induce spurious conclusions, since it is difficult to distinguish between the decision variables' information content and an omitted nonlinear effect of the initial exogenous variables. We discuss a pragmatic way of avoiding this difficulty; it consists in introducing among the regressors both the decision variables and their expected values computed from the initial information.

This approach is applied to the analysis of automobile accidents in Quebec and to prediction of the demand for life insurance in France. The lesson from these examples is that the additional information provided by the decision variables is rather weak and often insignificant, as soon as the nonlinear effect of the initial exogenous variables has been introduced in a suitable way. Other conclusions are summarized in the final section of the chapter.

Conditional Dependence and Independence

The problem of additional information may be treated by means of conditional dependence. In this section, we review the main results on this notion (see, e.g., Gourieroux and Monfort, 1995, vol. 2, pp. 458–475). We use Y to denote the endogenous variable of interest, X to denote initial K exogenous variables, and Z to denote the L decision variables.

Conditional Independence

The endogenous variable Y provides no additional information if and only if prediction of the Z decision variables based on both X and Y coincides with the prediction based on X alone. In a nonlinear framework, this condition has to be valid for any transformation of the Y variable and may be written in terms of conditional probability:

$$l(Z/X, Y) = l(Z/X), \tag{8.1}$$

where $l(./.,.)$ denotes a conditional pdf.

Z can represent the deductible and the coinsurance rate in health or automobile insurance or the type of life insurance coverage. Equation (8.1) can be rewritten to obtain

$$l(Y, Z/X) = l(Y/X)l(Z/X). \tag{8.2}$$

From (8.2), we deduce the symmetry of conditional independence in Y and Z. An equivalent form to (8.1) is the following:

$$l(Y/X, Z) = l(Y/X). \tag{8.3}$$

We see that this is equivalent to the Z variable's lack of additional informational content for predicting the random variable Y.

Measure of Conditional Dependence

It is also standard to define valid measures of conditional dependence in a nonlinear framework. These measures are based on the so-called information criterion, first evaluated conditionally to X and then possibly averaged on the values of the exogenous variables. More precisely, we define

$$M(Z, Y/X) = E\left[\log \frac{l(Y/X, Z)}{l(Y/X)} \,/\, X\right]$$

$$= \int\int \log \frac{l(y/X, z)}{l(y/X)} l(y, z/X)\, dy\, dz. \tag{8.4}$$

It is known that

$$M(Z, Y/X) = -E\left[E\left(\log \frac{l(Y/X)}{l(Y/X, Z)} \middle/ X, Z\right) \middle/ X\right]$$

$$\geq -E\left\{\log E\left(\frac{l(Y/X)}{l(Y/X, Z)} \middle/ X, Z\right) \middle/ X\right\}$$

(from the convexity inequality)

$$= 0.$$

Moreover, this nonnegative measure vanishes if and only if $l(Y/X, Z) = \lambda(X)l(Y/X)$, for some function λ. Since the pdf has unit mass, this condition is equivalent to $l(Y/X, Z) = l(Y/X)$—that is, to conditional independence.

$M(Z, Y/X)$ is a dependence measure between Z and Y, computed for the different homogeneous groups of individuals defined from the exogenous variables.

These measures may be summarized by a more global one corresponding to the whole population of interest by averaging on X

$$\overline{M}(Z, Y/X) = E \log \frac{l(Y/X, Z)}{l(Y/X)}$$

$$= E\left[E \log \frac{l(Y/X, Z)}{l(Y/X)}\right]$$

$$= E_X M(Z, Y/X).$$

The Effect of Exogenous Information
The value of introducing the additional decision variables is contingent on the initial exogenous information. A question of interest is what happens if, for instance, this information is increased.

Let us distinguish two sets of exogenous variables $X = (X_0, X_1)$. We get

$$\frac{l(Y/X, Z)}{l(Y/X)} = \frac{l(Y/X_0, Z)}{l(Y/X_0)} \frac{l(Y/X_0, X_1, Z)}{l(Y/X_0, Z)} \frac{l(Y/X_0)}{l(Y/X_0, X_1)}.$$

By taking the logarithm and the expectation of both sides, we derive a decomposition formula of the conditional dependence measure:

$$\overline{M}(Z, Y/X) = \overline{M}(Z, Y/X_0) + \overline{M}(X_1, Y/X_0, Z) - \overline{M}(X_1, Y/X_0), \tag{8.5}$$

where the terms $\overline{M}$ are nonnegative.

The additional information contained in the decision variables may increase or decrease depending on the new X_1 variables introduced in the exogenous information. We may select different more or less informative exogenous information sets such that the conditional independence hypothesis is satisfied.

Conditional Dependence or Misspecified Structure

Null and Alternative Hypotheses

The conditional independence hypothesis can be tested by either nonparametric or parametric techniques. This latter approach is generally retained for applications to finance and insurance decisions.

Indeed, the available exogenous variables are mainly qualitative variables, such as occupation, type of car, and class of historical risk. They are numerous, and the main problem is achieving an efficient cross-matching of these qualitative variables to detect the subclasses that are the least or the most risky and to construct appropriate rate scales. Nonparametric approaches such as the ones proposed by Robinson (1988) or Linton and Gozalo (1995) are not appropriate since they require a small number of variables with continuous values. The difficulty of introducing these approaches for a single quantitative exogenous variable combined with other qualitative covariates can be seen in the paper on credit scoring by Müller and Rönz (1999). The large number of individual observations (sometimes in excess of 200,000 in finance or insurance applications) does nothing to counter the curse of dimensionality. If we consider fifty dichotomous covariates (a standard number in this type of problems), the number of cross-classes is equal to 2^{50}, a number much larger than the number of observations.

The test requires a preliminary parametric modeling for the conditional distribution of the endogenous variable of interest Y, given the different explanatory variables X and Z. To simplify the presentation, we consider the case of dichotomous variables Y and Z_l, $l = 1, \ldots, L$. Typically, a parametric formulation gives the following conditional probability:[2]

$$P[Y = 1/X, Z] = F(g(X; b) + c'Z), \tag{8.6}$$

where F and g are given functions, F is a cumulative distribution function, and b and c are unknown parameters. In practice, the transformation F used to pass from a quantitative score $g(X, b)$ to a probability is a logistic or a probit transformation. The logistic form is generally preferred, since it allows for the use of standard software including automatic backward and forward selections of cross-effects and leads to an easier residual analysis.

In this framework, the conditional independence between Y and Z given X is characterized by the constraint $c = 0$. Under this null hypothesis $H_o = \{c = 0\}$, we get

$$P[Y = 1/X, Z] = P[Y = 1/X] = F[g(X; b_o)],$$

where b_o is the true value of the parameter.

The null hypothesis may be rejected as a consequence of either conditional dependence

$$P[Y = 1/X, Z] \neq P[Y = 1/X]$$

or a misspecified structural form

$$P[Y = 1/X] \neq F[g(X; b)], \quad \forall b.$$

This second reason may be avoided by selecting a sufficiently smooth specification, including cross effects. This is the point we are now going to discuss.

Example of the Linear Scoring Function
In practice, the scoring function $S(X; Z) = g(X; b) + c'Z$ is often written as a linear function $S(X; Z) = b'X + c'Z$, without introducing cross-effects of individual characteristics or by introducing a limited number of standard ones. These specifications are generally verified by applying standard specification tests. However, the implicit alternatives corresponding to these tests are not necessarily the most significant ones. The approach described below provides natural candidates for informative alternatives to be used before applying a specification test. We will see that these alternatives involve complicated cross-effects.

Note that in the framework of dichotomous qualitative covariates $x_1, x_2, \ldots, x_K$, an introduction of the cross-effects between x_1 and x_2, for instance, provides a specification

$$b_0 + b_{11}x_1x_2 + b_{12}x_1(1 - x_2) + b_{21}(1 - x_1)x_2 + b_3x_3 + \cdots + b_Kx_K,$$

which is linear in the transformed variables

$$1, x_1x_2, x_1(1 - x_2), (1 - x_1)x_2, x_3, \ldots, x_K.$$

More generally for qualitative covariates, a model with any type of cross-effects can always be written under a linear specification. To summarize, the score can always be specified as a linear function of unknown parameters, whereas it is nonlinear in the initial covariates.

Some similar specifications may also be introduced for the Z_l, $l = 1, \ldots, L$ variables:

$$P[Z_l = 1/X] = F(a_l'X).$$

Moreover, we may assume that the Z_l variables are independent. In practice, the transformation associated with the specification of the conditional distribution of Z_l is assumed to be the same as the transformation associated with the specification of the conditional distribution of Y, logit if logit, probit if probit. In this specification, the score $a_l'X$ is linear with respect to the parameters but may be nonlinear with respect to the basic explanatory variables if some cross-effects have already been introduced.

Let us now consider this modeling when the conditional dependence is small: $c \simeq 0$. The conditional distribution of Y, given only the exogenous variables X, is

$$P[Y = 1/X]$$

$$= \sum_{z_1=0}^{1} \cdots \sum_{z_L=0}^{1} \left\{ \prod_{l=1}^{L} (F(a_l'X)^{z_l}(1 - F(a_l'X))^{1-z_l}) F\left(b'X + \sum_{l=1}^{L} c_l z_l \right) \right\}$$

$$\simeq F(b'X) + \dot{F}(b'X) \sum_{z_1=0}^{1} \cdots \sum_{z_L=0}^{1} \prod_{l=1}^{L} (F(a_l'X)^{z_l}(1 - F(a_l'X))^{1-z_l}) \sum_{l=1}^{L} c_l z_l$$

$$= F(b'X) + \dot{F}(b'X) \sum_{l=1}^{L} c_l F(a_l'X)$$

$$\simeq F\left(b'X + \sum_{l=1}^{L} c_l F(a_l'X) \right),$$

where $\dot{F}$ is the derivative of F.

The general form of the conditional distribution $P[Y = 1/X]$ is very different from the linear scoring corresponding to the null hypothesis.[3] The linear introduction of the decision variables Z_l, $l = 1, \ldots, L$, inside the scoring function is an artificial way of introducing the cross-effects of the X variables, through the expectations $F(a_l'X)$, $l = 1, \ldots, L$. Indeed, the second-order derivative of the score with respect to variables X_1, X_2 (say) is equal to $(\partial^2 (b'X + \sum_{l=1}^{L} c_l F(a_l'X)))/(\partial X_1 \partial X_2) = \sum_{l=1}^{L} c_l \, a_{1l} \, a_{2l} F''(a_l'X)$ and is generally different from zero. This example shows that the linear scoring functions are too constrained and that rejection of the null hypothesis $\{c_l = 0\}$, $\forall l$, will likely detect the omission of cross-effects.

How to Smooth the Linear Scoring Functions
Modeling with linear scoring functions can be easily extended to avoid the main part of the previous difficulty. We simply have to consider a modified specification

$$P[Y = 1/X, Z]$$

$$= F\left[b'X + \sum_{l=1}^{L} d_l F(a_l'X) + \sum_{l=1}^{L} c_l Z_l \right],$$

in which the decision variables are introduced jointly with their X-conditional expectations. The introduction of decision-variables predictions among the explanatory variables is similar to the idea followed for defining the regression specification error test (RESET) (Ramsey, 1969; Godfrey, 1988, p. 106). The difference is that, in our case, the prediction introduced concerns other decision variables that can be non-linearly linked to the endogenous variable Y conditionally to X.

Applications

We apply the previous approach by comparing models in which the additional variables introduced in the linear scoring are the Z_l, $l = 1, \ldots, L$, only to models containing both these variables and their expectations. We will see that spurious conditional dependence may be exhibited if we omit the expectations (see Chiappori and Salanié, 1997, 2000, 2003, for a different approach to that proposed in this chapter).

Joint Analysis of the Distribution of Automobile Accidents and Deductible Choice

Literature Review For about forty years (Arrow, 1963), information problems have been discussed in the economic literature to explain the nature of transactions or contracts (insurance, banking, labor, industrial organization, and taxation).

However, very few empirical investigations of the significance of these problems were published before the 1990s. Part of the explanation for this lies in the availability of adequate data. The other part has to do with methodology.

Many authors have claimed to have found strong evidence of private information in a given market, but their results may be due to misspecification of the model (many control variables are not included in the model) or inadequate data (the control group does not exist); so many other interpretations of the results are possible.

Different tests on the presence of residual private information in insurance markets have been proposed in the economic literature recently (Puelz and Snow, 1994; Dionne and Doherty, 1994; Chiappori and Salanié, 2000; Dionne, Gouriéroux, and Vanasse, 2001; Dionne and Gagné, 2001; Abbring, Chiappori, and Pinquet, 2003; Dionne, Michaud, and Dahchour, 2004).

If we limit the discussion to single-period insurance contracting and private information in insurance markets, testing for the presence of residual private information in a given portfolio remains an interesting empirical question. In the presence of residual private information, the data should provide correlations between contracts and behaviors. The economic theory provides two causality relationships (Chiappori, 2000; Chiappori and Salanié, 2003; Chiappori, Jullien, Salanié, and Salanié, 2004):

• Under pure adverse selection, high-risk individuals self-select by choosing higher insurance coverage. This can be identified as the effect of unobserved heterogeneity on the forms of contracts.

• Under pure moral hazard, individuals choose fewer safety activities under higher insurance coverage. This is often identified as the incentive effect of contracts.

In both cases, we should observe a positive correlation between insurance contracting and accidents or state realizations when private information remains in the data. From the data we may observe one positive correlation, but from the theory we have two alternative explanations. At least one degree of freedom is missing (as mentioned above, differences in risk aversion and the presence of proportional loading factors may also explain different insurance-contract choices).

This is why recent contributions limited their interpretation to a test for residual private information in the data (Chiappori and Salanié, 2000; Dionne, Gouriéroux, and Vanasse, 2001).

One possible means of identifying the information problem is to have an exogenous allocation of individuals to contracts or to use a natural experiment as in Newhouse et al. (see Newhouse et al., 1987). But these studies are expensive.

Another possibility is to use panel data because the dynamics of behavior generates a structure for distinguishing moral hazard from adverse selection (Dionne and Gagné, 2001; Abbring, Chiappori, and Pinquet, 2003; Dionne, Michaud, and Dahchour, 2004).

In this study, however, the nature of the data (one period) is not appropriate for making such distinctions because we do not have enough degrees of freedom. So we are limited to checking for the presence of residual private information in the data.

In many insurance markets like the ones studied, insurers use observable characteristics to categorize individual risks. It was shown by Crocker and Snow (1986) that such categorization is welfare improving if its cost is not too high and if observable characteristics are correlated with hidden knowledge. The effect of risk categorization is to reduce the gap between the different risk types. It may also decrease the need for separation by offering the choice of different insurance coverages within the different risk classes, as in Rothschild and Stiglitz (1976).

In other words, if risk categorization is efficient enough, the insurer may not need additional instruments related to household decisions to select the different risks in an efficient manner.

This result suggests that a test for the presence of residual private information should be applied within different risk classes or by introducing categorization variables in the model (control of observable heterogeneity). It is known that risk classification variables such as age, territory, and type of car are costless to observe in the insurance industry. The correlation between these variables and individual risks is easily verified by the estimation of accident distributions (see appendix 8C).

Model   Puelz and Snow (1994) consider an ordered logit formulation for the deductible choice (Z) in which the observed number of accidents (Y) was introduced among the explanatory variables. The estimated coefficient of the Y variable is significant, and this leads them to conclude that adverse selection is present (that is, there is a conditional dependence between Y and Z). It can be noted that the test procedure was based on the indirect (8.1) and not the direct (8.3) characterization of conditional independence. Such a practice may be interpreted as the description of what the individual would decide if he had private knowledge of future risk.

We show that the conclusion derived is likely a spurious effect due to the overly constrained form of the exogenous effects. In fact, the linear specification of the ordered logit model contained only few variables. For this purpose, we consider the indirect form of the conditional distribution of Z given Y and X in which we introduce the linear effect of the X variables plus their nonlinear effect through an expected value of the number of accidents. This expectation is based on a preliminary negative binomial model estimated with only the X as explanatory variables (Gourieroux, Monfort, and Trognon, 1984; Dionne and Vanasse, 1992; Lemaire, 1995; Dionne, Gagné, Gagnon, and Vanasse, 1997; Pinquet, 2000) (see appendix 8C for the estimated model and Dionne, Gourieroux, and Vanasse, 1998, for more details).

The data come from a large private insurer in Quebec. Different contracts corresponding to various levels for a straight deductible are proposed, but the deductible choice really matters only for the $250 and $500 deductibles, and the $500 choice was made by only about 4 percent of the overall portfolio.

Figure 8.1 and table 8.1 indicate that the proportion of individuals who choose the $500 deductible varies between risk classes. These risk

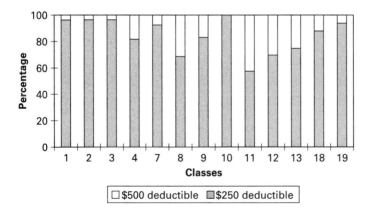

Figure 8.1
Observed deductible choices according to classes

Table 8.1
Deductibles and risk classes

| Class | $250 Deductible | | $500 Deductible | |
	n	Percentage of Class	n	Percentage of Class
1	14,015	96.32%	535	3.68%
2	13,509	96.53	486	3.47
3	4,538	96.49	165	3.51
4	756	81.82	168	18.18
7	1,515	92.66	120	7.34
8	11	68.75	5	31.25
9	287	83.19	58	16.81
10	5	100.00	0	0.00
11	53	57.61	39	42.39
12	164	69.79	71	30.21
13	308	74.94	103	25.06
18	175	87.94	24	12.06
19	855	93.96	55	6.04
Total	36,191	95.19%	1,829	4.81%

classes are not directly observable and were built up from observable variables such as age, sex, and territory. The question of interest is the following: Do these choices of deductible reveal private information on individual risk? To answer this question, we did the following analysis for classes 4 to 19, where the $500 deductible choice is significant.

The main exogenous variables introduced in the econometric specifications of the deductible choice equation (Z) are *Age* of the principal driver; *SexF* (1 if the principal driver is a female); *Gj*, a group of eight dummy variables representing the insurer's car classification groups; and *Occasional young male* (*YMALE*) driver, if there is such a driver in the household. All these variables and others have been introduced since the insurance company uses them in its pricing. Moreover, as in Puelz and Snow (1994), the number of current accidents $N(acc)$ is introduced in the first model, while in the second model, the expected number of accidents $E(acc)$ is added. We did also control for risk aversion by introducing wealth proxy variables Wi that indicate the liability coverage chosen. Finally, a price variable (GD) for the $500 deductible was obtained from the insurer's pricing book. This is the rebate for switching from the $250 to the $500 deductible (see appendix 8A for the complete list of variables).

Table 8.2
Probit on deductible choice (1 if $500 deductible)

Variable	Model 1 (Conditional on the number of claims)		Model 2 (Conditional on the number of claims and expected number of claims)	
	Coefficient	t-ratio	Coefficient	t-ratio
Intercept	−0.7505	−5.006	−0.4884	−3.111
Acc	−0.1579	−1.983	−0.1151	−1.436
E(acc)			−5.4637	−6.524
GD	−0.0099	−5.275	−0.0150	−7.299
SEXF	−0.5097	−8.296	−0.5968	−9.426
AGE	−0.0251	−7.975	−0.0241	−7.681
Liability limit				
W2	−0.0133	−0.177	−0.0360	−0.474
W3	−0.2016	−1.872	−0.2016	−1.860
W4	0.0115	0.172	0.0427	0.635
W5	−0.2337	−2.990	−0.1634	−2.063
Group of vehicles				
G9	0.1484	2.683	0.1266	2.268
G10	0.2428	3.359	0.2475	3.410
G11	0.4242	3.267	0.4905	3.754
G12	0.6934	4.346	0.8398	5.165
G13	0.7974	4.485	1.3053	6.709
G14	1.1424	4.937	1.0745	4.675
G15	1.0582	3.541	1.0690	3.551
YMALE	0.1127	0.734	0.0589	0.384
Number of observations	4,772		4,772	
Log-likelihood	−1,735.406		−1,713.091	

In a first step, probit models for the choice of a deductible of $500 were estimated for all drivers, first with the number of claims (over $500) only (model 1) and then jointly with the expected number of accidents (model 2).[4] The specifications of the two models do not contain all the available classification variables as in Puelz and Snow (1994). More variables are considered in model 3. The first columns of table 8.2 give the estimated coefficients, and the second ones give the associated student statistics.

The results indicate clearly that when the model is not correctly specified, a false conclusion can be made about the presence of residual asymmetric information in automobile insurance. Model 1 suggests that Y and Z are correlated or that the null hypothesis of conditional independence is rejected. Indeed, as in Puelz and Snow (1994), we obtain that the coefficient of $N(acc)$ is negative and significant, indicating that those who have more accidents chose the low deductible (adverse selection). It may also indicate that those with more coverage had less incentive for safety (moral hazard). These conclusions are, in fact, not appropriate. When we add the expected number of accidents $E(acc)$ in the model to test whether the prediction of a deductible choice conditional on X is appropriately specified, the coefficient of $N(acc)$ is no longer significant.[5] This means that when we take the nonlinearity of the risk-classification variables into account through $E(acc)$, the number of accidents is no longer significant in explaining the deductible choice. So we conclude that the residual asymmetric information in the risk classes vanishes. In other words, by an appropriate risk-classification procedure, the insurer, when using observable variables, is able to control for adverse selection and potential moral hazard and needs no additional self-selection or bonus-malus mechanism. Since these classification variables are all observable by the insurer, no residual asymmetric information remains on the individuals risks. Finally, model 3 in table 8.3 shows that we can eliminate the $E(acc)$ variable by using more classification variables, as insurers do.[6] Even the proxies for the wealth variables Wi used to control for risk aversion are no longer significant, whereas two categories were significant in models 1 and 2.

Life Insurance Coverage in France
The second application concerns portfolio allocation by French households. It is well known that individual portfolios are not well diversified (Hamburger, 1968; Shorrocks, 1982; King Leape, 1984; Gourieroux, Tiomo, and Trognon, 1996). This result is contrary to the standard financial theory (Markowitz, 1992), but it can be explained by transaction costs, the inaccessibility of short positions, the illiquidity of a number of assets (such as housing and human capital), the commercial strategies of banks and insurance companies, and asymmetric information in some markets (such as life insurance). Therefore, it is useful to begin a study of portfolio allocation by considering qualitative features such as the type of assets introduced in the portfolio.

    In the traditional literature on life insurance and adverse selection (see Villeneuve, 2000, for a recent literature review), risk-classification variables have been useful in approximating the individual risks.

Table 8.3
Probit estimates on deductible choice

| Variable | Model 3 (Conditional on the number of claims, expected number of claims and additional risk classification variables) | |
	Coefficient	t-ratio
Intercept	−0.47151	−0.777
Acc	−0.11166	−1.352
E(acc)	−2.62320	−0.772
GD	−0.00195	−0.530
SEXF	−0.08582	−0.571
AGE	−0.01352	−2.694
Liability limit		
W2	0.06720	0.837
W3	−0.12067	−1.054
W4	0.11830	1.621
W5	−0.03462	−0.395
Group of vehicles		
G9	0.16806	2.799
G10	0.29861	3.928
G11	0.48917	3.445
G12	0.75350	3.885
G13	1.07560	3.126
G14	1.10850	4.673
G15	1.29840	4.211
YMALE	0.29254	1.795
Territory		
T2	−0.12335	−0.357
T3	0.15908	0.775
T4	−0.01370	−0.042
T5	−0.18685	−1.202
T6	−0.32644	−1.100
T7	−0.55344	−2.595
T8	−0.21743	−0.577
T9	−0.85540	−3.372
T10	−0.38619	−1.391
T11	−0.14505	−0.466
T12	−0.20954	−0.607
T13	−0.14890	−0.710
T14	−0.43829	−1.621
T15	−0.49780	−1.376
T16	−0.58153	−1.341

Table 8.3
(continued)

	Model 3 (Conditional on the number of claims, expected number of claims and additional risk classification variables)	
Variable	Coefficient	t-ratio
T17	−0.27998	−0.391
T18	−0.29979	−0.975
T19	−0.27616	−0.796
T20	−0.32431	−0.889
T21	−0.32216	−1.327
T22	0.12731	0.534
Driver's class		
CL7	−0.40895	−3.557
CL8	0.47235	1.319
CL9	−0.09367	−0.871
CL10	−3.31830	−0.095
CL11	0.75389	4.824
CL12	0.38643	2.935
CL13	0.19255	2.036
CL18	−0.30438	−1.702
CL19	−0.66526	−4.364
NEW	−0.17552	−1.436
AGEAUTO	0.05828	3.328
Number of observations	4,772	
Log-likelihood	−1,642.626	

However, when individuals also differ in their risk aversion, more instruments are necessary to predict insurance demand. For example, interaction variables with income and total wealth (when available) can be used to increase the number of risk classes. Here we show that the decision variables of other financial securities do not provide strong additional information when the traditional exogenous variables are introduced in an appropriate way. In other words, residual risk aversion can be captured by appropriate classes of insureds.[7]

The data correspond to a sample of French households observed in 1995. Various kinds of information are available on the characteristics of individuals and on the type and amount of assets they have in their portfolio. These assets have been grouped in four classes—liquid assets (bank accounts, short-term T-bonds, short-term mutual funds), home-buyer saving schemes (HBS), stocks and bonds, and life insur-

Table 8.4
Diversification level of portfolios studied

Number of Different Assets	Combination of Assets	Proportion (Percentage)
0		9.2
1	Liquid asset	21.6
	HBS	2.4
	Life insurance	1.5
	Stock and bond	1.1
	Total	**26.6**
2	Liquid asset + HBS	10.2
	Liquid asset + life insurance	7.7
	Liquid asset + stock and bond	7.6
	HBS + life insurance	1.2
	HBS + stock and bond	0.8
	Stock and bond + life insurance	0.5
	Total	**28.0**
3	Liquid asset + HBS + life insurance	7.5
	Liquid asset + stock and bond + life insurance	5.7
	Liquid asset + HBS + stock and bond	7.8
	HBS + stock and bond + life insurance	0.8
	Total	**22.0**
4	Liquid asset + HBS + stock and bond + life insurance	12.4

ance. The fiscal conditions governing life insurance in France explain its return and why it competes with more traditional assets. In table 8.4, we give some information on the diversification level of the portfolios studied.

We are interested in the prediction of life insurance demand. Here the application is rather different from that for automobile insurance. We do not have information on deaths or the risk variable, so the focus is on risk aversion as a source of asymmetric information. Portfolio choices should reveal information on individual risk aversion (aymmetric information) just as deductible choice should reveal individual risk. Under asymmetric information, this demand is a function of nonobservable individual risk (approximated by exogenous risk-classification variables), risk aversion, and demand for other assets. In this study, the other decision variables concern the holding of three other categories of assets (a formal description of the variables is given in appendix 8B). The exogenous variables for risk classification are age and $(age)^2$ of the head of household (to account for life-cycle effect), current income, total financial wealth, sex (reference group: man); occupation (superior, intermediate, employees, workers, retired, nonactive) (reference group: others); type of district (rural, between 2,000 and 20,000 inhabitants, between 20,000 and 100,000, more than 100,000) (reference group: Paris); education level (technical, high school, graduate and postgraduate reference group: primary); type for housing (owner, lender) (reference group: free disposal); type of household one adult and children, couple with two active people without child, couple with two active people with children, couple without activity, couple with one active person (reference group: alone). This set of variables is used to estimate logit models separately for the three different decision variables and then is reintroduced in the logit formulation for the holding of life insurance. The two logit regressions estimated for life insurance with decision variables alone and jointly with their expectations are given in table 8.5. For each model, the first column gives the estimated coefficients, and the second one gives the corresponding Wald chi-square statistics, whose critical value is about 6.3 at 99 percent.

As in the previous example, without introducing the expected decision variables, all the choice variables (liquid assets, home-buyer saving schemes, and stocks and bonds) are highly significant. But they become almost nonsignificant when their expectations are introduced. From the analysis of the first logit model, (model 4), we may get the impression of some dependence between the choices conditional on the exogenous variables, whereas this is due mainly to the omission of some cross-effects taken into account by the expected variables of the second logit specification (model 5). The substitution effects are conditional on the initial information. The coefficients of the expected variables indicate that the more risk-averse decision makers (who hold liquid assets and home-buyer saving schemes) have a higher life insurance demand than the less risk averse (who hold stocks and bonds). But as in the previous example, since these coefficients were obtained from observable variables, the result also means that there is no significant residual asymmetric information about risk aversion in the data. Finally, as in the previous example, one can show that, by appropriate use of other classification variables or by interactions

Table 8.5
Estimation of the logit model for life insurance (1 if life insurance)

Variable	Model 4 (Conditional on the decision variables only)		Model 5 (Conditional on the decision variables and their expectations)	
	Coefficient	Wald Chi-Square Statistic	Coefficient	Wald Chi-Square Statistic
Intercept	−3.0340	101.1371	−16.1711	444.8785
Age 1	0.5480	28.4901	1.4229	65.9224
Age 2	−0.0610	35.0456	−0.1121	75.2270
Income	0.0134	11.3471	−0.0070	0.8014
Total wealth	2.5625	347.0983	−0.1809	1.2095
Sex	−0.0510	0.3684	−0.5577	25.6743
Occupation 2	0.1371	1.3144	−0.6870	20.5386
Occupation 3	0.1882	3.3965	−0.4583	14.2203
Occupation 4	0.0799	0.5534	−0.0869	0.3082
Occupation 5	0.0190	0.0378	0.2588	3.1969
Occupation 6	0.2370	3.4280	−0.5786	11.6255
Occupation 7	−0.4840	13.0765	−0.5138	8.4863
District 1	0.2260	8.6343	0.0120	0.0131
District 2	0.1817	5.0111	−0.0205	0.0441
District 3	0.2946	12.0767	−0.0938	0.9024
District 4	0.3225	20.4899	0.0223	0.0783
Education 2	0.0256	0.1500	−0.0776	1.1562
Education 3	0.0725	1.0913	−0.2713	12.6975
Education 4	−0.0613	0.3656	−0.0829	0.4958
Housing 1	0.1946	3.2427	0.0815	0.5018
Housing 2	−0.0424	0.1448	0.5807	18.6138
Household type 2	−0.2743	7.9454	0.8497	41.8249
Household type 3	−0.1452	2.2975	−0.5300	19.6440
Household type 4	−0.0270	0.0610	−0.7857	33.1828
Household type 5	−0.2688	7.2596	−0.3562	10.8407
Household type 6	−0.2687	8.1108	−0.2054	3.9184
Liquid asset	0.3964	38.9024	−0.1484	4.3335
HBS	0.3599	57.4634	−0.1288	6.0106
Stock and bond	0.4665	71.8624	0.1357	5.3426
Exp. liquid asset			13.6634	645.5160
Exp. HBS			3.9539	20.0459
Exp. stock and bond			−1.8813	30.0230
Log-likelihood	−6,161.030		−5,677.380	
Number of observations	10,818		10,818	

between available ones, the expected variables will themselves cease to be significant.

Conclusion

In this chapter, we introduce the notion of conditional independence and show how it can be applied to our framework of individual choices under asymmetric information. We show that spurious conclusions can be drawn in different applications, since it is difficult to separate the information content of a decision from complicated cross-effects of initial qualitative covariates.

Two applications to insurance decisions under asymmetric information (adverse selection and potential moral hazard) are presented. In the first one, we combine the analysis of automobile-accidents distribution and deductible choice. One prediction in the literature is that high-risk individuals should choose small deductibles inside risk classes when there remains residual asymmetric information. Another prediction is that all insureds should produce less prevention inside risk classes when there remains residual asymmetric information (moral hazard). We show, however, that risk classification is sufficient to eliminate asymmetric information on risk types or actions in the automobile insurance portfolio studied. We obtain a similar conclusion for the variables used to measure risk aversion in this example.

In the second example, we consider the joint decision of holding life insurance and other financial assets. In this example, since we do not have information on individuals' risks, the asymmetric information of interest is risk aversion. Under residual asymmetric information on risk aversion for life insurance holding, the decision on other assets may reveal information on risk aversion. Those who hold positions in more risky assets should be less risk averse and hold less life insurance. But assets-decision variables are almost nonsignificant when their expectations on observable variables are introduced. There is again no strong residual asymmetric information on risk aversion in the life insurance portfolio considered.

Of course, there is (marginal) asymmetric information in these markets. The message of this chapter is that appropriate combinations of exogenous variables are sufficient to capture the asymmetric information. In other words, when appropriate observable characteristics are used, no other mechanism (such as self-selection or bonus-malus)

seems necessary. However, the expected values of the decision variables (or different cross-combinations of the observable variables)
should be used to take into account nonlinearity between variables.

Acknowledgments

Comments by P. A. Chiappori, Pierre-Yves Geoffard, a referee, and
participants at the meetings of the Twenty-fourth Seminar of the European Group of Risk and Insurance Economists (Paris), the Delta-Thema
seminar on insurance economics in Paris, the Société Canadienne de
Science Économique (Montreal), the CESifo Workshop (San Servolo),
and department seminars at University of Toronto, University of Min-
nesota, Université du Québec à Montréal, Harvard University, and
Hautes Etudes Commerciales Montreal are acknowledged. This research was financed by the Fédération Française des Sociétés d'Assur-
ances, Social Sciences and Humanities Research Council, Centre de
recherche en économie et en statistique, Fonds pour la formation de
Chercheurs et l'Aide à la Recherche Quebec, and the Canada Research
Chair in Risk Management at HEC Montreal. Claire Boisvert improved
significantly the presentation of the article.

Appendixes

Appendix 8A: Definition of Variables for Automobile Insurance Example

AGE	Age of the principal driver.
SEXF	Dummy variable equal to 1 if the principal driver is a female.
MARRIED	Dummy variable equal to 1 if the principal driver of the car is married.
Z	Dummy variable equal to 1 if the deductible is $500 (equal to 0 for a $250 deductible).
T1 to T22	Group of twenty-two dummy variables for territories. The reference territory T1 is the center of the island of Montreal.
G8 to G15	Group of eight dummy variables representing the tariff group of the car used. The higher the actual market value of the car, the higher the group. G8 is the reference group.
CL4 to CL19	Driver's classes, according to age, sex, marital status, use of the car, and annual mileage. The reference class is 4.
NEW	Dummy variable equal to 1 for insured entering the insurer's portfolio.

YMALE	Dummy variable equal to 1, if there is a declared occasional young male driver in the household.
AGEAUTO	Age of the car in years.
N (acc)	Observed number of claims (for accidents where the loss is greater than $500) (range 0 to 3).
E (acc)	Expected number of claims obtained from the negative binomial regression estimates.
GD	Marginal price (rebate) for switching from the $250 to the $500 deductible. This amount is negative and comes from the insurer's tariff book.
W1 to W5	Chosen limit of liability insurance. W1 is the reference limit.
Alpha	Overdispersion parameter of the negative binomial distribution.

Appendix 8B: Definition of Variables in the Life Insurance Example

Age 1	Age of the head of household.
Age 2	$(\text{Age } 1)^2$.
Sex	Dummy variable equal to 1 if a female.
Income	Current income of the household.
Total Wealth	Total financial wealth of the household.
Occupation 1 to Occupation 7	Group of seven dummy variables for the occupation of the head of the household. The reference group (Occupation 1) is for others.
District 1 to District 5	Dummy variables for geographical areas defined by population, Paris (District 5) is the omitted category.
Education 1 to Education 4	Four classes of education. Primary school (Education 1) is the omitted class.
Housing 1 to Housing 3	Dummy variables for the type of housing. Free disposal (Housing 3) is the omitted category.
Household 1 to Household 6	Dummy variables for the type of household. The omitted category (Household type 1) is for an adult alone.

Appendix 8C: Negative Binomial on Automobile Accidents

Variable	Coefficient	t-ratio
Intercept	−1.86280	−6.832
SEXF	−0.27216	−2.294
MARRIED	0.11436	0.959
AGE	−4.47E-03	−0.763
NEW	0.31644	2.871
Group of vehicles		
G9	−4.58E-02	−0.381
G10	−1.78E-03	−0.011

G11	0.12375	0.447
G12	0.27727	0.833
G13	0.60915	1.708
G14	−7.47E-02	−0.112
G15	6.26E-02	0.078
Territory		
T2	−0.36545	−0.748
T3	−0.28546	−0.973
T4	−0.75719	−2.406
T5	−6.77E-02	−0.279
T6	−0.51594	−1.412
T7	−0.37108	−1.787
T8	−0.94753	−1.888
T9	−0.19458	−0.632
T10	1.32E-02	0.033
T11	−0.76729	−2.989
T12	−0.72699	−1.431
T13	−0.18672	−0.551
T14	−0.57162	−2.386
T15	0.22855	0.552
T16	−0.95952	−1.430
T17	0.47768	0.861
T18	−0.63773	−1.776
T19	−0.96049	−3.068
T20	−0.96003	−2.694
T21	−0.44106	−1.641
T22	−0.47611	−1.916
Alpha	0.36905	1.299
Number of observations	4,772	
Log-likelihood	−1,515.045	

Notes

1. On the combined demand for liability insurance and portfolio assets, see, for example, Mayers and Smith (1983). On insurance decisions in the presence of adverse selection with different risk-averse individuals, see Dionne, Doherty, and Fombaron (2000). On moral hazard, see Winter (2000).

2. The presentation can be extended to the case of discrete variables. In fact, in one application, Y is a count variable.

3. The previous expansion shows that the conditional distribution of Y and X may be derived simply by instrumenting the endogenous decision variables inside the scoring function. This result is valid only locally (for $c \simeq 0$), and such a practice will lead in

general to a misspecified formulation for $P[Y = 1/X]$ and to inconsistent estimators of the c parameters (see Pagan, 1984).

4. As in Puelz and Snow (1994), we did not consider the claims between $250 and $500 since they are not observable for those who choose the higher deductible.

5. Our second-step regression (deductible choice) contains a stochastic regressor, $E(acc)$. It is well known that such a two-step procedure will yield consistent estimates of the coefficients. However, the second-step estimation of standard errors based on this procedure will generally be biased. Murphy and Topel (1985) proposed a general correction to the estimated variance matrix to correct standard errors in two-step estimation. The application of the proposed correction (Murphy and Topel, 1985, p. 377) did not change our results: significant (nonsignificant) coefficients remain the same.

6. We did also estimate a model with $N(acc)$ only and with more classification variables than in model 1. Again, $N(acc)$ became nonsignificant.

7. Here the residual adverse selection on risk types cannot be studied since we do not have access to the data on accidents.

References

Abbring, J., P. A. Chiappori, and J. Pinquet. (2003). "Moral Hazard and Dynamic Insurance Data." *Journal of the European Economic Association* 1: 767–820.

Arrow, K. J. (1963). "Uncertainty and the Welfare Economics of Medical Care." *American Economic Review* 53: 941–969.

Chassagnon, A., and P. A. Chiappori. (1996). "Insurance under Moral Hazard and Adverse Selection: The Case of Pure Competition." Working Paper 28, DELTA.

Chiappori, P. A. (2000). "Econometric Models of Insurance under Asymmetric Information." In G. Dionne (Ed.), *Handbook of Insurance* (pp. 365–393). Boston: Kluwer.

Chiappori, P. A., B. Jullien, B. Salanié, and F. Salanié. (2004). "Asymmetric Information in Insurance: General Testable Implications." Working Paper, University of Chicago, CREST and Université de Toulouse. Forthcoming in *Rand Journal of Economics*.

Chiappori, P. A., and B. Salanié. (1997). "Empirical Contract Theory: The Case of Insurance Data." *European Economic Review* 41: 943–950.

Chiappori, P. A., and B. Salanié. (2000). "Testing for Asymmetric Information in Insurance Markets." *Journal of Political Economy* 108: 56–78.

Chiappori, P. A., and B. Salanié. (2003). "Testing Contract Theory: A Survey of Some Recent Work." In M. Dewatripont, L. P. Hansen, and S. J. Turnovsky (Eds.), *Advances in Economics and Econometrics, Theory and Applications, Eighth World Congress of the Econometric Society* (vol. 1, pp. 115–149).

Crocker, K. J., and A. Snow. (1986). "The Efficiency Effects of Categorical Discrimination in the Insurance Industry." *Journal of Political Economy* 94: 321–344.

Crocker, K. J., and A. Snow. (2000). "The Theory of Risk Classification." In G. Dionne (Ed.), *Handbook of Insurance* (pp. 245–276). Boston: Kluwer.

Dionne, G., and N. Doherty. (1994). "Adverse Selection, Commitment, and Renegotiation: Extension to and Evidence from Insurance Markets." *Journal of Political Economy* 102: 209–233.

Dionne, G., N. Doherty, and N. Fombaron. (2000). "Adverse Selection in Insurance Markets." In G. Dionne (Ed.), *Handbook of Insurance* (pp. 185–243). Boston: Kluwer.

Dionne, G., and R. Gagné. (2001). "Replacement Cost Endorsement and Opportunistic Fraud in Automobile Insurance." *Journal of Risk and Uncertainty* 24: 213–230.

Dionne, G., R. Gagné, F. Gagnon, and C. Vanasse. (1997). "Debt, Moral Hazard and Airline Safety: An Empirical Evidence." *Journal of Econometrics* 79: 379–402.

Dionne, G., C. Gouriéroux, and C. Vanasse. (1998). "Evidence of Adverse Selection in Automobile Insurance Markets." In G. Dionne and C. L. Nadeau (Eds.), *Automobile Insurance* (pp. 13–46). Boston: Kluwer.

Dionne, G., C. Gouriéroux, and C. Vanasse. (2001). "Testing for Evidence of Adverse Selection in the Automobile Insurance Market: A Comment." *Journal of Political Economy* 109(2): 444–453.

Dionne, G., P. C. Michaud, and M. Dahchour. (2004). "Separating Moral Hazard from Adverse Selection in Automobile Insurance: Longitudinal Evidence from France." Working Paper 04-05, Canada Research Chair in Risk Management, HEC Montreal.

Dionne, G., and C. Vanasse. (1992). "Automobile Insurance Ratemaking in the Presence of Asymmetrical Information." *Journal of Applied Econometrics* 7: 149–165.

Godfrey, L. G. (1988). *Misspecification Tests in Econometrics: The Lagrange Multiplier Principle and Other Approach.* Cambridge: Cambridge University Press.

Gouriéroux, C. (1999). "The Econometrics of Risk Classification in Insurance." *Geneva Papers on Risk and Insurance Theory* 24: 119–139.

Gouriéroux, C., and A. Monfort. (1995). *Statistics and Econometric Models* (vol. 2, pp. 458–475). Cambridge: Cambridge University Press.

Gouriéroux, C., A. Monfort, and A. Trognon. (1984). "Pseudo Maximum Likelihood Methods: Application to Poisson Models." *Econometrica* 52: 701–721.

Gouriéroux, C., A. Tiomo, and A. Trognon. (1996). "The Portfolio Composition of Households: Some Evidence from French Data." CREST.

Hamburger, M. J. (1968). "Household Demand for Financial Assets." *Econometrica* 56: 97–118.

King, M., and J. Leape. (1984). "Wealth and Portfolio Composition: Theory and Evidence." Working Paper NBER 2468.

Lemaire, J. (1995). *Bonus-Malus Systems in Automobile Insurance.* Boston: Kluwer.

Linton, O. B., and P. Gonzalo. (1995). "A Non-Parametric Test of Conditional Independence." Discussion Paper 1106, Cowles Foundation, Yale University.

Markowitz, H. (1992). *Portfolio Selection: Efficient Diversification of Investment.* 2nd ed. New York: Wiley.

Mayers, D., and C. W. Smith. (1983). "The Interdependence of Individual Portfolio Decisions and the Demand for Insurance." *Journal of Political Economy* 91: 304–311.

McFadden, D. (1973). *Conditional Logit Analysis of Qualitative Choice Behavior.* In P. Zarembka (Ed.), *Frontiers in Econometrics.* New York: Academic Press.

Müller, M., and B. Rönz. (1999). "Credit Scoring Using Semi-parametric Methods." Working Paper, Humboldt University, Berlin.

Murphy, K. M., and R. H., Topel. (1985). "Estimation and Inference in Two-Step Econometric Models." *Journal of Business and Economic Statistics* 3: 370–379.

Newhouse, J. P. et al. (1987). "Health Economics and Econometrics." *American Economic Review* 77: 269–274.

Pagan, A. (1984). "Econometric Issues in the Analysis of Regressions with Generated Regressors." *International Economic Review* 25: 221–247.

Pinquet, J. (2000). "Experience Rating for Heterogeneous Models." In G. Dionne (Ed.), *Handbook of Insurance* (pp. 459–500). Boston: Kluwer.

Puelz, R., and A. Snow. (1994). "Evidence on Adverse Selection: Equilibrium Signaling and Cross-Subsidization in the Insurance Market." *Journal of Political Economy* 102: 236–257.

Ramsey, J. (1969). "Test for Specification Errors in Classical Linear Least-Squares Regression Analysis." *Journal of the Royal Statistical Society* B, 31: 350–371.

Robinson, P. M. (1988). "Root-N-Consistent Semiparametric Regression." *Econometrica* 56: 931–954.

Rothschild, M., and J. Stiglitz. (1976). "Equilibrium in Competitive Insurance Markets: An Essay on the Economics of Imperfect Information." *Quarterly Journal of Economics* 90: 629–649.

Shorrocks, A. (1982). "The Composition of Asset Holdings in the United Kingdom." *Economic Journal* 92: 268–284.

Villeneuve, B. (2000). "Life Insurance." In G. Dionne (Ed.), *Handbook of Insurance* (pp. 901–931). Boston: Kluwer.

Wilson, C. A. (1977). "A Model of Insurance Markets with Incomplete Information." *Journal of Economic Theory* 16: 167–207.

Winter, R. (2000). "Moral Hazard in Insurance Markets." In G. Dionne (Ed.), *Handbook of Insurance* (pp. 155–183). Boston: Kluwer.

9

Rethinking the Sources of Adverse Selection in the Annuity Market

Irena Dushi and Anthony Webb

Introduction

Annuities are actuarially unfair to the general population in the sense that their expected present value to someone with population average mortality is less than the premium paid.[1] This is partly due to the costs that insurance companies face in providing annuities but also reflects the fact that annuitants have considerably lower mortality than the population as a whole. Although previous research has shown that the longevity insurance provided by annuities will be valuable to a risk-averse household facing an uncertain lifespan, only a very small part of the population voluntarily annuitizes.

One plausible explanation for the lower mortality of annuitants and the low rate of voluntary annuitization is that people take private mortality information into account when deciding whether to annuitize. If low-mortality people are more likely to purchase annuities, the cost of annuities will increase, further discouraging higher-mortality people from annuitizing and resulting in an equilibrium in which only those with exceptionally low mortality choose to annuitize.

In this chapter, we show that although there is evidence that information asymmetries contribute to the low mortality of annuitants and the small size of the voluntary annuity market, there is another equally important factor. This is that the high proportions of preannuitized wealth held by poorer and on average higher-mortality households lead them to place such a low value on the longevity insurance provided by annuities that they will find annuitization unattractive over a wide range of subjective mortality beliefs. Even when poorer households do annuitize, they may also annuitize smaller dollar amounts than the rich. In other words, the lower mortality of annuitants may be the result not only of traditional adverse selection arising out of asymmetric mortality information but also of passive selection in which an unobservable factor (wealth) affects both preferences and outcomes.

For plausible preference parameters, the proportion of the household's wealth that is held in preannuitized form is an important determinant of the value of annuitization. Under constant relative risk aversion, households with larger proportions of preannuitized wealth will value annuitization less highly. Dushi and Webb (2004) show that preannuitized wealth in the form of social security and employer pensions constitutes the majority of the nonhousing wealth of all but the wealthiest households. In contrast, the wealthy have much smaller proportions of preannuitized wealth. Dushi and Webb also show that at prevailing levels of actuarial unfairness, the proportion of preannuitized wealth held by the average household is, under plausible preference assumptions, and over a wide range of subjective mortality beliefs, sufficiently large to deter that household from ever annuitizing any of its unannuitized wealth.

We extend the above analysis and calculate that at prevailing degrees of actuarial unfairness, and assuming that the household believes it has population average mortality, the average proportion of preannuitized wealth of households in all but the top one or two wealth deciles is sufficiently high to deter annuitization. In fact, it is so high that households in all except the top one or two wealth deciles would, under plausible preference assumptions, generally decline even an actuarially fair annuity, subject only to a deduction for typical insurance company administrative expenses. We also show that most households in the bottom half of the wealth distribution, who typically have higher than average mortality, will decline annuitization if for no other reason than that they lack any significant amounts of annuitizable wealth.

On the other hand, we calculate that households with the average proportion of preannuitized wealth found in the top one or two wealth deciles will find annuitization worthwhile over quite a wide range of mortality beliefs. If these wealthy households have lower than average mortality, the annuity market may therefore be subject to passive selection on the basis of wealth.

We analyze the Asset and Health Dynamics Among the Oldest Old (AHEAD) panel of individuals born before 1924. We find that, in accordance with the predictions of our simulations, voluntary annuitization is concentrated among households in the top wealth deciles.

This correlation between wealth and voluntary annuitization may be the result not of wealth-related differences in tastes for annuitization but the fact that annuities usually offers the wealthy a higher "money's worth" as a result of their lower mortality.[2] But the calculations referred to above strongly suggest that private mortality information is not the deciding factor for most households.

This is not to say that information asymmetries contribute nothing to the actuarial unfairness of annuities. We place a lower bound on the impact of private mortality information on annuity prices by comparing annuitant mortality with the mortality of similarly wealthy nonannuitants. One way of doing this would be to compare the mortality rates of AHEAD annuitants with those of nonannuitants, controlling for wealth. There are relatively few annuitants in the AHEAD panel, and as a result, statistical tests of the relationship between mortality and annuitization lack power. We therefore adopt an alternative approach—namely, to calculate whether annuitant mortality, derived from annuitant life tables, is lower than that of the AHEAD sample, weighted to reflect the wealth deciles from which annuitants are drawn. We find that annuitant mortality is still significantly lower. Even if none of the relationship between wealth and annuitization is the result of the correlation between wealth and subjective mortality beliefs, then somewhat less than half of the difference between annuitant and nonannuitant mortality still results from the use of private mortality information.

In the United Kingdom, some insurance companies are experimenting with annuity underwriting on the basis of post code, a good predictor of wealth. Our calculations suggest that this may prove to be only a partial solution to the problem of adverse selection.

Identifying the sources of adverse selection in the annuity market has important policy implications. Friedberg and Webb (2005) show that in coming decades the proportion of household wealth that is preannuitized will decline considerably, not only among the wealthy who are currently most likely to annuitize but also in lower wealth deciles, as unannuitized defined contribution pension plans displace annuitized defined benefit plans. If the proportion of preannuitized wealth is a significant determinant of the annuitization decision, there may be an increase in annuitization among lower-wealth individuals who have higher average mortality. This may reduce the degree of actuarial unfairness of annuities. The likely magnitude of this change needs to be considered when evaluating calculations of the benefits that might be obtained from mandatory annuitization (for example, those of Brown, 2003).

The remainder of this chapter is organized as follows. We high-light some important features of the United States annuity market and discuss previous research, our methodology, our findings, and our conclusions.

The Annuity Market and Previous Research

Characteristics of the Annuity Market

Many features of the annuity market have been extensively docu-mented in previous research, including Poterba (2001) and Mitchell, Poterba, Warshawsky, and Brown (1999). More recent evidence con-firms earlier findings that voluntary annuitization is quite uncommon. The National Association for Variable Annuities (2002a) reports that immediate annuity sales were only $10.2 billion in 2001.[3] Brown and Poterba (2000) point out that approximately half of all immediate an-nuity sales are period certain rather than life-contingent, so we esti-mate sales of immediate life-contingent annuities at about $5.1 billion in 2001. We calculate that this amounts to only about $2,500 per person turning sixty-five in that year. This situation is not unique to the United States. A review by Impavido, Thorburn, and Wadsworth (2004) shows that rates of voluntary annuitization are extremely low in all the countries they studied.

Although voluntary annuitization is rare, annuitized wealth forms a large part, in most cases the majority, of the total financial wealth of households entering retirement. This is because the average household owns considerable amounts of compulsorily annuitized wealth through Social Security and employer pensions. Dushi and Webb (2004) con-struct balance sheets for Health and Retirement Study (HRS) house-holds turning sixty-five between 1994 and 2000, including housing wealth and the expected present value (EPV) of employer pensions and Social Security.[4] The mean total nonhousing wealth of the median 20 percent of married couples amounts to $513,525 in 2000 dollars. So-cial Security comprises $266,301 of this, and defined benefit pensions a further $145,050. Compulsorily annuitized wealth comprises 65 per-cent of total wealth and 82 percent of financial wealth. It is only in the top decile that mean preannuitized wealth falls to 49 percent of total fi-nancial wealth. We show that these high proportions of compulsorily annuitized wealth may contribute to the lack of demand for voluntary annuitization.

One feature of the voluntary annuity market that has received little comment is the almost total absence of underwriting prior to the issue of an annuity. In most insurance markets, insurers attempt to quantify the risk they face and relate premiums and policy terms to the perceived risk. Life insurance underwriters usually require detailed information about an individual's health before issuing policies for any significant amount and will frequently also require a medical examination.

In contrast, except for a small but growing market in "impaired life annuities," insurers underwrite annuities on the basis of age and gender alone and, for some annuity types, are even legally required to offer unisex rates.[5] A possible explanation for the lack of underwriting may be that insurers use policy terms to sort households according to risk, anticipating that individuals will use private information not only to decide whether or not to purchase insurance but also to choose a contract type.

Finkelstein and Poterba (2004) analyze data from the U.K. annuity market. They find evidence of the predicted relationship between policy characteristics and ex post mortality and also evidence that pricing reflects the effects of self-selection. The U.K. market offers level, increasing, and index-linked annuities, and annuities are also available with guarantee periods of various lengths. A greater proportion of the return on increasing and index-linked policies is conditional on surviving to collect the backloaded payments. Individuals with high expected mortality will obtain a higher EPV from guaranteed policies and low-mortality people a higher EPV from increasing and index-linked policies. The authors find that individuals who buy escalating annuities have lower mortality than those who buy level annuities and also that escalating annuities are more actuarially unfair than level annuities to someone with population average mortality.

This relationship may not necessarily be the result of individuals making use of private mortality information when selecting a contract type. An alternative explanation for the observed pattern of actuarial unfairness is that those with greater wealth and, on average, lower mortality can afford the immediate loss in income imposed by a joint life annuity and that selection is taking place on the basis of wealth rather than on the basis of private mortality information. Evidence in support of this interpretation of Finkelstein and Poterba's results is the finding of Johnson, Uccello, and Goldwyn (2005) that wealth is an important determinant of whether married individuals choose single or joint life annuities, a choice that involves a similar tradeoff between current and future income.

The Extent of Actuarial Unfairness in the Annuity Market

The actuarial unfairness of annuities is partly the result of the production costs that insurance companies face. A measure of the magnitude of these costs is the EPV of an annuity to someone with annuitant mortality. Mitchell et al. (1999) calculated that in 1995 the average after tax EPV of an annuity to a sixty-five-year-old couple with annuitant mortality equaled 84.1 percent when the income stream was discounted at the corporate bond rate of interest and 92.9 percent when the treasury strip term structure of interest rates was used. Thus, costs would appear to be in the order of 7.1 to 15.9 percent.

But individuals who invest in the bond market will also incur management charges if they invest through a mutual fund, although they can eliminate all charges, except broker's fees, by direct purchase of individual bonds. A proper comparison of the costs of annuitized with those of unannuitized investments should take account of such charges. According to Vanguard, the average long-term bond fund had an expense ratio of 102 basis points in 2003, but funds were also available with charges as low as 20 basis points. We calculate that for a married couple, ages sixty-five and sixty-two, these charges correspond to 2.0 and 10.1 percent in expected present value terms. If we believe it is more appropriate to discount annuities at the corporate bond interest rate than at the treasury strip rate, then a comparison of annuity and bond fund expense ratios suggests that annuitization results in additional costs of 5.8 to 13.9 percent.

The Extent of Adverse Selection in the Annuity Market

The standard test for adverse selection in insurance markets involves examining whether there is a positive correlation between insurance coverage and risk occurrence, conditional on information available to the insurer.[6] Risk occurrence in the context of annuities means realized mortality that the literature quantifies as EPV. One would therefore test for adverse selection by comparing the EPV of an annuity to someone with mortality equal to that of the average annuitant with its EPV to someone with population average mortality. This test has two important limitations.

First, it is not an accurate measure of the impact of adverse selection on the price faced by potential purchasers, defined as those who would wish to purchase insurance under conditions of symmetric information. We show many high-mortality households would not enter the annuity market even if offered a price that was, for them, actuarially fair, subject only to a deduction for insurance company administrative expenses. Many high-mortality households have no annuitizable wealth and are therefore clearly not going to participate in the market.[7] For plausible utility functions, the value of annuitization depends on the proportion of preannuitized wealth. We show that many other high-mortality households have such high proportions of preannuitized wealth that they would similarly not wish to annuitize, even under symmetric information. Even among the remaining households that would wish to annuitize under symmetric information, there is a likely negative correlation between mortality and the amounts they would wish to annuitize, so that the average degree of actuarial unfairness they face, weighted by the amounts they would wish to annuitize, is less than the unweighted average.

Second, the lack of correlation does not guarantee the absence of adverse selection, as there may be multiple forms of private information operating in different directions. For example, Finkelstein and McGarry (2003) find that after controlling for the insurance company's risk classification, an individual's assessment of his risk of requiring long-term care is a statistically significant predictor of subsequent nursing home use. On the other hand, they find no evidence of a correlation between long-term care insurance coverage and nursing home use and conclude that risk aversion, a characteristic not observable by the insurer, leads people to be more likely to purchase long-term care insurance but less likely to actually require care.[8]

Prior literature has identified a significant mortality difference between annuitants and the general population when that difference is quantified in EPV terms. Friedman and Warshawsky (1988) calculated that for 1983, the latest year they analyzed, the difference in EPVs for sixty-five-year-old males amounted to 8 percent when the income streams were discounted at the yield on twenty-year U.S. government bonds and 7 percent when the income streams were discounted at the average yield on corporate bonds held by insurance companies.

Mitchell et al. (1999) updated and extended the analysis using 1995 data. They calculated survival probabilities by first interpolating between the 1983 table A annuitant mortality table and the Annuity 2000 basic life table.[9] As these are period tables, they made an actuarial adjustment to create a series of annuitant cohort tables.[10] They assumed that premiums equaled the average of those charged by 100 major insurance companies. The difference in EPVs amounted to 10 percent when they discounted the income streams at the treasury strip interest rate and 8 percent when they used the corporate-bond interest rate, broadly consistent with the findings of ten years earlier.

The Relationship between Wealth and Mortality
There is a substantial body of literature that demonstrates a strong relationship between wealth and mortality risk. Menchik (1993) found a nonlinear realtionship, with individuals in the bottom quintile having much higher mortality than the remainder of the sample.

Attanasio and Hoynes (2000) also found that wealthier individuals have substantially lower mortality rates. Among households with heads aged eighty or more, mortality in the bottom wealth quartile was almost three times that in the top quartile.

Hurd, McFadden, and Merrill (2001) analyzed the AHEAD panel. They found a strong relationship between mortality and wealth quartile among those aged seventy to seventy-four. The relationship was weaker at older ages, although mortality was, except among the small number aged ninety plus, always highest among those in the lowest wealth quartile. Disney, Johnson, and Stears (1999) and Attanasio and Emmerson (2003) found similar relationships in the United Kingdom.

With the exception of Menchik (1993), whose data are old and who does not provide annual survival probabilities, all of the above research conditions on current or recent wealth rather than on initial wealth. Current wealth is certainly not exogenous, and its use also introduces survivor bias as Attanasio and Hoynes noted. However, the construction of annual survival probabilities for each percentile of initial wealth ideally requires an extremely long panel data set, one that will only gradually become available as the HRS cohort ages.

To summarize, the above research shows that wealthy households, who we know have, on average, much smaller proportions of pre-annuitized wealth, also have much lower mortality.

The Money's Worth of Individual Annuities
In the first of a series of papers, Mitchell et al. (1999) used numerical optimization to calculate a utility-based measure of the wealth equiva-

lent of an annuity. They defined the wealth equivalent as the expected present value of the annuity at which an individual would be indifferent between immediately annuitizing all his unannuitized assets and continuing to hold those assets in unannuitized form. If the individual chooses not to annuitize, then he is assumed to choose the asset decumulation path that maximizes his expected discounted lifetime utility. In the absence of other considerations, such as a desire to retain liquidity or a bequest motive, individuals should annuitize if and only if the EPV of the annuity, based on their subjective assessment of their survival probabilities, exceeds the wealth equivalent.

Assuming a real interest rate of 3 percent, an inflation rate of 3.2 percent, a rate of time preference of 1 percent, a coefficient of risk aversion equal to 1, and no bequest motive or preexisting annuities, they calculated the before tax wealth equivalent of a nominal annuity to be 0.659 for a single male with population mortality. At a coefficient of 2, the wealth equivalent fell to 0.619. If the individual held half his wealth in the form of a preexisting real annuity, the wealth equivalents increased to 0.730 and 0.695 under the same assumptions, resulting in a corresponding reduction in the value of annuitization. As the expected present value of an annuity typically exceeds its wealth equivalent, many individuals would appear, at the assumed proportion of preannuitized wealth, to be able to increase their expected utility by annuitizing their unannuitized wealth.

Longevity risk pooling causes married couples to value annuitization less highly than otherwise similar single individuals, particularly if much of the household's consumption is joint. Brown and Poterba (2000) extended the previous analysis to married couples considering the purchase of a joint life and survivor annuity, again assuming that either none or 50 percent of the household's wealth was preannuitized. They calculated "annuity equivalent wealth," the premium over expected present value at which a household would be indifferent between retaining and surrendering the right to purchase an actuarially fair annuity. When there are no preexisting annuities, annuity equivalent wealth is simply the reciprocal of the wealth equivalent. With preexisting annuities, this simple relationship breaks down.

Brown and Poterba calculated that annuity equivalent wealth for a sixty-five-year-old single man was 1.576, assuming population mortality, no preexisting annuities, a coefficient of risk aversion of 2, a rate of time preference and a real rate of interest both of 3 percent, and a rate of inflation of 3.2 percent. When none of the household's consumption is joint, they calculated the annuity equivalent wealth of a joint life and 50 percent survivor annuity to be 1.244 under the same assumptions. Marriage decreases the value of annuitization by 58 percent. When the coefficient of risk aversion equals 10, their comparable figures are 1.703, 1.407, and 42 percent.

As in the case of the single individual, preannuitized wealth reduces the value of further annuitization. When half the household's wealth is preannuitized, annuity equivalent wealth is 1.405 for a sixty-five-year-old single male, assuming a coefficient of risk aversion of 2. The comparable figure for a married couple is 1.153, a reduction of 63 percent.

This literature suggests the existence of an "annuity puzzle." One might not expect annuitization to be universal, but it is nonetheless puzzling that it is quite so uncommon. All of the above papers compared annuitizing at a fixed age, usually sixty-five, with the alternative of never annuitizing. If there are advantages to postponing annuitization, annuitizing at the optimal age will be even more valuable.

However, the papers invariably assumed that either none or one-half of the household's wealth was preannuitized. As we show, the annuity puzzle is much less of a puzzle when one incorporates actual and much higher proportions of preannuitized wealth. We emphasize that our findings hold only for the current cohort of retirees. The displacement of annuitized defined benefit by unannuitized defined contribution pension plans may substantially increase the value of annuitization for subsequent birth cohorts.

Methodology

We use numerical optimization techniques first applied in Dushi and Webb (2004) to calculate optimal annuitization strategies from age sixty-five onward for typical HRS households in each wealth decile. We show that the annuitization of unannuitized financial wealth will be attractive to households in the top one or two wealth deciles over a wide range of preferences and subjective mortality beliefs but that it will be attractive only to households in lower wealth deciles under quite restrictive assumptions.[11] In other words, there is no "annuity puzzle" over most of the wealth distribution, and most households in most wealth deciles appear to be behaving rationally when they choose not to annuitize.

We then use the model to demonstrate that, except in the top one or two wealth deciles, the proportion of wealth that is held in preannuitized form through employer pensions and social security is, given plausible assumptions regarding the level of insurance company administrative costs, sufficiently high to deter further voluntary annuitization, even if the household and the insurance company held symmetric mortality beliefs.

We then analyze the pattern of voluntary annuitization in the AHEAD and show that, as predicted by our simulations, annuitization is concentrated among the wealthiest households. As explained previously, wealth is likely to be correlated with private mortality beliefs, and the relationship between wealth and annuitization might reflect not only the direct impact of wealth on the value of annuitization but also the relationship between wealth and subjective mortality beliefs. We claim that the latter relationship is unlikely to have a significant effect because our simulations show that households in these lower wealth deciles would have to believe that they had exceptionally low mortality—about half the population average at age sixty-five—to make annuitization worthwhile.

We then investigate the relationship between wealth and mortality among the AHEAD households. Previous analyses that used measures of wealth that excluded employer pensions and social security showed a strong relationship. Our analyses show that the relationship continues to hold when one uses a broader measure that includes the expected present value of annuitized wealth.

We then consider whether annuitants have lower mortality than other similarly wealthy individuals—in other words, whether after controlling for the impact of both wealth and correlates with wealth on the annuitization decision, there is evidence of selection on the basis of private mortality information. One approach to answering this question would be to analyze the AHEAD mortality data to see whether, after controlling for wealth, AHEAD annuitants had lower mortality than nonannuitants. The problem with this approach is that because there are so few annuitants in the AHEAD, tests of the statistical significance of the annuitant coefficient lack power. We therefore adopt an alternative approach—namely, to test whether annuitant mortality is any lower than the average mortality of individuals in the wealth deciles from which annuitants are drawn. We compare annuitant mortality, as predicted by annuitant life tables, with the average mortality of individuals in the AHEAD, weighted by the probability that an individual in a particular wealth decile is an annuitant.

Calculating Optimal Annuitization Strategies

We apply the numerical optimization technique used in Dushi and Webb (2004) to calculate optimal annuitization strategies for households in various wealth deciles and to explore how the household's subjective mortality beliefs and degree of risk aversion might affect its strategy. In the papers considered in the previous section, the household was constrained to choose between annuitizing all of its unannuitized wealth at retirement and undertaking an optimal decumulation of its unannuitized wealth. In contrast, Dushi and Webb make the more realistic assumptions that the household can choose to annuitize only part of its wealth, that it can annuitize at any age, and that it can return to the annuity market as many times as it wishes. They retain the assumption that the decision to purchase an annuity is irreversible. Although annuities can be resold, the terms offered are quite unfavorable. In both Dushi and Webb and previous models, the financial asset is risk-free, households do not update their mortality beliefs, and the household does not suffer consumption shocks, and as a result, the household would never wish to commute its annuities on the same or less favorable terms than those on which they were purchased.

Dushi and Webb follow previous research by assuming the following constant relative risk aversion utility function:

$$U_m(C_t^m, C_t^f) = \frac{(C_t^m + \lambda C_t^f)^{1-\gamma}}{1-\gamma}, \quad U_f(C_t^f, C_t^m) = \frac{(C_t^f + \lambda C_t^m)^{1-\gamma}}{1-\gamma}, \quad (9.1)$$

where λ measures the jointness of consumption; C_t^m, C_t^f denote the consumption of the husband and wife at time t; and γ is the coefficient of risk aversion. When λ equals 1, all consumption is joint. When λ equals zero, none of the household's consumption is joint. The real rate of interest and the rate of time preference are both assumed to be equal to 3 percent. The annuity is priced by reference to the ages of the members of the household, the real rate of interest, and an expense load that is assumed not to vary with age. Dushi and Webb present evidence to justify the realism of this last assumption. They assume that the expense load is the average of the age sixty-five and age seventy-five values calculated by Mitchell, Poterba, Warshawsky, and Brown (1999). The simulation starts at age sixty-five, and in the case of married couples, the wife is assumed to be three years younger than the husband, the average age difference for this cohort.

Under constant relative risk-aversion, the optimal annuitization strategy is invariant to scaling parameters. We assume that the household had a real annuity equal to $18,000 a year, reducing to $12,000 on the death of either spouse, the survivor benefit corresponding to that payable under Social Security when the wife's pension is payable by reason of her husband's contributions. We then endow the household with an amount of unannuitized wealth such that the present value of the household's real annuity equals the appropriate percentage of the household's total wealth. For example, the present value of the real annuity referred to above is approximately $280,000 for a household with population average mortality, so if the mean proportion of preannuitized wealth of households in a particular wealth decile was 50 percent, we would endow the household with $280,000 of unannuitized wealth to obtain the required percentage.

A household's optimal annuitization strategy will also depend on its subjective mortality beliefs. Although it may be not only reasonable but also consistent with rational expectations to assume that the average household has population average mortality, it is less clear as to how one should model the subjective mortality beliefs of average households at other points on the wealth distribution.

One would ideally wish to calculate the distribution of subjective mortality beliefs held by households in each wealth decile. Although the HRS and the AHEAD contain data on subjective survival probabilities—individuals are asked to estimate their probabilities of living to certain ages—it is not clear how one should convert these responses into subjective mortality tables. Gan, Hurd, and McFadden (2005) propose a methodology, but their approach is difficult to apply because the four different and equally plausible sets of assumptions that they consider each produce quite different subjective mortality tables. We therefore consider two alternative assumptions—that households in each wealth decile believe they have either population average or annuitant mortality. For population mortality, we use Social Security Administration life tables for the 1930 male and 1933 female birth cohorts. For annuitant mortality, we follow Mitchell et al. (1999) by first interpolating the 1983 and 2000 annuitant life tables referred to previously and then converting the resulting period table into a cohort table.

As annuitants tend to be drawn from the top wealth deciles, a reasonable hypothesis might be that if annuitants are randomly drawn from these wealth deciles, then households in these wealth deciles believe, on average, that they have annuitant mortality. If, on the other hand, there is selection on the basis of private mortality information, then the average household in these wealth deciles probably believes that it has something in between population and annuitant mortality. The average household in the bottom deciles probably believes it has something worse than population mortality, so if annuitization is unattractive to households in these wealth deciles given population mortality, it will be even more unattractive given their actual beliefs.

Assuming annuitant mortality is equivalent to assuming that the household and the insurer symmetrically believe that the household has mortality equal to that of our adjusted annuitant life table. The results would however differ slightly if we assumed that the individual and the insurer symmetrically held some other beliefs—for example, that the individual had population mortality. The differences are not significant, and we therefore report only annuitant mortality results.

Patterns of Annuitization in the HRS and AHEAD
Our objective is to identify those individuals in the AHEAD who have voluntarily purchased immediate annuities, whether fixed or variable, qualifying or nonqualifying, and to calculate their distribution by wealth decile.[12] We calculate the total wealth of each AHEAD household in 1993, inclusive of the present value of employer pensions and Social Security.[13] We sort married couples and single women separately into total wealth deciles, there being too few single men to permit a similar analysis. In this chapter, we identify those AHEAD households containing individuals who have voluntarily annuitized by 2000 and calculate the percentages of such households in each of these wealth deciles. We use 1993 in preference to 2000 wealth data because we want, as far as possible, to observe preannuitization wealth. The relationship between annuitization and postannuitization wealth may differ if subjective mortality beliefs are correlated with both annuitization and the rate of asset decumulation.

We want to exclude deferred annuities, which are sold in much greater volumes than immediate annuities and which are not very annuity-like in that they do not involve the irrevocable transfer of a capital sum in return for longevity insurance.

The "financial respondent" in each HRS and AHEAD household is asked, in the following order, questions about their and their spouse's pension income, annuity income, and annuity wealth. These questions are phrased to minimize the risk of double counting, yet several risks remain. An obvious risk is that individuals may report annuity income from DC plans under the pension category. Another risk is that income from deferred annuities may be reported under the annuity category. In addition, there is the risk of general reporting error. As all immediate annuities pay an income, there should be little risk of them remaining unreported until the interviewer gets to the annuity wealth section.

It is particularly important to distinguish between individuals receiving income from immediate annuities and those taking withdrawals from deferred annuities. Brown and Poterba (2006) show that tax deferral is the major reason that most people buy deferred annuities. Taking a withdrawal would vitiate this tax advantage, and our analysis of National Association for Variable Annuities (2002b) data suggests that although there has been a rapid increase in the number of systematic withdrawal plans, they are still quite uncommon. However, the volume of deferred-annuity sales is much greater than that of immediate annuities, and a sizeable proportion of annuity income could still emanate from deferred annuities. The HRS and AHEAD ask a number of questions about annuity income—whether it is fixed or variable, for life or for a specified period, linked to the cost of living, and so on. These questions can be analyzed to determine annuity type. For example, a fixed lifetime income is almost certain to be from an immediate annuity, whereas given that there have been no sales of inflation-linked annuities in the United States, an income that is subject to cost-of-living increases almost certainly does not come from an annuity.[14] Where a response is missing, we assign a value using hot-deck imputation, using appropriate covariates.[15]

The Relationship between Wealth, Annuitization, and Mortality among the AHEAD Households
We calculate male and female mortality tables for the AHEAD sample, using mortality data covering the period 1993 to 2000. To correct for nonmonotonicity due to small cell sizes, we smooth mortality for men and women separately between age sixty-seven and ninety by estimating a Gompertz mortality function.[16] Previous research has shown that Gompertz mortality approximates quite closely to actual mortality, except at very advanced ages.

We then calculate the average mortality of the AHEAD sample, weighted by the probability that a household in any given wealth decile will be an annuitant.[17] We accomplish this by combining our estimates of the relationship between wealth decile and annuitization rates with estimates of the relationship between wealth and mortality. We obtain these latter estimates by estimating a Gompertz mortality model from AHEAD mortality data for individuals age ninety or less, controlling for gender, age at baseline, and wealth decile.

We then compare annuitant mortality, as shown by annuitant mortality tables, with the average mortality of people in the wealth deciles from which annuitants are drawn. We calculate annuitant mortality by taking the average of the 1983 and 2000 annuitant life tables referred to previously, weighted to produce a series of period mortality tables for the period 1993 to 2000, but for the purpose of this analysis do not convert the resulting period table into a cohort table.[18]

Results

Optimal Annuitization Strategies

Dushi and Webb (2004) analyzed the balance sheets of HRS households turning age sixty-five between 1994 and 2000, calculating wealth inclusive of the present value of employer pensions and Social Security. Their analysis included a calculation of the mean proportion of preannuitized wealth held by married couples and single women in each wealth decile.

As shown in the first row of table 9.1, the average proportion of preannuitized wealth held by married couples in each of the bottom five wealth deciles is extremely high, and the mean is still 49 percent in the top wealth decile. Under the assumption of constant relative risk aversion, households in the lower wealth deciles will value annuitization less highly than those in higher deciles.

The second to fifth rows of table 9.1 report the optimal annuitization strategy for the household with the mean proportion of preannuitized wealth in each wealth decile, assuming population mortality, a coefficient of risk aversion of either 2 or 5, and actuarial unfairness calculated by reference to either the treasury strip or the corporate bond rate of interest. At a coefficient of risk aversion of 2, annuitization is not worthwhile for households in any wealth decile under either of our two assumed levels of actuarial unfairness. At a coefficient of risk aversion of 5, annuitization is worthwhile for households in the top two wealth deciles when actuarial unfairness is calculated by reference to the treasury strip rate of interest but is worthwhile only for households in the top wealth decile when the corporate bond rate is used.

But the average household in the upper half of the wealth distribution might well believe that it had better than population average mortality. Rows six to nine report optimal annuitization strategies when

Table 9.1
Optimal annuitization strategies for Health and Retirement Study households turning 65 between 1994 and 2000

	Wealth Decile									
	1	2	3	4	5	6	7	8	9	10
Average proportion of preannuitized wealth[a]	94	91	90	85	83	81	72	65	63	49
Optimal Annuitization Strategy										
Population mortality										
Treasury strip interest rate:										
CRRA = 2	Never	Never	Never	Never	Never	Never	Never	Never	Never	Never
CRRA = 5	Never	Never	Never	Never	Never	Never	Never	At age 81	At age 79	At age 74
Amount annuitized								Almost 0	partial	partial
Corporate bond interest rate:										
CRRA = 2	Never	Never	Never	Never	Never	Never	Never	Never	Never	Never
CRRA = 5	Never	Never	Never	Never	Never	Never	Never	Never	Never	At age 83
Amount annuitized										partial
Annuitant mortality										
Treasury strip interest rate:										
CRRA = 2	Never	Never	Never	Never	Never	Never	Never	Never	At age 79	At age 76
Amount annuitized									Almost 0	partial
CRRA = 5	Never	Never	Never	At age 90	At age 89	At age 89	At age 75	At age 69	At age 70	At age 68
Amount annuitized				partial	partial	partial	partial	partial	partial	partial
Corporate bond interest rate:										
CRRA = 2	Never	Never	Never	Never	Never	Never	Never	Never	Never	Never
CRRA = 5	Never	Never	Never	Never	Never	Never	Never	Never	Never	At age 82
Amount annuitized										partial

Notes: Data from Health and Retirement Study, wave 2 to 5. Sample of married couples who turned 65 in any of the waves 2 to 5. Sample size: 1,418 observations. Figures are weighted using household weights. $\lambda = 0.5$, $B = 0.9709$, $r = 0.03$, wife three years younger than husband.

a. Dushi and Webb (2004, table 1a).

we assume annuitant mortality. When we calculate actuarial unfairness by reference to the corporate bond rate of interest, the results are almost identical to those obtained when we assume population average mortality. Annuitization is worthwhile only if the household is in the top wealth decile and also has a coefficient of risk aversion of 5. In other words, household behavior is unaffected by the change in the assumption about mortality beliefs or, equivalently, the substitution of symmetric for asymmetric mortality beliefs.

Things are a little different when we calculate actuarial unfairness by reference to the treasury strip rate of interest. When the coefficient of risk aversion equals 2, households in only the top two wealth deciles annuitize, but when the coefficient of risk aversion equals 5, it becomes optimal for households in most wealth deciles to annuitize small amounts. Households will generally find it optimal to delay annuitization until quite advanced ages. We conclude that annuitization can be worthwhile for low-wealth households under symmetric information or under favorable mortality beliefs, but it requires both a high degree of risk aversion and a low level of residual actuarial unfairness.

Who Annuitizes

Table 9.2 reports separately for married couples and single women, for each 1993 wealth decile, the percentages of AHEAD households containing individuals who had voluntarily annuitized by 2000, and the average age at which they first annuitized.

Married couples are more likely to have annuitized than single women, despite the fact that longevity risk pooling reduces the value of annuitization to married couples. By 2000, when the youngest age eligible member of the panel was age seventy-seven, the "own life" annuitization rate averages 9.1 percent among married couples and 6.3 percent among single women, a weighted average of 7.4 percent.[19] There is a strong relationship between wealth decile and the incidence of voluntary annuitization. We attribute the greater prevalence of voluntary annuitization among married couples to the fact that the single women have exceptionally high proportions of preannuitized wealth. Indeed, many of the single women lack any significant financial wealth at all.[20]

A significant proportion of households reported that they had annuitized only in recent years, consistent with our simulation results indicating that there are advantages to postponing annuitization. The married couples and single women in the AHEAD annuitize, on

Table 9.2
Annuitization patterns in the AHEAD

	Wealth Decile										All
	1	2	3	4	5	6	7	8	9	10	
Percentage of married couples in wealth decile where either spouse had annuitized by 2000	0.0	7.4	2.6	8.0	9.8	6.6	9.9	7.9	22.6	17.5	10.2
Mean age of husband at which household first annuitized											69.1
Percentage of single women in wealth decile who had annuitized by 2000	0.0	0.0	0.8	2.4	0.7	7.0	4.0	7.7	10.6	16.0	6.2
Mean age at which first annuity purchased											72.2

Notes: Sample size = 1,427 single women and 921 married men who were alive at wave 5 (2000) of the AHEAD and for whom annuitization decision and wealth deciles are not missing. Figures are weighted using person weights.

average at age sixty-nine and seventy-two, respectively. Although some AHEAD individuals who have not yet annuitized may choose to do so in the future, we don't believe the number will be significant, as mortality rates in the AHEAD have already started to rise substantially.

Despite some inconsistencies in responses across waves, there is reason to think that the data are of at least acceptable quality. The AHEAD is not a representative sample of the entire population of individuals over sixty-five, as it includes only those born in 1923 or earlier and their spouses of any age and excludes those institutionalized at baseline. Although we lack data, they were probably much poorer and with far higher mortality and far lower annuitization rates than the average. The overall annuitization rate among those age sixty-five and over may therefore differ from that observed in the AHEAD. In response to our enquiries, LIMRA estimated that only 3 percent of the over-sixty-five population hold immediate annuities, somewhat lower than the rate we observe in the AHEAD. But if individuals typically annuitize some time after retirement, we would expect to find a higher annuitization rate among the oldest old. Our analysis of 2000 Census data shows that this 3 percent equates to 6.4 percent of those over age seventy-five, close to the rate we calculate for the AHEAD. We conclude that we have a reasonable measure of annuitization among the elderly.

One possible source of bias is random reporting error that may tend to reduce the observed relationship between wealth and annuitization and result in us overestimating the effect of private mortality information on the annuitization decision.

The Relationship between Wealth, Annuitization, and Mortality among the AHEAD Households

Table 9.3 reports the results of our analysis of mortality in the AHEAD panel. As a benchmark, the first column shows male population mortality for the period 1993 to 2000, obtained by averaging the Social Security Administration period life tables for the relevant years. The seventh column shows corresponding data for women. The second and eighth columns shows annuitant mortality for the same period, obtained by interpolating the 1983 and 2000 annuitant life tables referred to previously. The third and ninth columns show annuitant as a percentage of population mortality. Annuitant mortality is considerably less than that of the population as a whole. At age sixty-five, annuitant mortality is just over half the population average, but the percentage increases with age. One possible explanation is that people in low-wealth deciles die younger so that at more advanced ages the mortality characteristics of the population tend to resemble those of annuitants. Or it may be that the predictive power of private mortality information declines with age.

The fourth and tenth columns report mortality for the AHEAD sample as a whole after mortality smoothing. Mortality is lower than the population average at younger ages but somewhat exceeds it at older ages. As mentioned previously, the sample excluded those who were institutionalized at baseline and who would have had much higher mortality. We suspect that their exclusion not only accounts for the lower than population average mortality at younger ages but also biases upward our estimate of the age-related increase in mortality.

We find that the relationships between wealth and mortality and between wealth and annuitization rates are both statistically significant. For example, for men and women combined, mortality rates in each of the first five wealth deciles exceed those in the top decile at the 5 percent level of significance and only twice fall a little short when men and women are analyzed separately. Although the relationship between annuitization rates and wealth decile is nonmonotonic, one can still reject the hypothesis of no correlation at the 1 percent level of significance. As a result, the weighted mortality among the AHEAD panel is considerably lower than the unweighted. The fifth and eleventh columns show AHEAD mortality, weighted by the probability that a household in a particular wealth decile is an annuitant.

Columns six and twelve show weighted AHEAD mortality as a percentage of population mortality. At age seventy, when AHEAD mortality is close to that of the population as a whole and the AHEAD sample is starting to annuitize, weighted mortality is some 24 percent less than the population average. This percentage can be compared with the 42 percent difference between population and annuitant mortality at the same age. The relative magnitudes of these two numbers suggests that at age seventy somewhat less than half of the lower mortality of annuitants is the result of private mortality information, and the other half or more is the result of correlates with variations in household wealth that we believe may largely reflect differences in tastes rather than differences in subjective mortality beliefs.

As mentioned previously, a substantial part of the lower mortality of annuitants results from the fact that many of the poor have little or no

Table 9.3
Annual mortality risk for individuals alive between 1993 and 2000

Age	Men					
	Population	Annuitant	Annuitant/ Population	AHEAD	AHEAD Weighted by Probability of Annuitizing	Weighted AHEAD/ Population
	(1)	(2)	(3)	(4)	(5)	(6)
65	0.0224	0.0117	0.5197	0.0201	0.0160	0.7109
66	0.0248	0.0129	0.5216	0.0220	0.0175	0.7065
67	0.0271	0.0144	0.5310	0.0242	0.0192	0.7094
68	0.0292	0.0160	0.5486	0.0265	0.0211	0.7211
69	0.0313	0.0179	0.5704	0.0291	0.0231	0.7373
70	0.0337	0.0199	0.5912	0.0319	0.0254	0.7523
71	0.0364	0.0222	0.6085	0.0350	0.0278	0.7639
72	0.0394	0.0246	0.6232	0.0384	0.0305	0.7742
73	0.0428	0.0272	0.6348	0.0421	0.0335	0.7826
74	0.0465	0.0300	0.6440	0.0462	0.0367	0.7895
75	0.0507	0.0330	0.6511	0.0507	0.0403	0.7945
76	0.0554	0.0364	0.6569	0.0556	0.0442	0.7981
77	0.0606	0.0401	0.6620	0.0610	0.0485	0.8009
78	0.0662	0.0435	0.6560	0.0669	0.0532	0.8031
79	0.0725	0.0487	0.6711	0.0734	0.0584	0.8048
80	0.0794	0.0536	0.6747	0.0805	0.0640	0.8061
81	0.0870	0.0590	0.6776	0.0884	0.0702	0.8071
82	0.0954	0.0648	0.6799	0.0969	0.0771	0.8081
83	0.1045	0.0712	0.6817	0.1064	0.0845	0.8094
84	0.1143	0.0781	0.6828	0.1167	0.0928	0.8113
85	0.1250	0.0854	0.6835	0.1280	0.1018	0.8142
86	0.1365	0.0933	0.6837	0.1404	0.1116	0.8181
87	0.1488	0.0969	0.6515	0.1541	0.1225	0.8233
88	0.1619	0.1106	0.6831	0.1690	0.1344	0.8301
89	0.1758	0.1200	0.6823	0.1854	0.1474	0.8384
90	0.1906	0.1299	0.6813	0.2034	0.1617	0.8483

Women					
Population	Annuitant	Annuitant/ Population	AHEAD	AHEAD Weighted by Probability of Annuitizing	Weighted AHEAD/ Population
(7)	(8)	(9)	(10)	(11)	(12)
0.0134	0.0073	0.5411	0.0119	0.0092	0.6581
0.0148	0.0080	0.5415	0.0133	0.0102	0.6905
0.0162	0.0088	0.5444	0.0147	0.0114	0.7022
0.0175	0.0096	0.5511	0.0164	0.0126	0.7220
0.0188	0.0105	0.5600	0.0182	0.0140	0.7454
0.0203	0.0115	0.5692	0.0202	0.0156	0.7670
0.0220	0.0127	0.5790	0.0224	0.0173	0.7849
0.0239	0.0142	0.5919	0.0249	0.0192	0.8016
0.0261	0.0159	0.6084	0.0277	0.0213	0.8174
0.0285	0.0179	0.6267	0.0307	0.0237	0.8314
0.0313	0.0201	0.6440	0.0341	0.0263	0.8413
0.0344	0.0227	0.6601	0.0379	0.0292	0.8487
0.0379	0.0256	0.6764	0.0421	0.0325	0.8563
0.0417	0.0289	0.6926	0.0467	0.0360	0.8642
0.0459	0.0325	0.7081	0.0519	0.0400	0.8716
0.0508	0.0366	0.7211	0.0577	0.0445	0.8761
0.0562	0.0412	0.7319	0.0641	0.0494	0.8781
0.0624	0.0463	0.7420	0.0711	0.0549	0.8794
0.0692	0.0520	0.7518	0.0790	0.0609	0.8806
0.0768	0.0584	0.7614	0.0878	0.0677	0.8817
0.0852	0.0656	0.7708	0.0975	0.0752	0.8826
0.0945	0.0737	0.7801	0.1083	0.0835	0.8833
0.1049	0.0828	0.7894	0.1203	0.0927	0.8843
0.1162	0.0929	0.7988	0.1336	0.1030	0.8861
0.1287	0.1038	0.8068	0.1484	0.1144	0.8891
0.1422	0.1155	0.8122	0.1648	0.1271	0.8938

annuitizable wealth and will therefore not annuitize regardless of their subjective mortality beliefs. For example, we calculate that only 2.3 percent of AHEAD married couples in the bottom wealth decile have $50,000 or more in annuitizable financial assets, compared to 84.7 percent of those in the top decile. When we weight the mortality rates of AHEAD married couple households by the probability that a household in any given wealth decile has $50,000 or more in annuitizable financial wealth, we arrive at male and female mortality rates of 70 and 74 percent of the sample average. This is further evidence that a sizeable part of the lower mortality of annuitants is clearly unrelated to private mortality beliefs.

Conclusions

Previous literature has suggested that adverse selection has a significant effect on the price of annuities. Traditional models of adverse selection attribute the lower mortality of annuitants to people's use of private information when deciding whether to annuitize. But the lower mortality of annuitants may also be the result of passive selection in which an unobservable factor (wealth) affects both preferences and outcomes. The two effects may, of course, interact, with passive selection increasing the actuarial unfairness of annuities and further discouraging people who believe they have high mortality from annuitizing.

Our analyses show that for plausible parameter values the wealthy will indeed value annuitization much more highly than the poor and that high proportions of preannuitized wealth combined with plausible levels of insurance-company administrative expenses would be sufficient to deter many poorer households from annuitizing, even in the absence of adverse selection. Many poorer households may also not participate in the annuity market for the simple reason that they lack annuitizable financial assets.

Our comparison of the mortality rates of annuitants with those of similarly wealthy people and with the population as a whole suggests that about one-half of the lower mortality rates of annuitants is attributable to the correlation between wealth and mortality, leaving the other half to be explained by traditional adverse selection on the basis of private mortality information.

An alternative measure, that we defer to future research, would be to express the difference in EPV terms, weighted by either annuitizable wealth or, alternatively, the amounts that households might wish to annuitize if offered actuarially fair terms, subject only to a deduction for insurance company administrative expenses.

Acknowledgments

The opinions and conclusions are solely those of the authors and should not be construed as representing the opinions or policy of Hunter College or the Center for Retirement Research at Boston College. Corresponding author: Anthony Webb, Center for Retirement Research, Hovey House, 258 Hammond Street, Chestnut Hill, MA 02467, webbaa@bc.edu.

Notes

1. We define *population average mortality* as a probability of dying between one birthday and the next that is equal to that predicted by the Social Security Administration for individuals of their gender and year of birth. We define an *actuarially fair annuity* as one that, at some assumed interest rate, offers someone with population average mortality an expected present value equal to the premium paid.

2. We define the *money's worth of an annuity* as being the expected present value, given the household's mortality, divided by the premium paid.

3. Sales of deferred annuities substantially exceed those of immediate annuities. A deferred annuity lacks the essential feature of an immediate annuity—namely, the irrevocable exchange of a capital sum in return for a lifetime income. Deferred annuities enable individuals to accumulate wealth with the benefit of tax-deferral. Individuals may subsequently withdraw the assets in the form of a lifetime income but rarely do so.

4. The Health and Retirement Study is a panel of over 12,000 individuals age fifty-one to sixty-one in 1992 who have been reinterviewed at two-year intervals.

5. The U.K. annuity market is more innovative than that in the United States. Ainslie (2000) reports that in 1998 the impaired life annuity market totaled £190 million, compared with an overall market of £6.095 billion. Of the £190 million, £130 million related to lives with low or moderate impairment, £50 million to lives with medium impairment and £10 million to severely impaired lives. U.K. insurers have recently started to underwrite on the basis of an individual's postcode, a good predictor of house value and therefore potentially of wealth and longevity in the United States. Pension plans, including 401(k) plans, are legally obliged to use unisex rates, although men can circumvent this requirement by rolling over into an IRA and buying a qualifying male life annuity within the IRA.

6. We are informed that in 1995 the market for impaired annuities was extremely limited and that in the nonimpaired market the information available to the insurer was limited to age and gender, the variables on which they conditioned their calculations of EPV.

7. We have taken annuitizable wealth to equal the household's financial assets. Housing wealth can be accessed through a reverse mortgage and then annuitized, although few households choose to do so. On the other hand, liquidity considerations may result in

some households, particularly those with modest amounts of wealth, wishing to retain part of their financial wealth in unannuitized form.

8. For a theoretical discussion, see Chiappori, Jullien, Salanie, and Salanie (2002).

9. A *basic life table* is one based on industry experience without an additional margin for conservatism or improvements in longevity.

10. A *period table* records the mortality experience of people of different ages who are alive in the reference year. A *cohort table* estimates the mortality experience of people who were born in a reference year.

11. A more ambitious objective would be to show that our model predicted the behavior of individual households. Data limitations and lack of computing power prevent us from doing so. We lack usable data on subjective mortality beliefs, and the HRS/AHEAD panel is not yet of sufficient length for us to observe individuals from age sixty-five to the ages that our model predicts annuitization can be advantageous. Our program takes twenty-four hours to run for a single household. Brown (2001) uses a numerical optimization model to explain the annuitization intentions of HRS household, but our model allows for a much richer variety of choices and as a result takes many times longer to run.

12. The return on a fixed annuity is, as its name suggests, fixed. It may either be level or be increasing at a predetermined rate. The return on a variable annuity depends on the performance of the underlying assets. Most variable annuities are deferred, but there is a small but growing market for variable immediate annuities. These offer the benefits of both longevity risk pooling and the equity premium. The fact that so few purchasers of immediate annuities choose a variable annuity is yet another manifestation of the equity premium puzzle.

13. The present value of a pension declines with age. To avoid a spurious correlation between age and wealth, we calculate the present value of each individual's pension wealth at the median age of the sample. The relationship between age and nonpension wealth is much less strong, and we do not attempt a similar age adjustment for such wealth.

14. We understand that one insurance company marketed such a product but withdrew it after making zero sales, and another has recently launched one. TIAA-CREF offers a variable annuity invested in treasury Inflation-Protected Securities, but it is not a true inflation-proofed product.

15. *Hot-deck imputation* involves filling in missing values by making a random draw from the subsample of individuals with similar characteristics. The HRS and AHEAD use it extensively but have not applied it to the annuitization data.

16. In a Gompertz model, mortality increases exponentially with age.

17. We excluded single households because it is difficult to know how to compare the wealth held by couples with that held by singles.

18. These life tables are period tables showing the mortality experience of annuitants of varying ages who were alive in 1983 and 2000, respectively.

19. Some of the single women will undoubtedly be receiving a survivor benefit from an annuity taken out on their deceased husband's life, while others will have acquired their own life annuity prior to the death of their husband.

20. As mortality is higher among low-wealth households, the AHEAD cohort will be a somewhat more select group than the corresponding HRS households turning age sixty-five.

References

Ainslie, R. (2000). "Annuity and Insurance Products for Impaired Lives." *Staple Inn Actuarial Society* (London) (May): 12–13.

Attanasio, O., and C. Emmerson. (2003). "Differential Mortality in the U.K." *Journal of the European Economic Association* 1(4): 821–850.

Attanasio, O., and H. Hoynes. (2000). "Differential Mortality and Wealth Accumulation." *Journal of Human Resources* 35(1): 1–29.

Brown, J. (2001). "Private Pensions, Mortality Risk, and the Decision to Annuitize." *Journal of Public Economics* 82(1): 29–62.

Brown, J. (2003). "Redistribution and Insurance: Mandatory Annuitization with Mortality Heterogeneity." *Journal of Risk and Insurance* 70(1): 17–41.

Brown, J., and J. Poterba. (2000). "Joint Life Annuities and Annuity Demand by Married Couples." *Journal of Risk and Insurance* 67(4): 527–553.

Brown, J., and J. Poterba. (2006, forthcoming). "Household Demand for Variable Annuities." *Tax Policy and the Economy*.

Chiappori, P., B. Jullien, B. Salanie, and F. Salanie. (2002). "Asymmetric Information in Insurance: Some Testable Implications." Mimeo, September.

Disney, R., P. Johnson, and G. Stears. (1999). "Asset Wealth and Asset Decumulation among Households in the Retirement Survey." *Fiscal Studies* 19(2): 153–174.

Dushi, I., and A. Webb. (2004). "Household Annuitization Decisions: Simulations and Empirical Analyses." *Journal of Pension Economics and Finance* 3(2): 109–143.

Finkelstein, A., and K. McGarry. (2003). "Private Information and Its Effect on Market Equilibrium: New Evidence from Long-Term Care Insurance." NBER Working Paper No. 9957, September.

Finkelstein, A., and J. Poterba. (2004). "Adverse Selection in Insurance Markets: Policyholder Evidence from the U.K. Annuity Market." *Journal of Political Economy* 112(1): 183–208.

Friedberg, L., and A. Webb. (2005). "Retirement and the Evolution of Pension Structure." *Journal of Human Resources* 40(2): 281–308.

Friedman, B., and M. Warshawsky. (1988). "Annuity Prices and Savings Behavior in the United States." In Z. Bodie, J. Shoven, and D. Wise (Eds.), *Pensions in the U.S. Economy* (pp. 53–77). Chicago: University of Chicago Press.

Gan, L., M. Hurd, and M. McFadden. (2005). "Individual Subjective Survival Curves." In D. Wise (Ed.), *Analyses in Economics of Aging* (pp. 377–411). Chicago: University of Chicago Press.

Hurd, M., D. McFadden, and A. Merrill. (2001). "Predictors of Mortality among the Elderly." In D. Wise (Ed.), *Themes in the Economics of Aging* (pp. 171–197). Chicago: University of Chicago Press.

Impavido, G., C. Thorburn, and M. Wadsworth. (2004). "A Conceptual Framework for Retirement Products: Risk Sharing Arrangements between Providers and Retirees." World Bank and Watson Wyatt Working Paper, February.

Johnson, W., C. Uccello, and J. Goldwyn. (2005). "Who Forgoes Survivor Protection in Employer-Sponsored Pension Annuities?" *The Gerontologist* 45(1): 26–35.

Menchik, P. (1993). "Economic Status as a Determinant of Mortality among Black and White Older Men: Does Poverty Kill." *Population Studies* 47(3): 427–436.

Mitchell, O., J. Poterba, M. Warshawsky, and J. Brown. (1999). "New Evidence on the Money's Worth of Individual Annuities." *American Economic Review* 89(5): 1299–1318.

National Association for Variable Annuities. (2002a). *Annuity Fact Book*. Reston, VA: NAVA.

National Association for Variable Annuities. (2002b). "Income for Life: The Unappreciated Benefit." *NAVA Outlook* 11(3): 1–5.

Poterba, J. (2001). "The History of Annuities in the United States." In J. Brown, O. Mitchell, J. Poterba, and M. Warshawsky, *The Role of Annuity Markets in Financing Retirement* (pp. 22–56). Cambridge, MA: MIT Press.

10   The Role of Risk Aversion in Predicting Individual Behavior

Luigi Guiso and Monica
Paiella

Introduction

The theory of choice under uncertainty implies that the attitude an individual has toward risk is decisive in a variety of contexts that are critical for understanding individual behavior. According to theory, differences in risk aversion among individuals should show up sharply in their occupational choices, their decisions on how to allocate accumulated assets, how much insurance to buy in the market, and how much to self-insure. In some cases—as in simple portfolio theory (Samuelson, 1969; Merton, 1969; Gollier, 2001b)—theory implies that all differences across individuals in observed portfolio composition should reflect differences in risk preferences. Thus, the well-documented massive heterogeneity in portfolio shares across households (Guiso, Haliassos, and Jappelli, 2000) could all be traced back to such differences. More generally, differences in risk aversion should affect individuals' investment choices with the more risk-averse being ready to forego relatively higher expected returns for returns with lower variability. The immediate implication is that more risk-averse individuals should have less variable earnings but end up, on average, poorer. One key question then is how much of the inequality in income and wealth distribution can be due to differences across individuals in their risk preferences. The answer clearly depends on how much attitudes toward risk differ across consumers and how important risk aversion is in explaining behavior toward other income determinants that may themselves differ significantly across individuals. To be able to provide evidence on these issues, one needs to be able to measure risk aversion at the individual level. However, individual willingness to bear risk is not normally observable, so researchers typically have assumed that individuals have identical risk preferences and have explained the observed differences in behavior and wealth by assuming some form of market friction or imperfection that affects individuals differentially.[1]

This chapter makes two contributions to help sort out the role of differences in risk preferences. First, we employ information on households' willingness to pay for a hypothetical risky security contained in the 1995 Bank of Italy Survey of Household Income and Wealth (SHIW) to recover a measure of the Arrow-Pratt index of absolute risk aversion of the consumer's lifetime utility function and check how much measured risk aversion differs across individuals. Second, we relate this measure to various behaviors that according to theory should be greatly affected by risk preferences. In particular, we focus on individuals' occupational and portfolio choices, their demand for insurance, their investment in education, the propensity to move or change jobs, and their exposure to chronic diseases. We find unequivocal evidence that risk preferences differ considerably across individuals and that these differences have substantial explanatory power as regards individual decisions.

Although the vast majority of the survey participants are risk-averse according to our measure, a small proportion (4 percent) are either risk-neutral or risk-loving (we will call this group *risk-prone*). In addition, even among the risk-averse there is a lot of heterogeneity in the degree of risk aversion, which shows that preferences for risk do differ significantly across individuals. Furthermore, these differences are systematically related to individual choices that involve risk. Differences in risk preferences are important for understanding differences in behavior across individuals. For instance, compared to the risk-prone, the risk-averse are six percentage points less likely to be self-employed (corresponding to 36 percent of the sample share of the self-employed), have a six-point lower chance of holding risky securities (corresponding to 42 percent of the sample mean), and have, on average, 110,000 euros less in total net worth, 75 percent of the sample mean. Correspondingly, individuals with a low degree of risk aversion (at the tenth percentile of the cross-sectional distribution) have earnings that are 60 percent more variable than those of highly risk-averse individuals (ninetieth percentile).

Our findings imply that individuals sort themselves out in such a way that the highly risk-averse face less risky prospects. This self-selection makes it problematic to assess the effect of risk on choice, an issue that arises, for instance, in evaluating the effect of income uncertainty on investment in risky assets or testing for precautionary savings. The problem here is that the risk that agents face is correlated with preferences for risk that are unobservable. This unobserved preference heterogeneity biases—normally toward zero—the measured effect of risk. Since we observe risk preferences directly, we can assess the importance of self-selection for estimates of the effect of risk on behavior, and we do this with reference to precautionary saving.

The rest of the chapter is organized as follows. We describe our measure of risk aversion, present descriptive evidence on risk aversion and individuals' choices in our cross-section of households, and summarize what theory says about the effect of risk aversion on a number of household decisions: occupational choice, portfolio allocation, insurance demand, investment in education, moving, and job change. Then we present the results of the estimates, look more closely at the link between attitudes toward risk and the mean and variance of individual income, and discuss self-selection induced by risk attitudes and illustrates its relevance for precautionary savings estimates.

Measuring Risk Aversion

To measure risk aversion, we exploit the 1995 wave of the Survey of Household Income and Wealth (SHIW), which is run every two years by the Bank of Italy. The 1995 SHIW collects data on income, consumption, real, and financial wealth and its composition, insurance demand, type of occupation, educational attainment, geographic and occupational mobility, and several demographic variables for a representative sample of 8,135 Italian households. Balance-sheet items are end-of-period values. Income and flow variables refer to 1995.[2]

The 1995 survey had a section designed to elicit attitudes toward risk. Each participant was offered a hypothetical negotiable asset and was asked to report the maximum price that he would be willing to pay for it:

We would like to ask you a hypothetical question that you should answer as if the situation were a real one. You are offered the opportunity of acquiring an asset permitting you, with the same probability, either to gain 10 million lire or to lose all the capital invested. What is the most that you would be prepared to pay for this asset?

Ten million lire is roughly equal to 5,000 euros. The expected gain from the investment is equal to 16 percent of average household's annual consumption. Thus, the investment represents a relatively large risk. Putting consumers face to face with a relatively large investment is a better strategy to elicit risk attitudes when one relies, as we do, on expected utility maximization to characterize risk aversion (see Rabin, 2000). In fact, expected utility maximizers behave risk-neutrally with respect to small risks even if they are averse to larger risks (Arrow, 1970).[3] The interviews are conducted personally at the consumer's home by professional interviewers. To help the respondent understand the question, the interviewers showed an illustrative card and were ready to provide explanations. The respondent could respond in one of three ways: (1) declare the maximum amount he was willing to pay for the asset, which we denote Z_i; (2) answer "don't know"; or (3) not answer.

Notice that the way the hypothetical asset is designed implies that with probability $1/2$ the respondent gets 10 million lire and with probability $1/2$ he loses Z_i. So the expected value of the hypothetical investment is $1/2(10 - Z_i)$. Clearly, $Z_i < 10$ million lire, $Z_i = 10$, and $Z_i > 10$ million lire imply risk aversion, risk neutrality, and risk loving, respectively. This characterizes attitudes toward risk qualitatively. Within the expected-utility framework, a measure of the Arrow-Pratt index of absolute risk aversion can also be obtained for each consumer. Let w_i denote household i's endowment. Let $u_i(\cdot)$ be its (lifetime) utility function and $\tilde{P}_i$ be the random return on the security for individual i, taking values 10 million and $-Z_i$ with equal probability. The maximum purchase price is thus given by

$$u_i(w_i) = \frac{1}{2}u_i(w_i + 10) + \frac{1}{2}u_i(w_i - Z_i) = Eu_i(w_i + \tilde{P}_i), \qquad (10.1)$$

where E is the expectations operator. Taking a second-order Taylor expansion of the right-hand side of (10.1) around w_i gives

$$Eu_i(w_i + \tilde{P}_i) \approx u_i(w_i) + u_i'(w_i)E(\tilde{P}_i) + 0.5u_i''(w_i)E(\tilde{P}_i)^2. \qquad (10.2)$$

Substituting (10.2) into (10.1) and simplifying, we obtain

$$R_i(w_i) \approx -u_i''(w_i)/u_i'(w_i) = 4(5 - Z_i/2)/[10^2 + Z_i^2]. \qquad (10.3)$$

Equation (10.3) uniquely defines the Arrow-Pratt measure of absolute risk aversion in terms of the parameters of the hypothetical asset of the survey.[4] For risk-neutral individuals (those reporting $Z_i = 10$), $R_i(w_i) = 0$, and for the risk-prone (those with $Z_i > 10$), $R_i(w_i) < 0$. Notice that since the loss Z_i or the gain from the investment need not be fully borne by or benefit current consumption but may be spread over lifetime consumption, our measure of risk aversion is better interpreted as the risk aversion of the consumer's lifetime utility.[5] As such, it reflects not only the preference parameters that affect the curvature of the period utility but also aspects of the constraint set, such as any liquidity constraints or background risk an individual faces, that affect an individual willingness to bear risk. To take this into account, in our empirical estimates we control for liquidity constraints and background risk.

A few comments on this measure and on how it compares with those used in other studies are in order. First, our measure requires no assumption on the form of the individual utility function, which is left unspecified. Second, it is not restricted to risk-averse individuals but extends to the risk-neutral and the risk lovers. Third, our definition provides a point estimate, rather than a range, of the degree of risk aversion for each individual in the sample. These features distinguish our study from that of Barsky, Juster, Kimball, and Shapiro (1997), who only obtain a range measure of (relative) risk aversion and a point estimate under the assumption that preferences are strictly risk-averse and utility is of the constant relative risk aversion (CRRA) type. However, their elicitation strategy allows them to recover a measure of the risk aversion of period utility instead of lifetime utility as we do. In this regard, our and their study should be viewed as complementary.[6]

Descriptive Evidence
The question on the risky asset was submitted to the whole sample of 8,135 heads of household, but only 3,458 answered and were willing to purchase the asset. Of the 4,677 who did not, 1,586 answered "do not know" and 3,091 refused to answer or to pay a positive price (twenty-five offered more than 20 million). This is likely to be due to the complexity of the question, which might have led some participants to skip it altogether because of the relatively long time required to understand its meaning and provide an answer. Non-responses also reflect the fact that the question was asked abruptly by the interviewers and was not prepared for by warm-up questions. However, this strategy has its advantages: first, the framing and timing of the introductory questions could affect the response to the main question, thus distorting the measure of the true preference parameter. Second, the abrupt approach avoids noise respondents (those with a poor understanding of the question), as would probably happen with

warm-up questions. Thus, while the high nonresponse rate signals that the question is complex and there may be cognitive problems, it does not mean that those who chose to respond gave erroneous answers. This is not to say that our gauge of risk aversion is free of measurement error. However, if this is of the classical type, it will bias our results toward finding small effects of risk aversion on behavior. Thus, our estimates should be regarded as lower bounds of the true effects of risk preferences on consumer decisions.[7]

Table 10.1 reports descriptive statistics for the sample of 3,458 respondents to the risky-asset question and for the subsamples of risk-averse individuals and of the risk-prone.[8] The risk-averse make up the great majority of respondents: 96 percent, in fact, set a maximum price lower than the potential gain. The risk-prone consists of 144 individuals, of whom 125 are risk-neutral and 19 are risk-loving. The mean reported price is 2.2 million lire (1.8 million for the risk averse and 11.2 million for the risk prone, panel A), about 36 percent of the expected gain from the lottery. There is, however, considerable heterogeneity. The value of the standard deviation is 2.7 million, larger than the average reported price, while the ninetieth percentile is 5 million lire, 100 times larger than the tenth percentile. This difference in willingness to pay translates into large differences in risk aversion: the ninetieth percentile of the cross-sectional distribution of the degree of absolute risk aversion is 2.5 times as great as the tenth percentile. We also report a measure of the degree of relative risk aversion obtained multiplying absolute risk aversion by household income. Median relative risk aversion is 5.8 (6.0 among the risk-averse) and ranges between 1.9 (tenth percentile) and 13.3 (ninetieth percentile), showing that there is considerable diversity in aversion to proportional risks too.[9]

Panel B reports summary statistics of the characteristics of the respondents. The two subsamples of risk-prone and of risk-averse consumers exhibit several interesting differences. The risk-averse are younger and less well educated. They are less likely to be male, to be married, and to be borne in the north of Italy and are more likely to have children.

Panel C shows summary statistics for the variables that in principle should be affected by individual preferences for risk. Strong differences emerge in the type of occupation: among the risk-averse the share of self-employed is 17.4 percent; among the risk-prone it is much higher at 29.2 percent. This ordering is reversed for public-sector employees.

Table 10.1
Descriptive statistics

Variable	Risk Averse	Risk Lovers and Neutral	Mean	Standard Deviation	10th Percentile	90th Percentile
			Total Sample of Respondents			
A. Risk aversion						
Value of Z	1.82	11.19	2.21	2.71	0.05	5.0
Absolute risk aversion	0.158	−0.005	0.1507	0.05	0.08	0.20
Relative risk aversion (median)	6.03	−0.40	5.83	5.83	1.92	13.25
B. Characteristics						
Age	48.50	49.34	48.54	13.61	31	68
Male (%)	79.24	93.75	79.84	40	0	1
Married (%)	78.58	87.50	78.95	41	0	1
Number of members	3.20	3.00	3.19	1.31	1	5
Children (%)	42.12	36.11	41.87	49	0	1
Area of birth (%)						
North	37.69	52.78	38.32	49	0	1
Center	21.61	19.44	21.52	41	0	1
South	39.20	25.69	38.64	49	0	1
Father (%)						
With fifth grade	76.67	66.67	76.26	42.56	0	1
Self-employed	31.20	32.64	31.26	46.36	0	1
Public employee	14.73	16.67	14.81	35.52	0	1
C. Choices						
Self-employed (%)	17.38	29.17	17.87	38.32	0	1
Entrepreneur (%)	14.70	19.44	14.89	35.61	0	1
Public employee (%)	27.55	27.08	27.53	44.67	0	1
Mover (%)	18.5	18.8	18.5	39	0	1
Job changer (%)	32.38	38.89	32.65	46.90	0	1
Years of education	9.25	10.81	9.31	4.28	5	16
Chronic disease (%)	19.76	36.11	20.45	40	0	1
Household net worth	275.22	537.28	286.13	431.65	3.91	641.01
Household income	47.45	72.02	48.48	36.23	17.49	84.60
Mean saving rate (%)	13.52	19.77	13.77	33.39	−23.20	48.52
Holders of (%):						
Risky assets	13.46	36.11	14.40	35.12	0	1
Life insurance	21.97	37.50	22.61	41.84	0	1
Health insurance	8.96	13.19	9.14	28.82	0	0
Other insurance	31.11	45.83	31.72	46.55	0	1

Table 10.1
(continued)

			Total Sample of Respondents			
Variable	Risk Averse	Risk Lovers and Neutral	Mean	Standard Deviation	10th Percentile	90th Percentile
Expected earnings:						
Mean	25.38	31.41	25.59	18.88	8.82	42.50
Standard deviation	1.02	1.39	1.03	2.51	0	2.04
Number of observations	3,314	144	3,458	3,458	3,458	3,458

Notes: All the variables refer to the household head, unless stated otherwise. *Z* denotes the amount households are willing to invest in the risky asset and is in million lira. *Children* denotes the share of household with members less than age eighteen. The variables under the heading *Father* denote the share of households whose head has a father with five years of schooling or less and who is or was self-employed or a public employee. *Self-employed* includes the entrepreneurs. *Mover* denotes the share of households whose head has moved from his or her region of birth. *Job changer* denotes the share of households whose head has changed jobs more than twice. *Chronic disease* refers to the share of households whose head is chronically ill. Net worth and income are in million lira. The mean of the *Saving rate* is computed excluding the top and bottom 1 percent of its distribution. *Risky assets* include private bonds, stocks, and mutual funds. *Other insurance* includes casualty and theft insurance. The mean and standard deviation of expected earnings refer to the subjective distribution of the household head (see Guiso et al., 2002, for details).

The risk-prone are public employees in 27 percent of cases; the risk-averse, in 28 percent. As we argue, these differences are likely to reflect self-selection, with more risk-averse individuals choosing safer jobs. Further, the risk averse are less likely to have changed jobs more than twice and to be chronically ill. On average, the risk-averse are significantly less wealthy than the risk-prone (275 million lire—142,000 euros—of mean net worth compared with 537 million—277,000 euros) and expect to earn lower but less variable salaries. Finally, they have a lower share of risky asset holders (13.5 percent compared to 36.1) but also of households holding life, health, or theft insurance.

Predicting Behavior with Risk Aversion: Theory

Attitudes toward risk should affect consumers' willingness to take risk in a variety of situations. In this section, we review theoretical arguments for the effects of risk preferences on individuals' behavior and then test whether our measure of risk preferences has predictive power with respect to consumer choices in ways consistent with theory.

Occupational Choice and Entrepreneurship
If different jobs differ not only in expected return but also in the riskiness of those returns, individuals should sort themselves into occupations on the basis of their risk aversion. One of the few theories of entrepreneurship, put forward by Kihlstrom and Laffont (1979), is indeed based on heterogeneity in risk aversion among individuals. Since running a business is equivalent to the choice of a risky prospect, the less risk-averse will become entrepreneurs while the relatively risk-averse will prefer to be employees and work for a fixed wage. Thus, heterogeneity in risk aversion may explain who becomes an entrepreneur in a society. Understanding the role of preferences in the decision to set up a firm compared with other possible explanations (such as the ability to combine factors of production as in Lucas, 1978, or access to the loan market as in Evans and Jovanovic, 1989) is of critical relevance for policy since if tastes for risk are innate and cannot be acquired, they can potentially be a formidable obstacle to the growth of business.

Portfolio Choice
Standard portfolio theory predicts that the amount of wealth an individual is willing to invest in risky assets depends on his degree of risk aversion. Given the return and riskiness of the risky assets, the more risk-averse should hold safer portfolios. Furthermore, under the conditions for the validity of the two-fund separation theorem, since all investors face the same distribution of asset returns, differences in portfolio composition across individuals should reflect only differences in their degree of risk aversion. Although the conditions for the two-fund separation theorem are rather severe (see Gollier, 2001b), we expect differences in risk aversion across individuals to help predict differences in portfolio holdings. Besides helping to explain why risky asset holders differ in the share of wealth invested in risky assets, differences in risk aversion may also help explain why some do not invest at all in risky assets (such as stocks). If there are fixed costs of acquiring risky assets, those who in the absence of these costs would optimally invest little in the risky assets—because they are strongly risk-averse—will find it unprofitable to incur the fixed cost and enjoy the excess return. Thus, differences in risk aversion should also help predict who will become a stockholder and who will not.

Insurance Demand

The classical model of the demand for casualty insurance elaborated by Mossin (1968) implies that risk-averse individuals should fully insure if insurance is offered at fair terms. If insurance is unfair, the amount purchased will depend on one's degree of risk aversion: the more risk-averse will demand more insurance coverage. Nevertheless, even some risk-averse may choose not to insure if departure from fairness is significant. Thus, differences in risk aversion should predict not only the amount of insurance demand among insurance holders but also the decision to buy an insurance policy among risk-averse consumers.

Investment in Education

Like all forms of investment, that in education entails risk. In fact, compared to accepting a current job offer at a known wage, the decision to obtain more education exposes the investor to a risk of failure—because the program may turn out more difficult than anticipated or because the individual later discovers he lacks the necessary ability. He may thus lose the sum invested (including the direct fees, the living costs, and the forgone salary in the alternative job). In addition, since the investment in education bears fruit only after a relatively long timespan, the investor also bears the uncertainty over the market value of the degree at time of completion. Thus, the less risk-averse individuals should be more likely to obtain higher education. Brunello (2002) shows formally that the number of years of education a person optimally chooses depends negatively on absolute risk aversion.[10]

Migration, Job Change, and Health

The decision to migrate or to change jobs and the consumer's health status (insofar as it depends on how cautious a consumer is) depend on attitude toward risk. Compared with staying in the area of birth, migrating to another area or country entails undertaking a risky prospect as it implies leaving a sure and known prospect for an unknown, though typically more promising future. Similarly, leaving a known job and taking a new one may imply incurring new risks. Thus, one expects more risk-averse individuals to be less likely to move and to change jobs than the risk-prone. Also, since risk-averse consumers should behave more prudently, they should have better health status. Consistent with this intuition, Eeckhoudt and Hammit (2002) show that individuals that are more averse to financial risk have a higher willingness to pay to reduce health risk.[11]

Results

Occupational Choice

Table 10.2 reports the results of estimating probit regressions for occupational choice. We focus on the household head's decision to be self-employed (first two columns), to be a bona fide entrepreneur (third and fourth columns) and to be a public-sector employee (last two columns). All regressions include as controls a second-order polynomial in the age of the household head; dummies for gender, education, and region of birth; and a full set of region of residence dummies to account for local factors that may affect job choice, such as differences in the degree of development of local financial markets (Guiso, Sapienza, and Zingales, 2004b). In addition, we include dummies for the occupation of the household head's father to capture any intergenerational links in occupational choice. For the analysis, we use a measure of absolute risk aversion, which may vary with household resources. Hence, to avoid capturing any correlation between the left-hand-side choice variable and an individual's wealth or income, in this and in all regressions that follow we control for the level of income and wealth of the household. In the case of occupational choice, for example, if wealth is not controlled for, absolute risk aversion may have a negative effect on the decision to become self-employed simply because it declines with wealth and poor individuals lack the financial muscles to set up a business in the presence of imperfect capital markets. Finally, to account for the fact that the risk-aversion measure reflects also aspects of the set of constraints that affect an individual willingness to take up risks, we insert a measure of the liquidity constraints an individual may be exposed to and a measure of the background risk he faces. As to the first, we pool together several years of the SHIW and compute the fraction of individuals in each province that applied for a loan and were turned down or were discouraged from borrowing (did not apply in the expectation that would have been turned down). Provinces with a high share of liquidity-constrained individuals are areas where raising funds is more difficult, which limits the opportunities to time-diversify any risk currently taken and can be expected to make individuals more reluctant to undertake actions involving extra risks. To measure background risk, we rely on per-capita growth in gross domestic product (GDP) at the provincial level for the period 1952 to 1992, which we employ to compute a measure of the variability of GDP growth in the province of residence. For each province, we regress (log) GDP on a

Table 10.2
Risk aversion and occupation choice

Variable	Self-employment (Probit regressions)		Entrepreneur (Probit regressions)		Public-Sector Employee (Probit regressions)	
	(1) Whole Sample	(2) The Risk Averse	(3) Whole Sample	(4) The Risk Averse	(5) Whole Sample	(6) The Risk Averse
Risk averse	-0.256**		-0.121		0.122	
	(0.130)		(0.145)		(0.127)	
Absolute risk aversion		-1.268**		-0.838		1.298**
		(0.644)		(0.692)		(0.590)
Income	-0.114	-0.196*	-0.328***	-0.433***	0.153*	0.260***
	(0.098)	(0.110)	(0.101)	(0.124)	(0.088)	(0.098)
Wealth	0.080***	0.093***	0.092***	0.109***	-0.028***	-0.033***
	(0.008)	(0.009)	(0.008)	(0.010)	(0.008)	(0.008)
Liquidity constraints	1.924	2.407	5.070**	5.925**	-1.360	-2.426
	(2.358)	(2.436)	(2.515)	(2.598)	(2.078)	(2.131)
Background risk	-6.821	-5.710	-5.546	-5.374	0.936	0.732
	(5.104)	(5.287)	(5.540)	(5.738)	(4.280)	(4.478)
Age	0.068***	0.067***	0.099***	0.092***	0.059***	0.061***
	(0.018)	(0.018)	(0.020)	(0.020)	(0.013)	(0.013)
Age squared	-0.097***	-0.096***	-0.129***	-0.122***	-0.051***	-0.054***
	(0.018)	(0.019)	(0.021)	(0.021)	(0.012)	(0.012)
Gender	-0.529***	-0.534***	-0.475***	-0.493***	-0.057	-0.053
	(0.083)	(0.085)	(0.089)	(0.091)	(0.064)	(0.065)
High school diploma	-0.219***	-0.222***	-0.417***	-0.401***	0.610***	0.637***
	(0.068)	(0.070)	(0.072)	(0.075)	(0.059)	(0.060)

University degree	-0.247**	-0.300***	-1.343***	-1.651***	1.258***	1.232***
	(0.104)	(0.111)	(0.171)	(0.215)	(0.089)	(0.093)
Chronic	-0.165**	-0.178**	-0.134	-0.131	0.043	0.028
	(0.080)	(0.084)	(0.085)	(0.089)	(0.065)	(0.067)
Father						
Self-employed	0.393***	0.406***			-0.031	-0.031
	(0.061)	(0.062)			(0.056)	(0.058)
Public employee	-0.126	-0.131	-0.185*	-0.154	0.320***	0.315***
	(0.089)	(0.092)	(0.101)	(0.105)	(0.070)	(0.071)
Entrepreneur			0.367***	0.391***		
			(0.065)	(0.067)		
Constant	-1.840***	-1.951***	-2.578***	-2.481***	-2.937***	-3.060***
	(0.433)	(0.438)	(0.480)	(0.481)	(0.353)	(0.351)
Number of observations	3,374	3,234	3,374	3,234	3,374	3,234

Notes: The left-hand-side variable is a dummy equal to 1 if the household head is a self-employed (first two columns), an entrepreneur (third and fourth column), or a public employee (last two columns). *Risk averse* is a dummy for whether the individual is risk averse. *Absolute risk aversion* is the measure of absolute risk aversion discussed in the text and is defined only for the risk averse. Income and wealth are in hundred million lira. The occupation dummies under the heading *Father* refer to the occupation of the father of the household head. Dummies of the region of birth and for that of residence are also included. Standard errors in parentheses.

* Significant at 10 percent.
** Significant at 5 percent.
*** Significant at 1 percent.

time trend and compute the residuals. We then calculate the variance of the residuals and attach this estimate to all households living in the same province. The variance of GDP growth in the province is an estimate of aggregate risk and should be largely exogenous to the individual risk attitude unless risk-averse consumers move to provinces with low-variance GDP.

The first column of table 10.2 reports the regression results based on the whole sample. The attitude toward risk is measured using a dummy for risk-averse consumers. The benchmark is the group of risk-prone. The left-hand-side variable is set equal to 1 if the household head is a bona fide entrepreneur, both in manufacturing and retailing, or a professional (such as a doctor or a lawyer). Risk-averse consumers are less likely than the risk-prone to be self-employed, and the coefficient is statistically significant at less than the 5 percent confidence level. The differences are economically substantial: being risk-averse rather than risk-prone lowers the probability of being self-employed by six percentage points, or 36 percent of the sample share of self-employed. This evidence suggests that self-selection into occupations triggered by differences in individuals' preferences is indeed an important feature of reality, an issue to which we return when we examine the correlation between the degree of absolute risk aversion and a subjective measure of the variance of earnings. The second column restricts the sample to risk-averse households and uses as explanatory variable our measure of absolute risk aversion. Since the risk-prone group includes relatively few observations, we feel more confident exploiting the variability in the degree of risk aversion rather than differences in the regime of attitudes toward risk. Within the class of risk-averse individuals, those who are more strongly risk-averse should be less likely to choose risky jobs. This is confirmed by the estimates, which imply a negative coefficient for the degree of risk aversion: increasing absolute risk aversion by one standard deviation lowers the probability of being self-employed by 1.2 percentage points (7 percent of the unconditional probability).

In the third and fourth columns, we focus on pure business entrepreneurs, where the amount of risk-taking is probably greater than for other categories of self-employed. Results are qualitatively similar to those reported in the first two columns for the self-employed: the risk-averse are less likely than the risk-prone to be an entrepreneur, and the more risk-averse are less likely than the less risk-averse to be entrepreneurs. The inclusion of the self-employed in the control group, together with employees, may explain why we lose precision in the estimation of the coefficients.

The fifth and sixth columns look at the probability of being a public-sector employee for the whole sample and for the sample of risk-averse individuals. Consistent with the general perception that public jobs are more secure,[12] our estimates show that risk-averse individuals are more likely than the risk-prone to work in the public sector, though the coefficient is significant only at the 34 percent level. Among the risk-averse, the probability of choosing the safer occupation is an increasing and statistically significant function of the degree of risk aversion: increasing the latter by one standard deviation raises the probability of being a public-sector employee by little less than two percentage points (about 7 percent of the sample mean), suggesting again that risk preferences have a strong impact on job choice.

It is worth noticing that in all regressions the occupation of the father of the household head is highly significant statistically and shows a strong positive correlation with the son's current occupation. Sons of entrepreneurs or the self-employed are more likely to become themselves entrepreneurs or self-employed and less likely to be public employees, and similarly for the sons of public employees. The effects are also important economically: having a self-employed father raises the chances of the son being self-employed by nine percentage points, 50 percent of the unconditional mean; if he is a bona fide entrepreneur, the chances that the son also becomes an entrepreneur are higher by seven percentage points and those of becoming a public employee, if the father is one, rise by eleven points. These remarkable effects are obtained after we control for individual preferences toward risk; thus, they do not reflect intergenerational correlation in individuals willingness to deal with risk but other factors that affect occupation choice, such as access to information or the inheritance of one's father's business or professional practice, thus shedding light on the debate started by Galton (1869) on the correlation in fortunes across generations.[13] Finally, it is interesting to note that our measure of background risk has a negative effect on the probability of being an entrepreneur or self-employed and a positive effect on the probability of being a public-sector employee, consistent with the idea that background risk discourages independent risk taking. On the other hand, the proxy for liquidity constraints has the wrong sign (positive for the self-employed and negative for the public employees). This might reflect the fact that, when deciding whether to extend credit to a household, an applicant's occupation is a proxy for income stability and the self-employed have a more variable income than public-sector employes. However, for both variables the estimated coefficients are poorly estimated.

Asset Allocation

Table 10.3 shows the effect of the risk-attitude indicators and of the degree of risk aversion on the ownership and portfolio share of risky financial assets (private bonds, stocks, and mutual funds). The right-hand-side variable set includes total net worth, nonasset income (both measured in hundred million lira), liquidity constraint and background risk indicators, a second-order polynomial in age, and dummies for gender, education, region of birth, and of residence. The risk-averse indicator has a negative effect on the risky-asset ownership decision, and its coefficient is highly significant. When estimated on the whole sample of households, the probability of holding risky financial assets (first column) is almost half as great among risk-averse consumers as among the risk-prone. Compared to the latter, risk-averse investors have a six-point lower chance of holding risky securities, corresponding to 42 percent of the sample mean (equal to 14.4 percent).[14] Among risk-averse consumers (second column), the probability of holding risky assets is a decreasing function of our measure of absolute risk aversion, and the coefficient is precisely estimated. A one-standard-deviation increase in absolute risk aversion lowers the probability of holding risky assets by 1.1 percentage points (7.8 percent of the unconditional probability). The third and fourth columns report Tobit estimates of the portfolio share of risky assets (ratio of risky to total financial assets). This set of results confirms the probit estimates: the share invested in risky assets declines as the degree of risk aversion increases and is lower among the risk-averse than among the risk-prone. Consistent with the predictions of the classical theory of portfolio choice, differences in risk attitudes prove to be powerful determinants of portfolio composition.

Insurance Demand

We report the estimates of the effect of risk attitudes on the demand for insurance in table 10.4, distinguishing among life, health, and casualty insurance. Standard insurance theory predicts that, provided that insurance premiums depart from fair pricing, differences in risk aversion should predict both the decision to buy insurance and the amounts bought, with more risk-averse individuals being more likely to take out insurance and to hold more of it when they do. We test these pre-

Table 10.3
Risk aversion and portfolio choice

Variable	Ownership of Risky Assets (Probit regressions)		Portfolio Share of Risky Assets (Probit regressions)	
	(1) Whole Sample	(2) The Risk Averse	(3) Whole Sample	(4) The Risk Averse
Risk averse	−0.319** (0.130)		−0.165** (0.074)	
Absolute risk aversion		−1.731** (0.699)		−1.306*** (0.424)
Income	0.897*** (0.107)	0.899*** (0.115)	0.335*** (0.051)	0.409*** (0.061)
Wealth	0.021*** (0.007)	0.019** (0.008)	0.011*** (0.004)	0.010** (0.004)
Liquidity constraints	−0.305 (2.843)	0.374 (2.995)	0.289 (1.713)	0.779 (1.848)
Background risk	−1.420 (6.284)	−0.374 (6.870)	−0.407 (3.775)	−1.689 (4.245)
Age	0.023 (0.016)	0.027 (0.017)	0.014 (0.009)	0.016 (0.010)
Age squared	−0.021 (0.015)	−0.024 (0.016)	−0.013 (0.009)	−0.014 (0.010)
Gender	−0.127 (0.081)	−0.133 (0.082)	−0.100** (0.049)	−0.099* (0.051)
High school diploma	0.416*** (0.071)	0.425*** (0.074)	0.252*** (0.043)	0.256*** (0.046)
University degree	0.498*** (0.102)	0.510*** (0.106)	0.326*** (0.059)	0.307*** (0.064)
Chronic	−0.024 (0.082)	−0.034 (0.087)	−0.006 (0.049)	−0.017 (0.052)
Constant	−1.939*** (0.421)	−2.127*** (0.433)	−1.090*** (0.255)	−1.171*** (0.268)
Number of observations	3,374	3,234	3,009	2,877

Notes: See note to table 10.2. *Risky assets* include stocks, private bonds, and mutual funds. The left-hand-side variable for the regressions in the first two columns is a dummy equal to 1 if the household head owns risky assets. *Risk averse* is a dummy for whether the individual is risk averse. *Absolute risk aversion* is the measure of absolute risk aversion discussed in the text and is defined only for the risk averse. Income and wealth are in hundred million lira. The left-hand-side variable for the regressions in the tobit (last two columns) is the share of financial assets held in risky assets. Standard errors in parentheses.
*Significant at 10 percent.
**Significant at 5 percent.
***Significant at 1 percent.

Table 10.4
Risk aversion and demand for insurance

Variable	Insurance Ownership (Probit regressions)			Insurance Premiums as a Share of Consumption (Tobit regressions)		
	(1) Life Insurance	(2) Health Insurance	(3) Other Insurance	(4) Life Insurance	(5) Health Insurance	(6) Other Insurance
Absolute risk aversion	-0.617 (0.608)	-2.090*** (0.761)	-1.900*** (0.576)	-0.052 (0.039)	-0.073*** (0.026)	-0.055*** (0.016)
Income	0.496*** (0.103)	-0.016 (0.123)	0.426*** (0.102)	0.023*** (0.006)	-0.000 (0.004)	0.002 (0.002)
Wealth	0.031*** (0.008)	0.016* (0.008)	0.052*** (0.008)	0.001*** (0.000)	0.000 (0.000)	0.001*** (0.000)
Liquidity constraints	0.340 (2.277)	1.244 (3.065)	3.326 (2.268)	0.081 (0.145)	-0.017 (0.103)	0.053 (0.063)
Background risk	2.953 (4.652)	5.155 (6.825)	0.297 (4.907)	0.210 (0.294)	0.214 (0.234)	-0.171 (0.140)
Age	0.120*** (0.018)	0.058*** (0.021)	0.025* (0.013)	0.007*** (0.001)	0.002*** (0.001)	0.001 (0.000)
Age squared	-0.145*** (0.019)	-0.070*** (0.022)	-0.030** (0.013)	-0.009*** (0.001)	-0.002*** (0.001)	-0.001* (0.000)
Gender	-0.145** (0.073)	-0.166* (0.096)	-0.153** (0.065)	-0.005 (0.005)	-0.003 (0.003)	-0.003* (0.002)
High school diploma	0.167*** (0.064)	0.329*** (0.081)	0.124** (0.062)	0.011*** (0.004)	0.009*** (0.003)	0.004** (0.002)
University degree	0.052 (0.097)	0.255** (0.126)	0.100 (0.096)	0.006 (0.006)	0.009** (0.004)	0.004 (0.003)

Self-employed	0.395***	0.682***	0.100	0.030***	0.026***	0.008***
	(0.066)	(0.080)	(0.070)	(0.004)	(0.003)	(0.002)
Chronic	−0.179**	0.055	0.099	−0.013**	0.002	0.001
	(0.078)	(0.097)	(0.070)	(0.005)	(0.003)	(0.002)
Siblings	−0.026*	0.020	−0.016	−0.002**	0.001	−0.000
	(0.014)	(0.019)	(0.014)	(0.001)	(0.001)	(0.000)
Constant	−3.284***	−2.286***	−0.630*	−0.205***	−0.078***	−0.015
	(0.423)	(0.518)	(0.332)	(0.028)	(0.018)	(0.009)
Number of observations	3,234	3,234	3,238	3,238	3,238	3,223

Notes: See note to table 10.2. The left-hand-side variable is a dummy equal to 1 if the household head owns a life insurance (first column), a health insurance (second column), or a theft or casualty insurance (third column). *Absolute risk aversion* is the measure of absolute risk aversion discussed in the text and is defined only for the risk averse. Income and wealth are in hundred million lira. The left-hand-side variable for the tobit regressions are the ratios of the insurance premiums to household consumption. Standard errors in parentheses.

* Significant at 10 percent.
** Significant at 5 percent.
*** Significant at 1 percent.

dictions by focusing on the subsample of risk-averse individuals and estimate a probit model for whether the household has insurance and a Tobit model for the amount of insurance purchased (i.e., the value of insurance premiums) scaled with consumption. To account for differences in household endowments and in human capital, wealth and income are included among the right-hand-side variables. In all cases, we find that more risk-averse consumers are less likely to hold insurance, that they buy less of it, and that the effect is in most cases statistically significant. This puzzling finding contradicts the predictions of the simple models of insurance demand.[15] The proxy for background risk has a positive effect of the decision to have insurance and on the amount to buy, consistent with theoretical predictions, though the high standard errors of the coefficient do not allow reliable inference. As for liquidity constraints, their effect is in principle ambiguous: they make individuals more risk averse and thus more prone to insure, but at the same time, when the household faces a high shadow interest rate, paying premiums now for possible insurance benefits later could be a bad deal. The estimates seem to suggest that the first effect dominates, but the coefficients are never statistically significant.

Investment in Education
We report the effects of risk attitudes on the investment in education in table 10.5. Our left-hand-side variable is the number of years of education an individual has obtained. The set of controls includes individual income and wealth, a second-order polynomial in age (or year of birth) to account for differences in the return to schooling across different cohorts, a dummy for gender and a full set of regional dummies to proxy for differences across areas in the return to education. In addition, we insert four dummies for the educational attainment of the father of the household head to account for intergenerational persistence in education, finding strong supportive evidence. As shown in the first column, compared to the risk-prone, risk-averse individuals invest less in education, and the effect is statistically significant: being risk-averse lowers education by over one year, on average. Among the risk-averse, those who are more averse invest less in education, and again the effect is strongly significant (second column).

Moving, Job Changes, and Health Status
Table 10.6 shows the results for the decisions to migrate and change jobs and for health status. The first two columns estimate a model for

Table 10.5
Risk aversion and the investment in education

	Years of Schooling	
Variable	(1) Whole Sample	(2) The Risk Averse
Risk averse	−0.321**	—
	(0.165)	
Absolute risk aversion	—	−4.667***
		(1.346)
Income	2.960***	3.355***
	(0.198)	(0.220)
Wealth	0.032**	0.024
	(0.016)	(0.017)
Liquidity constraints	−1.304	−1.180
	(4.906)	(4.977)
Background risk	3.162	5.810
	(10.365)	(10.691)
Age	−0.050*	−0.064**
	(0.028)	(0.029)
Age squared	−0.019	−0.006
	(0.027)	(0.028)
Gender	−0.279*	−0.209
	(0.146)	(0.147)
Chronic	−0.409***	−0.463***
	(0.151)	(0.155)
Father		
Elementary school	2.415***	2.322***
	(0.142)	(0.143)
Junior high school	4.267***	4.203***
	(0.207)	(0.212)
High school diploma	5.751***	5.652***
	(0.249)	(0.253)
University degree	7.163***	6.952***
	(0.372)	(0.387)
Constant	8.781***	9.252***
	(0.792)	(0.776)
Number of observations	3,312	3,177
R-squared	0.428	0.436

Notes: See note to table 10.2. The left-hand-side variable is the number of year of schooling reported by the household head. *Risk averse* is a dummy for whether the individual is risk averse. *Absolute risk aversion* is the measure of absolute risk aversion discussed in the text and is defined only for the risk averse. Income and wealth are in hundred million lira. The education dummies under the heading *Father* refer to the education attainment of the father of the household head. Standard errors in parentheses.
*Significant at 10 percent.
**Significant at 5 percent.
***Significant at 1 percent.

Table 10.6
Risk aversion, moving, changing jobs, and one's health

Variable	Moving to Another Region (Probit regressions)		Propensity to Change Job (Probit regressions)		Health (Probit regressions)	
	(1) Whole Sample	(2) The Risk Averse	(3) Whole Sample	(4) The Risk Averse	(5) Whole Sample	(6) The Risk Averse
Risk averse	−0.105 (0.145)		−0.074 (0.116)		−0.591*** (0.122)	
Absolute risk aversion		−0.996** (0.430)		−0.764** (0.310)		0.582 (0.641)
Income	0.001 (0.099)	0.001 (0.111)	−0.023 (0.088)	−0.072 (0.098)	0.018 (0.093)	0.111 (0.108)
Wealth	0.014* (0.007)	0.016** (0.007)	−0.011 (0.007)	−0.007 (0.007)	0.000 (0.007)	−0.002 (0.008)
Liquidity constraints	19.833*** (2.112)	21.573*** (2.187)	8.092*** (2.025)	8.962*** (2.084)	4.330** (2.260)	4.551* (2.322)
Background risk	50.948*** (3.775)	48.865*** (3.871)	4.343 (4.210)	2.391 (4.397)	6.434 (4.667)	6.676 (4.869)
Age	0.023 (0.014)	0.019 (0.014)	0.031** (0.012)	0.032** (0.013)	0.039*** (0.014)	0.042*** (0.015)
Age squared	−0.021 (0.014)	−0.017 (0.014)	−0.043*** (0.012)	−0.044*** (0.012)	−0.004 (0.013)	−0.007 (0.013)
Gender	0.115 (0.070)	0.102 (0.071)	−0.460*** (0.064)	−0.454*** (0.064)	0.158** (0.066)	0.171** (0.067)
High school diploma	−0.050 (0.068)	−0.049 (0.070)	−0.233*** (0.057)	−0.245*** (0.059)	−0.101 (0.067)	−0.111 (0.070)

University degree	0.165*	0.130	−0.414***	−0.433***	−0.013	−0.039
	(0.099)	(0.103)	(0.092)	(0.096)	(0.100)	(0.105)
Chronic	0.083	0.087	0.215***	0.208***		
	(0.072)	(0.074)	(0.062)	(0.064)		
Constant	−1.125***	−0.988***	−0.786**	−0.759**	−2.643***	−3.500***
	(0.384)	(0.373)	(0.322)	(0.322)	(0.396)	(0.408)
Number of observations	3,374	3,234	3,378	3,238	3,374	3,234

Notes: See note to table 10.2. The left-hand-side variable is a dummy equal to 1 if the household head lives in a region different from the one where he or she was born (first two columns), if he or she has changed jobs at least twice over his or her working life (third and fourth column), or if he or she is affected by a chronic disease (last two columns). *Risk averse* is a dummy for whether the individual is risk averse. *Absolute risk aversion* is the measure of absolute risk aversion discussed in the text and is defined only for the risk averse. Income and wealth are in hundred million lira. The regressions in the first two columns include the dummies for the region of birth but not for the region of current residence. Standard errors in parentheses.
*Significant at 10 percent.
**Significant at 5 percent.
***Significant at 1 percent.

the probability that an individual has moved from his region of birth to another region. In the sample, 18.5 percent of household heads were born in a region different from the one where they currently live. Since the regressions include a full set of dummies for region of birth, local factors affecting the decision to move (such as labor-market conditions and wage prospects in the area) are accounted for. We also control for age, gender, and education. Compared to the risk-prone, the risk-averse are less likely to have moved, but the effect is not statistically significant (first column). The second column reports the estimates for the restricted group of risk-averse individuals. The degree of risk aversion has a negative and significant effect on the probability of having moved; increasing the degree of risk aversion by one standard deviation lowers the probability by one percentage point, or 5.5 percent of the sample mean.[16]

The third and fourth columns show the results for the propensity to change jobs. The left-hand-side variable is a dummy equal to 1 if the household head has changed jobs at least twice and 0 otherwise. About 33 percent of the consumers in our sample have changed jobs more than twice. Being risk-averse compared to being risk-prone lowers the probability of being a job changer, but the coefficient is not precisely estimated. Within the group of risk-averse individuals, however, a higher degree of risk aversion has a negative and statistically significant effect on the probability of changing jobs; a one-standard deviation increase in risk aversion lowers the probability of taking the risks connected to changing job by 1.2 percentage points. The last two columns report probit regressions for the probability of being affected by a chronic disease. When the total sample is used, the estimates indicate that the risk-averse are significantly less likely than the risk-prone to incur a chronic disease, with an effect equal to nineteen percentage points, about 91 percent of the sample share of households with a chronic disease. When the sample is restricted to the risk-averse, the degree of risk aversion has the wrong sign.

Overall, the evidence in tables 10.2 to 10.6 implies that attitudes toward risk have considerable explanatory power for several important consumer decisions. In some cases, such as occupational and portfolio choice, our evidence strongly suggests that leaving out measures of risk aversion in an empirical analysis of household behavior is likely to be a substantial problem.

Risk, Return, and Risk Aversion

The results in the previous section show that risk-averse individuals tend to undertake safer actions when they choose their occupation, invest in education, allocate their savings, and decide to move or change jobs. Choosing safer actions means, in equilibrium, choosing prospects with a lower but more predictable payoff. As a consequence, the more risk-averse the individual, the lower but the less variable his income, on average. To check these implications, we focus on the sample of risk-averse consumers and exploit information available in the 1995 SHIW on the subjective probability distribution of future earnings[17] to construct a measure of expected earnings and their variance and correlate it with consumers' risk aversion. Since the subjective probability questions were put to only half of the sample, these regressions are based on a much smaller sample.

Table 10.7, in the first column, reports the results of the estimates where expected earnings is the left-hand-side variable. We control for age to account for experience and its productivity effects on wages, for gender, for family size, and for differences in economic development (and thus wage levels) across areas by inserting a full set of regional dummies. We also control for education to account for differences in returns arising from differences in human capital. Finding a negative correlation between expected future earnings and absolute risk aversion may reflect decreasing absolute risk aversion rather than choice of low-income-safer jobs by the more risk-averse. To partially address this reverse-causality issue, we insert in the regression the level of individual wealth. Being more risk-averse translates into lower expected labor income, and the effect is statistically significant and economically important: having a risk-aversion coefficient equal to the ninetieth percentile implies a level of expected earnings that is 5.4 million lire lower than that for the tenth percentile (21 percent of mean expected earnings). These results are consistent with the idea that the more risk-averse will, on average, end up poorer.

The second column shows the regression for the standard deviation of expected earnings. After controlling for age, gender, education, region of residence, and accumulated wealth, more risk-averse consumers face lower earnings variance, and the effect is highly significant. Economically, those with a degree of risk aversion in the ninetieth percentile of the cross-sectional distribution face an income risk, as

Table 10.7
Return, risk, and risk aversion

Variable	(1) Expected Earnings	(2) Earnings Uncertainty	(3) Earnings Uncertainty
Absolute risk aversion	−49.838***	−6.665***	−1.370
	(11.880)	(1.769)	(1.250)
Family wealth	0.014***	0.002***	0.001***
	(0.001)	(0.000)	(0.000)
Expected earnings			0.106***
			(0.003)
Age	1.232***	−0.024	−0.154***
	(0.463)	(0.069)	(0.048)
Age squared	−1.372**	0.008	0.154***
	(0.540)	(0.080)	(0.056)
Gender dummy	6.967***	0.433**	−0.307**
	(1.448)	(0.216)	(0.153)
High school diploma	6.164***	0.120	−0.535***
	(1.146)	(0.171)	(0.121)
University degree	17.056***	0.499**	−1.314***
	(1.625)	(0.242)	(0.179)
Constant	−7.457	1.626	2.418**
	(9.912)	(1.476)	(1.035)
Number of observations	1,027	1,027	1,027
R-squared	0.298	0.132	0.574

Notes: The left-hand-side variable is household expected earnings in the first column, and earnings uncertainty in the second and third columns. Earnings uncertainty is the standard deviation of the subjective distribution of the household head expected earnings, as from Guiso et al. (2002). *Absolute risk aversion* is the measure of absolute risk aversion discussed in the text and is defined only for the risk averse. Dummies for the region of residence are also included. Standard errors are reported in parentheses.
*Significant at 10 percent.
**Significant at 5 percent.
***Significant at 1 percent.

measured by the standard deviation of expected earnings, that is 70 percent lower than that of those at the tenth percentile. The last column further refines these results by adding to the regression the expected value of future income and considering the risk and return options faced by individuals. Since expected income represents the premium the market offers for bearing more risk, once one controls for expected earnings, risk aversion should no longer affect the variance of earnings. And this is indeed the case. Once expected earnings is added to the regression, the coefficient of the degree of risk aversion becomes six times smaller and is no longer statistically significant. While these results are consistent with more risk-averse individuals earning less because they choose safer jobs, the possibility of being driven by reverse causality cannot be ruled out by these estimates, even if we control for the level of individual accumulated assets. For this, more research is needed that brings exogenous variation in risk aversion.

Preferences about Risk: The Consequences of Self-Selection

The evidence presented in the previous sections shows that risk attitudes have important effects on observable behavior and that risk-averse individuals sort themselves into activities that entail lower exposure to risk. This self-selection is relevant in many situations where one is interested in studying the effect of risk on choice. For instance, hours worked will in general depend on wage riskiness (see Block and Heineke, 1973, and Killingsworth, 1983), and higher wage variability may reduce leisure. Similarly, precautionary savings decisions will be affected by the income risk faced by prudent consumers (Leland, 1982; Drèze and Modigliani, 1972). Labor income risk may also affect portfolio choice and insurance demand, inducing investors to pick up safer portfolios or demand more insurance to reduce overall exposure to risk (Kimball, 1993). To assess the relevance of risk for consumers' decisions, one needs variation in risk. This is often unobserved and has thus been proxied with observable variables. Typically, since Friedman (1957)'s study of the consumption function, labor income risk has been measured with occupational dummies (e.g., Skinner, 1988). More recently, starting with the work of Guiso, Jappelli, and Terlizzese (1992), survey measures of the subjective probability distribution of future income have been used to obtain indicators of the expected value and riskiness of an individual's labor income. These measures have then been used to test for precautionary savings and for the effects of background risk on insurance demand and portfolio choice. The problem with these studies is self-selection: labor income risk is endogenous because more risk-averse individuals sort themselves into safer occupations. If risk aversion is unobservable, estimates of the effect of labor income risk on choice will be inconsistent because the measure of risk is correlated with the error term that contains the (unobserved) preference parameter.

In this section, we offer evidence on the importance of self-selection in estimating precautionary savings by proxying risk with a dummy for self-employment.[18] We estimate a saving function based on a life-cycle model extended to allow for precautionary savings due to earnings uncertainty. Under a set of somewhat restrictive assumptions, the model has a closed-form solution for the saving rate where the precautionary motive is additive with respect to life-cycle savings (Caballero, 1991), which we approximate as follows:

$$s_i = a_0 w_i + a_1 y_i + a_2 z_i + a_{3i}\sigma_i + u_i, \tag{10.4}$$

where s_i is household i savings, y_i is its labor income, w_i is the household's net worth, and z_i is a vector of demographic variables. The precautionary saving component is captured by the fourth term on the right-hand side, where household labor income risk σ_i is proxied by a dummy variable for self-employment. The coefficient a_{3i} reflects the strength of the precautionary motive, as measured by the degree of absolute prudence, which (if preferences are of the constant absolute risk aversion (CARA) variety) is equal to the degree of absolute risk aversion; this is why a_{3i} is household-specific. Self-selection emerges because strongly risk-averse individuals choose safer jobs and will be less exposed to income risk. If risk aversion is unobservable, it will show up in the residual and will bias the precautionary motive estimate downward. Since we observe individuals' risk aversion, we can assess the importance of the self-selection bias in estimates of precautionary savings.

To illustrate, table 10.8 shows the results of the estimates where variables are scaled by household earnings. The first column reports the estimates when the self-selection problem is ignored. The self-employment dummy—our proxy for labor income risk—is statistically significant but carries a negative coefficient. This is contrary to the precautionary savings hypothesis but is consistent with a strong self-selection bias if risk aversion has a strong effect on individual occupational choice. To check whether the result is indeed driven by self-selection, we interact our measure of risk aversion (scaled by labor income) with the self-employment dummy and use this variable as a measure of risk in the regression. The results, shown in the second column of table 10.8, reveal a positive and statistically significant effect of this risk-aversion-weighted measure of risk consistent with the predictions of precautionary savings models. Computed at the sample mean of risk aversion, being self-employed raises the saving rate by 5.2 percentage points, or about 28 percent of the median saving rate in the

Table 10.8
Risk aversion, precautionary savings, and self-selection

Variable	(1)	(2)
Wealth	−0.0117***	−0.0130***
	(0.0009)	(0.0009)
Self-employed head	−0.0399**	—
	(0.0159)	
Self-employed * absolute risk aversion	—	0.0090***
		(0.0015)
Age	0.0095***	0.0092***
	(0.0029)	(0.0029)
Age squared	−0.0051*	−0.0044
	(0.0028)	(0.0028)
Gender dummy	0.0445***	0.0355**
	(0.0147)	(0.0146)
High school diploma	0.1186***	0.1204***
	(0.0136)	(0.0135)
University degree	0.2001***	0.1933***
	(0.0197)	(0.0199)
Household size	0.0223***	0.0195***
	(0.0056)	(0.0056)
Dummy for children	−0.0622***	−0.0575***
	(0.0152)	(0.0152)
Number of observations	3,197	3,197

Notes: The left-hand-side variable is household saving rate. We exclude the top and bottom 1 percent of the distribution. Dummies for the region of birth and for the region of residence are also included. The sample is restricted to the risk averse. Standard errors are reported in brackets. Standard errors in parentheses.
*Significant at 10 percent.
**Significant at 5 percent.
***Significant at 1 percent.

sample, suggesting that precautionary saving exists and is relevant, once self-selection is properly addressed.

Conclusions

Theory of choice under uncertainty implies that preferences for risk should strongly affect individuals' choices in a variety of contexts. Thus, differences in risk attitudes across individuals should be important in explaining observed differences in behavior. In some instances, theory suggests that differences in attitudes toward risk could be the only factor affecting differences in behavior. We have used a survey-based measure of individuals' willingness to pay for a hypothetical risky asset to construct a measure of the Arrow-Pratt index of absolute risk aversion at the individual level. We have then related this measure to a number of choices under uncertainty. Our results show that this measure has strong predictive power on some key consumer decisions (including occupational choice, portfolio allocation, investment in education, job change, and moving decisions) in ways that are consistent with what theory predicts. In some cases, the effects are extremely substantial. For instance, being risk-averse, as opposed to being risk-neutral or risk-loving, raises the probability of being self-employed by as much as 36 percent of the sample mean and the chances of holding risky assets by 42 percent of the sample mean. Our evidence shows strongly that individuals differ markedly in their attitudes toward risk and that these differences lead them to sort themselves out in such a way that the more risk-averse choose lower returns in exchange for lower risk exposure when they invest their assets, choose their occupation, decide to invest in education, migrate or change jobs, or take precautions against illness. How important, then, are differences in risk aversion in explaining income inequality? One way to answer is to look at how much of the variability in expected earnings is explained by differences in risk aversion compared to other factors. A regression of expected earnings on a second-order polynomial in age, a set of dummies for place of birth, and a dummy for gender explains 6.4 percent of the sample variability in expected earnings. Adding risk aversion explains an additional 2.2 percent of the sample variability, about a third of what is explained by age, gender, and area of birth. Furthermore, if dummies for father's occupation are included as proxies for intergenerational transmission of inequality, they can explain an additional 1.2 percent of the variability. Thus, differences in attitudes on risk are at least as important in explaining differences in average income across individuals as are such variables as age, gender, place of birth, and family of origin, which are deemed to have a substantial explanatory power on income levels.

Overall, these results suggest that it pays to devote resources to collect data on individual preferences toward risk. However, in future research it will be important to jointly elicit information on the absolute risk aversion of the value function (as done in the SHIW) and the relative risk aversion of the underlying felicity function (as pursued in the Health and Retirement Survey). This would help to clarify many issues, including the possibility of distinguishing between preference for risk and aspects of the environment that affect individuals' willingness to bear risk (such as imperfections in credit markets and uninsurability of labor income risk).

Appendix

The SHIW

The Bank of Italy Survey of Household Income and Wealth (SHIW) collects detailed data on demographics, households' consumption, income, and balance-sheet items. The survey was first conducted in the mid-1960s and has been available on tape since 1984. Over time, it has gone through a number of changes in sample size, design, sampling methodology, and questionnaire. However, sampling methodology, sample size, and the broad contents of the information collected have been unchanged since 1989. Each wave surveys a representative sample of the Italian resident population and covers about 8,000 households, although at times specific parts of the questionnaire are asked to only a random subsample. Sampling occurs in two stages—first at the municipality level and then at the household level. Municipalities are divided into fifty-one strata defined by seventeen regions and three classes of population size (more than 40,000, 20,000 to 40,000, and less than 20,000). Households are randomly selected from registry office records. They are defined as groups of individuals related by blood, marriage, or adoption and sharing the same dwelling. The head of the household is conventionally identified with the husband, if present. If the person who would usually be considered the head of the household works abroad or is absent at the time of the interview, the head of the household is taken to be the person responsible for managing the household's resources. The net response rate (ratio of responses to households contacted net of ineligible units) was 57 percent in the 1995 wave. Brandolini and Cannari (1994) present a detailed discussion of sample design, attrition, and other measurement issues and compare the SHIW variables with the corresponding aggregate quantities.

Expected Earnings and Their Variance

The variance and the expected value of individual earnings are computed as in Guiso, Jappelli, and Pistaferri (2002) and are based on the following questions that were asked in the SHIW.

• "Do you expect to voluntarily retire or stop working in the next 12 months?"

If the answer is yes, the interviewer goes on to the next survey section. If the answer is no, each respondent is asked the following questions:

1. "What are the chances that in the next 12 months you will keep your job or find one (or start a new activity)? In other words, if you were to assign a score between 0 and 100 to the chance of keeping your job or of finding one (or of starting a new activity), what score would you assign (0 if you are certain not to work, 100 if you are certain to work)?"

2. "Suppose you will keep your job or that in the next 12 months you will find one. What is the minimum annual income, net of taxes and contributions, that you expect to earn from this job?"

3. "Again suppose you will keep your job or that in the next 12 months you will find one. What is the maximum annual income, net of taxes and contributions, that you expect to earn from this job?"

4. "What are the chances that you will earn less than X [where X is computed by the interviewer as [(item 2 above) + (item 4 above)] ÷ 2]? In other words, if you were to assign a score between 0 and 100 to the chance of earning less than X, what score would you assign (0 if you are certain to earn more than X, 100 if you are certain to earn less than X)?"

Acknowledgments

Luigi Guiso acknowledges financial support from Ministero dell'Universita e della Ricerca Scientifica e Tecnologica (MURST) and the European Commission (EEC) for the Training and Mobility of Researchers (TMR) research project "Specialization versus Diversification: The Microeconomics of Regional Development and the Spatial Propagation of Shocks in Europe." Cristiana Rampazzi provided excellent research assistantship. Only the authors are responsible for the contents of this chapter, which does not reflect the opinion of the Community or of the Bank of Italy.

Notes

1. For instance, inequalities in income and wealth have been related to limited access to financial markets—either because of the fixed costs of investing in assets with high expected yield (Guvenen, 2002) or because of rationing in credit markets arising from information and commitment problems (Cagetti and De Nardi, 2002).

2. The appendix to this chapter describes the survey contents, sample design, interviewing procedure, and response rates in more detail.

3. Although we assume individuals are expected utility maximizers, it is fair to say that there is no common experimental evidence that shows that individulas behave as predicted by the expected utility model (see Camerer, 1995).

4. The approximation for R_i is good only if the risk is relatively small compared to wealth. Thus, the approximation is likely to be less satisfactory for relatively poor households. We have checked our results excluding households in the first decile of the wealth distribution and found no significant departures.

5. In a related paper (see Guiso and Paiella, 2001), we study the determinants of risk aversion and find that, once we control for the agent's endowment, individual charactersitics (such as age, sex, education, and place of birth) have limited explanatory explanatory power and attitudes toward risk are characterized by massive unexplained heterogeneity.

6. Tiseno (2002) shows that knowledge of the maximum subjective price function for a risk is sufficient to identify the risk aversion of a consumer lifetime utility. He also shows that under certain conditions the risk aversion of lifetime utility and that of period utility are proportional.

7. The reported prices are likely to be affected by a well-known problem in experimental economics: individuals asked to price hypothetical lotteries (or risky assets) tend to report lower buying than selling prices (see Kagel and Roth, 1995, pp. 68–86). If the true willingness to pay or accept for a lottery is in between the reported bid and ask prices, the reported willingness to pay (sell) will lead to upward (downward) biased estimates of individual risk aversion. Since our survey elicits the willingness to pay, it is likely that our individual risk-aversion measures are biased upward. But experiments are silent on whether the extent of the bias (or the difference between bid and ask prices) is correlated with some observable individual characteristics. If the bias is proportional to the reported price and constant across individuals, our results will be unaffected.

8. Those who answered have somewhat different characteristics than nonrespondents. They are on average six years younger than the total sample, are slightly better educated (1.3 more years of schooling), have higher shares of male-headed households (79.8 compared to 74.4 percent) and of married people (78.9 and 72.5 percent), and are significantly more likely to have children (41.9 and 31.6 percent, respectively).

9. Since our risk-aversion measure is the risk aversion of the lifetime utility function, strictly speaking the measure of relative risk aversion that we report is correct if consumers have a one-year horizon. If consumers have a lifetime horizon, then the proper scale variable should be lifetime wealth. We also compute a measure of relative risk aversion (RRA) that relies on a measure of lifetime wealth. Estimating lifetime wealth is fraught with problems. To construct one, we take current consumption, assume that individuals have a flat consumption profile over the life cycle, assume that maximum lifespan is eighty years (about life expectancy at birth), and assume that all die without wealth. For each individual in our sample, we compute the present value of consumption from current age to age eighty assuming a discount rate of 10 percent (which incorporates both the rate on borrowing and the probability of dying before age eighty) and use this to compute relative risk aversion. The median relative risk aversion of the value function estimated this way is 16.

10. Compensation for risk may thus be an additional reason why education carries a higher return (Hartog and Vijverberg, 2001).

11. In the discussion in the text, we have ignored the possibility that risky decisions may interact. For instance, the amount of insurance one is willing to buy may depend on the level of portfolio risk one is exposed to, so that endogenous exposure may act as a form of background risk. This possibility, noted by Eeckhoudt and Gollier (1999) and Gollier (2001a), is not directly addressed by our estimates. However, insofar as these interactions exist, they should be reflected in our measure of risk aversion, in the sense that individuals who are already more exposed to endogenous risks will be less willing to pay for the hypothetical security and thus turn out to be more risk averse. We have also run regressions inserting as explanatory variables some of the risk choices that we attempt to explain—for example, by using occupational dummies in the portfolio regressions and vice versa. These regressions, not reported but available on request, leave our results unaffected.

12. In Italy, for instance, public-sector employees cannot be laid off except in a few extreme circumstances of misconduct. In addition, public-sector jobs provide less variable on-the-job wages (see Guiso, Jappelli, and Pistaferri, 2002).

13. It can be shown that this result is unaffected when our measure of risk aversion is measured with error, provided the parent's occupational choice is uncorrelated with the measurement error in the risk aversion of the individual, a reasonable assumption.

14. Thus, differences in risk aversion can help understand the "stockholding puzzle"— that is, the well-documented feature of household portfolios that few households invest in stocks.

15. The implication that more risk-averse individuals should buy more insurance has a strong intuitive appeal and not finding it in the data is somewhat disappointing. At the moment, we have no convincing explanation for the finding. Two admittedly unsatisfactory possibilities are the following. One is that insurance companies are able to price-discriminate on the basis of customers' risk aversion. This would lead to higher premiums for more risk-averse consumers, who would then reduce insurance demand. This explanation—which we consider unlikely—relies on the assumption that personal risk aversion is observable. Another tentative explanation is that individuals can act to self-insure against the consequences of adverse events. This leads them to replace market insurance with self-insurance. If market insurance is sold at highly unfair prices, while self-insurance is relatively efficient—in the sense that one extra euro of current spending results in a large reduction in the loss—an increase in risk aversion can reduce market insurance and increase self-insurance. If this explanation were true, self-insurance (which is not observed in our data and cannot be controlled for) would be picked up by our measure of risk aversion, which reflects substitutability between self-insurance and market insurance, giving rise to a negative correlation between risk aversion and market insurance demand. A third, perhaps more appealing, explanation for the negative coefficient is reverse causality. If lack of insurance is due to highly unfair pricing that is originated by unobserved and uncontrolled local insurance-market characteristics, then individuals in these locations will face a greater background risk, which makes them less willing to take on the risks proffered by the question, resulting in a higher measured risk aversion.

16. As pointed out by Daveri and Faini (1999), migration may be triggered by households' need to diversify their sources of income, spreading income earners geographically. The implication is that members of households (heads) that are more risk-averse will tend to work in different geographical locations rather than bunch in the same place.

We cannot test this prediction since in our data a household groups only the individuals who live in the same house.

17. Four questions on income expectations were put to half of the overall sample after excluding the retired and people not in the labor force (a total of 4,799 individuals). The employed, the unemployed, and the job seekers were asked to state, on a scale from 0 to 100, their chances of having a job in the twelve months following the interview. Each individual assigning a positive probability to being employed was then asked to report the minimum and the maximum he or she expects to earn if employed and the probability of earning less than the midpoint of the support of the distribution. The exact wording of these questions is reported in the appendix to this chapter. The answers are then used to compute expected earnings and their variance (see Guiso, Jappelli, and Pistaferri, 2002, for details on the computation).

18. Fuchs and Schündeln (2003) address the relevance of self-selection for estimates of precautionary saving by comparing the saving behavior of East and West German households after unification. They argue that under Communism, job allocation in East Germany was essentially exogenous and not driven by individual preferences. They compare the effect of being self-employed (their proxy for earnings risk) on the propensity to save in the two countries after unification and argue that the stronger effect found for East German households is an estimate of the effect of self-selection.

References

Arrow, Kenneth J. (1970). *Essays in the Theory of Risk Bearing*. Amsterdam: North Holland.

Barsky, Robert B., Thomas F. Juster, Miles S. Kimball, and Matthew D. Shapiro. (1997). "Preference Parameters and Behavioral Heterogeneity: An Experimental Approach in the Health and Retirement Study." *Quarterly Journal of Economics* 112: 537–580.

Block, M. K., and J. M. Heineke. (1973). "The Allocation of Effort under Uncertainty: The Case of Risk Averse Behavior." *Journal of Political Economy* 81: 376–385.

Brandolini, Andrea, and Luigi Cannari. (1994). "Methodological Appendix." In Albert Ando, Luigi Guiso, and Ignazio Visco (Eds.), *Saving and the Accumulation of Wealth*. Cambridge: Cambridge University Press.

Brunello, Giorgio. (2002). "Absolute Risk Aversion and the Returns to Education." *Economics of Education Review* 21: 635–640.

Caballero, Ricardo. (1991). "Earnings Uncertainty and Aggregate Wealth Accumulation." *American Economic Review* 81: 859–871.

Cagetti, Marco, and Cristina De Nardi. (2002). "Entrepreneurship, Frictions and Wealth." Federal Reserve Bank of Minneapolis Working Paper No. 620.

Camerer, Colin. (1995). "Individual Decision Making." In John H. Kagel and Alvin E. Roth (Eds.), *The Handbook of Experimental Economics*. Princeton, NJ: Princeton University Press.

Daveri, Francesco, and Riccardo Faini. (1999). "Where Do Migrants Go?" *Oxford Economic Papers* 51: 595–622.

Drèze, Jean, and Franco Modigliani. (1972). "Consumption Decisions under Uncertainty." *Journal of Economic Theory* 5: 308–335.

Eeckhoudt, Louis, and Christian Gollier. (1999). "Are Independent Risks Substitutes?" Mimeo, University of Toulouse.

Eeckhoudt, Louis, and James K. Hammitt. (2004). "Risk Aversion and Mortality Risks." *Journal of Environmental Economics and Management* 47: 13–29.

Evans, David S., and Boyan Jovanovic. (1989). "An Estimated Model of Entrepreneurial Choice under Liquidity Constraints." *Journal of Political Economy* 97: 808–827.

Friedman, Milton. (1957). *A Theory of the Consumption Function*. Princeton, NJ: Princeton University Press.

Fuchs, Nicole, and Matthias Schündeln. (2003). "Precautionary Savings and Self-Selection: Evidence from the German Reunification Experiment." Mimeo, Yale University.

Galton, Francis. (1869). "Hereditary Genius: An Inquiry into Its Laws and Consequences." London: MacMillan.

Gollier, Christian. (2001a). *The Economics of Risk and Time*. Boston: MIT Press.

Gollier, Christian. (2001b). "What Does the Classical Theory Have to Say about Portfolio Choice?" In Luigi Guiso, Michael Haliassos, and Tullio Jappelli (Eds.), *Household Portfolios*. Boston: MIT Press.

Guiso, Luigi, Michael Haliassos, and Tullio Jappelli (Eds.). (2000). *Household Portfolios*. Boston: MIT Press.

Guiso, Luigi, and Tullio Jappelli. (2000). "Household Portfolios in Italy." In Luigi Guiso, Michael Haliassos, and Tullio Jappelli (Eds.), *Household Portfolios*. Boston: MIT Press.

Guiso, Luigi, Tullio Jappelli, and Luigi Pistaferri. (2002). "An Empirical Analysis of Earnings and Employment Risk." *Journal of Business and Economic Statistics* 20: 1–13.

Guiso, Luigi, Tullio Jappelli, and Daniele Terlizzese. (1992). "Earnings Uncertainty and Precautionary Saving." *Journal of Monetary Economics* 30: 307–337.

Guiso, Luigi, and Monica Paiella. (2001). "Risk Aversion, Wealth and Background Risk." CEPR DP No. 2728.

Guiso, Luigi, Paola Sapienza, and Luigi Zingales. (2004a). "Does Local Financial Development Matter?" *Quarterly Journal of Economics* 119: 929–969.

Guiso, Luigi, Paola Sapienza, and Luigi Zingales. (2004b). "The Role of Social Capital in Financial Development." *American Economic Review* 94: 526–556.

Guvenen, Fatih. (2002). "Reconciling Conflicting Evidence on the Elasticity of Intertemporal Substitution: A Macroeconomic Perspective." Mimeo, Rochester University.

Hartog, Joop, and Wim Vijverberg. (2001). "Do Wages Really Compensate for Risk Aversion and Skewness Affection?" Mimeo, University of Texas.

Kagel, John H., and Alvin E. Roth (Eds.). (1995). *The Handbook of Experimental Economics*. Princeton, NJ: Princeton University Press.

Kihlstrom, Richard E., and Jean Jaques Laffont. (1979). "A General Equilibrium Theory of Firm Formations Based on Risk Aversion." *Journal of Political Economy* 87: 719–748.

Killingsworth, Mark R. (1983). Labor Supply. Cambridge: Cambridge University Press.

Kimball, Miles S. (1993). "Standard Risk Aversion." *Econometrica* 3: 589–611.

Leland, Hayne E. (1982). "Savings and Uncertainty: The Precautionary Demand for Saving." *Quarterly Journal of Economics* 82: 465–473.

Lucas, Jr., Robert E. (1978). "On the Size Distribution of Business Firms." *Bell Journal of Economics* 2: 508–523.

Merton, Robert C. (1969). "Lifetime Portfolio Selection under Uncertainty: The Continuous-Time Case." *Review of Economics and Statistics* 3: 247–257.

Mossin, Jan. (1968). "Aspects of Rational Insurance Purchases." *Journal of Political Economy* 91: 304–311.

Pratt, John W., and Richard Zeckhauser. (1987). "Proper Risk Aversion." *Econometrica* 55: 143–154.

Rabin, Matthew. (2000). "Risk Aversion and Expected-Utility Theory: A Calibration Theorem." *Econometrica* 68: 1281–1292.

Samuelson, Paul A. (1969). "Lifetime Portfolio Selection by Dynamic Stochastic Programming." *Review of Economics and Statistics* 3: 239–246.

Skinner, Jonathan. (1988). "Risky Income, Life Cycle Consumption and Precautionary Savings." *Journal of Monetary Economics* 22: 237–255.

Tiseno, Andrea. (2002). "Using Wealth, Consumption and Shadow Prices to Identify Intertemporal Preferences." Mimeo, University of Chicago.

11

Insurance and Incentives
in Sharecropping

Luis H. B. Braido

Introduction

The term *insurance* is used to describe formal and informal arrangements designed to mitigate the risk of harmful events. Risk has always been a major human concern, and many practices in primitive tribes can be seen as insurance mechanisms. This chapter discusses some recent empirical papers on one of these ancient insurance mechanisms, sharecropping, which is used to share the risk posed by nature to agricultural activities.

Sharecropping is a form of land leasing in which a tenant and landlord share the final output as compensation for the managerial labor supplied by the former and the land capital supplied by the latter. This contract was used in ancient societies and is still in use in modern economies. For instance, Warriner (1962), Hodkinson (1992), and Huson (2000) describe the use of this system in ancient Mesopotamia, Egypt, and Greece; Hoffman (1984) notes a dramatic expansion of sharecropping in France between the Middle Ages and the seventeenth century; Ackerberg and Botticini (2000) present an empirical analysis of the risk-sharing properties of sharecropping in early Renaissance Tuscany; and Canjels (1998b) and Allen and Lueck (2003) discuss the importance of this contractual form in the present organization of the farming sector in the United States.

Classical View

Adam Smith is one of the first classical authors to extensively comment on the incentive aspects of the sharecropping practice.[1] In the first volume of *An Inquiry into the Nature and Causes of the Wealth of Nations*, Smith discussed hindrances to agriculture in Europe and emphasized the lack of incentives inherent in the sharecropping system. Sharecropping tenants (or metayers) bear most of the input costs (especially labor costs) and receive only a fraction of the final output. This induces them to undersupply these inputs. Furthermore, tenure insecurity reduces their incentive to improve the land. In Adam Smith's (1996, book 2, chap. 2, pp. 412, 414) words:

> To the slave cultivators of ancient times, gradually succeeded a species of farmers known at present in France by the name of Metayers.... It could never, however, be to the interest even of this last species of cultivators to lay out, in further improvement of the land, any part of the little stock which they might save from their own share of the produce, because the lord, who laid out nothing, was to get one-half of whatever is produced.

Smith's point of view has influenced many other classical authors. John Stuart Mill (1936, book 2, chap. 8, p. 304) wrote, "The metayer has less motive to exertion than the peasant proprietor, since only half the fruits of his industry, instead of a whole, are his own." But Mill also acknowledges the existence of mechanisms that are available to landlords to mitigate the sharecropping inefficiency. After mentioning the very critical view of Anne R. J. Turgot, Arthur Young, John R. McCulloch, Richard Jones, and M. Destutt de Tracy, Mill describes the view of M. de Sismondi (a landowner from Tuscany) defending the metayer system for protecting tenants from land disputes with their neighbors. Such disputes would be part of the landlord's responsibilities. The fact that different generations of the same family live as tenants on some lands is also mentioned as being able to reduce the problems caused by tenure insecurity.

In line with Adam Smith's view, Alfred Marshall (1961, book 6, chap. 9, p. 644) wrote, "For, when the cultivator has to give to his landlord half of the returns to each dose of capital and labor that he applies to the land, it will not be to his interest to apply any doses the total return to which is less than twice enough to reward him." However, Marshall also acknowledges that the sharecropping technical inefficiency would be mitigated if the tenants' actions were costlessly monitored.

Taking a different perspective, Karl Marx (1967) condemned sharecropping, considering it a feudal institution that is incompatible with capitalism. Curiously, the idea of a noble landlord leasing lands to poor farmers to avoid being involved in productive activities does not seem to fit in a dynamic capitalist system, but absentee shareholders hiring managers to run a company became a main characteristic of modern capitalism.

In spite of the disadvantages noted by classical economists, the sharecropping lease remained in use throughout the Old World and became even more popular in the New World. Intriguingly, share contracts in the twentieth century tended to have a short duration, contrary to the classical arguments for tenure stability. Noticing this fact, D. Gale Johnson (1950) stressed an important incentive aspect of short-term leases: they must be frequently renewed. Moving is costly for tenants, and landlords tend to renew contracts based on relative performance (by comparing the productivity of sharecropped farms with those of similar lands owned or leased under fixed rent). Repeated contracting could induce sharecropping tenants to supply the appropriate amount of labor and other inputs. Furthermore, the landlord should be willing to pay for land-specific investments, which alter the long-term productivity of the land and therefore its rental price. Under these premises, sharecropping generates no loss of efficiency in resource allocation. In Johnson's (1950, p. 120) words,

With a short-term lease renters are obviously aware that landlords have the alternative of renting their land for a cash rent independent of current output. Consequently, the tenant must plan to produce an average output per acre that will provide a rental payment, if yields are average, equal to the possible cash rent plus any additional payment required to compensate the landlord for the uncertainty that he bears.... Once he has found a farm, he may fear that his lease will not be renewed unless sufficient rent is actually paid.

Modern Theory
From Adam Smith to D. Gale Johnson, the debate was concentrated mainly on the sharecropping incentives for proper allocation of resources. Cheung (1969) shifted the focus of the discussion toward the insurance properties of sharecropping.[2] He argued that efficient resource allocation would be obtained whenever landlords were able to monitor tenants' activities. Under this premise, sharecropping is presented as an efficient way of sharing the production risk between landlords and tenants. In equilibrium, the share of risk borne by landlords and tenants would be determined by the difference in their level of risk aversion (see also Cheung, 2002).

In 1974, Joseph E. Stiglitz published an influential analysis of the sharecropping problem. Share contracts were viewed as the optimal solution for an insurance problem in a scenario with moral hazard. Tenants usually choose privately observed variables that affect productivity, and the optimal share rate should balance the incentives for exerting this hidden effort and the costs of risk bearing. Works by Stiglitz (1974), Holmstrom (1979), Grossman and Hart (1983), and Holmstrom and Milgrom (1987) showed that the optimal tenancy contract should balance incentives and insurance in environments with moral hazard. Similar to the predictions of Adam Smith and other classical authors, sharecropping would in fact not induce the maximum output per unit of land. However, this productivity loss would be compensated by the welfare gain of sharing risk.

By connecting the early discussion of resource allocation with Cheung's analysis of optimal contract design, the literature on moral hazard set the basis for our modern understanding of tenancy contracts. This literature together with the works on asymmetric information developed by Akerlof (1970), Spence (1973), and Rothschild and Stiglitz (1976) became the core of modern insurance theory.

However, insurance and incentives are not the only motives raised in the economic literature to explain the design of tenancy contracts. Rao (1971) and Prendergast (2002) argue that the value of managerial effort and entrepreneurial activities is much higher in risky environments. Risky farms should then be rented under contracts with high incentive power (that is, contracts in which a high share of the output is retained by the tenant). This prediction is in sharp contrast with those based on insurance. In a different vein, part of the literature stresses the importance of labor-market imperfections to the choice of tenancy contracts (see Otsuka, Chuma, Hayami, 1992, for an extensive discussion on this topic and Ray, 1999, for a recent contribution). Furthermore, the literature on transaction costs lists a number of different features that can affect the contract choice. For instance, negotiations to determine the rental price in a fixed-rent contract can destroy trust between the parties, since landlords usually have better information about the land (see Williamson, 1979; Murrell, 1983). Also, nonlinear supervision costs can explain systematic variation in the incidence of share contracts (see Alston, Datta, and Nugent, 1984) and costs for measuring the final output tend to discourage share contracts (see Allen and Lueck, 1992).

New aspects of the agency problem have been pointed out recently. Eswaran and Kotwal (1985) and Bhattacharyya and Lafontaine (1995) model the environment where the landlord also exerts productive activities.[3] In this case, sharecropping would not only share the risk between the two parties but also provide incentives for both of them. For this reason, share contracts promote better allocation of resources than fixed-rent contracts in the presence of double-sided moral hazard. Laffont and Matoussi (1995) stress that when dealing with a poor and credit-constrained tenant, sharing the output might be the only way the landlord has to extract the tenant's surplus. Hence, the sharecropping technical inefficiency would be related to the lack of enforceable mechanisms available to the principal to extract the tenant's surplus. Sengupta (1997) and Ghatak and Pandey (2000) show that sharecropping is the optimal tenancy contract in environments with limited liability in which the tenant controls the average productivity and the riskiness of the farm—since limited liability makes the tenant's willingness to take risk be increasing in the contract's incentive power.

Some other aspects related to Johnson's (1950) analysis were also recently formalized. For instance, Lazear and Rosen (1981) and Green and Stokey (1983) show that compensation schemes based on relative performance can in fact alleviate incentive problems in environments with shocks that are common to all tenants. Moreover, eviction threats provide incentives for actions affecting the current revenue, and as shown by Banerjee and Ghatak (2004), there are scenarios in which these threats also induce long-term investment. Repeated contracting is another tool used to improve the efficiency of resource allocation in lands under sharecropping. First-best efficiency is approximately achievable in environments where contracting agreements are infinitely repeated and tenants are sufficiently patient, as shown by Rubinstein and Yaari (1983) and Radner (1985). In finite-horizon settings, Lambert (1983) and Rogerson (1985) show that the optimal finite-horizon dynamic contract is history dependent, provides intertemporal insurance for the tenants, but also imposes some risk on them within each period, similarly to Holmstrom (1979). However, first-best results could also be approximated in finite-horizon scenarios if one works with the epsilon-equilibrium concept defined by Radner (1981).

All these theoretical advances have raised the sophistication level of the debate about sharecropping, making empirical investigation even more crucial to test the relevance of each argument. Recently, the availability of well-built databases as well as the development of new identification strategies have brought some light to the debate. This chapter is intended to discuss some of these contributions.

There are many comprehensive surveys of land contracts: see Otsuka and Hayami (1988), Otsuka, Chuma, and Hayami (1992), Binswanger,

Deininger, and Feder (1995), and Deininger and Feder (1997), among others. This chapter instead focuses on recent empirical contributions regarding two particular aspects of this debate—(1) the effects of the contractual form (incentive power and contract length) on resource allocation and farm performance and (2) the exogenous elements behind the choice of different contractual forms. Some empirical articles and working papers on these two topics, written in the last decade, have been selected to be discussed here. A few classic papers are also included to provide a perspective of the current trends. An advantage of this strategy is that, by narrowing the focus of the essay, one is able to provide a more extensive presentation of the selected papers.

The remainder of this chapter discusses the empirical research on resource allocation by comparing the impact of different share rates on input use and farm productivity and by studying the effects of tenure stability on land improvements. It also presents papers that test different arguments raised to explain the design of tenancy contracts and concludes with a brief summary discussing a few policy implications.

Resource Allocation

The main elements of tenancy contracts are (1) the contract incentive power (described by the share of the final output retained by the tenant and the shares of different input costs borne by the tenant) and (2) the contract length.

Share contracts display lower incentive power than ownership and fixed-rent contracts, since sharecropping tenants receive only a fraction of the total output and fully bear the costs of many inputs. Even when the landlord shares the costs of observed inputs, the tenant still bears the effort cost of managerial activities. In the absence of dynamic incentives and threats, farmers under share contracts would underuse those inputs whose costs are not shared with the landlord. Consequently, their farms would be less productive.

Furthermore, since sharecropping and fixed-rent tenants face uncertainty of tenure security, fear of expropriation would lead them to make suboptimal levels of noncontractible long-term investments. Note that this issue is not exclusive to sharecropping. In many developing countries, even owners and tenured tenants fear expropriation due to land reforms. Hence, at some level, this issue is related to a broader debate about property rights.

Incentive Power
This section studies the effects of incentive power on input use and farm productivity. It starts with a paper by Rao (1971) that contains an investigation of the productivity difference between owner-operated and share-rented farms in India. The results are not conclusive; owner-operated farms produce more output per acre, but sharecroppers are more productive than owners when farm-size level is held constant. In another important work, Shaban (1987) uses data from the International Crops Research Institute for Semi-Arid Tropics (ICRISAT) in India to study differences in resource allocation across owned and sharecropped lands cultivated by the same farmer. He finds that farmers are more productive and use inputs more intensively on their own lands, suggesting the existence of incentive problems. Next, Laffont and Matoussi (1995) theorize that, under limited liability, poor sharecroppers would tend to retain a lower fraction of the output and thus exert less effort and be less productive. They provide evidence from Tunisia supporting their theory.

The last work presented here, Braido (2004a), suggests that the incentive problems measured by comparing land productivity and input use across farms under different contracts can be biased by land-quality heterogeneity. In situations where land quality is not randomly distributed across different contracts, one must be careful when interpreting differences in the per acre value of each input used and output produced. Typically, tenants cultivate lands with lower value, which directly reduces their productivity as well as the marginal return of each input. Hence, the fact that sharecroppers are less productive and employ lower amounts of each input does not necessarily imply the existence of shirking behavior. That working paper uses ICRISAT data to revisit Shaban's conclusions from this new perspective. The results raise some doubts over the belief that sharecroppers shirk systematically.

Rao (1971): Part I An important part of Rao's paper refers to optimal contract design and is left to a later section of this chapter. Here, I present another investigation carried out in that paper (p. 588) testing the average productivity difference between owner-operated and share-rented farms. The work uses farm-level data from the Studies in Economics of Farm Management in India. In this part of the paper, the author uses 137 observations from two different cropping years (1957 to 1958 and 1958 to 1959) in ten different villages (seven of them in the rice zone and three in the tobacco zone).

The author argues that land quality (measured by imputed values of land resources) and other inputs are highly correlated. Hence, he estimates a Cobb-Douglas production function where land quality is the only independent variable (capturing the joint effect of land quality and other inputs).

The results are ambiguous. Output per acre is higher in the owner-operated fields than in share-rented farms, but observed land quality explains around 90 percent of this variation. Moreover, the elasticity coefficients indicate the existence of diminishing marginal productivity among owner-operated plots and constant marginal productivity under sharecropping. Rao then estimates the effect of the contract on the average per acre output at each farm-size level, and unlike before, the productivity is higher in sharecropped lands than in owner-operated farms of corresponding sizes.

Shaban (1987) This work tests two theoretical models of sharecropping—the Marshallian approach versus Cheung's monitoring approach. The Marshallian approach assumes a prohibitively high cost of monitoring the tenant's activities. Nonmonitored farmers tend to use inputs less intensively in their sharecropped lands relative to their owned lands, which leads to a lower output per acre in sharecropped farms. The monitoring approach, on the other hand, theorizes that if landlords accessed an effective and inexpensive monitoring technology, they would stipulate all relevant actions to be followed by tenants. In this scenario, there would be no misallocation associated with sharecropping.

The empirical investigation uses farm-level data from the ICRISAT's Village-Level Studies, which contain detailed farming information from eight villages in India. The database contains a subsample of sharecroppers who simultaneously own and sharecrop different fields, allowing one to control for household heterogeneity. Shaban compares the average per acre values of the output produced and the different inputs used across owned and sharecropped lands of the same household. Higher output and input intensities on owned land would support the Marshallian approach, while equal values for owned and sharecropped lands would favor Cheung's monitoring approach.

The results indicate significant differences. Controlling for irrigation, plot value, and some observed soil characteristics, one finds that the per acre output is higher by 16.3 percent on owned lands relative to

sharecropped lands of the same household. Farmers also use significantly more of each input on each acre of their owned farms.

Laffont and Matoussi (1995): Part I This paper develops a model of
sharecropping with the objective of explaining contracts observed in El
Oulja, a rural area of Tunisia. The key aspect of the model is the presence of financial constraints that limit the tenants' ability to pay up
front rents and invest in productive inputs. Thus, fixed-rent contracts,
which induce appropriate levels of effort, might not be feasible for
landlords dealing with poor tenants. In their theory, share contracts
have the function of providing effort incentives and solving financial
constraints. They show that the share of the product retained by the
tenant, the level of effort exerted, and the output produced are decreasing in the tenant's working capital.

These predictions are tested using data collected with the help of the
Tunisian National Institute of Statistics in 1986 from the rural area of El
Oulja, Tunisia.[4] The empirical part can be divided into two subparts—
one studying productivity across contracts and another one investigating the determinants of contract design. Here I focus on the
productivity discussion, leaving the part on contract choice for later in
this chapter.

The database contains information on the general characteristics of
100 families (including wealth and income) and detailed farming information on each plot operated by these families (including plot size,
type of crop, tenancy status, and production and input levels). The
authors estimate a log-linear production function using output (per
hectare) as the dependent variable. The control variables include the
amount of hired labor, family labor, and other inputs (evaluated per
hectare) and dummies for the contractual characteristics—namely, two
dummy variables describing the contract form (sharecropping versus
owner or fixed rent) and, for sharecropping contracts, a variable
describing the number of months of the relationship between the landlord and the sharecropper. They acknowledge the fact that the contract
is endogenous and attempt to solve potential endogeneity biases by
means of instrumental variables. They claim that the type of crop
(such as, tomato, potato, melon, or vegetable), the tenant's wealth, and
the number of active members in the family are good instruments for
the contractual characteristics. For that to be true, these variables
should be correlated to the tenancy contract and not correlated to
unobserved features affecting output. The Instrumental Variable (IV)

estimates for the contract-dummies coefficients are similar (namely, 4.8 for fixed rent and 4.4 for sharecropping; see p. 391) but statistically different from each other. Since the coefficients of the contract dummies measure the impact of each contract on expected output, this result suggests that sharecroppers exert less effort than fixed-rent tenants. It is also found that, in sharecropped fields, productivity is positively related to the number of months of the landlord-tenant relationship.

Braido (2004a) Land characteristics vary considerably across farms under different tenancy status. Typically, lands leased out to tenants (under sharecropping or fixed rent) have lower quality than those cultivated by the owners. Some authors argue that good lands are cultivated by owners because they display larger scope for soil exploitation (see, for instance, the papers by Allen and Lueck, 1992, 1993, and Dubois, 2002, discussed later in this chapter).

Most of the literature on incentive power compares the amount of different inputs used and output produced (evaluated per unit of land) across fields under different contracts. However, in the presence of land heterogeneity, comparing quantities (or values) is not a valid procedure to test the existence of incentive problems. It is usually optimal to use inputs less intensively on lands with lower quality, and this relationship is not necessarily linear (as assumed by Shaban, 1987) or log-linear (as assumed by Rao, 1971). Furthermore, many land characteristics are privately observed and so are not available in the data. Thus, whenever sharecropping is associated with lower-quality lands, these farms will naturally employ inputs less intensively and be less productive (even after controlling linearly or log-linearly for observed land characteristics).

Braido (2004a) acknowledges this fact and uses the ICRISAT's Village Level Studies (India) to revisit the incentive-power analysis from this perspective (see also Braido, 2002). To better illustrate the main point of that paper, consider the following Cobb-Douglas production function:

$$y_i = A_i k_i^\alpha \exp(\varepsilon_i), \tag{11.1}$$

where i indexes the plots in a certain period, y_i represents the output produced per unit of land, A_i is a productivity factor related to observed land quality, k_i represents all inputs used per unit of land, $\alpha \in (0, 1)$, and ε_i is an error term accounting for productive shocks as well as for hidden actions (such as managerial effort) and unobserved characteristics of landlords, tenants, and lands.

Define $\theta_i = E\left(\frac{p}{r}\exp(\varepsilon_i)\,|\,\mathscr{I}_i\right)$, where p and r represent the prices for y_i and k_i (respectively), and $\mathscr{I}_i$ is the information set available to the farmer cultivating plot i. Notice that θ_i is not constant across plots due to differentiated information about characteristics of landlords, tenants, lands, and expected prices and shocks.

For general production functions, profit-maximization conditions establish an implicit relationship between k_i and $A_i\theta_i$. For the Cobb-Douglas, this relationship is explicitly given by

$$k_i = (\alpha A_i \theta_i)^{1/(1-\alpha)}. \tag{11.2}$$

A few important features are worth noticing from (11.2). First, lower land quality (A_i) implies lower input use and thus lower output per unit of land. Second, even minor differences in land quality (A_i) may significantly impact productivity (y_i), since this effect is amplified through input choices.

Under a Cobb-Douglas technology, the profit-maximizing input choice would make $\ln(k_i)$ and $\ln(A_i)$ colinear if and only if θ_i were constant across plots (that is, $\theta_i = \theta$). In this case, one could ignore inputs when estimating the reduced form of (11.1). However, there are reasons for θ_i to vary across plots, so that ignoring inputs (k_i) introduces a serious problem in the estimation of (11.1).

The paper then proceeds in the following manner. First, it tests the effect of the contract form on productivity when observed land quality and input choices are used as control variables. The results show that the entire productivity gap across contracts is explained by differences in input use. This could be due to the fact that tenants shirk in their input choices or that these choices reflect land-quality heterogeneity. One must then test whether input choices were distorted.

If inputs were chosen to maximize profits, the marginal productivity of each factor should be the same across farms under different tenancy contracts, regardless of the unobserved characteristics of the land, the tenant, the landlord, and the environment. In this sense, a test procedure based on the marginal productivity of each input is free of selection problems. Moreover, when the production function is Cobb-Douglas, the marginal productivity is easily measured by $\alpha\frac{y_i}{k_i}$. The empirical results for the ICRISAT data do not reject the hypothesis that the marginal productivity of labor and nonlabor inputs are constant across plots under ownership, fixed rent, and sharecropping.

Contract Length

The review here begins with the paper by Besley (1995), which studies the relation between land-specific investments and property rights in Ghana. The results support the hypothesis that land rights and investments are positively correlated. This finding is indirectly related to tenure status since, like better-defined property rights, tenure stability avoids expropriation of long-run investments. The second paper discussed, Banerjee, Gertler, and Ghatak (2002), uses a unique quasi-experiment to study the effect of land tenure on resource allocation. The authors use an exogenous change in property rights in West Bengal that increased tenure stability of tenants and subsequently increased the incentive power of tenancy contracts and the lands' average productivity.[5] The next paper discussed, Jacoby, Li, and Rozelle (2002), uses a statistical procedure to estimate the plot-level hazard of expropriation and shows that this measure is positively correlated to the use of organic fertilizer in China. Among authors of recent working papers, Manyong and Houndékon (2000) find that land tenure was positively related to the adoption of a new resource management system in Benin Republic (West Africa); Jacoby and Mansuri (2003) suggest that owned lands tend to receive more specific investments than leased lands in Pakistan; and Bandiera (2004) shows that Nicaraguan farmers are more likely to grow trees in combination with annual crops in their owned lands (as opposed to leased lands).

Besley (1995)   This work examines the correlation between investment and land rights in Ghana. The author lists three possible channels driving this correlation. First, land rights would affect investments through fear of expropriation. Second, better-defined land rights may facilitate land being collateralized, reducing interest rates faced by landowners and increasing land investments. Finally, there is a link between investment and land rights through gains from trade. Superior land rights improve the market for selling and renting the land. This amplifies the effects of new investment on the land's price and rent, increasing the incentives to invest.

The empirical analysis is based on farm-level data from two regions of Ghana—namely, Wassa and Anloga. The main product grown in Wassa is cocoa, and the only significant investment made to improve the land is planting tree crops. In Anloga, most agriculture is devoted to growing shallots (a type of small onion), and land improvements are much more diverse than in Wassa. The database contains information on land and household characteristics, a binary variable indicating whether land investments were made, and discrete variables describing household rights on each operated field. There is significant variation in property rights as a consequence of Ghana's transition from a traditional system (where land ownership was communal and controlled by a tribal chief) to a more modern system that emphasizes individual claims. These rights fall into six categories—rights to sell, rent, gift, mortgage, pledge, and bequeath—each of them with or without lineage approval. In many parts of the paper, property rights are aggregated into two categories—number of rights with and without need of approval.

The author starts by investigating the relationship between investment and land rights by means of a discrete-choice model. Estimations are conducted with and without household fixed effects.[6] A number of variables describing the mode of acquisition of each farm (such as purchased, appropriated, or gifted) and the number of years since the acquisition are used as instrumental variables for property rights. The results for Wassa indicate that land rights do influence investment: better rights significantly raise the probability of land investments. The results for Anloga are less robust but are still broadly in line with the theory.

Extensions attempt to assess which of the channels previously listed drive this relationship. In such extensions, the author makes use of the disaggregated definition of household rights. Being allowed to use a particular field as collateral does not necessarily imply that the investments will occur in that specific field. Thus, if the relationship between investments and land rights were driven by the effects of property rights on access to credit markets, investments should be related to rights enjoyed in all fields, rather than field-specific rights. Next, under the gains-from-trade argument, some land rights (such as the right to sell or rent the field) should have a greater impact on investments than other rights (such as the right to mortgage, for instance). The empirical results do not strongly support any of these two particular theoretical views.

Banerjee, Gertler, and Ghatak (2002) In the late 1970s, there was a major change in property rights in West Bengal, India, due to a reform of tenancy laws known as Operation Barga. The reform, carried out by a newly elected left-wing administration, increased tenants' bargaining power and secured land tenure. The election of this new administration in West Bengal is interpreted by the authors as a national response to the party in power, which had ruled India since its independence, rather than a local particularity. Operation Barga is thus interpreted as an exogenous change in property rights and used to examine the relationship between tenancy laws and efficiency.

The paper first develops a theoretical approach to the landlord-tenant relationship based on moral hazard and limited wealth of tenants, which is used to analyze the potential effects of the reform on contractual relationships. The reform increased tenants' reservation utility, since they could not be evicted by the landlord anymore and could choose to retain the share of the output accorded before the reform. Due to limited liability, a higher outside option increases the optimal share rate retained by the tenant. The authors present evidence showing that the incentive power of tenancy contracts has in fact increased after the reform. Greater tenure security and a higher share rate induce the tenant to increase the supply of effort and noncontractible land-specific investments. On the other hand, after the reform the landlord loses the possibility of using the threat of eviction as a credible incentive device.

The effect of Operation Barga on productivity was estimated using two approaches. The first is a quasi-experiment that uses Bangladesh as a control. The authors argue that Bangladesh may be used as a control because it did not introduce tenancy reform; it is very similar to West Bengal in terms of agroclimatic conditions, prevalence of tenancy, and agricultural technology; and it had growth rates similar to West Bengal during the period before the reform. The second approach compares the productivity growth in districts in which Operation Barga was implemented intensively to districts in which the implementation was less intensive.[7] The results from both approaches indicate a positive impact of Operation Barga on sharecropping productivity.

The productivity increase that followed the land reform in West Bengal is due to a combination of two effects—tenure stability and higher incentive power. Hence, this paper is also related to the previous discussion in this chapter.

Jacoby, Li, and Rozelle (2002) This study is based on a survey conducted by the World Bank containing information on 3,113 plots of

727 households from thirty-one villages in the Northeast region of China in 1995. Unlike other papers in the literature, risk of expropriation is not measured in this paper by land rights or tenure status. Instead, the authors estimate a hazard model and predict the risk of expropriation associated with each land. This predicted hazard of expropriation is then shown to be positively correlated to the use of organic fertilizers (which has long-term impact on soil quality). The same result is not found for the use of chemical fertilizers (whose effects on soil quality do not last for long) and for maintenance investments.

Manyong and Houndékon (2000) In 1987, a group of international institutions introduced a new land-improving technology to the farmers of Benin Republic (in West Africa). Using data collected six years later, Manyong and Houndékon (2000) identify land tenure as an important element explaining the adoption of this technology on different farms.

Jacoby and Mansuri (2003) Using data from the Pakistan Rural Household Survey completed in 2001, Jacoby and Mansuri (2003) study whether farmers tend to invest more in their own lands than in the lands they lease (under sharecropping and fixed rent). Land-specific investment is measured by the amount of farmyard manure (FYM) used per acre cultivated during the year. The authors argue that FYM improves land quality and its effects last for many seasons; FYM is not portable once incorporated into the soil; and FYM is usually collected as a by-product of farmers' own livestock and manuring is very labor intensive. Thus, under imperfect monitoring, farmyard manure could be interpreted as a noncontractible land-specific investment.

The database contains a subsample of mixed tenants (that is, households that cultivate both owned and leased lands). This feature makes it possible to compare investment behaviors across plots of the same household, avoiding potential biases caused by unobserved characteristics of the tenant. In addition to this, one must also worry about selection bias caused by soil-quality heterogeneity. The authors use information about the landlord (such as total landholdings and tractor ownership) as instruments for the leasing decision. These instrumental variables capture characteristics of the landlord that are correlated to the leasing decision. Moreover, if the landlords did not interfere in the investments made in their leased lands, these variables would also be uncorrelated to unobserved aspects of FYM investments (the dependent variable). The results indicate that FYM investments are lower on leased (as opposed to owned) lands cultivated by the same household, which supports the existence of a holdup problem.

Bandiera (2004) Cultivation of trees in combination with regular crops is costly but preserves soil fertility and reduces soil erosion (a benefit not fully appropriated by untenured tenants). Using household data from the 1998 Nicaragua Living Standards Measurement Survey, Bandiera (2004) analyzes the choice of farmers who may or may not grow trees.

A subsample of farmers who own and rent different plots is used to control for nonrandom heterogeneity in household characteristics. Since land characteristics are not available, three different strategies are used to address potential selection bias due to land-quality heterogeneity. First, the opportunity cost of the land (reported by owner and tenant farmers) is used as a proxy variable for land quality. Second, subsamples of geographically close farms (among which the soil type could be more similar) are analyzed. Third, the author introduces a control variable indicating whether a particular owned farm was originally acquired via land reform (rather than through purchase or inheritance). Owned lands acquired via land reform were originally leased before the reform, being thus similar to currently leased farms.

The results indicate that owned lands are more likely to have trees together with annual crops. The tenant's wealth is not a significant determinant of tree cultivation, which suggests that limited liability and risk sharing are not crucial aspects of the problem. Since wealth is endogenous, the value of the house and the number of bedrooms are used as instruments.

Comments and Perspectives on Resource Allocation
Our understanding about the effects of different contractual elements on resource allocation has considerably improved in the last decade. Yet definitive conclusions are far from being reached. Conclusive experiments, in the molds of natural sciences, are difficult to be implemented, and the existing empirical tests are based on market data. Hence, the contracts studied are endogenously designed, and their

observed characteristics (incentive power and length) are probably related to unobserved characteristics of landlords, tenants, lands, crops, and other features of the environment (such as taxes, laws, and traditions).

The empirical literature in the last decade has attempted to develop different techniques to deal with selection and endogeneity issues. The paper by Rao (1971), discussed earlier, does not account for endogeneity issues, while Shaban (1987) uses tenants who simultaneously cultivate multiple plots under different contracts to account for endogenous heterogeneity in household characteristics. The paper by Laffont and Matoussi (1995) uses the method of instrumental variable to deal with all types of endogeneity problems (such as heterogeneity in landlord and tenant characteristics, land quality, and institutions). The difficulty of this method is that it strongly relies on the quality of the instrument (a variable that must be correlated to the contract design and not related to any unobserved feature affecting the dependent variable). A truly exogenous instrumental variable is often difficult to be found. Braido (2004a) uses the economic theory to derive a testable prediction that is free of endogeneity considerations. Instead of comparing the amount of inputs used, this paper compares the marginal productivity of each input across lands cultivated by owners, fixed-rent tenants, and sharecroppers. This type of structural test, however, depends on parametric assumptions on the production function. In fact, there is an intense debate in economics regarding the use of reduced form models estimated by instrumental variables versus the use of tests based on structural economic models.

The literature on contract length essentially relies on instrumental variables to deal with the endogeneity problem. Hence, the validity of those analyses depends on the quality of the instruments used. A remarkable case is found in Banerjee, Gertler, and Ghatak (2002), where a quasi-experiment is constructed from an exogenous reform of tenancy laws. As with experiments in the natural sciences, this quasi-experiment uses exogenous treatment and control groups to test a certain theoretical prediction, but this type of quasi-experiment is not replicable and does not allow the researcher to control the variables to be exogenously changed.

Increasing our capability to deal with selection issues, with a special focus on replicability, is certainly an important goal for future research. Creative identification strategies coupled with the development of new data surveys are likely to be the key elements in this process.

Contract Design

This section reviews the debate on the designs of tenancy contracts. The two main characteristics of tenancy contracts are, again, incentive power and length. The literature however has mainly focused on the former, and Bandiera (2003) is the only paper discussed here that explicitly addresses the latter issue.

Regarding incentive power, there are three different classes of arguments commonly used to explain it. First, agency theory (see Holmstrom and Milgrom, 1987) stresses the tradeoff between incentives and risk. Holding tenants' risk aversion constant, high-powered contracts are more likely to be used in fields with low exogenous risk. On the other hand, delegation theory (see Rao, 1971, and Predengast, 2002) predicts exactly the opposite: since the scope for entrepreneurship is higher in high-risk fields, incentives are also more important in these farms. Finally, arguments based on transaction costs predict that crops with lower costs for monitoring effort and for measuring the inputs and the final output are more likely to be rented under sharecropping.

The review starts with the part of Rao (1971) that was purposely omitted in the previous section. Rao finds a positive association between farm risk and incentive power, supporting the delegation theory. Next, three papers on transaction costs are discussed: Hoffman (1984) suggests that vine plots are usually rented under sharecropping due to lower costs of monitoring the tenant; Allen and Lueck (1992) stress aspects related to soil exploitation and costs of measuring the final output as important in explaining tenancy contracts; and Allen and Lueck (1993) extend this analysis to explain the share rate for input costs in sharecropping contracts. I discuss a small part of Laffont and Matoussi (1995) that shows the contractual incentive power is affected by the tenant's working capital but not by the tenant's wealth—emphasizing the relative importance of financial constraints over insurance motives to explain contract designs. Allen and Lueck (1999) also present evidence against the risk-sharing theory of sharecropping. Unlike these findings, Ackerberg and Botticini (2002) find that the contract power is positively affected by the tenant's wealth in Renaissance Tuscany. Dubois (2002) studies how share contracts dynamically balance risk-sharing, effort incentives, and incentives for land-quality maintenance. Chaudhuri and Maitra (2002) provide further evidence that landowners tend to personally cultivate their most valued plots. Finally, some recent working papers by Canjels (1998a), Pandey (2001), Dubois (2001), Bandiera (2003), and Braido (2004b) are presented.

Rao (1971): Part II Let us examine now the part of Rao's (1971) paper that is related to contract design. The argument developed by the author is based on the idea that tenants perform a variety of different entrepreneurial functions. Fixed-rent contracts permit the tenant to capture the returns associated with decision making and protect the landlord against possible risk arising from the production decisions of the tenant. Hence, these contracts should be observed in environments with high risk and significant scope for entrepreneurship. On the other hand, in low-risk scenarios, where the scope for entrepreneurial decisions is restricted, sharecropping arrangements insure tenants against risk.

This theory is tested against data from the Studies in Economics of Farm Management collected by the government of India in three different years—1957 to 1958, 1958 to 1959, and 1959 to 1960—in seven villages of the rice zone and three of the tobacco zone. Sharecropping and fixed rent coexist in the villages studied, the former being predominant in the rice zone and the latter being more common in the tobacco zone. The estimated variance of profits is much higher for the tobacco zone (where fixed rent is predominant) than for the rice zone (where sharecropping is predominant). Furthermore, irrigation pattern, variation in rainfall, and variation in prices also suggest that tobacco as a riskier crop than rice. Hence, scope for entrepreneurship rather than risk sharing is viewed as the key element explaining the design of share contracts.

Hoffman (1984) In this work, the author argues that, due to costs of supervising the tenant, landlords are more likely to lease distant lands under higher-powered contracts. Moreover, crops requiring a close landlord are more likely to be rented under lower-powered contracts. These predictions are tested against historical data from eighty-three contracts, dated between 1533 and 1633 in France.

Logit estimations show that distant lands are more likely to be rented under fixed rent relative to sharecropping and to sharecropping relative to wage labor (confirming the first theoretical prediction). Moreover, vines are more likely to use wage labor than tenancy and, among the fields leased, sharecropping is more common than fixed rent. The author argues that vines require present landlords regardless of the tenancy contract. Considerable damage could be caused if the tenant neglected buildings and fences. Moreover, by cutting the vines very short, one increases return in that season at the cost of reducing productivity thereafter. Hence, the cost of monitoring other farming activities is significantly lower in vines, and the fact that these lands are leased under lower-powered contracts supports the second theoretical prediction.

Allen and Lueck (1992)   Due to insecurity of tenure, tenants have incentives to overuse the land. Sharecropping alleviates this distortion relative to fixed rent because sharing the output reduces the tenant's gains in overusing the land. However, to implement share contracts, the landlord must incur the costs of measuring the final output.

This is the basic tradeoff studied by Allen and Lueck (1992). Under this theory, sharecropping is expected to occur in environments with high possibilities for soil exploitation and where the cost of dividing the output is low. The authors test this prediction using a sample with 3,432 leasing contracts from the 1986 Nebraska and South Dakota Leasing Survey. Measurement costs are proxied by the type of crop cultivated. Hay crops are more difficult to measure, since they are typically sold through private sales in contrast to other cultures that are publicly sold at local markets. Scope for soil exploitation is measured by proximity to urban areas and presence of irrigation. Proximity to urban areas provides alternative uses for the land, making concerns about soil exploitation less important. Irrigation makes soil exploitation less likely. Thus, proximity to urban areas and irrigation should be positively correlated to fixed rent.

A logit analysis is conducted, and the results support the underlying theory. In addition, the authors find that sharecropping is positively related to corn and wheat. Since corn is a crop with high profit variability and wheat is a low-risk culture, the authors argue that this evidence does not support the risk-sharing motives commonly associated with sharecropping.

Allen and Lueck (1993)   Here, the analysis of the previous paper is extended to understand not only the share rate used to divide output but also the share of input costs borne by the landlord. Agricultural production depends on land and productive inputs. Assuming a production function that is separable in each factor, fixed rent induces proper use of inputs. However, since the opportunity cost of using the land is typically lower for untenured tenants as opposed to owners, fixed-rent contracts induce land overuse. Sharecropping, on the other hand, alleviates the incentives for land overuse but implies costs of measuring the output. Share contracts also distort incentives for the proper use of other inputs, but this could be solved by sharing input costs between landlords and tenants at the same rate used to share the output.

In this setting, one should expect sharecropping to be associated with lower costs of measuring output and high possibilities for soil exploitation. Moreover, for easily measured inputs, sharecropping landlords would share costs at a rate equal to the crop-share rate. Finally, fixed-rent contracts would be associated with environments with few possibilities for soil exploitation and high measurement costs.

These predictions are tested using data from the 1986 Nebraska and South Dakota Land Leasing Survey. Evidence shows that, in general, tenants either bear input costs alone or share them with the landlord at the same rate as the output share. Tenants retain a higher share of the output when they bear input costs alone.

Moreover, logit estimates show that inputs purchased in the market are more likely to be shared than those provided by the farmer (those harder to measure). The probability of having an input being shared is negatively affected by the land's value, which proxies for scope of soil exploitation, and by the fraction of the total area cropped under the current contract: the more lands from the same landlord, the lower the tenant's ability to shirk on the use of shared inputs.

Laffont and Matoussi (1995): Part II   This paper has multiple aims, some of them already discussed earlier in this chapter. Here, I focus on a small part of it (pp. 395–397) that uses an ordered probit model to study the selection of contracts. Evidence from El Oulja, in Tunisia, shows that incentive power is negatively related to the landlord's working capital, positively related to the tenant's working capital, and not significantly related to the tenant's wealth. The authors conclude that financial constraints are more important than risk aversion in explaining the design of tenancy contracts.

Allen and Lueck (1999)   The authors use four different land-leasing surveys (from Nebraska, South Dakota, British Columbia, and Louisiana) to test the relationship between risk and incentive power. They have data on the form of the tenancy contract (fixed rent versus share-cropping) and the fraction of crop retained by the sharecropping tenant. Exogenous risk is measured by the variability of crop yield across plots of a certain region. A logit analysis shows that risk does not have a positive impact on the probability of a crop being leased under sharecropping. Tobit regressions also indicate that, in general, the tenant's share rate does not decrease with risk.

Ackerberg and Botticini (2002) The possibility of endogenous matching between landlords' and tenants' unobservable characteristics is addressed in this paper by means of a historical data set from Renaissance Tuscany. Endogenous matching happens when there are reasons leading landlords and tenants to contract with each other. For instance, if tenants were heterogeneous in their level of risk aversion and plots differed in their level of riskiness, it could possibly be the case that less risk-averse tenants match with more risky plots. Since the rule governing the matches is unknown, using proxies for tenants' risk aversion and plot risk is not enough to account for the endogeneity bias.

The paper uses geographical-based instruments to account for the endogeneity bias. The underlying assumption is that exogenous differences across regions affect the matching between tenants and landlords, without affecting the contract design (the dependent variable) through other channels. Once this matching is taken into account, the authors find a positive correlation between the contract share and the tenant's wealth. Assuming that wealth is a proxy for risk aversion, this evidence supports insurance motives for share contracts.

Dubois (2002) This paper develops a dynamic principal-agent model for agricultural tenancy where the optimal contract design balances risk sharing, effort incentives, and concerns about land-quality maintenance. In the model, land fertility is noncontractible and evolves over time. Moreover, contracts expire at the end of each season, and long-term contracts are not enforceable.

The author derives testable predictions that relate contract choice and land value in environments where production effort can reduce land fertility due to land overuse. The analysis is implemented using data from rural areas of the Philippines, collected by the International Food Policy Research Institute (Washington) and the Research Institute for Mindanao Culture (Xavier University, Philippines).

Results reject the pure risk-sharing model and the pure transaction-costs approach. The tradeoff between productivity and land-quality maintenance is supported by the data. Nonparametric estimation shows that the probability of leasing out a plot is inverse U-shaped with respect to the land's value. Among the leased plots, landlords choose more incentive-powered contracts for more valuable plots and for cropping patterns that are less likely to induce land overuse.

Chaudhuri and Maitra (2002) This paper uses ICRISAT data from India and finds that the probability of a land being leased out to a tenant decreases with its value. Among the tenants, sharecropping is positively correlated to the plot's value.

Canjels (1998a) This work uses a panel from the 1998 Agricultural Economics and Land Ownership Survey in the United States to construct regional measures for the yield risk due to weather variation. It shows that the likelihood of a plot being under a share contract is positively related to this measure of risk.

Pandey (2001) The effects of technology on the design of share contracts are studied by means of a database collected by the author in 1996 and 1998 in four villages of North India. The sample contains plot-level data on output and inputs of 270 randomly selected plots cultivated under sharecropping and ownership. The design of share contracts varies across villages in terms of the share of the output received by the tenant, the share of costs borne by them, and the renewal (or not) of the contract from one period to the next.

The author constructs different measures of noise, based on the standard deviation of the error term in a linear regression of output on different regressors (such as plot characteristics and dummy variables for the tenancy contract, year, village, and crop). Risk aversion is proxied by the tenant's caste. The author finds that the probability of having a share contract repeated from one period to the next is negatively related to the output noise. Moreover, sharecroppers' rewards are lower powered when the output is noisier.

Dubois (2001) This paper uses data from Pakistan to assess the risk-sharing properties of household consumption. A structural model for the households' preferences is used to construct the coefficients of absolute risk aversion. The author shows that more risk-averse house-holds are more likely to sign contracts with lower incentive power.

Bandiera (2003)   This article studies the determinants of the design of tenancy contracts (incentive power and length) by means of a historical data set containing information on the characteristics of tenants, land-lords, and crops of 705 tenancy contracts written between 1870 and 1880 in the district of Syracuse, Italy.

The empirical results indicate that the tenant's wealth is positively related to long-term and fixed-rent contracts; female and aristocratic landlords (with high monitoring costs) tend to lease their lands under long-term and fixed-rent contracts; and the most maintenance-intensive crops tend to be leased under long-term contracts, combined with either sharecropping (for poor tenants) or fixed rent (for rich tenants).

This work is important for studying different elements of tenancy contracts, instead of focusing exclusively on their incentive-power dimension.

Braido (2004b)   Two of the main difficulties in testing the relationship between risk and incentive power are that measures of risk based on output variability are usually affected by the farmer's actions and risk aversion is heterogeneous across farmers. Braido (2004b) uses data from the ICRISAT's Village-Level Studies in India to address these issues.

Exogenous risk is measured by the variability of the error term of a stochastic Cobb-Douglas production function. This measure of risk controls for variability caused by endogenously chosen inputs, crop-ping pattern, irrigation, and cropped area, among other factors. Plot-fixed effects were also introduced in these estimations, exploring the panel nature of the data.

Once a metric for exogenous risk is constructed, the paper tests the risk-incentive relationship. Risk-aversion heterogeneity is taken into account by means of farmers who simultaneously own and sharecrop different plots in a same period. Holding the farmer code and period of time constant, the owned farms are riskier than the sharecropped lands. This evidence does not support the risk-sharing argument for sharecropping.

Comments and Perspectives on Contract Design
The literature on contract design tests the predictions derived from the-oretical models of market equilibrium. If the model indeed captured all

relevant aspects of the problem, there should be no special concern about selection issues (selection would be part of the equilibrium prediction). However, the multiple features affecting the contract design are not easily incorporated into a parsimonious model. This fact leads many authors to focus on particular aspects of the contracting problem and use the available techniques to control for heterogeneity in the other dimensions of the problem.

Ignoring the contract-length dimension of the problem is a common feature in most of the papers discussed (exceptions include Laffont and Matoussi, 1995, and Bandiera, 2003). This is mainly because most databases do not have information about the length of each contract. Moreover, many of the existing theoretical results are based on static models, and there is no conclusive theory about how contract length and incentive power interact in a dynamic environment.

While the development of new empirical methods is central in some of the literature, the research agenda on contract design might tend to focus on the development of new testable predictions that are robust to the different features of the contracting environment. New data, with more detailed information on the contract design and on the environment, are also likely to be crucial for future research.

Final Remarks and Policy Implications

The insurance literature has seen numerous theoretical contributions whose predictions have been tested against data from many different markets. Sharecropping is regarded as a classic example of insurance, and this chapter has discussed some papers that study the impact of different contractual characteristics on resource allocation and other papers that test different theories used to explain the design of land-leasing contracts. This final section briefly comments on some of the policy implications derived from these papers.

In the studies that discuss whether the lower incentive power of share contracts distorts the allocation of input resources, the evidence presented by most of the literature suggests that share contracts induce lower productivity. Considering the arguments in Braido (2004a), one may still have doubts on this issue. This debate, however, generates no particular policy implication. Even if share contracts did induce lower productivity, they could still be necessary to solve the trade-off between incentives and risk sharing (see Stiglitz, 1974) or to mitigate soil exploitation (see Allen and Lueck, 1992, 1993). A different conclusion would follow if share contracts were determined by other market imperfections.

Some studies suggest that land investments made by tenants are affected by tenure insecurity (through fear of expropriation). There is a relative consensus among economists that better-defined property rights encourage investment decisions. It is also widely believed that a reliable legal system (that is able to enforce contracts and to define property rights unambiguously) should positively impact land-leasing efficiency. Besides that, there are papers suggesting that better-defined rights could also reduce the amount of nonutilized lands (see Berry and Cline, 1979; Assunção, 2002). In some developing countries, land-holding is used as a store of value (due to capital-market imperfections). Fearing land reforms, some of these investors prefer to keep the land unproductive instead of leasing it out to a tenant. Therefore, improving the legal system to expand the set of feasible contracts can lead societies to more efficient allocations.

Finally, in discussing the determinants of tenancy contracts, many authors suggest that contract designs are determined by market imperfections, such as transaction costs (e.g., Allen and Lueck, 1992, 1993) and credit-market imperfections (e.g., Laffont and Matoussi, 1995). In these cases, policies reducing transaction cost and promoting the development of capital markets would be desirable.

Microeconomic inefficiencies have been neglected for many years in the debate over public policy and economic development. Recently, growth theory has suggested that differences in total factor productivity account for most of the income inequality across countries (see Parente and Prescott, 2000). Microeconomic distortions, such as trade barriers, rent seeking, market power,[8] and informational asymmetries are among the variables affecting a country's productivity. Therefore, besides evaluating the relevance of different insurance theories, the empirical research on asymmetric information also contributes to a broad agenda in public policy and development economics.

Acknowledgments

I am thankful to Helena S. Perrone for excellent research assistance. Her efforts and comments are reflected throughout this essay. I also thank the referee for helpful suggestions. I am solely responsible for all errors and omissions.

Notes

1. Other contemporaneous authors (such as Anne R. J. Turgot) have also analyzed this practice along similar lines.

2. Higgs (1894) had already suggested that sharecroppers face more stable income than owner farmers, but Cheung (1969) was the first to use insurance to explain the design of share contracts.

3. Reid (1977) argued that landlords supply managerial advice to sharecroppers.

4. A later data collection was carried out in 1988, but as the authors do not seem to trust these more recent data, they are used only to test the robustness of the results.

5. Note that this paper links the exogenous change in the tenure status to the contract's incentive power. Consequently, it is also related to the topic of the previous section.

6. Household fixed effects account for farmer heterogeneity but rule out the identification of effects that depend on the average rights (as in the collateral-based theory).

7. Intensity is measured by the number of sharecroppers who registered with the Department of Land Revenue (a necessary condition for the tenant to be entitled to permanent and inheritable land tenure).

8. Harberger (1954) estimates that distortions associated with monopolistic behavior in U.S. industry would amount to approximately 0.1 percent of the U.S. gross national product. A subsequent work by Harberger (1959) shows that this value would amount to about 15 percent of the GNP in the Chilean economy.

References

Ackerberg, Daniel A., and Maristella Botticini. (2000). "The Choice of Agrarian Contracts in Early Renaissance Tuscany: Risk Sharing, Moral Hazard, or Capital Market Imperfections?" *Explorations in Economic History* 37(3): 241–257.

Ackerberg, Daniel A., and Maristella Botticini. (2002). "Endogenous Matching and the Empirical Determinants of Contract Form." *Journal of Political Economy* 110(3): 564–591.

Akerlof, A. George. (1970). "The Market for 'Lemons': Quality Uncertainty and the Market Mechanism." *Quarterly Journal of Economics* 84(3): 488–500.

Allen, Douglas W., and Dean Lueck. (1992). "Contract Choice in Modern Agriculture: Cash Rent versus Cropshare." *Journal of Law and Economics* 35(2): 397–426.

Allen, Douglas W., and Dean Lueck. (1993). "Transaction Costs and the Design of Cropshare Contracts." *RAND Journal of Economics* 24(1): 78–100.

Allen, Douglas W., and Dean Lueck. (1999). "The Role of Risk in Contract Choice." *Journal of Law, Economics, and Organization* 15(3): 704–736.

Allen, Douglas W., and Dean Lueck. (2003). *The Nature of the Farm: Contracts, Risk and Organization in Agriculture*. Cambridge, MA: MIT Press.

Alston, Lee J., Samar K. Datta, Jeffrey B. Nugent. (1984). "Tenancy Choice in a Competitive Framework with Transaction Costs." *Journal of Political Economy* 92(6): 1121–1133.

Assunção, Juliano J. (2002). "Eficiência Agrícola e Política Agrária no Brasil." Ph.D. dissertation, Pontifical Catholic University of Rio de Janeiro.

Bandiera, Oriana. (2003). "Contract Duration and Investment Incentives: Evidence from Land Tenancy Agreements." Mimeo, London School of Economics.

Bandiera, Oriana. (2004). "Land Tenure, Incentives and the Choice of Techniques: Evidence from Nicaragua." Mimeo, London School of Economics.

Banerjee, Abhijit, Paul Gertler, and Maitreesh Ghatak. (2002). "Empowerment and Efficiency: Tenancy Reform in West Bengal." *Journal of Political Economy* 110(2): 239–280.

Banerjee, Abhijit, and Maitreesh Ghatak. (2004). "Eviction Threats and Investment Incentives." *Journal of Development Economics* 74(2): 469–488.

Berry, Albert, and Willian R. Cline. (1979). *Agrarian Structure and Productivity in Developing Countries.* Baltimore: Johns Hopkins University Press.

Besley, Timothy. (1995). "Property Rights and Investment Incentives: Theory and Evidence from Ghana." *Journal of Political Economy* 103(5): 903–937.

Bhattacharyya, Sugato, and Francine Lafontaine. (1995). "Double-Sided Moral Hazard and the Nature of Share Contracts." *RAND Journal of Economics* 26(4): 761–781.

Binswanger, Hans P., Klaus Deininger, and Gershon Feder. (1995). "Power, Distortions, Revolt, and Reform in Agricultural Land Relations." In Jere Behrman and T. N. Srinivasa (Eds.), *Handbook of Development Economics.* New York: Elsevier.

Braido, Luis H. B. (2002). "Essays on Moral Hazard." Ph.D. dissertation, University of Chicago.

Braido, Luis H. B. (2004a). "Evidence on the Incentive Properties of Share Contracts." Mimeo, Getulio Vargas Foundation.

Braido, Luis H. B. (2004b). "Evidence on the Relationship between Incentives and Exogenous Risk." Mimeo, Getulio Vargas Foundation.

Canjels, Eugene. (1998a). "Does Risk Affect the Choice between Share and Fixed Rent Contracts?" Mimeo, New School University.

Canjels, Eugene. (1998b). "Share Contracts in Modern U.S. Agriculture." Mimeo, New School University.

Chaudhuri, Ananish, and Pushkar Maitra. (2002). "On the Choice of Tenancy Contracts in Rural India." *Economica* 69(275): 445–459.

Cheung, Steven N. S. (1969). *The Theory of Share Tenancy.* Chicago: University of Chicago Press.

Cheung, Steven N. S. (2002). "Sharecropping." In Daniel F. Spulber (Ed.), *Famous Fables of Economics: Myths of Market Failures.* Oxford: Blackwell.

Deininger, Klaus, and Gershon Feder. (1997). "Land Institutions and Land Markets." In Bruce L. Gardner and Gordon C. Rausser (Eds.), *Handbook of Agricultural Economics.* New York: Elsevier.

Dubois, Pierre. (2001). "Consumption Insurance with Heterogeneous Preferences: Can Sharecropping Help to Complete Markets?" Mimeo, INRA.

Dubois, Pierre. (2002). "Moral Hazard, Land Fertility and Sharecropping in a Rural Area of the Philippines." *Journal of Development Economics* 68(1): 35–64.

Eswaran, Mukesh, and Ashok Kotwal. (1985). "A Theory of Contractual Structure in Agriculture." *American Economic Review* 75(3): 352–367.

Ghatak, Maitreesh, and Priyanka Pandey. (2000). "Contract Choice in Agriculture with Joint Moral Hazard in Effort and Risk." *Journal of Development Economics* 63(2): 303–326.

Green, Jerry R., and Nancy L. Stokey. (1983). "A Comparison of Tournaments and Contracts." *Journal of Political Economy* 91(3): 349–364.

Grossman, Sanford J., and Oliver D. Hart. (1983). "An Analysis of the Principal-Agent Problem." *Econometrica* 51(1): 7–45.

Harberger, Arnold C. (1954). "Monopoly and Resource Allocation." *American Economic Review Paper and Proceedings* 44(2): 77–87.

Harberger, Arnold C. (1959). "Using the Resources at Hand More Efficiently." *American Economic Review* 49(2): 134–146.

Higgs, Henry. (1894). "'Metayage' in Western France." *Economic Journal* 4(13): 1–13.

Hodkinson, Stephen. (1992). "Sharecropping and Sparta's Economic Exploitation of the Helots." In J. Sanders (Ed.), *Philolakôn Lakonian Studies in Honour of Hector W. Catling*. Oxford: British School at Athens.

Hoffman, Philip T. (1984). "The Economic Theory of Sharecropping in Early Modern France." *Journal of Economic History* 44(2): 309–319.

Holmstrom, Bengt R. (1979). "Moral Hazard and Observability." *Bell Journal of Economics* 10(1): 74–91.

Holmstrom, Bengt, and Paul Milgrom. (1987). "Aggregation and Linearity in the Provision of Intertemporal Incentives." *Econometrica* 55(2): 303–328.

Hudson, Michael. (2000). "Mesopotamia and Classical Antiquity: Taxation History." *American Journal of Economics and Sociology* (December): 3–26.

Jacoby, Hanan G., Guo Li, and Scott Rozelle. (2002). "Hazards of Expropriation: Tenure Insecurity and Investments in Rural China." *American Economic Review* 92(5): 1420–1447.

Jacoby, Hanan G., and Ghazala Mansuri. (2003). "Incomplete Contracts and Investment: A Study of Land Tenancy in Pakistan." Mimeo, World Bank.

Johnson, D. Gale. (1950). "Resource Allocation under Share Contracts." *Journal of Political Economy* 58(2): 111–123.

Laffont, Jean-Jacques, and Mohamed S. Matoussi. (1995). "Moral Hazard, Financial Constraints and Sharecropping in El Oulja." *Review of Economic Studies* 62(3): 381–399.

Lambert, Richard A. (1983). "Long-Term Contracts and Moral Hazard." *Bell Journal of Economics* 14(2): 441–452.

Lazear, Edward P., and Sherwin Rosen. (1981). "Rank-Order Tournaments as Optimum Labor Contracts." *Journal of Political Economy* 89(5): 841–864.

Manyong, Victor M., and Victorin A. Houndékon. (2000). "Land Tenurial Systems and the Adoption of Mucuna Planted Fallow in the Derived Savannas of West Africa." Mimeo, International Institute of Tropical Agriculture.

Marshall, Alfred. (1961). *Principles of Economics.* Edited by C. W. Guillebaud. London: Macmillan. (Original work published in 1890).

Marx, Karl. (1967). *Capital.* Edited by Frederick Engels. New York: International Publishers. (Original work published in 1887).

Mill, John S. (1936). *Principles of Political Economy.* Edited by W. J. Ashley. London: Longmans. (Original work published in 1848).

Murrell, Peter. (1983). "The Economics of Sharing: A Transactional Cost Analysis of Contractual Choice in Farming." *Bell Journal of Economics* 14(1): 283–293.

Otsuka, Keijiro, Hiroyuki Chuma, and Yujiro Hayami. (1992). "Land and Labor Contracts in Agrarian Economies: Theories and Facts." *Journal of Economic Literature* 30: 1965–2018.

Otsuka, Keijiro, and Yujiro Hayami. (1988). "Theories of Share Tenancy: A Critical Survey." *Economic Development and Cultural Change* 37(1): 31–68.

Pandey, Priyanka. (2001). "Effects of Technology on Incentive Design of Share Contracts." Mimeo, Pennsylvania State University.

Parente, Steven L., and Edward C. Prescott. (2000). *Barriers to Riches.* Cambridge, MA: MIT Press.

Prendergast, Canice. (2002). "The Tenuous Tradeoff between Risk and Incentives." *Journal of Political Economy* 110(5): 1035–1070.

Radner, Roy. (1981). "Monitoring Cooperative Agreements in a Repeated Principal-Agent Relationship." *Econometrica* 49(5): 1127–1148.

Radner, Roy. (1985). "Repeated Principal-Agent Games with Discounting." *Econometrica* 53(5): 1173–1198.

Rao, C. H. Hanumantha. (1971). "Uncertainty, Entrepreneurship, and Sharecropping in India." *Journal of Political Economy* 79(3): 578–595.

Ray, Tridip. (1999). "Share Tenancy as Strategic Delegation." *Journal of Development Economics* 58(1): 45–60.

Reid, Jr., Joseph D. (1977). "The Theory of Share Tenancy Revisited—Again." *Journal of Political Economy* 85(2): 403–407.

Rogerson, William P. (1985). "Repeated Moral Hazard." *Econometrica* 53(1): 69–76.

Rothschild, Michael, and Joseph E. Stiglitz. (1976). "Equilibrium in Competitive Insurance Markets: An Essay on the Economics of Imperfect Information." *Quarterly Journal of Economics* 90(4): 629–649.

Rubinstein, Abreu, and Menahem E. Yaari. (1983). "Repeated Insurance Contracts and Moral Hazard." *Journal of Economic Theory* 30(1): 74–97.

Sengupta, Kunal. (1997). "Limited Liability, Moral Hazard and Share Tenancy." *Journal of Development Economics* 52(2): 393–407.

Shaban, Radwan A. (1987). "Testing between Competing Models of Sharecropping." *Journal of Political Economy* 95(5): 893–920.

Smith, Adam. (1996). *An Inquiry into the Nature and Causes of the Wealth of Nations*. Edited by Edwin Cannan. Chicago: University of Chicago Press. (Original work published in 1776).

Spence, A. Michael. (1973). "Job Market Signaling." *Quarterly Journal of Economics* 87(3): 355–374.

Stiglitz, Joseph E. (1974). "Incentives and Risk Sharing in Sharecropping." *Review of Economic Studies* 41(2): 219–255.

Warriner, Doreen. (1962). *Land Reform and Development in the Middle East: A Study of Egypt, Syria and Iraq*. London: Oxford University Press.

Williamson, Oliver E. (1979). "Transaction-Cost Economics: The Governance of Contractual Relations." *Journal of Law and Economics* 22(2): 233–261.

12

Asymmetric Learning in Insurance Markets

Paul Kofman and Gregory P. Nini

Auto insurance is often considered an industry likely to be plagued by information asymmetries: drivers seem to vary in ability, insurers collect large amounts of data about their customers, and insurers seem to use a variety of screening devices (such as a menu of choices for the amount of insurance) to illicit private information. Yet recent empirical work has frequently found little evidence consistent with the theoretical predictions of models with private information. Chiappori (2000) reviews the literature testing a prediction of the Rothschild and Stiglitz (1976) model that risk and coverage are positively correlated. In general, the data do not lead to a rejection of the null of independence.[1] Simultaneously, theoretical models of both insurance and banking markets have considered that private information may reside with an incumbent supplier relative to other competitors in the market.[2] Given the repeated nature of insurance contracting and the large amounts of data collected by insurers, it is natural to conjecture that insurance companies may develop information monopoly power over their customers.

This purpose of this chapter is to identify empirically testable predictions from a theoretical model of asymmetric learning, characterized by an incumbent insurance company gaining private knowledge about the risk of their customers. Three time-series predictions are developed and tested on a large set of policy-level data from a single insurance company. In total, the data are not consistent with the model of asymmetric learning. The results indicate that this market has developed an efficient mechanism for sharing relevant information through the use of a publicly available set of rating characteristics.

The theoretical model adapts the literature on relationship banking to an insurance environment and is similar to Kunreuther and Pauly (1985), the original paper to address the concept of asymmetric learning.[3] The important result from this work is that information monopoly power can result in consumer "lock-in," where prices rise over time because consumers are unable to credibly reveal information that has been learned by the incumbent supplier.[4] In a model closely related to that in Sharpe (1990), with an equilibrium similar to that in von Thadden (2001), two additional positive empirical predictions are developed. First, insurance claims and consumer switching should be contemporaneously positively correlated. The revelation of "bad" information is more likely for higher-risk insureds, who are more likely to receive an attractive offer from a competitor. Second, the risk associated with a particular cohort of insureds should decrease over time as riskier consumers strategically choose to switch more often than less risky consumers. The incumbent insurer generates positive profits from low-risk consumers and makes price offers designed to keep them. Most important, all of the hypotheses are conditional on publicly available information, since the model's predictions result from the incumbent insurer having private information.

The empirical application utilizes a dataset comprised of contract-level information from a single large Australian insurance company. The data cover the insurer's entire book of business for a single policy year, allowing identification of policies that lapse (leave the insurer's portfolio for an unknown reason) and renew during the sample period. The empirical tests use this time dimension to examine the correlation between claims and lapses, changes in average risk, and changes in average profitability. The data contain all relevant rating variables and policy provisions, which are observable to competitor insurers, and the results highlight the importance of controlling for observable information.

While aggregate statistics are consistent with the predictions of the model, the multivariate tests do not lead to a rejection of the null hypothesis that average risk and average profitability are constant over time. Similar to the results from Chiappori and Salanie (2000) and Dionne, Gourieroux, and Vanasse (2001), this result is likely a consequence of the underwriting process in the examined market. The Australian market has developed an experience rating mechanism that assigns a score to each consumer based on the consumer's claim history. This rating is public information and contributes to the amount of information that is publicly available about the risk profile of the consumer. Regardless of the motivation for developing such a mechanism, the public nature of this information has eliminated any information advantage of incumbent insurers.[5]

While the econometric tests reject the hypothesis of asymmetric learning, the data indicate an interesting pattern over time. Claiming and lapsing are contemporaneously correlated, but the policies that do not lapse do not show an improvement in the subsequent period. This suggests that lapsing is not due to the revelation of information concerning future claim risk but rather that a simple contemporaneous (possibly causal) relationship exists. Second, observably less risky consumers are more likely to renew with the incumbent insurer, so cohorts improve in average riskiness as they age. This makes auto insurance, with frequent recontracting, different than other financial services that are often plagued by worsening risk over time.[6]

The remainder of the chapter is structured as follows. A theoretical model is presented along with comparisons to related insurance and banking literature. The equilibrium pricing strategies of an insurance market characterized by asymmetric learning are followed by empirical predictions concerning claiming and lapsing rates, the evolution of average risk over time, and the impact that policy aging has on the average price and profitability of insurance. The empirical application finds little support for the predictions generated by an asymmetric learning model. The chapter's conclusions include suggestions for future research generated from the interesting patterns in the data.

A Model of Asymmetric Learning

A continuum of risk-averse consumers is faced with a single source of risk of loss to their wealth. The loss occurs with probability p, and the probability of loss is assumed to vary across consumers. For simplicity, assume that consumers are either *high risk* or *low risk*, identified by their probability of loss. High-risk consumers have a higher probability of loss than low-risk consumers, $p_H > p_L$. In the population of consumers, it is common knowledge that a proportion $b \in (0, 1)$ are low risk. Consumers are assumed to behave very simply. They have completely inelastic demand and always purchasing insurance I at the lowest price received.[7]

Two risk-neutral insurance companies exist to provide insurance. At a price π, an insurer will provide coverage I in the event a loss occurs.[8] Prior to contracting with the consumer, each insurer has the option to perfectly learn the consumer's true riskiness. However, at most one insurer will become *informed*, leaving an *uninformed* insurer only knowing the unconditional probability of loss, $\bar{p} = bp_L + (1 - b)p_H$. The informed insured observes an imperfect signal concerning the consumer's true risk type. The signal $\tilde{s}$ is stochastic, providing improved but imperfect information about risk type. Specifically, assume the following distribution for $\tilde{s}$:

$$\Pr(s = l|\text{low risk}) = \Pr(s = h|\text{high risk}) = \frac{1 + \theta}{2}$$

$$\Pr(s = h|\text{low risk}) = \Pr(s = l|\text{high risk}) = \frac{1 - \theta}{2}.$$

(12.1)

The parameter θ captures the differential in information between the competing insurers. For $\theta = 0$, the signal provides no additional information, and for $\theta = 1$, the signal perfectly reveals the consumer's riskiness.[9] Assume that $\theta \in (0, 1)$ so that the signal is always imperfectly informative.

Given a signal $s \in \{l, h\}$, the informed insurer forms Bayesian updated beliefs about a consumer's riskiness. Denote b_s as the insurer's belief that a consumer is low risk, given a signal s. Using (12.1), the updated beliefs are given by

$$b_l = \left(\frac{b}{\lambda}\right)\left(\frac{1 + \theta}{2}\right), \quad b_h = \left(\frac{b}{1 - \lambda}\right)\left(\frac{1 - \theta}{2}\right),$$

(12.2)

where $\lambda = \frac{1}{2} + \theta\left(b - \frac{1}{2}\right)$ is the unconditional probability of observing a signal l. It is easily verified that $b_h < b < b_l$. Given updated beliefs, the insurer forms updated conditional loss probabilities as $\bar{p}_s = b_s p_L + (1 - b_s)p_H$, which is the average loss probability for the pool of consumers generating signal s. The conditioning information is informative because $\bar{p}_l < \bar{p} < \bar{p}_h$, but it is imperfect because $\bar{p}_l > p_L$ and $\bar{p}_h < p_H$.

For an updated loss probability p, the insurer values contracts, $\{\pi, I\}$, according to the expected profit from the contract, $I \cdot (\pi - p)$.[10] For any price $\pi > p$, the insurer makes positive expected profits.

The interaction is modeled as a single-shot game over two periods. In the first period, insurers bargain over the ability to become informed. In the second period, contracting occurs, with the informed insurer (I) and the uninformed insurer (U) each simultaneously making price offers, denoted $\pi^I = (\pi_l^I, \pi_h^I)$ and π^U, where only the informed insurer can condition on the observed signal. Consumers choose the lowest price offer and purchase insurance I. Finally, the insurance premium πI is paid, the loss is realized, and the indemnity is paid from the insurer to the consumer.

Note that the insurers do not offer contracts during the first stage of the game. With a risk-averse consumer, the most efficient contract would fully insure the consumer against two sources of risk: the risk of wealth destruction due to incurring the loss L and the classification risk generated by the information revealed over time. Without contracting in the first stage, long-term contracts that reduce both sources of risk are infeasible. In fact, it is shown below that the equilibrium of the game involves considerable ex ante price risk to the consumer.[11]

The interaction in stage 2 is modeled as a standard game of incomplete information. While the uninformed insurer will offer one price, the informed insurer will offer two prices (one for each signal). For the informed insurer, a pure strategy is a set of price offers, $\pi^I = (\pi_l^I, \pi_h^I)$, and a mixed strategy is a probability distribution over such offers, denoted $F_l^I(\pi)$ and $F_h^I(\pi)$. For the uninformed insurer, a pure strategy is a single price offer π^U, and a mixed strategy is a probability distribution over such offers, denoted $F^U(\pi)$.

Payoffs to insurers are given by the expected profits from the contract, conditional on the purchase decision. Specifically, the payoffs to the insurer are

$$\Pi_U(\pi^U, \pi_l^I, \pi_h^I) = \lambda I(\pi^U - p_L) + (1 - \lambda)I(\pi^U - p_H)$$
$$\text{if } \pi^U < \pi_l^I \text{ and } \pi^U < \pi_h^I$$
$$= (1 - \lambda)I(\pi^U - \bar{p}_h) \quad \text{if } \pi^U \geq \pi_l^I \text{ and } \pi^U < \pi_h^I$$
$$= \lambda I(\pi^U - \bar{p}_l) \quad \text{if } \pi^U < \pi_l^I \text{ and } \pi^U \geq \pi_h^I$$
$$= 0 \quad \text{if } \pi^U \geq \pi_l^I \text{ and } \pi^U \geq \pi_l^I$$
$$\Pi_I(\pi^U, \pi_l^I, \pi_h^I) = 0 \quad \text{if } \pi^U < \pi_l^I \text{ and } \pi^U < \pi_h^I$$
$$= \lambda I(\pi_l^I - \bar{p}_l) \quad \text{if } \pi^U \geq \pi_l^I \text{ and } \pi^U < \pi_h^I$$
$$= (1 - \lambda)I(\pi_h^I - \bar{p}_l) \quad \text{if } \pi^U < \pi_l^I \text{ and } \pi^U \geq \pi_h^I$$
$$= \lambda I(\pi_l^I - \bar{p}_l) + (1 - \lambda)I(\pi_h^I - \bar{p}_l)$$
$$\text{if } \pi^U \geq \pi_l^I \text{ and } \pi^U \geq \pi_l^I.$$

A stage 2 Nash equilibrium is defined in a standard fashion. The strategy of each insurer must maximize the above payoff, conditional on the strategy of the other insurer. A mixed-strategy equilibrium maximizes expected payoffs, conditional on the mixed strategy of the other insurer. At stage 1, the equilibrium bids for the right to acquire the signal are given by standard bidding under symmetric information.

Equilibrium Strategies

Proposition 12.1 provides an important result concerning equilibrium strategies in a game of Bertrand bidding under asymmetric information. The following proposition has been previously affirmed in slightly different forms in Kunreuther and Pauly (1985) and von Thadden (2001).

Proposition 12.1   In a game of incomplete information where an informed insurer observes updated loss probabilities $\bar{p}_l$ and $\bar{p}_h$ but an uninformed insurer observes only the average loss probability $\bar{p} = bp_L + (1 - b)p_H$, Bertrand competition results in the following:

1. No pure-strategy Nash equilibrium;

2. A mixed-strategy Nash equilibrium given by

$$F_h^I(\bar{p}_h) = 1$$

$$F_l^I(\pi) = 1 - \left(\frac{1 - \lambda}{\lambda}\right)\left(\frac{\bar{p}_h - \pi}{\pi - \bar{p}_l}\right) \quad \pi \in [\bar{p}, \bar{p}_h]$$

$$F^U(\pi) = 1 - \left(\frac{\bar{p} - \bar{p}_l}{\pi - \bar{p}_l}\right) \quad \pi \in [\bar{p}, \bar{p}_h)$$

$$f^U(\bar{p}_h) = \left(\frac{\bar{p} - \bar{p}_l}{\bar{p}_h - \bar{p}_l}\right),$$

(12.3)

where $\lambda = \frac{1}{2} + \theta\left(b - \frac{1}{2}\right)$ is the unconditional probability of observing signal l.

Proof   Part 1 is an interesting result since the strategy spaces are nonempty, compact, convex subsets of Euclidean space, so the game appears to satisfy the pure-strategy existence theorem (Debreu, 1952). However, the game does not satisfy all of the requirements of the theorem, as the payoff functions are not upper semicontinuous (Dasgupta and Maskin, 1986).

A formal proof for the nonexistence of a pure-strategy Nash equilibrium is given in Kunreuther and Pauly (1985). The derivation of the equilibrium-mixed strategies is given by a modification of the proof in von Thadden (2001), which is shown in the appendix to this chapter. □

The mixed-strategy equilibrium has an intuitive structure. The informed insurer offers a zero-profit price to the high types but randomizes on profitable offers to the low types. The uninformed insurer randomizes on the same support and places sufficient probability mass on the high-type break-even price. Since the informed insurer is randomizing on offers to consumers with lower risk, the uninformed insurer makes positive profits on the random occasions when its offer is less than the informed insurer. The randomization reduces the impact of the winner's curse, since success may be random rather than a perfect indicator that the consumer is unprofitable at the offered price. In expectation, the uninformed insurer makes zero profits (shown in the appendix to this chapter), providing maximal competition to the informed insurer. The informed insurer makes positive expected profits by utilizing the information advantage on the low risks.[12]

Strategies in the first stage are given by standard competitive bidding under symmetric information. The proof of proposition 12.1 shows that the informed insurer earns positive expected profits on the low-risk consumers. The profit level is $I(\bar{p} - \bar{p}_l)$, which is earned on all signal l consumers. In the population, a fraction λ of the consumers generate signal l, yielding total expected profits from becoming informed of $\lambda I(\bar{p} - \bar{p}_l)$, which is strictly positive.

Proposition 12.2 In the first stage of the game, each insurer offers $\lambda I(\bar{p} - \bar{p}_l)$. The signal is randomly allocated, and the winning insurer pays for the period 2 expected profits in the period 1 bid.

Proposition 12.2 confirms the temporal profit patter identified in Kunreuther and Pauly (1985) and D'Arcy and Doherty (1990). The information advantage of the informed insurer generates positive profits in period 2. Competition results in zero profits over the two periods, so insurers pay for the expected profits in period 1. Note that the level of learning achieved by the informed insurer (that is, the level of θ) does not affect the two-period expected payoffs of the insurers. With competition in the first period, total payoffs are always zero regardless of the size of the period 2 rents. However, the level of θ does affect the difference in rents across the two periods. Further, the equilibrium strategies given in (12.3) indicate that the uninformed insurance company acquires some consumers from the informed insurer in equilibrium. In fact, this implication is necessary to overcome the winner's curse problem that plagues pure strategies. These theoretical results are used to generate empirically testable predictions.

Empirical Development

The equilibrium outlined in propositions 12.1 and 12.2 yields several positive empirical predictions about the temporal patterns of profitability and average risk in an insurer's portfolio, even assuming that the econometrician does not observe the source of the insurer's private information. Without observing the informed insurer's private information, the model is tested by deriving necessary conditions on the relationship between commonly observable variables such as claiming behavior, consumer insurance choices, and insurer profitability.

Some care is necessary in generalizing the model to real-world insurance contracting, since the model consists of only one period of contracting. Nevertheless, the implications are straightforward under the assumption that private information is acquired through the repeated provision of insurance. In a repeated contracting situation such as with auto insurance, the incumbent insurer could receive private signals concerning consumers' true risk, potentially leading to the information monopoly game outlined above. Rather than direct bidding for the right to become informed, insurance companies compete by offering lower prices and, in the course of providing insurance, become privately informed about the risk of their customers. This private information then factors into future pricing decisions. With each contract, insurers quote a premium that reflects both the current level of private information and the expected benefit from future monopoly power. With this generalization in mind, simple comparative statics on the equilibrium result in several testable predictions.

Hypothesis 12.1: Contemporaneous Claiming and Switching Insurers

First, the model makes a prediction about the distribution of types that choose the uninformed insurer. With positive probability, both signal types receive price offers from the uninformed insurer that are lower than the price offer from the informed insurer. However, the probability of choosing the uninformed insurer is larger for the consumers generating signal h than for consumers generating signal l. With an informative signal, signal h consumers are higher risk than signal l consumers, so the model predicts that the uninformed insurer receives a pool of consumers with higher average risk. Given the analogy to actual contracting, choosing the uninformed insurer is equivalent to switching from an incumbent insurer to an alternative insurer, so the model predicts contemporaneous positive correlation between having a claim and switching insurance companies.

Type h consumers switch whenever the uninformed insurer offers a price below p_H, which happens with probability $\Pr(\pi^U < \bar{p}_h) = 1 - f_s^U(\bar{p}_h)$, which is greater than zero since $\bar{p}_h > \bar{p}$, because the signal is informative. Some algebra shows that

$$\Pr(switch|h) = \Pr(\pi^U < \bar{p}_h) = 1 - f_s^U(\bar{p}_h) = \lambda.$$

Low-risk types switch when the uninformed price offer is strictly less than the informed price offer, which happens with probability $[1 - f^U(\bar{p}_h)] \cdot \Pr(\pi^U < \pi_l^I | \pi^U < \bar{p}_h)$. The second term in the probability is strictly less than 1 when $\theta < 1$. Integrating the probability by parts and simplifying yields

$$\Pr(switch|l) = \Pr(switch|h) \cdot \Pr(\pi^U < \pi_l^I) = \tfrac{1}{2}\lambda^2.$$

Since $\lambda < 1$, it is always true that $\tfrac{1}{2}\lambda^2 < \lambda$, so type h consumers switch more often than type l consumers. Intuitively, type h face incumbent prices at least as high, and sometimes higher, as the prices faced by type l, yet both types receive an alternative price drawn from the same distribution. With some probability, the uninformed alternative price falls in between the high and low incumbent prices, causing just the high risks to switch.

Empirically, the above result suggests a positive correlation between the incidence of a claim and the incidence of a consumer switching insurers.[13] In particular, the observation of a consumer switching insurers results in an updated loss probability given by

$$\Pr(claim|switch) = \bar{p}_l \Pr(l|switch) + \bar{p}_h \Pr(h|switch)$$

$$= \bar{p}_l \frac{1 - \lambda}{1 - \lambda + \tfrac{1}{2}\lambda^2} + \bar{p}_h \frac{\tfrac{1}{2}\lambda^2}{1 - \lambda + \tfrac{1}{2}\lambda^2},$$

where the updated probabilities are given by Bayes law. Since $\lambda < 1$, this conditional probability is strictly greater than the unconditional probability of a claim, $\Pr(claim) = \bar{p}_l\lambda + \bar{p}_h(1 - \lambda)$, implying a positive correlation between claiming and switching:

H1 The model of asymmetric learning implies a contemporaneous, positive correlation between claims and switching.

Note that the hypothesis does not depend on the claim being the source of private information. H1 holds even if the occurrence of a claim is public information. The positive correlation results from an unobservable factor that is related to both claiming and switching: high risks are more likely to switch insurers and, by definition, more likely to have claims.

Hypothesis 12.2: Policy Persistence and Average Risk

While H1 concerns the contemporaneous relationship between claiming and switching, the model also yields an empirical prediction concerning the claiming behavior of insureds that remain with the informed insurer. In particular, assuming that insureds' claim type does not change, the average risk of a cohort of insureds should decrease on renewal with an incumbent insurer.

Similar to the analysis above, the probability of a claim, conditional on the insured remaining with the informed insurer, is given by

$$\Pr(claim|stay) = \bar{p}_l \Pr(l|stay) + \bar{p}_h \Pr(h|stay)$$

$$= \bar{p}_l \frac{\left(1 - \frac{1}{2}\lambda^2\right)\lambda}{\left(1 - \frac{1}{2}\lambda^2\right)\lambda + (1 - \lambda)^2} + \bar{p}_h \frac{(1 - \lambda)^2}{\left(1 - \frac{1}{2}\lambda^2\right)\lambda + (1 - \lambda)^2}.$$

The conditional probability is strictly less than the unconditional claiming probability, $\Pr(claim) = \bar{p}_l\lambda + \bar{p}_h(1 - \lambda)$, as long as $\frac{1}{2}\lambda^2 < \lambda$, which is true for $\lambda < 1$.

Empirically, this result suggests that the average riskiness of a cohort of insureds should decrease with each successive renewal with an incumbent insured. At the culmination of each contracting period, the incumbent insurer retains a higher percentage of low-risk consumers, resulting in average risk decreasing over time. This result does not predict autocorrelation in risk over time but rather a change in portfolio composition that creates a decrease in average risk over time. The following hypothesis formally states the result:

H2 The model of asymmetric learning implies that average risk decreases over time as insureds renew their policies with an incumbent insurer.

This result is unique from H1 in that H1 may be true yet H2 false.[14] H1 predicts contemporaneous correlation between risk and switching, while H2 predicts correlation between switching (or the failure to switch) and future risk. The theoretical foundation is that lower-risk customers are less likely to switch, but risk is understood to be a permanent type associated with a particular customer. Risk must be lower both in the current period (contemporaneous correlation) and in future periods (decreasing average risk). Rejection of either is evidence contrary to the model.

Hypothesis 12.3: Policy Persistence and Price
The final hypothesis is related to the temporal pattern of prices as hypothesized in Kunreuther and Pauly (1985) and Dionne and Doherty (1994). Proposition 12.2 shows that the informed insurer makes positive expected profits in period 2, since low-risk types are charged more than the actuarially fair premium. Moreover, the informed insurer has to pay for the expected future rents with a first-period bid that offsets the future gains. Empirically, this suggests that an incumbent insurer will charge a higher average price to policies that renew compared with the average price charged to all policies in the previous period.[15]

The degree of change over time is related to the size of the information advantage possessed by the informed insurer. Proposition 12.2 shows that the size of the period 2 expected profits are $\lambda I(\bar{p} - \bar{p}_l)$. Expected profits increase as the conditional loss probability $\bar{p}_l$ decreases, which happens when θ increases since the updated belief that a consumer with signal l is a low-risk increases. However, the unconditional probability of generating signal l, $\lambda = \frac{1}{2} + \theta(b - \frac{1}{2})$, may decrease with θ for $b < \frac{1}{2}$. The combined effect is given by the derivative with respect to θ

$$\frac{2(p_H - p_L)b(1 - b)}{(1 + 2\theta b - \theta)^2}.$$

As expected, as the quality of the signal increases, expected second-period profits to the informed insurer increase. Given the result from proposition 12.2, this suggests that the change in profits over the two periods becomes larger.

Empirically, incumbent insurers are setting prices in consideration of both expected claims cost and expected future rents earned from private information. Consequently, the relationship between insurance premiums and claims costs will change with the level of private information and the expected future benefits of private information.

Insureds choosing to remain with an incumbent insurer will, on average, have a higher ratio of premiums to claims than in the prior period.

H3   The model of asymmetric learning implies that average profitability increases over time as insureds renew their policies with an incumbent insurer.

Hypothesis H3 results when insurers do not insure against classification risk. Without a long-term contract, informed insurers utilize their information advantage by increasing prices as relevant information is revealed to them. Competition for these future rents results in earlier-period losses that offset later gains. Note that the hypothesis does not make a prediction about premium levels but rather the relationship between premiums and claims, a measure of profitability. D'Arcy and Doherty (1990) use the inverse of this measure, termed the *loss ratio*, in their empirical work, and they find a negative relationship between policy age and loss ratio in a cross-section of policies for several insurers.

Empirical Application

The three hypotheses are tested using a large dataset from a single Australian automobile insurance company. While the data have a large cross-section of policies, they cover only one year in time. Nevertheless, the data can be segmented into two distinct periods, allowing a comparison of policies before and after renewal. Three sets of tests are conducted to examine the contemporaneous correlation between claiming and lapsing, the change in average risk between the new and late periods, and the change in average profitability between the new and late periods. In all tests, a large set of control variables is used to remove the impact of publicly observable information, which is shown to be quite important.

Data-Set Construction

Policy-level data from a single Australian auto insurer are used to test the empirical hypotheses. The data set is comprised of all comprehensive auto policies in effect during the year July 1, 1996, through June 30, 1997. Comprehensive policies provide first-party protection for damage to the covered auto, including at-fault accidents, nonfault accidents, theft, and various other perils. All policies in force during the year are included in the sample, with policies included in the sample having inception dates as early as July 1, 1995, and as late as June 30, 1997, a two-year period.[16] Accidents related to these policies are included only if they occur during the one-year period from July 1, 1996, to June 30, 1997. Consequently, observations are heterogeneous with respect to their exposure to loss during the sample period.

The full data set contains in excess of 900,000 observations. However, the same insured often results in two separate observations—one related to the policy beginning before the sample period and one beginning during the sample period. The sample is split into two distinct time periods to identify observations related to the same underlying insured. Policies written during the period July 1, 1995, to June 30, 1996, are termed *early*, and policies written during the period July 1, 1996 to June 30, 1997, are termed *late*. Every early policy either renews and generates another observation or leaves the insurer.[17] A *persisting* policy is an early policy with a corresponding late policy. A *lapsing* policy is an early policy without a corresponding late policy. Not all late policies have a corresponding early policy, since the insurer generates new business during the sample period. A *new-business* policy is late policy that has no corresponding early policy. Persisting policies provide a balanced sample over two periods. Including the lapsing policies and the new business policies creates an unbalanced sample. Due to the short nature of the time series, the empirical work focuses on the difference in average risk and premiums between the early and late policies.

For each observation, a large set of observable consumer characteristics is available in the data set. These variables include common characteristics known to be correlated with the expected claims costs, including the insured's age, gender, and residence and the automobile's value, crash worthiness, and intended use. Two variables related to the amount of coverage are included: the deductible level and an indicator that the policy provides coverage for a contractually specified agreed amount rather than market value.[18] The data also include a single measure of the insured's claim history, termed the *no-claims discount* (NCD) in the Australian market. Australian auto insurance utilizes a bonus-malus pricing scheme, with prices being determined by rating class (a function of age, gender, residence, and so on) and the consumer-specific NCD rating. NCD ratings take up to fifteen different levels and provide up to a 60 percent premium benefit for consumers in the best class. In short, every driver begins as level 7 and improves by one step for each year without a claim and drops by three steps for each year with a claim. The data provides the NCD level,

Table 12.1
Observable explanatory variables in early and late policies (Description and sample statistics)

		Early Policies		Late Policies	
Variable	Description	Persist	Lapse	Persist	New
Insured Age	Age of insured measured in years	47.4	42.4	48.2	38.6
		(10.4)	(11.2)	(11.2)	(8.4)
Amount Insured	Value of vehicle measured in	12.1	11.7	12.6	15.0
	A$1,000	(6.7)	(7.1)	(7.2)	(7.2)
Vehicle Age	Age of vehicle measured in years	9.6	10.4	9.6	7.8
		(3.9)	(4.3)	(4.2)	(3.5)
Policy Age	Consecutive years the particular	3.4	2.5	4.4	0.0
	policy has been in force	(2.6)	(2.6)	(2.8)	(0.0)
Rating	NCD rating of primary driver,	3.8	5.1	3.4	6.4
	raging from 1 (best) to 15 (worst)	(2.1)	(2.4)	(2.0)	(2.0)
Male	Indicates primary driver is male	58.4	63.0	58.4	59.2
Rate Protection	Indicates purchse of NCD rating	7.1	8.1	6.4	4.4
	protection				
Agreed Value	Indicates policy provides an	9.2	13.4	9.9	11.0
	agreed amount in event of total				
	loss				
Group 1	Indicates insured fully owns the	90.8	85.0	91.2	79.6
	covered vehicle				
Group 2	Indicates insured is financing the	6.9	11.4	6.7	15.7
	covered vehicle				
Class 1	Indicates private use is primary	93.5	93.9	94.4	90.5
	purpose of vehicle				
Claim frequency		8.7	17.9	9.6	13.0

Notes: Statistics are sample means. For continuous variables, sample standard deviations are below the sample means in parentheses. Early policies have inception dates prior to the sample period, and late policies have inception dates during the sample period. Persisting policies renew and become late policies; lapsing policies leave the data. New policies enter the data during the late period.

termed *rating*, for the primary driver of each policy. Finally, the data set includes the full premium charged to the insured as well as the number of claims made during the sample period along with their associated costs.

Table 12.1 presents list of the variables included in the data set, along with sample means by time period. The statistics are also presented separately for policies that lapse and new policies. All of these variables are considered exogenous. The important assumption is that all of these variables are observable to outside insurance companies, which means that all information available to the econometrician is publicly available information and not a source of private information.[19] Consequently, the econometric tests will focus on changes created by the entry and exit of policies after controlling for other variables.

Test 12.1: Contemporaneous Correlation between Claiming and Lapsing

The first prediction of the model concerns the distribution of customers who choose to leave the insurer, with the model predicting positive contemporaneous correlation between a policy with a claim and a policy lapsing. Since the data on early policies provide information on the number of claims and an indicator if the policy lapsed, the hypothesis is tested by examining the correlation between these two variables. For this section only, claim risk is captured by a dummy variable that indicates the occurrence of at least one claim.[20]

In the aggregate, the claiming random variable and the lapsing random variable are not statistically independent. For the sample of early policies, the lapsing policies report a claim 19 percent of the time, while persisting policies report a claim only 9 percent of the time.[21] Similarly, policies with no claims lapse at a 6 percent rate, while policies with a claim lapse at an 11 percent rate. The standard Pearson statistic for independence in a two-way table is 1360, which leads to rejection of the null hypothesis of independence under any reasonable significance level. However, since the model predicts positive correlation due to the impact of unobservable information, aggregate tests do not provide a true test of the model. In particular, the correlation may be due to the impact of observable information.

Following Richaudeau (1999) and Chiappori and Salanie (2000), the independence assumption is tested via a parametric bivariate probit model. The model specification relies on a pair of probit equations to explain the occurrence of a claim and the decision to lapse. All of the explanatory variables are used in each equation, and the model is estimated by maximum likelihood, assuming bivariate normally distributed latent random variables. Conditional correlation is captured by the sample estimate of the correlation between the latent random variables. The null hypothesis of independence is tested against the one-sided alternative that unobserved correlation is positive. To account for the varying exposure periods, observations on claim occurrence are weighted by the portion of the year during which insurance is provided, unless a claim occurs, in which case the observation is given full weight.[22]

Table 12.2 presents the results from the bivariate probit model. Most important, the estimated correlation between the latent random variable is .201, with a 99 percent confidence interval given by (.186, .216). Further, a likelihood ratio test strongly rejects the hypothesis that the equations can be estimated independently. The evidence is strong in favor of residual heterogeneity that created positive correlation between claiming and lapsing.

Test 12.2: Policy Persistence and Average Risk
While the data indicate a contemporaneous negative correlation between risk and policy persistence, the theory of asymmetric learning predicts that the decrease in risk is permanent. Essentially, the group of policies that persist should have a lower average claims rate in the second period than the group of early policies in the first period. This hypothesis is tested by comparing the sample average claims rate of early policies with the sample average claims rate of persisting policies. Controlling for observable characteristics remains important, so both parametric and semiparametric models are estimated to isolate just the impact of policy aging.

Claim frequency risk is modeled as an extension of the above occurrence probit model to incorporate differences in exposure across observations. Consider an observation i insured for D_i days during the sample period, and suppose the probability of a claim during one day is given by $p_i = \Phi(X_i'\beta)$. The probability of N_i claims, $N = 0, 1, 2, \ldots$, is given by $\begin{pmatrix} D \\ N \end{pmatrix}(p)^D(1-p)^{N-D}$, where i subscripts have been suppressed. With this formation, the contribution of each observation to the log likelihood of observing a large sample of observations on $\{X_i, D_i, N_i\}$ is

$$\ln L_i = D \ln[\Phi(X'\beta)] + (N - D) \ln[1 - \Phi(X'\beta)].$$

Estimation of β is performed by maximizing $\sum_i \ln L_i$ with respect to β. Among the variables in X is a dummy variable indicating that the observation is for a late policy. This variable captures shifts in the average after removing the impact of observable characteristics. Identification results from the heterogeneity present in the observable characteristics within each of the two time periods. A significantly negative value of the coefficient would be consistent with the theoretical model, indi-

Table 12.2
Contemporaneous correlation between claiming and lapsing (Bi-probit model)

Variable	Claim Occurrence Coefficient (Standard error)	Lapse Coefficient (Standard error)
Insured Age	−0.002 (0.002)	−0.016** (0.001)
Insured Age squared	0.000 (0.000)	0.0001** (0.0000)
Male Dummy	0.019* (0.008)	0.093** (0.006)
Amount Insured	0.001 (0.001)	0.003** (0.001)
Amount Insured squared	0.000 (0.000)	0.000* (0.000)
Vehicle Age	0.001 (0.002)	0.043** (0.002)
Vehicle Age squared	−0.0003** (0.000)	−0.0005** (0.000)
Rate Protection dummy	0.124** (0.015)	−0.061** (0.012)
Agreed Value dummy	0.035** (0.012)	0.011 (0.010)
Group 1 dummy	−0.044 (0.023)	−0.219** (0.017)
Group 2 dummy	0.030 (0.025)	0.048* (0.019)
Class 1 dummy	0.011 (0.016)	0.101** (0.012)
NCD Rating dummy variables	Yes	Yes
Policy Age dummy variables	Yes	Yes
Location dummy variables	Yes	Yes
Residual correlation	0.201** (0.006)	
Number of observations	362,795	

Notes: Table reports maximum-likelihood estimates of coefficients from a bi-probit model. Observations are weighted by the exposure during the sample period.
*Significant at the 5 percent level.
**Significant at the 1 percent level.

cating that late policies have claims less often on average. An insignificant coefficient or a positive coefficient would be sufficient to reject the model, however, since renewing policies should have lower risk.

Table 12.3 reports the maximum likelihood estimation results using the entire sample of observations, excluding the new policies from the second period. Two sets of results are presented—one incorporating the age of the policy as an explanatory variable and one ignoring the age of the policy. Since insureds may not be able to credibly communicate policy age to an outside insurer, policy age may be a potential source of private information. Moreover, since each persisting policy ages one year when moving from early to late, including policy-age dummy variables results in the late effect being identified by comparing policies that began their relationships exactly one year apart. Without the policy-age variables, policies of all ages are grouped together, so identification is not conditional on the length of the relationship. Since there may be important time-series effects, removing the dummy variables provides a robustness check.

In both empirical models, the coefficient on the late dummy is positive and significant, indicating that policies that renew are more risky on average. However, the point estimates suggest that the change is economically rather small. Using the model without policy-age indicators, the annual change in claim frequency is only a positive .22 percentage points (or roughly 2 percent on the average claim frequency) as the group of policies age one year.[23] The unconditional difference in claim frequency is a negative .25 percentage points, suggesting that changes in observable characteristics are creating a decrease in realized claim frequency, roughly negative .47 percentage points on average. In other words, observably less risky consumers are more likely to stay with the incumbent insurer. Furthermore, the data cannot reject the hypothesis that the change due to unobserved factors is zero or positive. The evidence is not consistent with a model of asymmetric learning.

As a final robustness check, the probit model is estimated by rating class and policy age to control for the potential endogeneity of these variables. Since rating class is based on the history of claims of a particular insured, it is possible that the variable is correlated with unobserved factors affecting driving ability and claim experience, resulting in biased coefficient estimates.[24] The data are split into fifteen rating classes and fifteen policy-age groupings, resulting in 225 unique combinations of rating and policy age.[25] The probit model is estimated for each cell with enough data, restricted to twenty-five years of exposure

Table 12.3
Effect of policy persistence on claim risk (Adjusted probit model)

Variable	Model 1 Coefficient (Standard error)	Model 2 Coefficient (Standard error)
Late policy indicator	0.014** (0.003)	0.007* (0.003)
Insured Age	−0.002* (0.001)	−0.001 (0.001)
Insured Age squared	0.00002** (0.00000)	0.000 (0.000)
Male dummy	0.009** (0.003)	0.010** (0.003)
Amount Insured	0.001* (0.000)	0.001** (0.000)
Amount Insured squared	0.000 (0.000)	0.000 (0.000)
Vehicle Age	0.005** (0.001)	0.003** (0.001)
Vehicle Age squared	−0.0003** (0.0000)	−0.0003** (0.0000)
Rate Protection dummy	0.070** (0.006)	0.071** (0.006)
Agreed Value dummy	0.024** (0.005)	0.034** (0.005)
Group 1 dummy	−0.025** (0.009)	−0.023* (0.010)
Group 2 dummy	0.025* (0.010)	0.028** (0.010)
Class 1 dummy	0.011 (0.007)	0.015* (0.007)
NCD Rating dummy variables	Yes	Yes
Policy Age dummy variables	Yes	No
Location dummy variables	Yes	Yes
Number of observations	686,135	686,135
Number of exposures	338,315	338,315
Number of claims	32,753	32,753

Notes: Table reports maximum-likelihood estimates of coefficients of the adjusted probit model that incorporates the effect of exposure. Coefficients are for the latent variable, the probability of making a claim in a single day. Model 2 excludes dummy variables for the age of the policy.
*Significant at the 5 percent level.
**Significant at the 1 percent level.

in the results discussed below. Each cell results in a coefficient estimate on the late dummy variable, along with associated standard error, t-statistic, and p-value. Aggregating the statistics is done in several ways.

Of the 225 cells, 142 have at least 25 years of exposure. The claiming model is estimated for each of these cells, resulting in 142 independent coefficient estimates, 142 independent t-statistics, and 142 independent p-values. Of the 142 t-statistics, 14 fall into the upper or lower 5 percent of a t distribution with one degree of freedom. However, only two of the fourteen are associated with negative values of the coefficient on the late dummy variable, offering no evidence that late policies are less risky on average. The mean p-value is .57, with well less than half of the observations below .5.[26] Again, there is no evidence to reject the hypothesis that late policies are no less risky than early policies.

The estimation is also done for each rating class alone, without controlling for policy age. This results in just fifteen cells, with fourteen of the fifteen rating classes having over fifty years of exposure are available.[27] Of these fourteen rating classes, the estimated coefficient is significantly positive at the 95 percent level for only one class. Alternatively, the coefficient is significantly negative in four of the classes. The sample average p-value is .64, which is not significantly different from .5. On balance, there is no evidence that persisting policies are of better average risk.

Test 12.3: Policy Persistence and Insurer Profit
The final prediction of the model concerns the evolution of the informed insurer's profit. The model predicts that the profit earned by the incumbent insurer increases as policies renew. Empirically, this hypothesis is tested by comparing the average *loss ratio*, defined as total claim costs per total premium, for all early policies with the average loss ratio on persisting policies in the second period. The loss ratio is a measure of profit, with smaller values indicating larger profits. Since other observable factors may also affect the loss ratio, it remains important to control for the other variables in the data set.[28] This is done nonparametrically by grouping policies according to several variables and examining the change in loss ratio for each cell.

The loss ratio for a particular policy is given by $r_i = \frac{l_i}{\pi_i}$, where l is the realized value of claims paid and π is the *earned premium* for the policy, the total premium multiplied by the exposure of the policy.[29] Since policies with less exposure during the sample period are likely to be more variable than policies with more exposure, a weighted sample mean is used to estimate population expected values. For the loss ratio, the sample mean, along with the first two moments of the sampling distribution are given by

$$\bar{r} = \frac{\sum r_i \pi_i}{\sum \pi_i} = \frac{\sum l_i}{\sum \pi_i}$$

$$E(\bar{r}) = \frac{E(r) \sum \pi_i}{\sum \pi_i} = E(r)$$

$$Var(\bar{r}) = \frac{Var(r) \sum \pi_i^2}{\left(\sum \pi_i\right)^2}.$$

The weighted mean is an unbiased and consistent estimator of the population expected value, with the standard error a slight modification of the usual result.

For the sample as a whole, the loss ratio for early policies is 69.0 percent, and the loss ratio for the persisting policies is 66.8 percent. However, the standard error of the difference in means is 2.1 percent, so the 2.2 percent increase is not statistically different from zero, falling at the eighty-fifth percentile of the null distribution. However, the point estimate of the difference is economically large, indicating a nearly 5 percent increase in the mark-up of premiums over expected losses.[30] As before, multivariate methods are needed to remove the impact of observable information.

Policies are grouped together to perform comparison of means tests, which are robust to the highly skewed distribution of the loss ratio per policy. Four variables are used to create homogeneous cells: the age of the insured (five categories), the insured's NCD rating (nine categories), vehicle age (four categories), and gender (two categories). This results in 360 potential cells.[31] Restricting attention to cells with at least ten years of exposure in both the early and late periods results in 282 usable cells. In each cell, sample mean-loss ratios are computed for both the early and late periods, along with an estimate of the sampling standard error for the difference in means.

The results of this nonparametric exercise provide no evidence that persisting policies are more profitable than early policies. Of the 282 cells, 146 (51.7 percent) have an average loss ratio that decreases on renewal, with the remainder having a loss ratio that increases. In other words, the median change in loss ratio is slightly below zero. However, the distribution is slightly skewed to the right, so the average difference in loss ratios is slightly positive, .4 percent. Most important, there is no statistical evidence to reject the null hypothesis that the difference in means is zero. Only eight of the observations fall into the outer 5 percent of the null distributions, well within the expected range given 282 observations.[32] Under the null hypothesis of no difference in means, the average difference in average loss ratios falls at the 49.3 percentile of the null distribution, again providing no evidence of any statistical difference in loss ratios.[33]

For the sake of comparison, OLS regressions of the loss ratio on the set of explanatory variables are reported in table 12.4. Assuming the linear specification is accurate, the coefficient estimates are consistent despite the significant skew in the residuals. Standard errors are biased, so the focus is on the coefficient of the late indicator, which is estimated to be .4 percent using policy-age dummy variables and −.1 percent without the policy-age dummies. Since these estimates are close to zero, there is again no evidence that policies become more profitable over time. The estimated coefficients are quite close to the average change across cells in the nonparametric test (.4 percent). The loss-ratio regressions also show that several observable variables have large effects on loss ratios. In particular, loss ratios vary substantially across the NCD rating categories, ranging from 52 percent to 73 percent just within the first five rating classes (results not shown).[34]

Summary of Empirical Results

While the empirical results are not consistent with the theoretical prediction of the asymmetric learning model, they provide an interesting picture about the dynamics of the market. Two results are of particular note: (1) policies without a claim are more likely to persist, yet they are not less likely to have a claim in the future; and (2) observably less risky policies are more likely to persist than observably more risky policies.

Claiming and lapsing are contemporaneously correlated, but the effect is transitory since persisting policies are no less risky in the subsequent period. This suggests more of a causal relationship between claiming and lapsing rather than an underlying factor that is correlated with both (as in the asymmetric learning model). The direction of the causality is not clear. In an alternative learning story, making a claim may reveal relevant information to the insured about the insurance

Table 12.4
Effect of aging on loss ratio (OLS)

Variable	Model 1 Coefficient (Standard error)	Model 2 Coefficient (Standard error)
Late policy indicator	0.004 (0.024)	−0.001 (0.021)
Insured Age	−0.005 (0.004)	−0.005 (0.004)
Insured Age squared	0.000 (0.000)	0.000 (0.000)
Male dummy	0.036 (0.022)	0.039 (0.022)
Amount Insured	0.004* (0.002)	0.004** (0.002)
Amount Insured squared	0.000 (0.000)	0.000* (0.000)
Vehicle Age	0.040** (0.007)	0.027** (0.007)
Vehicle Age squared	−0.001** (0.000)	−0.001** (0.000)
Rate Protection dummy	0.048 (0.045)	0.036 (0.045)
Agreed Value dummy	0.209** (0.033)	0.244** (0.033)
Group 1 dummy	0.055 (0.064)	0.045 (0.064)
Group 2 dummy	0.103 (0.070)	0.107 (0.070)
Class 1 dummy	−0.064 (0.048)	−0.059 (0.048)
NCD Rating dummy variables	Yes	Yes
Policy Age dummy variables	Yes	No
Location dummy variables	Yes	Yes
Number of observations	686,135	686,135
Adjusted R-squared	0.0066	0.0067

Notes: The left-hand-side variable is the loss ratio per policy, and the table reports OLS estimates. While the estimates are consistent, standard errors are biased due to the non-normality of residuals. Significance is based on the OLS standard errors.
*Significant at the 5 percent level.
**Significant at the 1 percent level.

company, permitting a more informed decision that leads to more frequent switching. Conversely, knowledge that lapsing is likely may exacerbate moral hazard by affecting the insured's incentives to make a claim. In either case, the important result is that policies that persist are no less likely to have claims in the future than the group of policies previously insured.

Controlling for observable information is shown to be important, since the changes in average risk and average profitability are different in univariate tests than in the multivariate results. This suggests that the observable composition of policies is different in the early and late time periods, with lower risk and lower loss-ratio policies more likely to persist. Table 12.1 confirms this result. From the early sample, policies that lapse have different characteristics than persisting policies. Most important, lapsing policies are more likely to be younger drivers, male drivers, shorter policy ages, and over a one NCD rating worse than persisting policies. Table 12.3 (plus results not shown on the effect of NCD ratings and policy age) confirms that these drivers have claims more frequently. Since these factors are all observable, the changes are not due to the revelation of private information, since competitor insurers will understand the risk associated with the lapsing policies. Indeed, the new policies in the late period of the data are for younger drivers with significantly worse NCD ratings, but these can be identified as more risky using the data on just early policies.

Conclusion

The failure to confirm the model of asymmetric learning is subject to several caveats. Most important, the empirical tests are of the joint hypothesis that incumbent insurers gain private information and have pricing behavior as described the model. If the insurer is choosing not to use private information, either due to implicit long-term contracting or a strategic desire to prevent the market from inferring the information, the effect would not show up in our tests. A longer time series would be useful in adding statistical power to the tests. Nevertheless, the prediction that lower-risk insureds are more likely to persist is robust to many theoretical model specifications yet is not apparent in the data.

Perhaps the result is not surprising, given the lack of conclusive evidence that insureds themselves possess private information. Insurance companies spend considerable resources acquiring information about their consumers, and the result seems to be that residual information asymmetries have become quite small. It seems as if the first line of defense against information disparities is to acquire information. Future research needs to address the information-acquisition process and identify the unique characteristics of markets where residual adverse selection seems to persist (Finkelstein and Poterba, 2004, provide evidence of adverse selection in annuity markets).

Finally, the patterns in observable characteristics suggest that auto insurance remains an interesting market to study. Why are claiming and lapsing positively correlated? Why do observably less risky insureds tend to persist more than riskier insureds? Why does the loss ratio vary with observable characteristics? Future empirical research needs to test the robustness of these results, exploring other lines of business and other regulatory environments. Future theoretical research should continue to explore alternative-market frictions that may create such patterns in the data. For example, Israel (2003a, 2003b) considers auto insurance as an experience good, with consumers learning about the quality of the supplier only occasionally when claims are made. Empirical results suggest that lapsing tends to decrease with the length of the relationship and is mostly explained by a gradual matching process that only slowly results in consumers finding the optimal supplier. The infrequent occurrence of claims inhibits the learning process and results in consumer lock-in. Israel's work highlights the fact that insurance markets are unique in dimensions other than the potential presence of asymmetric information.

Appendix

Recall that the game is one of Bertrand competition with incomplete information. An uninformed insurer observes only the unconditional average loss probability $\bar{p} = bp_L + (1 - b)p_H$, and an informed insurer observes conditional loss probabilities $\bar{p}_l = b_l p_L + (1 - b_l)p_H$ and $\bar{p}_h = b_h p_L + (1 - b_h)p_H$. The proposed mixed-strategy equilibrium is

$$F_h^I(\bar{p}_h) = 1$$

$$F_l^I(\pi) = 1 - \left(\frac{1 - \lambda}{\lambda}\right)\left(\frac{\bar{p}_h - \pi}{\pi - \bar{p}_l}\right) \quad \pi \in [\bar{p}, \bar{p}_h]$$

$$F^U(\pi) = 1 - \left(\frac{\bar{p} - \bar{p}_l}{\pi - \bar{p}_l}\right) \quad \pi \in [\bar{p}, \bar{p}_h)$$

$$f^U(\bar{p}_h) = \left(\frac{\bar{p} - \bar{p}_l}{\bar{p}_h - \bar{p}_l}\right),$$

where $\lambda = \frac{1}{2} + \theta\left(b - \frac{1}{2}\right)$ is the unconditional probability of observing signal l.

First note that the proposed mixed strategies are valid probability distributions:

$$F_l^I(\bar{p}) = 0, \quad F_l^I(\bar{p}_h) = 1, \quad F^U(\bar{p}) = 0 \quad \text{and} \quad \lim_{\pi' \to \bar{p}_h} F^U(\pi') = 1 - f_U(\bar{p}_h).^{35}$$

Also, the distribution functions are strictly increasing, $\frac{\partial}{\partial \pi} F_l^I(\pi) > 0$ and $\frac{\partial}{\partial \pi} F^U(\pi) > 0$, on the ranges where they are continuous.

Fix the strategy of the uninformed insurer, and consider the set of best responses by the informed insurer. For consumers with expected loss probability $\bar{p}_h$, the informed insurer is indifferent among all offers $\pi_h \geq \bar{p}_h$, since the informed insurer either makes a sale and zero profits or does not make a sale. Any lower offer makes negative profits. For consumers with expected loss probability $\bar{p}_l$, any offer $\pi_l \in (\bar{p}_l, \bar{p}]$ makes a sale and strictly positive profits. The profit-maximizing price is $\pi_l = \bar{p}$ and yields profit $(\bar{p} - \bar{p}_l)$. Now consider an offer $\pi_l \in (\bar{p}, \bar{p}_h)$, which yields expected profits $[1 - F^U(\pi_l)](\pi_l - \bar{p}_l)$, incorporating the probability of making a sale. Substituting the equilibrium distribution of the uninformed insurer and simplifying yields expected profits of $(\bar{p} - \bar{p}_l)$ for all offers $\pi_l \in (\bar{p}, \bar{p}_h)$. Finally, consider the offer $\pi_l = \bar{p}_h$. Again, substituting the equilibrium strategy of the uninformed insurer yields expected profits $(\bar{p} - \bar{p}_l)$. The informed insurer is indifferent to all offers in the interval $[\bar{p}, \bar{p}_h]$ and can do no better with any offer outside this interval.

Now fix the strategy of the informed insurer and consider the set of best responses by the uninformed insurer. Any offer $\pi < \bar{p}$ captures all consumer but earns negative profits. Any offer $\pi > \bar{p}_h$ captures no consumers and earns zero profits. Consider offers in the interval $[\bar{p}, \bar{p}_h]$. Such offers earn expected profit $\lambda[1 - F_L^I(\pi)](\pi - \bar{p}_l) + (1 - \lambda) \cdot [1 - F_H^I(\pi)](\pi - \bar{p}_h)$, incorporating both the probability of making a sale and also the conditional probability of dealing with a type l consumer or type h customer.[36] Substituting equilibrium strategies, $F_L^I(\pi^U)$ and $F_H^I(\pi^U) = 0$, expected profits reduce to zero for all $\pi^U \in [\bar{p}, p_H]$. The uninformed insurer earns zero expected profit and can do no better by deviating from this interval.

Conditional on the strategy of the other insurer, both the informed and the uninformed insurer are indifferent between all of the prices in the support of the equilibrium distributions. Further, each price in the support is in the set of best responses to the mixed strategy of the other. Since the distributions are valid probability distributions, the strategies identified constitute an equilibrium.

Notes

1. Cohen (2003a) is a notable exception. In the Israeli market, more experienced drivers exhibit a positive correlation between risk and coverage. The result suggests that private information may be learned over time.

2. See Boot (2000) for a review of the relationship banking literature and Dionne, Doherty, and Fombaron (2000) for a review of the theoretical literature on insurance markets.

3. Sharpe (1990) and Rajan (1992) consider asymmetric learning in banking markets, where incumbent banks privately learn about the quality of their loan portfolio.

4. This result is also a consequence of the assumption that suppliers cannot write long-term contracts and therefore use learned information to subsequently raise prices. Dionne and Doherty (1994) allow partial commitment to long-term contracts and generate the opposite theoretical pattern for prices.

5. Padilla and Pagano (1997) allow the sharing of information to be endogenous and show that increased communication may be Pareto improving.

6. Life insurance and loan markets are typically plagued with the opposite problem: consumers becoming better risks opt out of long-term insurance policies and long maturity loans. Intermediaries understand this phenomenon and will charge for the option that consumers receive.

7. Completely inelastic demand is certainly an unrealistic assumption but permits a focus on just the production side of the market. Villeneuve (2000, 2003) addresses a model where insurers are (symmetrically) better informed than consumers but consumers update their assessment and willingness to pay based on price offers.

8. The price π is a per unit price. For a given quantity of insurance I, the total insurance premium is πI.

9. This information structure is used in Sharpe (1990).

10. The insurer is assumed to have no costs other than claims costs.

11. Cooper and Hayes (1987) and Dionne and Doherty (1994) allow for long-term contracts and address the commitment and renegotiation issue. Cooper and Hayes assume that the insurer can commit to a multiperiod insurance contract, while Dionne and Doherty allow for renegotiation of the initial contract.

12. Cohen (2003b) analyzes a similar model with asymmetric learning about consumer riskiness but finds an equilibrium in pure strategies. Cohen uses the assumption from Greenwald (1986) that some fraction of consumers switches insurers for exogenous reasons. When the exogenous switchers are indistinguishable, the effect is similar to the informed insurer using a mixed strategy: the winner's curse is abated since a new insured is not definitely unprofitable at the offered price. Such a model results in similar empirical predictions.

13. This result holds because the source of private information is not observable. Conditional on the signal, claiming and switching are independent, by assumption.

14. However, if H2 is true, H1 is likely true as well.

15. Recall that *price* here refers to the insurance premium per expected loss. The actual insurance premium may fall, but if expected loss also falls, the price may increase.

16. The longest policy period is one year. The insurer writes a small number of six-month policies, but these have been excluded for consistency.

17. The data do not include a reason for a policy's departure from the sample. In addition to purchasing a policy from another insurer, customers leaving the sample may not purchase insurance at all. Consequently, the empirical indicator is not identical to the theoretical concept of switching insurers.

18. In all subsequent empirical analysis, the sample is restricted to policies with an A\$400 deductible, which slightly reduces the sample size (roughly 85 percent of the policies carry an A\$400 deductible). Since the deductible is potentially a tool used to screen private information, it is appropriate to restrict attention to policies with the same deductible. Moreover, the deductible level affects the decision to file a claim, an important variable in the empirical analysis.

19. This assumption is consistent with the opinion of insurance professionals working in the Australian market. The data set contains information that all insurers would use to underwrite an auto insurance policy. Of particular interest is the no-claims discount that captures a portion of an insured's claim history. This variable is designed to be transparent and easily transferable to competing insurers.

20. In the sample, very few policies have more than one claim. Conditional on having a claim, fewer than 5 percent of the policies report more than one claim.

21. All occurrence rates are reported at an annual rate. Recall that no observation is actually observed for an entire year.

22. The weighting strategy is to discount the importance of observations covered for only a short period of time. However, if a claim occurs, valuable information is revealed that should not be discounted. Further, if a claim occurs during the first six months of a policy, then a claim is guaranteed to occur during the entire year of the policy. A similar statement cannot be made for the lack of a claim.

23. This is the sample average of the estimated probability impact of changing the late dummy from 0 to 1.

24. Chiappori and Salanie (2000) address this issue by focusing on just younger drivers, where claim history is shorter and the endogeneity less of a concern.

25. Policy ages range from zero through twenty-four years. At the older ages, two or more years are combined to preserve sufficient sample size, resulting in fifteen groups. Results are robust to the exact nature of the grouping.

26. The *p*-value is the probability of observing the estimated coefficient under the null hypothesis that the late variable is unrelated to claim frequency. Under the null, *p*-values are uniformly distributed on $[0, 1]$, with low values indicating negative estimates and high values indicating positive estimates.

27. The worst rating class has only seven years of exposure and is not used.

28. For example, some of the variables may be correlated with the elasticity of demand, and monopoly power may result in profit differences.

29. Using earned procedure implicitly assumes a constant expected loss throughout the life of the policy. Examination of the data revealed no seasonal effects.

30. The mark-up is the inverse of the loss ratio less 100 percent.

31. Incorporating other explanatory variables results in many more cells with small sample size. The results are robust to excluding observations from smaller cells: policies with rating protection, policies with an agreed value endorsement, and policies not from group 1 and class 1.

32. Of the eight extreme observations, four show a loss ratio increase and four show a decrease.

33. Under the null that the difference in means is zero within each cell, the p-values for the difference in means test are distributed uniformly on $[0, 1]$. A chi-square cannot reject the hypothesis that the p-values are uniformly distributed.

34. These differences likely partially reflect a fixed cost of providing insurance. Since the fixed cost is larger relative to losses for policies with lower expected losses, these policies tend to have a lower loss ratio. In general, the coefficient in the loss-ratio regression increases monotonically with risk.

35. Note that $f^U(\bar{p}_h) < 1$, since the signal is informative.

36. Note that the uninformed insurer offers a single price but does update the loss probability after successfully capturing a consumer. This is simply the Nash assumption.

References

Boot, Arnoud. (2000). "Relationship Banking: What Do We Know?" *Journal of Financial Intermediation* 9: 7–25.

Brisy Eric, Georges Dionne, and Louis Eeckhoudt. (1989). "More on Insurance as a Giffen Good." *Journal of Risk and Uncertainty* 2: 415–420.

Chiappori, Pierre-Andre. (2000). "Econometric Models of Insurance under Asymmetric Information." In Georges Dionne (Ed.), *Handbook of Insurance Economics*. London: Kluwer.

Chiappori, Pierre-Andre, and Bernard Salanie. (2000). "Testing for Asymmetric Information in Insurance Markets." *Journal of Political Economy* 108: 56–78.

Cohen, Alma. (2003a). "Asymmetric Information and Learning: Evidence from the Automobile Insurance Market." Discussion Paper No. 371, John M. Olin Center for Law, Economics, and Business, April.

Cohen, Alma. (2003b). "Profit and Market Power in Repeat Contracting: Evidence from the Insurance Market." May.

Cooper, Russell, and Beth Hayes. (1987). "Multi-period Insurance Policies." *European Economic Review* 34: 303–310.

D'Arcy, Stephen P., and Neil A. Doherty. (1990). "Adverse Selection, Private Information, and Lowballing in Insurance Markets." *Journal of Business* 63: 145–164.

Dasgupta, Partha, and Eric Maskin. (1986). "The Existence of Equilibrium in Discontinuous Economic Games, I: Theory." *Review of Economic Studies* 53: 1–26.

Debreu, G. (1952). "A Social Equilibrium Existence Theorem." *Proceedings of the National Academy of Sciences* 38: 886–893.

Dell'Ariccia, Giovanni, Friedman, Ezra, and Robert Marquez. (1999). "Adverse Selection as a Barrier to Entry in the Banking Industry." *RAND Journal of Economics* 30(3): 515–534.

Dionne, Georges, and Neil A. Doherty. (1994). "Adverse Selection, Commitment, and Renegotiation: Extensions to and Evidence from Insurance Markets." *Journal of Political Economy* 102(2): 209–235.

Dionne, Georges, Neil Doherty, and Nathalie Fombaron. (2000). "Adverse Selection in Insurance Markets." In Georges Dionne (Ed.), *Handbook of Insurance Economics*. London: Kluwer.

Dionne, Georges, Christian Gourieroux, and Charles Vanasse. (2001). "Testing for Evidence of Adverse Selection in the Automobile Insurance Market: A Comment." *Journal of Political Economy* 109(2): 444–453.

Dionne, Georges, and C. Vanasse. (1992). "Automobile Insurance Ratemaking in the Presence of Asymmetrical Information." *Journal of Applied Econometrics* 7: 149–165.

Finkelstein, Amy, and James Poterba. (2004). "Adverse Selection in Insurance Markets: Policholder Evidence from the U.K. Annuity Market." *Journal of Political Economy* 112(1): 183–208.

Fombaron, N. (1997). "No-Commitment and Dynamic Contracts in Competitive Insurance Markets with Adverse Selection." Working Paper.

Greenwald, Bruce C. (1986). "Adverse Selection in the Labour Market." *Review of Economic Studies* 53: 325–347.

Hendel, Igal, and Alessandro Lizzeri. (2000). "The Role of Commitment in Dynamic Contracts: Evidence from Life Insurance." NBER Working Paper 7470.

Hoy, Michael, and Arthur Robson. (1981). "Insurance as a Giffen Good." *Economics Letters* 8: 47–51.

Israel, Mark (2003a). "Consumer Learning about Established Firms: Evidence from Automobile Insurance." Working Paper, Northwestern University, July.

Israel, Mark (2003b). "Tenure Dependence in Consumer-Firm Relationships: An Empirical Analysis of Consumer Departures from Automobile Insurance Firms." Working Paper, Northwestern University, June.

Kunreuther, Howard, and Mark Pauly. (1985). "Market Equilibrium with Private Knowledge: An Insurance Example." *Journal of Public Economics* 26: 269–288.

Marquez, Robert. (2002). "Competition, Adverse Selection, and Information Dispersion in the Banking Industry." *Review of Financial Studies* 15(3): 901–926.

Nilssen, Tore. (2000). "Consumer Lock-In with Asymmetric Information." *International Journal of Industrial Organization* 18: 641–666.

Padilla, A. J., and M. Pagano. (1997). "Endogenous Communication among Lenders and Entrepreneurial Incentives." *Review of Financial Studies* 10: 205–236.

Rajan, Raghuram G. (1992). "Insiders and Outsiders: The Choice between Informed and Arm's Length Debt." *Journal of Finance* 47: 1367–1400.

Richaudeau, Didier. (1999). "Automobile Insurance Contracts and Risk of Accident: An Empirical Test Using French Individual Data." *Geneva Papers on Risk and Insurance Theory* 24(1): 97–114.

Rosenthal, Robert W., and Andrew Weiss. (1984). "Mixed-Strategy Equilibrium in a Market with Asymmetric Information." *Review of Economic Studies* 51: 333–342.

Rothschild, Michael, and Joseph Stiglitz. (1976). "An Essay of the Economics of Imperfect Information." *Quarterly Journal of Economics* 629–649.

Sharpe, Steven A. (1990). "Asymmetric Information, Bank Lending and Implicit Contracts: A Stylized Model of Customer Relationships." *Journal of Finance* 45: 1069–1087.

Villeneuve, Bertrand. (2000). "The Consequences for a Monopolistic Insurance Firm of Evaluating Risk Better Than Customers: The Adverse Selection Hypothesis Reversed." *Geneva Papers on Risk and Insurance Theory* 25: 65–79.

Villeneuve, Bertrand. (2003). "Competition between Insurers with Superior Information." *European Economic Review* 49(2): 321–340.

von Thadden, Ernst-Ludwig. (2001). "Asymmetric Information, Bank Landing and Implicit Contracts: The Winner's Curse." Mimeo, Universite de Lausanne.

Contributors

Luis H. B. Braido, Graduate School of Economics, Getulio Vargas Foundation, Rio de Janeiro, Brazil

Mark J. Browne, University of Wisconsin–Madison

Pierre-André Chiappori, Columbia University

Georges Dionne, HEC Montreal, CIRPÉE, CREF, and CRT, Montreal

Irena Dushi, Hunter College, Department of Economics, New York

Roland Eisen, Johann Wolfgang Goethe–Universität Frankfurt am Main

Lucien Gardiol, Institute for Health Economics and Management (IEMS), University of Lausanne

Pierre-Yves Geoffard, DELTA (joint research unit of Centre National de la Recherche Scientifique, Ecole Normale Supérieure, and Ecole des Hautes Etudes en Sciences Sociales), Paris; Institute for Economics and Management (IEMS), University of Lausanne; and Center for Economic Policy Research, London

Christian Gouriéroux, CREF, CREST, CEPREMAP, and University of Toronto

Chantal Grandchamp, Institute for Economics and Management (IEMS), University of Lausanne

Erik Grönqvist, Stockholm School of Economics

Luigi Guiso, University of Sassari, Ente Luigi Einaudi, and Center for Economic Policy Research, London

Paul Kofman, University of Melbourne

Hansjörg Lehmann, Socioeconomic Institute, University of Zurich

Gregory P. Nini, Federal Reserve Board, Washington

Monica Paiella, Bank of Italy Ente
Luigi Einaudi, Rome

Mark V. Pauly, The Wharton
School, University of
Pennsylvania, Philadelphia

Charles Vanasse, TD Asset
Management

Anthony Webb, Center for
Retirement Research, Boston
College

Peter Zweifel, Socioeconomic
Institute, University of Zurich

Index